W9-CGS-728

THE
BUSINESS
OF
MASSAGE

The Business of Massage

The Complete Guide
to Establishing Your Massage Career

Second Edition

A publication written by and for practitioners
of the massage therapy profession

Published by
American Massage Therapy Association®

Published by:
American Massage Therapy Association®

500 Davis Street, Suite 900
Evanston, IL 60201-4695
www.amtamassage.org
Phone 877-905-2700
Fax 847-864-1178

© 2009

Development Team
Textbook development: Words Unleashed, Glen Ellyn, Illinois
(wordsunleashed2@comcast.net)
Design: Eightyproof, Chicago, Illinois

All rights reserved.

No part of this publication may be reproduced, stored in a retrieval system,
or transmitted, in any form or by any means, whether electronic, mechanical,
photocopying, recording or otherwise, without the prior written permission
of the publisher (AMTA).

This publication is intended to provide general guidance and information and is not
meant to be a substitute for professional legal, financial, or tax advice, which should
be obtained through consultation with appropriate professionals in your state or
province. The information contained herein is provided "as is" and AMTA makes no
representation or warranty that the information will be timely or error free. Please
direct any comments, questions, or suggestions regarding this book to AMTA, The
Business of Massage, at the address above.

ISBN: 978-1-929947-00-3

BRIEF TABLE OF CONTENTS

TABLE OF CONTENTS

PREFACE

Congratulations on preparing to enter the profession of massage! The Business of Massage, Second Edition, was written to help you learn the business basics you will need to operate your practice. The first edition, published in 2002, was based on a series of business manuals, the American Massage Therapy Association Massage Therapy Career Guide Series. AMTA Professional members recommended that similar material be made available in textbook format for the benefit of students who will be starting their own practice as massage therapists.

To say that the profession of massage therapy has changed since the career guide series was first introduced is an understatement. In the rapidly changing professional climate in which massage therapists work, maintaining up-to-date information about regulation, requirements for credentials, continuing education, and regulatory requirements is a never-ending challenge. All survey data have been updated that represent consumers' and other health professionals' acceptance of massage, and that reflect how massage therapists operate their businesses. In every case where information might have changed since the book was printed, the text offers good places to go for updates, either via website links or names of organizations to contact.

As in the first edition, the business basics found in this book are tailored specifically to the massage therapy profession. This book covers business concepts that are applicable to any small business, such as how to find a job, how to maintain financial records, and how to find and keep customers. Of essential use to the massage therapist, it covers such topics as ethics, research, insurance claims administration, and choice of business space within the context of their unique, sometimes subtle and complex, applications within the profession of massage.

New and Expanded Coverage
Feedback to the first edition and reviewers' input prompted significant changes to the second edition. The book's organization has been restructured such that chapters are now in the sequence taught by most business classes in massage schools and training programs. Rather than present the business basics at the beginning of the book, the second edition first presents the subject matter a massage therapist must appreciate—choosing an appropriate setting in which to practice, understanding the nature of therapeutic relationships, learning the importance of self-care—before hitting the hard-business subject matter.

The overall tone and style of the second edition is chattier and friendlier, without slacking off on any of the serious responsibility to present the appropriate level of detail required to operate a massage therapy practice.

Acknowledgement of changes to the settings and climate within which massage therapists practice is reflected in significantly expanded coverage of the following topics:

- Laws and regulations
- Ethics and boundaries
- Corporate and franchise massage businesses
- Practical suggestions for maintaining good client relationships
- Sustainable practices that reflect the value of caring for the environment
- Buying, selling, and closing a practice
- Client insurance, billing, and receiving reimbursement
- Translational research
- Professional development business plan

New Features

This book adds three new features that will help readability and applicability of the content.

- *Key Concepts*—margin notes capture the essence of major ideas that are important in the lives of massage therapists.
- *Real Touch*—vignettes of real massage therapists describe the evolution of their careers and a typical day in their life, and give students a realistic view of the profession—not idealized, not discouraging, but realistic.
- *Spotlight on Business*—some topics are expanded to enhance the information described in the text narrative; for instance, how to how to start a workplace massage program, information on massage franchises, how to incorporate "green" into your practice, etc.

A feature that personalized the first edition of *The Business of Massage* was Shared Wisdom, a compilation of advice "tidbits" proffered by experienced massage therapists. Those quotes continue to be valid in massage therapists' current working environments and are now contained in Appendix A.

ACKNOWLEDGEMENTS

The Business of Massage, Second Edition, would not be nearly as complete or as helpful to readers were it not for instructors', specialists', and other readers' feedback regarding its content.

Particular thanks go to: Vivian Madison-Mahoney for her extensive contribution to the section on insurance reimbursement; to Diana Thompson for her careful review of insurance reimbursement; to Jenn Sommermann and Meg Darnell for keeping not just the accuracy of content but the spirit and intent of the message in clear focus in the chapters on launching and managing a career; and to Pete Whitridge for his careful reading and insightful comments for Chapters 4–7.

The following individuals were selfless in offering critiques and reviews, in terms of the accuracy of the content's tone as well as its facts. For revision input small and large, AMTA owes a debt of gratitude to:

Reviewers and Contributors

Barry Antoniow, RMT, Mountain State School of Massage, Charleston, West Virginia

John Balletto, LMT, NCTMB, Center for Muscular Therapy Inc., Pawtucket, Rhode Island

Meg Darnell, LMT, Director of Alumni Services, Swedish Institute, College of Health Sciences, New York, NY

Linda Derick, Connecticut Center of Massage Therapy, Newington, Connecticut

Dora Fronek, CMT, Lakeside School of Massage Therapy, Milwaukee, Wisconsin

John Kaiser, CPA, Cray, Kaiser, Ltd., Oakbrook Terrace, Illinois

Debra Locker, Public Relations Director, ISPA, Lexington, Kentucky

Vivian Madison-Mahoney, LMT, Massage Insurance Billing, Gatlinburg, Tennessee

National Certification Board for Therapeutic Massage and Bodywork (NCBTMB), Oakbrook Terrace, Illinois

Debra Persinger, Executive Director, Federation of State Massage Therapy Boards (FSMTB), Overland Park, Kansas

Jenn Sommermann, LMT, Swedish Institute, New York, New York

Diana Thompson, LMP, Hands Heal, Seattle, Washington

Pete Whitridge, Florida School of Massage, Gainesville, Florida

Reviewers of the First Edition

The Business of Massage, Second Edition, is the outgrowth of a substantive first edition whose content was greatly influenced by the following individuals, for whose contribution we continue to be grateful:

Steve Albertson, Chicago School of Massage, Chicago, Illinois

Christopher Alvarado, Chicago School of Massage, Chicago, Illinois

Barry Antoniow, RMT, Kiné-Concept Institute Maritimes, Fredericton, New Brunswick

John Balletto, Center for Muscular Therapy, Providence, Rhode Island

James E. Barr Jr., CPA, Overland Park, Kansas

Patricia Benjamin, Chicago School of Massage, Chicago, Illinois

Sue Brown, Illinois School of Health Careers, Chicago, Illinois

Kristin Chou, etopa, and ISPA, Hammond, Louisiana

Leslie Ciaccio, Kishwaukee College, Malta, Illinois

Judy Dean, Agua Dulce Center and Spa, Prescott, Arizona

René Evers, Baltimore School of Massage, Maryland

Réal Gaboriault, Kiné-Concept Institute, Montreal, Quebec

Claude Gagnon, Lakeside School of Massage Therapy, Milwaukee, Wisconsin

Ian Kamm, Sutherland-Chan School & Teaching Clinic, Toronto, Ontario

Carole Ostendorf, COMTA executive director, Evanston, Illinois

Jerry Pearce, Desert Institute of the Healing Arts, Tucson, Arizona

Sarah Rehwalt, COMTA commissioner, Portland, Oregon

Rhonde Reich, Boulder School of Massage, Boulder, Colorado

Demara Stamler, Potomac Massage Training Institute, Washington, DC

Diana Thompson, Hands Heal, Seattle, Washington

Diane Trieste, ISPA, and COMTA commissioner, Canyon Ranch, Arizona

Jean Wible, Baltimore School of Massage, Maryland

Your Feedback Is Welcomed

Already looking forward to the third edition, the authors of *The Business of Massage* would greatly appreciate any feedback you have regarding the book's content and features and how it might be improved in its next revision. Send your comments to AMTA at 500 Davis Street, Suite 900, Evanston, IL 60201, or to businessofmassage@amtamassage.org.

Chapter 1

Taking Stock of Your Career Options

In this chapter, you'll look at two pieces of a puzzle:
  1. Your career options as a massage therapist
  2. Yourself—your aptitudes, values, and aspirations
The resulting big picture is different for each individual.

CHAPTER OVERVIEW

- Overview of Profession
- Career Trends in Massage Therapy
- Career Settings
- Professional Credentials
- Self-Evaluation
- Career Transitions
- Summary

CHAPTER OBJECTIVES

1 Gain an appreciation for the history of the massage therapy profession.
2 Describe at least two trends in the massage therapy profession.
3 Describe the various settings in which massage therapy is practiced.
4 Identify the pros and cons of working in specific career settings.
5 Identify self-assessment strategies for examining how your needs, behaviors, beliefs, and attitudes are relevant to the practice of massage therapy.
6 Identify the credentials that are required or available for the practice of massage therapy.

Few professions offer the variety or flexbility of options you'll find in massage therapy. Before you start to explore these options, get your bearings by looking at the big picture. How did the practice of massage begin? How did it evolve? Where does it stand now, where is it going, and—most importantly— where and how do you plan to take your place in it?

You are entering a profession with a legacy rich in compassion, dedication to health and well-being, and high performance standards.

Massage is widely defined as the manipulation of soft tissue for therapeutic effect.

OVERVIEW OF PROFESSION

As you complete your studies in anatomy, physiology, hands-on techniques, ethics, and other subjects, there's a good chance that you hold an image of yourself someday providing massage to benefit many people. You might have a particular type of client in mind— clients who appreciate the cumulative wellness effects of massage, women and men who seek relaxation and rejuvenation at spas, or athletes seeking relief from pain and injury.

Only a few years ago, books and articles about massage therapy referred to the massage therapy profession as "emerging." The popularity of massage therapy has skyrocketed since the early 2000s, with more than 2 million people trying massage for the first time each year, and three-quarters of clients saying they'd recommend massage therapy to someone they know.[1] Now, as an increasing number of research studies show evidence of far-reaching benefits for massage therapy recipients, massage therapists who have strong business skills are in a better position than ever to establish a thriving practice.

Increased demand for massage therapy, however, doesn't guarantee a successful business practice. The U.S. Bureau of Labor Statistics reports that of all new businesses that opened between 1998 and 2002, 66 percent were still in existence two years after start-up, and 44 percent survived beyond four years.[2] Practitioners who care enough about staying in the profession must take seriously the work required to operate a profitable business.

DEFINITION OF MASSAGE

All definitions of massage include the concept of manipulation of soft tissue for therapeutic effect. Within this broad description lie many varieties of soft tissue manipulation, known as *modalities*. Many modalities coexist, mostly harmoniously, under the umbrella of massage (Figure 1.1). Each modality has its own technique and its own philosophy of why it is effective.

Many schools and programs of massage therapy instruct their students in some level of several modalities. However, most modalities require in-depth training specific to their techniques and philosophies, and require that a student complete a series of trainings before he or she can claim to perform that modality.

HISTORY OF MASSAGE

The recorded history of massage goes back at least 4,000 years. Written and pictorial records from the ancient civilizations of Sumer, Egypt, China, India, Greece, and Rome contain descriptions of massage. Forms of massage developed originally in ancient China and India continue to this day in more modern forms of Asian bodywork, and the heritage of Greece and Rome is found in today's Western massage.

The development of massage therapy in modern Western culture can be traced to the 19th century, and the work of Pehr Henrik Ling of Sweden and Johann Georg Metzger of Amsterdam. The combined systems of Ling and Metzger, Swedish movements and massage, form the basis of today's Western massage.

In America in the first half of 20th century, massage could be found at spas and hot springs, Turkish baths, natural healing resorts, health clubs, beauty salons, and Swedish

FIGURE 1.1
Massage Modalities

MASSAGE MODALITIES

CRANIO-SACRAL: A technique for finding and correcting cerebral and spinal imbalances or blockages that may cause sensory, motor or intellectual dysfunction.

DEEP TISSUE: Releases the chronic patterns of tension in the body through slow strokes and deep finger pressure on the contracted areas, either following or going across the grain of muscles, tendons and fascia. It is called deep tissue, because it also focuses on the deeper layers of muscle tissue.

EFFLEURAGE: A stroke generally used in a Swedish massage treatment. This smooth, gliding stroke is used to relax soft tissue and is applied using both hands.

FRICTION: The deepest of Swedish massage strokes. This stroke encompasses deep, circular movements applied to soft tissue causing the underlying layers of tissue to rub against each other. The result causes an increase in blood flow to the massaged area.

MYOFASCIAL RELEASE: A form of bodywork that is manipulative in nature and seeks to rebalance the body by releasing tension in the fascia. Long, stretching strokes are utilized to release muscular tension.

ON-SITE MASSAGE (also known as chair massage, or workplace or corporate massage): Administered while the client is clothed and seated in a specially designed chair. These chairs most often slope forward allowing access to the large muscles of the back. On-site massage usually lasts between 15 and 30 minutes and is intended to relax and improve circulation.

PETRISSAGE (also called kneading): Involves squeezing, rolling and kneading the muscles and usually follows effleurage during Swedish massage.

REFLEXOLOGY: Massage based around a system of points in the hands and feet thought to correspond, or "reflex," to all areas of the body.

ROSEN METHOD: Utilizes gentle touch and verbal communication to help clients to release suppressed emotions and subsequently muscular tension in some instances.

SHIATSU AND ACUPRESSURE: Asian-based systems of finger-pressure that treat special points along acupuncture "meridians" (the invisible channels of energy flow in the body).

SPORTS MASSAGE: Massage therapy focusing on muscle systems relevant to a particular sport.

SWEDISH MASSAGE: A system of long strokes, kneading and friction techniques on the more superficial layers of the muscles, combined with active and passive movements of the joints.

TAPOTEMENT: Executed with cupped hands, fingers or the edge of the hand with short, alternating taps to the client.

TRIGGER POINT THERAPY (also known as Myotherapy or Neuromuscular Therapy): Applies concentrated finger pressure to "trigger points" (painful irritated areas in muscles) to break cycles of spasm and pain.

Source: Glossary of Terms, American Massage Therapy Association (available at http://www.amtamassage.org/about/terms.html).

massage establishments. The Greek and Roman tradition of massage for athletes was continued by athletic massage practitioners and trainers.

During the 1950s the practice of massage in the United States went into a period of decline. "Massage parlor" and "masseuse" changed from neutral descriptions to terms associated with prostitution, and damaged the image of legitimate massage practitioners. Advances in conventional medicine overshadowed natural healing methods well respected in previous times, including massage.

During the 1960s and '70s, interest in massage enjoyed a revival in the United States. The human potential movement and counterculture of that time produced a simplified and popular form of Swedish massage called Esalen massage. In addition, health practices from other cultures, including China, Japan, and India, that included forms of massage were introduced to the general public. Athletes rediscovered sports massage as a way to improve performance, as well as help prevent and speed recovery from injuries. People began seeking more natural, holistic, and wellness-oriented approaches to health.

The growing interest in massage on a number of fronts in the 1970s fueled the revival of an economy related to massage that has gained in momentum. Fundamental to this economy was the increasing demand by the general public for massage, and the viability of massage therapy as a rewarding career. In the beginning of the 21st century, massage is again part of mainstream health practices. Massage practitioners are recognized as better educated, more professional, and better skilled than ever before.[3]

As you explore the wide variety of career options in massage therapy, you might want to give a nod of gratitude toward those who paved the way. Their legacy is your future in a rewarding career.

> Many earlier practitioners of massage therapy helped create today's thriving acceptance of massage, when the cultural climate was not as welcoming as it is today.

EMBARKING ON A MASSAGE CAREER

Many massage therapists are extremely good at running a business and supporting themselves financially, which enables them to practice the profession they love. But, if u.s. Bureau of Labor Statistics data that are true of small businesses in general hold true for massage therapy practices, for every 10 massage therapists who are successful in their practices or careers, there are as many as six who aren't.

Some massage therapists support themselves within a year of opening a private practice. Those are the therapists who work hard, are flexible and open-minded, and who have solid business and marketing skills. When successful practitioners were asked to offer advice to new massage therapists entering the profession, many recommended spending at least 2 or 3 years working for someone else before opening their own practice. One long-time practitioner put it in terms of having to "survive the apprenticeship" before you can fully and confidently find yourself an integrated member of this thriving and satisfying profession.

The most frequently cited reasons for advising new massage therapists to work as employees before opening their own practices were:

- To gain extensive hands-on practice to refine their techniques—to establish confident touch and a comfortable rhythm and sequence of performing massage.
- To build stamina by working on as many as five to seven clients a day, an experience most students do not acquire in school practice clinics.
- To gain skill-building relationships with a diversity of clients. Nowhere else will a practitioner gain such broad exposure to working with the public as she will as an employed massage therapist, such as for a fitness center, chiropractic clinic, or spa.

Many practitioners emphasize the need for enduring the rigors of apprenticeship in order to emerge as a fully functioning—in all facets of body, mind, and spirit—massage therapist. The reason seasoned professionals stress that newcomers be realistic in their expectations is that they know how richly satisfying total integration into the profession is, and that can't happen unless you know how to succeed in it.

Before deciding the specific details of how you plan to practice massage therapy, it will be helpful to take a broad view of today's career environment.

CAREER TRENDS IN MASSAGE THERAPY

CONSUMER TRENDS

The 2007 Massage Therapy Consumer Survey Fact Sheet[4] (Figure 1.2) reports the following facts:

- Almost a quarter of all adult Americans (24 percent) had a massage at least once in the last 12 months.
- More than a third (34 percent) of all adult Americans received massage in the last five years.
- Almost one-third of adult Americans say they have used massage therapy at least one time for pain relief—just behind chiropractic (38 percent) and physical therapy (44 percent).
- Of people who had at least one massage in the last five years, 30 percent report that they did so for health conditions such as pain management, injury rehabilitation, migraine control, or overall wellness.
- By comparison, only 22 percent had massages for simple relaxation, and just 13 percent for a "special indulgence."
- Survey respondents aged 45 to 64 have had an average of almost seven massages during the past 12 months; aged 18 to 44 have had an average of five.
- Women (32 percent) are more likely than men (23 percent) to give a gift of a massage.

Parallel to the nationwide trend of people living longer and healthier lives, massage among older baby boomers (ages 55 to 64) has tripled since 1997. It's not just seniors who are increasing their use of massage, but people in Gen X (ages 25 to 34) and Gen Y (ages 18 to 24) as well. Men and women in these younger age brackets are more apt to view massage as beneficial to their health, versus as purely a luxury. They are also three times more likely to choose massage over medication to deal with pain.[5]

Another trend in massage is the increased funding of research into the benefits of alternative therapies. One of the predominant sources of funding for complementary and alternative medicine (CAM) research is the National Center for Complementary and Alternative Medicine, under the auspices of the National Institutes of Health. Its predecessor, the Office of Alternative Medicine, started with a budget of $2 million in 1991. The largest budget jump occurred in 2003, when NCCAM funding went from $44.3 in 2002 to $113.4 in 2004, more than two-and-a-half times the previous year. Since 2005, funding has more or less plateaued, but still remains at an all-time high, $121.6 million in 2008.[6] This increased interest in alternative therapies has implications for massage therapists who want to become more involved in research, and is discussed in more depth in Chapter 8.

Research funding for complementary and alternative medicine has increased more than 250% since 2003.

Heightened interest also raises public awareness of the benefits of massage. Along with these trends, the use of complementary medicine, including massage, is on the rise, as are wellness programs. As public awareness rises, more people will seek massage for the first time, and you will have the opportunity to develop a long-term therapeutic relationship with them.

All these reasons for rapid growth are good news for you as a new practitioner. Your clients may be infants or adults, athletes, integrative health care patients, or even animals. Among the many options for a massage career are practices devoted exclusively to massage in integrative health care settings such as clinics and hospitals, and other facilities such as cruise ships, resorts, and fitness centers.

FIGURE 1.2
Consumer Trends in Massage Therapy

WHY PEOPLE HAVE MASSAGE

Medical reasons: 30%

Relaxation/stress reduction: 22%

Pampering: 13%

AWARENESS OF MASSAGE THERAPY'S ROLE IN HEALTH AND WELLNESS

Have used massage for pain management (of those who have had massage within the past 5 years): 30%

Agree that massage can be effective in reducing pain: 87%

Agree that massage can be beneficial to health and wellness: 85%

Would like to see their insurance plans cover massage therapy: 59%

CONSUMER AGE DIFFERENCES AND THEIR USE OF MASSAGE

Ages 45 to 64 who received massage for medical reasons: 38%

Ages 18 to 44 who received massage for medical reasons: 25%

Ages 45 to 64 who have discussed massage therapy with their doctors or health care providers: 23%

Ages 18 to 44 who have discussed massage therapy with their doctors or health care providers: 18%

Source: AMTA: 2007 Massage Therapy Consumer Survey Fact Sheet. Available at http:// www.amtamassage.org/media/consumersurvey_factsheet.html.

DEMOGRAPHICS OF MASSAGE THERAPISTS

Trends regarding where massage therapists spend their time, and how they spend it, correlate roughly with consumer demand trends. While not downplaying the importance of massage for relaxation and stress management, massage therapists are broadening their professional viewpoints to the bigger picture of prevention and wellness. Additionally, as evidence-based research verifies the health benefits of massage, massage therapists are finding more opportunities to not only focus on rehabilitation or integrative-health-care-related massage, but more opportunities to be paid for it by clients' insurance coverage.

A profile of "a typical massage therapist" does not exist. As the data in Figure 1.3 show, massage therapists work in a variety of settings, both massage and non-massage related, and can be self-employed, employed, and sometimes both.

While pay isn't necessarily the motivating factor for choosing a career in massage therapy, many (43%) earn enough to support themselves financially. Going rates differ depending on where you live and who your clients are. An average frequently quoted is $1 per minute, though this is generally lower in rural areas and generally higher in urban areas.

One of the most attractive features of a career in massage is its flexibility. As shown in the following examples of massage therapists' career development and daily schedules, Real Touch 1.1 and Real Touch 1.2, no one style fits all. Once you have earned your credentials to practice massage, there are many "mix and match" approaches to making a living—some using massage as the main focus, and others using it to supplement other skills or work.

Hourly massage rates differ depending on location and type of massage, but many sources quote $1 a minute as a general guideline.

FIGURE 1.3

Demographics of Massage Therapy
Profession

AREA SURVEYED	RESULTS
Gender[1]	83% female
	17% male
Age[1]	Mid-40s, on average
Full-time vs. Part-time[2]	Full-time defined as working 27 hours per week on average.
	About 19 hours per week is spent giving massages.
% of Work Day Spent Performing Massage Therapy[2]	72% giving massages
	7% time spent marketing
	10% general business tasks
	11% other tasks
Earnings[2]	Employees average $30 per hour plus $9 tip = $39/hour avg.
	Self-employed average $44 per hour plus $9 tip = $53/hour avg.
	Employers who pay the majority of the massage therapists' expenses pay on average $15 per hour.
First Careers[2]	76% of massage therapists had other careers before becoming massage therapists.
	24% entered massage therapy as their first career.
Work Settings[2]	Work in own home: 33%
	Spa/salon: 29%
	Work in my own massage place of business: 28%
	Health care setting: 24%
	Health club/athletic facility: 7%
	Massage franchise: 5%
	Other: 5%
	Note: Percentage totals exceed 100% because some massage therapists work in more than one setting.
Self-employed vs. Employee[2]	76% self-employed
	30% employee (either full-time or part-time)
	Note: Percentage totals exceed 100% because some massage therapists are part-time employees and also self-employed.
Work Other Jobs[2]	43% work only as massage therapists.
	57% also earn income from another profession or job.
Expected Growth Rate[3]	20% employment increase projected from 2006 to 2016.
Number of Schools[3]	1,500 massage therapy postsecondary schools, college programs, and training programs in the United States.
Employment[3]	Massage therapists held about 118,000 jobs in 2006 (in the United States).
	64% were self-employed.

Sources: [1]AMTA Massage Therapy Industry Fact Sheet (2005); [2]2007 Massage Therapy Industry Evaluation Trend Report (November 2007), conducted by North Star Research on behalf of American Massage Therapy Association; [3]Bureau of Labor Statistics, U.S. Department of Labor, Occupational Outlook Handbook, 2008–09 Edition, Massage Therapists, at http://www.bls.gov/oco/ocos295.htm.

Background	Helicopter pilot with the National Guard before becoming a massage therapist.
Oct. 1998	Graduated from Pennsylvania Institute of Massage Therapy.
Mar. 1999	Passed the National Certification Exam. Although Pennsylvania is not regulated (legislation is pending), she wanted the professional credential, and to have her certification in the event they become regulated at some point.
Oct. 1998–May 2000	Practiced massage therapy in fitness centers and a chiropractor's office, taught up to 12 aerobic classes a week, and served 5 to 10 hours a week in the National Guard. (As a helicopter pilot, she was required to maintain flight hours.) She was full-time mom to two sons, ages 2 and 5.
May 2000	Went into military full-time. Newly divorced and needed consistent income and health insurance. Massage took a back seat, but she continued to maintain her national certification.
2001	Began 4-year program of training in traditional hands-on-healing techniques. Says this training gave her the courage to retire from military and practice the healing arts full-time.
June 2004	Established home-based practice. After a period of time trying to center her efforts, she realized she needed a map, otherwise known as a business plan.
Lucky break	Began doing chair massages at a local gym. When the gym moved locations, they provided a massage room for her to use. The gym is franchising and has offered her the opportunity to grow with them.
Advice to new massage therapists	DON'T wait to take the National Certification Exam. Sit for the exam as soon as you can upon graduating from school while your knowledge is fresh.
	Also, work with a trusted supervisor. Burnout is very common in our profession. She knew she was burning out when her thumbs started to hurt and her mind kept wandering during a session rather than totally focusing on her work. Her supervisor's guidance and support helps her mentally, emotionally, and spiritually, which expands her healing practice.

DAY IN THE LIFE OF

5:00 a.m. three days a week, 7:00 a.m. two days a week	Day begins
6:00 a.m.	Three days a week: Teach fitness class at gym.
	Two days a week: Appointments with clients at home-based clients. These might be for massage or for holistic healing.
7:30 a.m.	Return home, shower, take sons to camp or school.
8:00 a.m.	Return to gym and see massage clients, sometimes up until 6:00 p.m.

12:30 p.m.	Break for lunch.
Afternoon	On the days she's not with massage clients at the gym, she's doing paperwork, laundry, and paying bills.
4:00 p.m.	Pick up sons.
Fees	Income demographics (a farming area) where Bobbi lives allow her to charge a rate of $35/half hour, $55/hour, and $80/hour-and-a-half.
General comments	Flexibility allows her to schedule around her family's needs.
	Time spent seeing clients: 25–33%
	Remainder of time: commuting to gym, doing laundry (including sheets for the practice), doing paperwork for the practice, teaching fitness classes, maintaining her own personal fitness, volunteering for AMTA, and taking care of her family.

Chronology of a Massage Career – Meet Ruth Lang   *Real Touch 1.2*

Background	After graduating from high school in 1989, studied graphic design and photography part-time at the University of Minnesota and worked as a bus driver part-time. Married in 1992, had three children by 1997, still drove a bus, and began massage school at the Aveda Institute Minneapolis part-time.
1998	Completed massage therapy training and started working as a massage therapist at a salon in St. Paul, MN. She did not take national certification when she finished training because it's not required in her state, plus "it was too expensive and I was too busy. Now I wish I had taken it just to have it."
2003	Spent one month in Hawaii learning facial rejuvenation. Got divorced, and started giving massages to friends and family at home to bring in extra income.
2005–08	Employed at salon 32 hours a week on average.
Advice to new massage therapists	Keep learning new things—this keeps you alert and interested! Keep receiving services of all kinds—this reminds you how wonderful the work is, and how much more you have to learn!
	Be grateful every time a person puts themselves into your hands—they are all a gift—even the grumpy ones, sometimes them most of all because they have the greatest potential for transformation.
	If you don't love it, do something else. This needs to be an expression of your playful, spiritual, physical, joyful, intuitive, connective, releasing self. Open to the needs of all different types of people—if that doesn't do it for you, figure out what does and go do that.

DAY IN THE LIFE OF

6:30 a.m. weekdays	Drive 15-year-old daughter to high school, drop 13-year-old son at bus stop, have breakfast with 11-year-old daughter and then drive her to school.

8:30 a.m.	Start work day at salon
Client appointments 9:00 a.m.– 6:45 p.m.	Client appointments Monday/Wednesday at 9:00, 11:15, 11:30, 1:00, 2:15, 3:30, 5:30, and 6:45. Salon makes all appointments, and clients are checked in and out by the front desk staff. All linens are sent out, all oils candles, etc. are provided. Employees are given business cards and have ads in magazines, billboards, radio, etc.
	She teaches massage classes to newer employees on such topics as hot stone massage, hydrotherm massage, body wraps, and a treatment called the PPE (pressure point experience). Classes usually happen on Mondays and are a nice diversion from taking clients.
	Kids go to their dad's house after school. Ruth takes the kids to their many sports events and attends most of them.
8:45 p.m.	Get home from work. Have dinner with fiancé, also a massage therapist, who is studying to get his degree in naturopathic medicine.
11:00 p.m.	In bed by 11 most nights.
Weekends	Mostly weekends are spent at sports events with the kids, but sometimes she'll take a massage guest for a home appointment on Sunday evenings.
Fees	Ruth currently charges $106 for 60 min. massage for which she schedules 1 hour and 15 minutes. As an employee, she keeps $54 of that $106 before taxes. The employer offers health insurance and dental, a 401K, and 3 weeks paid vacation after 6 years employment.

CAREER SETTINGS

The variety of settings in which you can perform massage is broad enough to suit a wide range of career interests. In this section, we look at opportunities in the field for practitioners in these settings:

- Wellness (includes workplace and chair massage)
- Integrative Health Care
- Sports /Fitness
- Spa
- Corporate/Franchise
- Specialty
  - Equine/Animal
  - Pregnancy/Infant
  - Elderly

Because types of work settings vary in their philosophies of how massage should be integrated to support their clients, and because there is a great deal of variance among businesses within the same type of setting, it is up to you to ask questions to establish realistic expectations. Some of the questions you should ask are:

- What are the requirements to work here?
- Will I be asked to give a demo massage?
- How would I be paid?

- Would I work here as an employee or as an independent contractor?
- How does this business market the service of massage therapy?
- What professional standards does this business adhere to?
- Who provides supplies?
- Who does the scheduling?
- How are clients assigned to massage therapists?
- Is insurance provided?
- Who is liable in the event of problems?

There is probably as much variation within each of these types of work settings as there is between them, but the following section describes general attributes of each.

WELLNESS SETTINGS

The emphasis of wellness programs is on promoting and maintaining health rather than on treating illness or disease. Wellness programs are based on models that focus attention on mind, body, and spirit, and to the total environment in which a person lives. The emphasis on wellness rather than on disease has been shown to reduce employee absenteeism, reduce the number of sick days and hours lost from work, and reduce overall health care costs.[7]

The National Wellness Institute recommends the "Six-Dimensional Wellness Model," developed by Bill Hettler, M.D.[8] (Figure 1.4). The six dimensions are:

- *Environmental*—Emphasizes interdependence between others and nature, and encourages contributing to one's environment and community. Social wellness follows the tenets "It is better to contribute to the common welfare than to think only of ourselves," and "It is better to live in harmony with others and our environment than to live in conflict with them."
- *Occupational*—Recognizes personal satisfaction through work. Its tenets are "It is better to choose a career that is consistent with our personal values, interest, and beliefs, than to choose one that is unrewarding to us."
- *Spiritual*—Recognizes our search for meaning and purpose in human existence. Its tenets are "It is better to ponder the meaning of life for ourselves and be tolerant of others' beliefs than to close our minds," and "It is better to live in a way that is consistent with our values and beliefs than to do otherwise and feel untrue to ourselves."
- *Physical*—Recognizes the need for regular physical activity. Its tenets are "It is better to consume foods and beverages that enhance good health rather than those that impair it," and "It is better to be physically fit than out of shape."
- *Intellectual*—recognizes one's creative, stimulating mental activities. Its tenets are "It is better to stretch and challenge our minds than to become self-satisfied and unproductive," and "It is better to identify potential problems and choose appropriate courses of action than to wait, worry, and contend with major concerns later."
- *Emotional*—Recognizes awareness and acceptance of one's feelings. Its tenets are "It is better to be aware of and accept our feelings than to deny them," and "It is better to be optimistic than pessimistic."

Promoting wellness surpasses the benefits of simply feeling good. A 2005 meta-analysis of 16 studies reporting cost/benefit ratios showed returns of $5.93 for every $1.00 invested in wellness programs (that is, for every $1.00 invested in wellness programs, a company reduced its expenses by $5.93[9] in terms of such things as reduced sick days, on-the-job injuries, etc., as shown below), and a 2006 article in American Journal of Health Promotion reported a payback of $10 for every $1 spent on wellness programs.[10] These data are based on savings in such areas as:

- Reduction in average days of sick leave
- Reduction in number of hospital admissions

Businesses have a vested
interest in helping their
employees stay healthy:
For every $1.00 spent
on wellness programs,
businesses save as much
as $10.00.

- Reduction in number of physician visits
- Reduction in per capita health costs
- Reduction in injury incidence
- Reduction in per capita workers' compensation cost

Wellness programs vary widely in their makeup; Figure 1.5 shows components that are frequently included. It is not surprising that many companies and organizations that recognize the benefits of wellness also recognize that massage can be an important and appreciated component of a wellness program.

One attribute common to all wellness settings is the focus on the health of the entire person. While it is important that a massage therapist be a self-care role model in any setting in which she works, it is especially important in wellness settings. Clients will be alert to a wellness practitioner's eating habits, mental and emotional well-being, and physical health and vitality.

Among the benefits of working in a wellness setting is that many of them create

FIGURE 1.4
Six Dimensions of Wellness

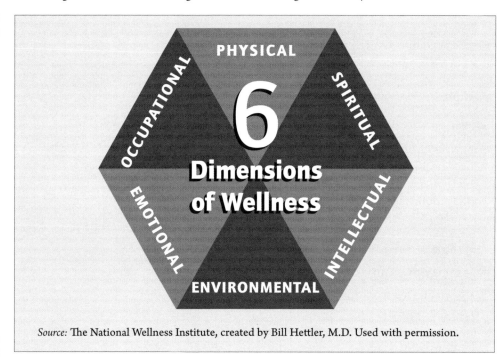

Source: The National Wellness Institute, created by Bill Hettler, M.D. Used with permission.

FIGURE 1.5
Components of Wellness Programs

art appreciation	health club classes	mental health counseling
bicycle programs (encouraging bike to work)	health evaluation/screening	Pilates classes
blood pressure screening	group/intramural sports (golf, volleyball, softball, etc.)	smoking cessation
breast examination	job counseling	strength conditioning
cholesterol screening	massage	stress reduction training
creative movement/dance	nap rooms	stretch breaks
diversity training	nature appreciation	substance abuse counseling
ergonomics training	nutrition counseling	tai chi
fitness training and classes	martial arts	weight-loss clinics
healing gardens	meditation classes	workplace safety
		yoga

opportunities for client education. Clients are likely to be interested in knowing how massage and related holistic health practices affect their health. Working in a wellness setting also can provide opportunities to partner with other health professionals, such as nutrition specialists, yoga and other fitness or spiritual practitioners, and meditation leaders, to provide your clients with a well-rounded menu of wellness practices.

Types of businesses and organizations that are likely to offer wellness programs include:

- college and university health centers
- community-based wellness centers (park districts, seniors programs, recreational centers)
- company work sites
- state and local government offices
- hospitals
- independent wellness centers
- integrative health centers
- medical clinics
- retirement communities
- substance abuse centers
- women's health centers

Workplace Massage

One specialty setting of massage under the wellness umbrella is workplace massage, also known as corporate massage. Reasons a company might make massage available to employees include reduced absences, increased productivity, reduced workplace injuries, reduced health care costs, and higher employee retention rates. In its 18th annual survey, *Working Mother* magazine (2003) reported that 77 percent of the best companies for working mothers to work for offered massage as an employee benefit, compared to 11 percent of all companies in general, nationwide, that offer massage."

RESOURCES FOR WELLNESS PROGRAMS

ASSOCIATIONS AND ORGANIZATIONS

Association for Worksite Health Promotion: www.awhp.org

Health Enhancement Research Organization: www.the-hero.org

HealthWorld Online: www.healthy.net

National Wellness Institute: www.nationalwellness.org

Wellness Councils of America: www.welcoa.org

WEBSITES AND PUBLICATIONS

American Journal of Health Promotion: www.healthpromotionjournal.com

FitWell Associates: www.fitwellinc.com

Wellness Web: www.wellweb.com

Workplace massage can take on many forms:

- Employer pays entire fee, or employer and employee share the fee.
- Massage therapist comes to the workplace, or the employee goes to the massage therapist's site.
- Massages are offered in the workplace on a given day each month or week, or employees receive a coupon that they can redeem x number of times in a given period, with any one of several designated massage therapists. This can be a great resource for you to network for your own practice.

- In general, corporate massage programs imply chair massage. If employees go to the massage therapist's site, they will more likely receive a table (full body) massage.

Finding out if a company already has a workplace massage program might take some digging. Steps you might take are:

- Call the company's human resources department to ask if they have a corporate massage program.
- If the company already has a program in place, request the name of the massage therapist who operates the program so you can contact him or her.
- Offer to be that massage therapist's backup when he or she is unavailable.
- If the company does not have a program, consider starting your own. Starting a workplace massage business from scratch requires a willingness to meet with potential clients and sell them on your idea. Because workplace massage is a growing area of opportunity for massage therapists, there are many resources available to help you get started. See Spotlight on Business, "How to Start a Workplace Massage Business."

SPOTLIGHT ᐧᐧᐧᐧᐧON BUSINESS

How to Start a Workplace Massage Program

Taking massage into the workplace can offer great benefits for you, and for employees and employers alike. Some massage therapists base their entire practice on workplace massage, and many others spend one or two days a week at an employer's location and work in their private practices on other days.

THREE STEPS TO GET STARTED

Generating interest in workplace massage—especially on the part of the employer, who must agree to the program—is at the heart of getting your program started. Here are the basic steps to follow:

1 Make a list of prospective employers who might be your corporate customers, and find out how to contact their human resources or employee benefits manager.
2 Send an introductory letter. Include materials that help educate the employer about the benefits of workplace massage.
3 Follow up by phone and personal visits.

INTRO LETTER

Your intro letter should be brief and concise. In it, you will:

1 Describe the benefits of workplace massage to the employer.
2 Your letter should address liability, an issue of concern to all employers.
3 Describe how such a program could work at this company. Suggest 20-minute on-site chair massages, which could be paid for by the employer or split half and half between employer and employee. Another option is that the employer would provide certificates for the employees to schedule off-site massage with you, again at either the full price or at some percentage of the price.
4 Offer to set up a workplace massage program for this employer.
5 Tell the employer you will call within the next week to answer any questions and to discuss setting up a program.

A sample letter can be found on the AMTA Members Only website at http://www.amtamassage.org/member/chairltr.html.

Also, consider including additional materials, such as a brochure that tells about massage or an article that discusses workplace massage specifically. (You may request permission to reprint "Massage Is in Business," which appeared in the Spring 2004 issue of *mtj*. It is downloadable in pdf format at http://www.amtamassage.org/journal/spring04_journal/MassageIsInBusiness.pdf.)

Keep a prospect tracking sheet on each employer to note his or her response when you call back. On the prospect sheet, in addition to including the employer's address, phone number, e-mail, and date of contact, note the employer's questions and whether he or she is interested in offering on-site chair massage or off-site certificates.

Consider your options for hiring other massage therapists to supplement your appointment coverage when the program begins.

Don't be discouraged if some employers do not at first seem receptive to your ideas. After you have established a successful track record at one or more companies, you might ask one of your corporate clients if he or she would be willing to write a letter of recommendation that describes that company's experience with workplace massage. Use the letter to help encourage other employers to give it a try!

Source: Adapted from American Massage Therapy Association

Chair Massage

Chair massage is the most common type of massage offered in the workplace—but the workplace isn't the only place appropriate for a chair massage. There is a small industry built up around chair massage business opportunities, owing to the convenience and portability of chair massage, its relatively low business start-up costs, not to mention its client satisfaction qualities. Many sources credit David Palmer, founder of TouchPro, with developing a chair that is comfortable and suited to massage, and promoting the industry that is now known as chair massage.

The advantage to clients is that they can get a "quick fix" and feel refreshed and invigorated after receiving just a 15-minute massage. Plus, they remain fully clothed, and no oils or lotions are used, so there's no worry about getting residue on their clothes. The advantage to the massage therapist is that your business goes where you go—to workplaces, retail stores, fund-raising walks, community events, airport kiosks, art fairs. Anywhere people will be, you can be, too.

RESOURCES FOR CHAIR MASSAGE

BOOKS, ARTICLES, TRAINING

Osborn, Karrie. (Feb/Mar 2006). "Massage for the Masses." *Massage & Bodywork*.

Palmer, David. (Winter 2000). "Negotiating an Agreement." *mtj*.

Stephens, Ralph (2005). *Therapeutic Chair Massage*. Philadelphia: Lippincott Williams & Wilkins.

TouchPro, The Websource for Professional Chair Massage: www.touchpro.com

VIDEOS

Chair Massage with Connie Scholl, 40 minutes (At Peace Videos): www.atpeacemedia.com.

Chair Massage with George Sprague, 45 minutes (George Sprague Productions), available from multiple sources. Google name of video.

Relax to the Max, 14 minutes (Eric Brown): www.chairmassagetraining.com.

INTEGRATIVE HEALTH CARE SETTINGS

The practice of massage therapy is growing in acceptance not only by consumers but by the medical community as well, and with it, opportunities for massage therapists. A survey conducted by the American Massage Therapy Association in 2006 reported that 9 million more people discussed massage therapy with their doctor than they did just five years earlier. Perhaps even more significantly, almost twice as many doctors recommended massage to their patients than they had 5 years before. In the field of health care, physicians are the most inclined to recommend massage therapy (59 percent), followed by chiropractors (48 percent) and physical therapists (47 percent).[12] In a similar vein, consumers reported that using massage for medical purposes (30 percent) had surpassed relaxation (26 percent) as their main motivation for getting a massage.[13] Medical purposes might include injury recovery, pain reduction, headache control, and overall health and wellness. These combined trends—doctors recommending massage and consumers seeking massage for health care—might suggest that those Americans (63 percent) who said they would be more inclined to try massage therapy if it were offered in conjunction with other health care treatments will one day get their wish. See the section "Client Insurance Billing and Reimbursement" in Chapter 6 for more information on this business practice.

The same survey previously cited reported that more than one-quarter of the population ranked medication and massage as the best form of treatment for relief from pain. In fact, nearly half (46 percent) of the survey participants had a massage at some time to relieve pain, and this percentage was even greater for people in the 18-to-34-year-old age group.[14]

As health benefits of massage become more broadly accepted, there are more opportunities to collaborate with medical practitioners. An organization named the Hospital-Based Massage Network offers extensive support to massage therapists seeking this type of section (see Spotlight on Business, "Hospital-Based Massage Network"). One avenue for combining massage and integrative health care practices is to work as an independent contractor at an integrative health care establishment, or to accept and make referrals. For the massage therapist interested in working in an integrative health care setting, the possibilities include such places and practices as the following:

- addiction counseling centers (mostly volunteer)
- athletic training
- chiropractic practice
- hospices (mostly volunteer)
- medi-spas
- integrative medical centers
- hospitals
- medical clinics
- naturopathic practice
- nursing homes
- obstetric practice
- oncology centers
- orthopedic physician practice
- pediatric practice
- physical therapy clinics
- physician family practice
- rehabilitation centers
- retirement centers
- rheumatology practice
- sports medicine clinics

Hospital-Based Massage Network

Founded in 1995, HBMN publishes books specifically aimed at helping massage therapists and hospitals find each other and provide benefits to patients.

Tel.: 970-407-9232

Website: www.HBMN.com

E-mail: Editor@HBMN.com

PUBLICATIONS BY HBMN

Koch, Laura (Ed.) *Hospital-Based Massage Programs in Review.*

Koch, Laura (Ed.) *Exploring Hospital-Based Massage:* Selected Articles from HBMN Quarterly 1995-2000.

Koch, Laura (Ed.) *1001 Sources to Build Your Hospital-Based Massage Program.*

GETTING STARTED IN HOSPITAL-BASED MASSAGE (TOPICS EXCERPTED FROM *1001 SOURCES* BOOK)

Consultants

Insurance Reimbursement

Manuals

Organizations

Research

Training: In-Hospital/In-Patient; Touch for Seriously Ill, Elderly, and Dying; Therapeutic Touch; Cancer Patients; Geriatric Patients; HIV/AIDS; Manual Lymph Drainage; Pregnancy and Infant Massage.

Universal Precautions: Health and Safety Standards

ONLINE FEATURES

Join the Network: Colleague registration form

Message Board

Register Your Hospital Program

Do your homework before contacting professionals who work in integrative health care settings. As is true of any good communication between people who work in different settings, knowing as much as you can about the specialty in which you want to work will help you present yourself credibly. Credibility requires knowing the terminology, understanding the concepts, and being familiar with the research. You will want to be familiar not only with current research about the effects of massage on particular conditions, but also about the administrative side of health care settings, such as payment options, health insurance coverage, and the issues of dealing with insurance companies. When discussing particular research studies, as emphasized in Chapter 8, you will want to be knowledgeable about research methodology so you can determine whether a particular study is credible or not.

Many schools of massage therapy today provide specialty training in massage practiced in integrative health care settings. Subjects most commonly taught to students who want to provide complementary massage within an integrative health care setting include:[15]

> Allied professionals who work in integrative health care settings will know you are a professional when you use medical terminology correctly and you know results of recent massage research.

- *Pathophysiology*—This is the study of specific medical conditions. Massage therapists need to understand not only the appropriate massage techniques for a particular condition but also the medical treatment. Knowledge of pathophysiology helps you determine cautions and contraindications for a variety of medical conditions, and to know when it is appropriate to refer a client to another specialist.
- *Medical Modalities*—Learn about modalities used in medical settings, such as electrotherapy, ultrasound, electrical stimulation, and pharmacology. Learn your state's regulations that govern various modalities. For example, in some states, massage therapists are allowed to perform ultrasound tests. In others, they cannot.

- *Techniques*—Learn appropriate techniques for a variety of medical conditions and diseases. Neuromuscular work is most common. Some medical conditions, such as burns, require non-touch types of body therapy, such as energy modalities.
- *Communication Skills and Recordkeeping*—Familiarity with terminology and recordkeeping specific to different types of medical practice is key to gaining credibility in these settings. Good communication also requires understanding organizational structures and chains of command typical in particular medical settings.

The quality and availability of resources that describe how to practice massage in an integrative health care setting have grown steadily in recent years.

RESOURCES FOR MASSAGE IN AN INTEGRATIVE HEALTH CARE SETTING

BOOKS

Chaitow, Leon. (2007). *A Massage Therapist's Guide to Lower Back and Pelvic Pain.* Elsevier.

Curties, Debra. (1999). *Massage Therapy and Cancer.* Moncton, NB: Curties-Overzet. Toll-free 1-888-649 5411 or www.curties-overzet.com

Fritz, Sandy, Leon Chaitow, & Glen Hymel (2008). *Clinical Massage in the Healthcare Setting,* Elsevier/Mosby.

Hendrickson, Thomas (2002). *Massage for People with Orthopedic Conditions.* Philadelphia: Lippincott Willliams & Wilkins.

Lowe, Whitney (2003). *Orthopedic Massage,* Elsevier.

MacDonald, Gayle. (1999). *Medicine Hands: Massage Therapy for People with Cancer.*

MacDonald, Gayle. (2004) *Massage for the Hospital Patient and Medically Frail Client.* Philadelphia: Lippincott Williams & Wilkins.

Walton, Tracy. Medical Conditions in Massage Therapy. (in press). Philadelphia: Lippincott Williams & Wilkins.

Werner, Ruth. (2008). *A Massage Therapist's Guide to Pathology* (4th ed). Philadelphia: Lippincott Williams & Wilkins.

Persad, Randal. (2001). *Massage Therapy and Medications.* Toronto: Curties-Overzet.

Wible, Jean. (2005). *Pharmacology for Massage Therapy.* Philadelphia: Lippincott Williams & Wilkins.

TRAINING

Walton, Tracy. Cancer and Massage Therapy Training: www.tracywalton.com/trainingschedule

Zazeski, Jim. Oncology Massage Certificate Program (accredited by COMTA): www.massageprogram.com.

SPORTS/FITNESS SETTINGS

The last several decades have witnessed a dramatic rise in the level of athletic performance. Many believe this increase can be attributed to improved technology and equipment, enhanced understanding of how nutrition fuels the body, enlightenment about psychological aspects of competition, and scientific advances in the study of body structure and function. The growing awareness of sports massage as a valuable addition to other physical therapies has become a key component in athletes' training regimens.

Extensive scientific research has yet to be conducted regarding the effects of massage on athletic performance and recovery, although some research has shown limited effects. For example, one study[16] looked at the effect of massage on delayed-onset muscle soreness in athletes and determined that the passage of time between strenuous exercise and relief from pain, rather than massage, was the greater factor. However, anecdotal evidence suggests that some benefits of sports massage to the athlete or fitness enthusiast might be:

- Reduced chance of injury, both through education about preparation, as well as through deep tissue massage;
- Improved range of motion, strength, performance times;
- Shortened recovery time between workouts;
- Maximized supply of nutrition and oxygen through increased blood flow.

Careers in fitness/sports massage can be found in many of the following settings:

- college and university sports teams
- professional sports teams
- sports massage clinics
- health and fitness centers
- rehabilitation clinics
- athletic resorts
- golf resorts and clubs

RESOURCES FOR SPORTS MASSAGE

ASSOCIATIONS

Canadian Sport Massage Therapists Assn., P.O. Box 1330, Unity, Saskatchewan, S0K 4L0 Canada (306) 228-2808; www.csmta.ca.

International Sports Science Association: www.issaonline.com

BOOKS

Archer, Pat. (2006). *Therapeutic Massage in Athletics.* Philadelphia: Lippincott Williams & Wilkins.

Karageanes, Steven. (2004). *Principles of Manual Sports Medicine.* Philadelphia: Lippincott Williams & Wilkins.

Benjamin, Patricia, & Scott Lamp. (2005). *Understanding Sports Massage.* Champaign, IL: Human Kinetics.

VIDEO

Massage for Sports Health Care. (1998). 45 minutes. Champaign, IL: Human Kinetics.

TRAINING

Online Sports Injury Clinic. Describes contraindications for sports massage, and shows basic sports massage tutorials. Available at: www.sportsinjuryclinic.net

Sports Massage Program. (2008). Offered by Natural Wellness: 1-800-364-5722;

www.naturalwellnessonline.com

Sports massage practice can be categorized as maintenance or as event-related. Maintenance is integrated into a client's training program. It is regularly scheduled and proactive. A sports massage practitioner needs to have a thorough understanding of anatomy and kinesiology, along with expert knowledge of which muscles are used in a given sports and which are likely candidates for trouble. Zeroing in on particular muscle systems and working specific tissues helps build optimal conditioning and prevent strain and injury. The objective of a maintenance program is to help the athlete reach optimal performance through injury-free training.

Sports massage is used pre-event, when it supplements an athlete's warm-up to enhance circulation and reduce excess muscle and mental tension prior to competition. It improves tissue pliability and assists in metabolic exchange, readying the athlete for top performance. It is also used post-event, when it is geared toward reducing the trauma that occurs after the cessation of vigorous exercise. Helped by massage, the body is able to gradually slow down yet maintain oxygen flow to tired muscles still requiring elevated levels of oxygen.

If you've always loved sports or participated in sports, this specialty might be satisfying to you.

SPA SETTINGS

The spa industry was one of the fastest growing segments of career opportunity for massage therapists in the years 2002 to 2007. According to the 2007 Spa Industry Study,[17] conducted by the International Spa Association (ISPA), the number of spas in the United States (14,600) has nearly tripled since 2002. Of the estimated 100 million active spa-goers in the United States, women make up the greater proportion of spa clients (69 percent). Other findings of the study included:

- Day spas receive the majority of visits (in 2006, there were an estimated 111 million spa visits in the United States, and in Canada 17 million).
- In 2006, the U.S. spa industry generated $9.4 billion and Canada $1.03 billion (both stated in U.S. dollars).
- The average price of a spa treatment in the United States is $79 U.S. dollars, in Canada $63 Canada dollars.
- Environmentally sustainable practices are carried out in 76 percent of U.S. spas and 86 percent of Canada spas. Such practices include on-site organic gardens, products made from locally grown fruits, vegetables, herbs and plants; mineral makeup, and green building tactics.

Many massage therapists view spas as a really good way to gain experience when they first start their careers. In fact, the percentage of massage therapists who work in a spa setting has nearly doubled since 2005, and was reported to be 29 percent in 2007.[18] A massage therapist can gain invaluable experience working in an efficient business setting and learning good skills at communicating effectively with a broad variety of clients. But don't make the mistake of assuming that spas are only for entry level careers. The best spas have excellent massage therapist longevity. When you interview for a position, ask whether massage therapists work there as employees or independent contractors. (See the list of questions at the beginning of this "Career Settings" section.)

Types of spas can essentially be categorized into four segments:

- *Destination spa*—This means that the spa is "the whole event" —it is all-inclusive, and guests usually select one of several packages of services for an entire week or partial week.
- *Day spa*—Day spas make up about three-quarters of the spa industry. This is where you'll find a salon of spa services, and you go by appointment. This could even be at a fitness center. You do not stay overnight.
- *Resort spa*—The spa is located within a hotel or complex; the spa is almost always independently owned and managed. It may focus on a specialty, such as fitness, burnout, rejuvenation, or beauty.
- *Cruise ships*—Most cruise ships have spas, which are basically like resort spas except that they are on cruise ships.

The well-managed spa is designed to serve its clients in a manner that is both relaxing and efficient. An essential attribute of spa profitability is productivity. Efficiency on the part of spa staff is necessary because of the need to seamlessly schedule multiple clients to take the most advantage of spa services and to improve profitability of the business.

If you desire to work in the spa industry but your school does not provide this type of training, you might check out opportunities to take continuing education at regional conferences or other schools or programs of massage therapy. Keep in mind that learning more modalities makes you more employable and offers the opportunity for greater profitability.

Probably the biggest learning curve a massage therapist encounters when she accepts a job at a spa is the fact that she will be expected to work in addition to massage. Most spas are not geared to staffing employees who perform only one specialty service; they must rely on their employees to perform a broad range of functions. These functions might include providing guest services such as reception duties, changing linens, or selling retail products. Performing a variety of functions helps to reduce burnout, as you are expanding your skills in actually running a business, while you get necessary breaks from performing end-to-end massages.

Spa workers generally perform some business support functions as well as massage, which add to their overall business skills and position them well for future career growth.

RESOURCES FOR MASSAGE IN SPA SETTINGS

ASSOCIATIONS

Day Spa Association (affiliated with International Medical Spa Association), 310 17th St., Union City, NJ 07087; 201-865-2065; www.dayspaassociation.com

International Medical Spa Society; 1-866-MEDISPA; www.medicalspasociety.com

International SPA Association (ISPA), 2365 Harrodsburg Rd., Suite A325, Lexington, KY 40504; 1-888-651-4772; www.experienceispa.com.

BOOKS

Bankowski, Linda, & Julie Register. (2007). *International Standards of Spa Excellence.*

Capellini, Steve. (2006). *Massage Therapy Career Guide for Hands-On Success.* Milady Salon Ovations.

Miner, Nanette & Gina Moncada. *101 Media and Marketing Tips for Spa Owners, Stylists, and Managers*

MAGAZINES

American Spa

Healing Lifestyles and Spas Magazine

Luxury SpaFinder Magazine: www.spafinder.com

Spa Life Magazine (a national Canadian magazine)

WEBSITES

Discover Spas with Julie Register: www.discoverspas.com

Spa Jobs: www.spajobs.com

An important thing to remember at a spa is that you are essentially working in a corporate environment. This means that your options for career growth are almost unlimited in terms of branching out in many directions within the health and wellness environment. In a well-run spa, you need to be an enthusiastic team player whose energy is directed to helping the spa serve its guests in the best way possible, both from a guest satisfaction and a profitability standpoint.

Spas are an excellent place to start a massage therapy career, for two reasons of significance to the beginning massage therapist. One, they give the new massage therapy practitioner an opportunity to build stamina and techniques from the experience of working on numerous clients. And two, spas expose the new massage therapist to a wide diversity of clients, allowing the practitioner to refine his or her personal interaction and customer service skills.

CORPORATE/FRANCHISE SETTINGS

A relatively new area of massage careers is the corporate/franchise setting. In a trend that started in the late 1990s, some massage businesses capitalized on the concepts of volume pricing, location convenience, and nationwide name recognition, by franchising their operations.

One of the earliest entrants to franchising was The Great American Back Rub,[19] which was started in 1998 in Toronto. Massage Envy, a frontrunner in extending massage franchising nationwide, has more than 660 franchise operations throughout the United States. Other examples of franchises are represented in all areas of the United States, including Hand and Stone Massage Spa[20] (started in Toms River, New Jersey), Keep in Touch Massage (regional Minneapolis), Elements Therapeutic[21] (started in Aurora and Centennial, Colorado), and Massage Heights (Baltimore, Maryland).

Key to many massage franchises' marketing is their appeal to clients' busy schedules and cost-consciousness. For instance, Massage Envy advertises, "Get a great massage that fits your busy schedule and budget," and Hand and Stone Massage Spa's tagline is "Love Thyself for Less." Franchises advertise their rates beginning at around $39.99 for an hour massage. The concept of most massage franchises is that clients will become "members" and will buy an annual membership. The introductory rate applies only for the first massage, and then continues at that rate only if the client buys a membership. Memberships usually offer other benefits in addition to low rates, such as incentives for bringing in other members and the ability to buy gift certificates at membership rates.

The focus on low cost is not the only concern of the well-run massage franchise. Franchise management and employees must also focus on providing customer satisfaction, or the franchise couldn't maintain and increase memberships. See Spotlight on Business, "More about Massage Franchises" for more detail about the pros and cons of owning and/ or working at a franchise.

SPOTLIGHT ⋔⋔⋔⋔ON BUSINESS

More About Massage Franchises

Investment required to buy a franchise license: Ranges from about $100,000 to $360,000
- This covers such costs as the franchise fee, space improvements and deposits, equipment and supplies, advertising and promotion, management training, and computerized operations support.

Pros and Cons of Working at a Franchise

Pros
- The franchise handles all your marketing and promotions.
- Most franchises provide all equipment, supplies, laundry, music, and session rooms.
- The franchise makes appointments on your behalf and handles all client administration (intake forms, billing, etc.)
- Encourages regular massages.
- Many franchises encourage low-cost, affordable, no-frills massage to people who might not otherwise consider it.

Cons

- Your take-home pay is generally X% of what the client pays, which is in most cases lower than you could earn if you were charging a private client.
- The work location may or may not be convenient for you.
- The hours your are asked to work may or may not be convenient for you.

See Real Touch 1.3 to read about one massage therapist who works at a Massage Envy location, to learn about his experience as a contractor to a franchise.

Chronology of a Massage Career – Meet Jerry Schobeloch	*Real Touch 1.3*
1968–1995	Worked for the Veterans Administration for 27 years, where he worked in the Dietetics, Radiology, Medical Records, and Library Services. While he was working for the VA, he also earned a B.A. in Education.
1995	Started getting neuropathy in both hands, and went to a chiropractor for help. Ended up getting his first massage, and the neuropathy, which turned out to have been stress related, was relieved. Took early retirement from the VA, and "tried to really retire, but couldn't." Over several years, worked at a jewelry store, a fraternal life insurance, and spent a lot of time gardening.
2000–2004	Enrolled in Travis Technical Center, Lakeland, Florida, and completed a 550-hour, 6-month massage therapy training program. Passed the NCTMB exam and received national certification. Then enrolled in East West College of Natural Medicine in Sarasota and earned acupuncture degree.
2000–2004	Had a private practice, home based, in Sarasota and Lakeland. Decided to move back to Midwest, his home base, because Florida "is pretty saturated with massage therapists and hurricanes."
2004–2006	Started private practice in a western suburb of Chicago; built back up to "a healthy business" within two years. Then a flood damaged his home, and the next year or better was spent repairing and renovating.
2007	As Jerry was rebuilding his home-based practice, he accepted a position with a new Massage Envy franchise outlet, where he is one of 19 massage therapists. Jerry's practice is now 75% Massage Envy, 25% private practice. Here are the things he appreciates about working for a franchise: Set hours, guaranteed paycheck, a 401K plan Opportunity to work with a diversity of clients The franchise does all the marketing, so Jerry doesn't have to The franchise takes care of business operations—scheduling appointments, laundry, billing, accounting, etc. Ability to develop clientele and have regular return clients
Advice to new massage therapists	After completing a 15-week class on how to develop a business, his expectation was that if he just put himself out there—through advertising, free coupons, gift certificates—clients would come. They didn't. Until someone works for someone else and learn the ropes, it's very difficult to run a profitable business. He feels that he's excellent at what he does—massage and shamanic healing—but he prefers to have someone else with business skills manage the business. He believes that people really benefit from what he does—so he lets someone else do the things he doesn't like to do.

Fees	Massage therapists earn approximately $17 an hour as employees of Massage Envy, depending on years of experience. They keep 100% of their tips and earn $5 for each membership they sell. In addition, they have 401K programs, and they earn cash bonuses after so many hours of massage. Jerry charges $50 an hour at his home-based practice.

SPECIALTY SETTINGS

In addition to the varied mainstream environments in which to practice massage therapy, several specialties have emerged that broaden your options further. These specialties may be practiced as sole pursuits, or in conjunction with a general practice. Specific training is available in all of these areas.

Pregnancy and Infant Massage

Women can benefit from massage while they are pregnant, during labor, and after the birth. Pregnancy has a significant impact, not only on the mother's habits and lifestyle, but on her body, too, as it alters to accommodate the new life within it. Finding ways to manage extra stress during this time is essential at every stage of pregnancy, from conception to birth, and afterward during the postpartum period. Massage has also been shown to be beneficial to infants.

BENEFITS BEFORE THE BIRTH
- Reduces stress
- Increases flow of oxygen and blood to tissues, accelerating nutrients to mother and baby
- Relieves backaches and other pains often experienced with pregnancy
- Decreases swelling and edema as it can drain toxins from the mother's body
- Helps in coming to terms with evolving body image
- Promotes mother's comfort
- Provides education and awareness
- Helps prepare muscles for delivery

BENEFITS DURING LABOR
- Reduces discomfort of repeatedly tensing muscles
- Revitalizes by relaxing the mother between contractions
- A partner or spouse can learn simple techniques to aid labor in this way
- Provides nurturing and supportive touch

BENEFITS AFTER THE BIRTH
- Speeds recovery from stress
- Helps relieve muscle pain from birth
- Helps relieve back pain from nursing

BENEFITS OF MASSAGING BABY
- Helps infant digest feedings better
- Helps build muscle tone, coordination and brain functioning
- Stimulates circulation, helping to heal any birth-related trauma
- Calms the baby's nervous system
- Establishes a pattern of relaxation at an early age
- Counterbalances frightening, negative messages about touch
- Helps the mother or partner and the baby grow closer to each other

RESOURCES FOR PREGNANCY AND INFANT MASSAGE

BOOKS AND TRAINING

Condon, Susanrachel and Richard. Niara Healing Arts Massage Therapy and Perinatal Support Services. *Advanced Pregnancy Massage Techniques* (DVD): www.niara.org

Jordan, Kate. *Bodywork for the Childbearing Year.*

Osborne-Sheets, Carole. (1998). *Pre- and Perinatal Massage Therapy: A Comprehensive Practitioner's Guide to Pregnancy, Labor, Postpartum.* Body Therapy Associates.

Stager, Leslie. (2009). *Nurturing Massage for Pregnancy: A Practical Guide to Bodywork for the Perinatal Cycle.* Philadelphia: Lippincott Williams & Wilkins.

Stillerman, Elaine, Diana Kurz (illustrator). (2006). *Mother Massage.*

Stillerman, Elaine. (2008). *Prenatal Massage,* Elsevier.

Tiran, Denise. (2000). *Clinical Aromatherapy for Pregnancy and Childbirth,* Elsevier.

ORGANIZATIONS

International Association of Infant Massage (IAIM): U.S. Chapter, 1891 Goodyear Avenue, Suite 622, Ventura, CA 93003; Tel. 805-644-8524; Fax 805-644-7699; www. iaim-us.com. This site shows the schedule for CIMI training throughout the United States.

International Association of Infant Massage – Canada Chapter: http://www.idpofbc. ca/Infant%20Massage%20Vancouver%20Jan%2008.pdf

For more information about pregnancy and infant massage, see the Resources box for Pregnancy and Infant Massage.

Equine/Animal Massage

Sometimes massage therapists develop animal massage as a specialty area, and sometimes veterinarians or veterinary technicians become certified in animal massage specialties so they can integrate these skills into their regular vet practices. The most common animal specialties are in canine (dog) and equine (horse) massage.

The International Association of Equine Sports Massage Therapists has approved a curriculum for this type of specialty, which results in a certificate in Equine Sports Massage Therapy. Benefits of equine massage are particularly helpful to performance horses that need to be in top form to compete. Equine massage also helps horses heal faster from muscle injuries than if they hadn't received massage. Practitioners trained in equine massage might work for owners and trainers in the horse racing world as well as the show arena.

In equine massage, you might find need for massage services at boarding stables, racetracks, and with law enforcement agencies that use horses in their line of work. If you practice canine massage, some of the options available to you are in working at dog agility trials, dog shows, dog flyball, doggie day care, and at vets' offices.

The reported benefits of massage to animals are:[22]

- maintaining muscle tone and flexibility
- increased blood and lymph circulation
- relieving discomfort from arthritis, lameness and hip dysplasia
- preventing injuries
- recovery from skeletal and muscular surgery or injury
- preventative overall health care
- relieving muscle pain by releasing endorphins

Before performing animal massage, it is essential that you be familiar with the scope of practice of massage therapy in your state or municipality. While in most states, veterinarians and massage therapists cooperate fully in providing the best possible care to animals, there are other regions or localities where veterinarians have protested that massage therapists are not qualified to perform massage on animals. Be aware that some states specifically prohibit massage therapists from practicing massage on animals. South Carolina regulations, for example, cite that massage is governed by the Board of Veterinary Practice and is not within the scope of practice for massage therapists. The International Association of Animal Massage and Bodywork maintains a website that tracks by state what the regulations are regarding animal massage: http://www.iaamb.org/reference/state-laws-2006.html.

> Animal massage is not within the massage therapy scope of practice in every state—be sure to verify your state's regulations.

RESOURCES FOR ANIMAL AND EQUINE MASSAGE

ASSOCIATIONS

Equine Sports Massage Therapy Certification Program: www.equissage.com.

Equinology, Inc.: www.equinology.com.

International Association of Animal Massage and Bodywork; 800-903-9350; www.iaamb.org.

BOOKS

Furman, Sue C. (2003) *Balance Your Dog: Canine Massage.* Ft. Collins, CO: Wolfchase.

Hourdebaigt, Jean-Pierre. *Dog Massage: A Complete Reference Manual.* New York: Dogwise; available through Massage Awareness, Inc. (author is founder of this organization): www.massageawareness.com.

TRAINING PROGRAMS

Many schools offer training in small animal, dog, and equine massage. These are just a few examples.

Bancroft School of Massage Therapy, Small Animal Massage Certification Program, Worcester, MA: www.bancroftsmt.com.

Boulder College of Massage Therapy, Canine Massage Certificate, Boulder, CO: www.bcmt.org

Healing Touch Therapy of Dog Massage, also offers online dog massage course (developed by Sue Furman, Ph.D., author of *Balance Your Dog*), Kinmundy, IL: www.holistictouchtherapy.com/online-classes.html

Massage Awareness Inc., Wellington, FL, Dog and Equine Massage classes and programs: www.massageawareness.com.

Treetops Animal Wellness Institute, Equine and Canine Massage Certification, St. Norbert, New Brunswick, Canada: www.treetopsweb.com.

Western Montana Equine Massage, Certified Equine Massage Therapist Program: www.equinetouchmontana.com.

Massage for Elderly

People over 75 years old constitute the fastest growing segment of the U.S. population. According to the U.S. Census Bureau projections:[23]

... a substantial increase in the number of older people will occur when the Baby Boom generation (people born between 1946 and 1964) begins to turn 65 in 2011. The older population is projected to double from 46 million in 2003 to 72 million in 2030, and to increase from 12 percent to 20 percent of the population in the same time frame. (2005, p. 5)

Growth in the elderly segment of the population offers massage therapists opportunities in two ways. One, given the adage that "70 is the new 50, and 80 is the new 60," implying that "old" isn't what it used to be, many people in the older age group are healthy and vital—and will benefit from massage in the same ways their younger counterparts do. Second, because many nonprofit services are established for the primary purpose of providing some type of service to people who are elderly, there may be opportunities for grant funding. See Real Touch 1.5 for one example of a massage therapy program that is funded through grants.

The Weaver's Tale Retreat Center

Real Touch 1.5

WWW.WEAVERS-TALE-RETREAT.ORG

Edie Seyl founded the Weaver's Tale Retreat Center in Portland, Oregon, in 1993. As a licensed massage therapist with a master's degree in occupational therapy, Edie believed that seniors' lives could be greatly enhanced with intentional sensory stimulation. Her goal was to get them outdoors experiencing nature, and combine that experience with other sensory stimulations such as music and massage.

At some point during their day-long outing to a retreat center set in an old growth rain forest typical of the Pacific Northwest, seniors receive a 15-minute chair massage. Seyl has a pool of about 25 massage therapists who vie for the opportunity of participating in the retreats. "I send an e-mail out that we're having a retreat on such-and-such date, and we sign up the first two massage therapists that reply. In addition to providing about two hours of massage, they also act as companions to the seniors, they help set up and take down the room and help load everyone back on to the bus at the end of the day. We all climb aboard the bus, sing 'Happy Trails to You,' and then say goodbye. The massage therapists get paid $75 for the day—not nearly what they're worth, but they do it out of love."

Edie performs the roles of executive director, marketing, fund-raising, budgeting, strategic planning, and administrative manager, pays herself $800 a month, and works 24 hours a week at a home-health job to earn benefits and living expenses. She is the first one to say it's not about the pay, it's about the love.

Sources of Funding

Grants have been awarded from the Massage Therapy Foundation, Portland General Electric, and Northwest Natural Gas. Most of Weaver's financial support comes from its annual fall fund raising, which is a silent and live auction that usually attracts about 150 faithful supporters.

Advice from Edie about finding funding possibilities

"What I did was to check with local universities for grant writing workshops (students can find out if there is a non-profit resource group in the vicinity, which Portland does have). I took a few classes; best research for suitable foundations is on the Web. There are grant-seeking reference books at libraries too but it's now all on the Web as well. Best to have conversations with grant giving source contact person. They are eager to give money away and want to give you the info you need if they think your program is a good match."

Possibilities for finding opportunities for massage and the elderly exist at businesses and organizations that provide services that are especially for people who are older, or at mainstream businesses during the hours when people who are retired might be there. One example of the latter might be golf courses that have leagues. Many men and women play golf well into their 70s, 80s, and even their 90s. Because they have the luxury of playing during hours when younger people are at work, you might find that a golf-course partnership would funnel after-golf customers to you during what might otherwise be a slow time for your business. Other places you might consider include:

- retirement communities
- municipal, county, and state senior service organizations
- seniors groups at churches and synagogues
- hospitals
- hospice organizations

Opportunities for income might be less than in some other areas, but the satisfaction of providing relief from stress, distraction from aches and pains, and a general sense of well-being to people who are elderly is real.

RESOURCES FOR MASSAGE FOR THE ELDERLY

Gentle Massage in Home and Facility Care (brochure), available from Information for People, www.info4people.com.

Nelson, Dawn. (2006). *From the Heart through the Hands: The Power of Touch in Caregiving,* available through www.amazon.com.

Rose, Mary (2009). *Comfort Touch: Massage for the Elderly and the Ill.* Phildelphia: Lippincott Williams & Wilkins.

PROFESSIONAL CREDENTIALS

Whether you want someone to hire you, be your client, or lend you money, you want to be able to demonstrate that you are a professional. One way to do that is with professional credentials. Credentials are accepted statements from a credible authority saying you are qualified to give massage. Credentials convey trustworthy information about the level of your competence. For clients, they also signal that you will provide safe and reliable care.

Because there are important distinctions between one type of credential and another, the concept of credentials can be confusing. When you see a massage therapist's business card, you might see the person's name followed by a string of initials, such as LMT, AMTA, NCTMB. Here is a brief guide to help you understand the type of credentials you might want or need as a massage therapist.

Learning the appropriate terminology at the early stages of your career will serve you well for many years. It's confusing at first, but you might just as well accept that every profession deals with similar distinctions, and knowing accurate terminology will distinguish you as a professional.

> Learning to use the terminology of credentials accurately distinguishes you as a professional in your field.

STATE AND PROVINCE

Regulation of the massage therapy profession, and the credentials required in order for an individual to practice, differ depending on where you practice. For additional details regarding the requirements in each state, go to the website of the regulatory agency of that state. For information about regulations in the United States, go to http://www.amtamassage.org/about/lawstate.html. For information about regulations in Canada, go to Canadian Massage Therapist Alliance, at www.cmta.ca.

CERTIFICATION

To be *certified* means that you have met the requirements of an organization that tests applicants on a core body of knowledge and requires them to uphold ethical and professional standards. For example, when a massage therapist says she's "nationally certified," she may be referring to either the NCTMB credential (Nationally Certified in Therapeutic Massage & Bodywork) or the NCTM credential (Nationally Certified in Therapeutic Massage), which many states accept as one criterion to practice in that state. These credentials are given when participants pass an exam administered by NCBTMB (National Certification Board for Therapeutic Massage & Bodywork), as well as meet standards for ongoing education and recertification every four years. To learn about NCBTMB certification, go to www.ncbtmb.com. See the Continuing Education section in Chapter 7 for more information about ongoing requirements to maintain certification.

Another way you might hear the word *certification* used is in reference to certificates you earn as a result of taking and passing courses of study in a particular modality, as in a "certificate of completion" that verifies you completed the coursework satisfactorily

LICENSURE

A *license* is a document issued to an individual or business by a governmental agency. In states that regulate massage therapy, an individual is required to be professionally licensed in order to practice. Some people confuse a *professional license* (which gives you the authority to practice massage) and a *business license* (which gives you the authority to operate a business). If you operate your own massage therapy practice, you may be required to have both types of licenses. Municipalities and states have different licensing and/or regulatory requirements for massage therapists. Check with your local regulatory agency to find out the requirements that apply to you.

In Canada, professional licensing is a credential that is required by three provinces (British Columbia, Ontario, and Newfoundland/Labrador).

Students seeking state licensure must pass the MBLEX (Massage & Bodywork Licensing Examination, through the Federation of State Massage Therapy Boards [FSMTB]), the NESL exam (National Examination for State Licensing, through the NCBTMB), or a state-developed exam. Some state regulatory boards require the NCTM or NCTMB exam rather than the NESL.

The MBLEX and NESL test comprehension in the following subject matter areas:

- Anatomy, physiology, and kinesiology
- Body systems
- Pathology
- Client assessment
- Methods and techniques
- Ethics, business practices, laws and regulations

Each state has rules regarding how to continue or renew licensure after a certain period of time, usually regarding the number of continuing education credits one must earn in order to maintain one's licensure.

REGISTRATION

In Canada, registration is a credential that meets accepted standards in the health-related fields. It defines a body of knowledge common to all who are registered. Most provinces require a minimum 2,200 hours of training; British Columbia requires a minimum 3,000 hours. Some provinces use Canada's registration standards as their licensing examination, which in some cases opens the door for reciprocity between provinces. As of late 2007, three provinces (British Columbia, Ontario, and Newfoundland/Labrador) regulated massage therapy and required practitioners to be registered after having met certification standards in order to practice massage therapy, and all provinces require registration status in order to secure insurance. Practitioners must renew registrations periodically as required by the governing agency.

Some states in the United States also require that massage therapy practitioners be registered in order to legally use the term "massage therapist" on their business cards and in their business. Find out if your state is one of them.

SCHOOL CERTIFICATES AND DEGREES

Institutions and programs of massage therapy award certificates or degrees to students upon successful completion of their curriculums. Most certificates and diplomas indicate the number of hours the student has completed in professional training.

MEMBERSHIP

Membership in a professional association is also a form of credential. At the national level, the major professional organizations for massage therapists are the nonprofit American Massage Therapy Association (AMTA, www.amtamassage.org), and the for-profit organizations Associated Bodywork and Massage Professionals (ABMP, www.abmp.com) and the International Massage Association (IMA, www.imagroup.com).

When citing membership in AMTA, it is important that you designate AMTA *Professional Member* or AMTA *Student Member,* because your type of membership conveys a distinction that you have certain qualifications for being one or the other. Professional associations also exist at local, state, and regional levels, and specific to many modalities. See Chapter 8 for a description of benefits you can derive from being a member of an organization with your professional peers.

ACCREDITATION—FOR SCHOOLS AND PROGRAMS ONLY, NOT FOR INDIVIDUALS

Accreditation means that an educational institution has met particular standards established by an accrediting organization. This credential applies only to institutions and programs, and never to individuals. School accreditation must be renewed periodically to assure continued compliance with standards. It is incorrect to say that you are "accredited" as a massage therapist.

USING ABBREVIATIONS

Abbreviations such as LMT are great when you're communicating with your peers in the profession, but most clients will not be familiar with what they mean. If you are a licensed massage therapist, whenever possible spell out Licensed Massage Therapist on your business cards, letterhead, and other documents that clients see.

The National Certification Board for Therapeutic Massage & Bodywork specifies that individuals use the letters NCTMB or NCTM following the name of the certified practitioner. The credential NCTMB stands for Nationally Certified in Therapeutic Massage & Bodywork and the NCTM stands for Nationally Certified in Therapeutic Massage. For clarity, when space allows, you might want to spell out Nationally Certified in Therapeutic Massage and Bodywork or Nationally Certified in Therapeutic Massage.

LANGUAGE OF CREDENTIALS

Using the terminology of credentials is similar to learning a foreign language. These sentences are all examples of correct usage:

- "The school I attend is *accredited* by COMTA."
- "When I complete my school's curriculum, I will receive a *diploma.*"
- "After passing my certification exam, I will be *certified* NCTMB."
- "I took the MBLEX, offered by the FSMTB, to get my *professional license.*"
- "My state requires that I pass the NESL before I can get my *professional license.*"

- "Before I can open my office for business, I will apply to the county for my *business license.*"
- "I am a *member* of a professional association."
- "I am a *registered* massage therapist in this province."

Correct usage is a fine point, and it reflects well on those whose speech reflects a solid grounding in professional terminology.

Spell out acronyms on your business card so your clients don't have to guess what they mean.

RESOURCES FOR MASSAGE THERAPY NATIONAL CERTIFICATION

National Certification Board for Massage Therapy and Bodywork (NCBTMB): www.ncbtmb.com

> 1901 South Meyers Road, Suite 240
> Oakbrook Terrace, IL 60181
> Tel.: 630-627-8000 or toll-free 1-800-296-0664
> E-mail: info@ncbtmb.com
> *Provider of the National Certification for Massage Therapy and the National Certification for Massage Therapy & Bodywork*

LICENSURE (NOTE: ALWAYS CHECK INDIVIDUAL STATE REQUIREMENTS)

Federation of State Massage Therapy Boards (FSMTB): www.fsmtb.org

> 7111 W 151st Street, Suite 356 Overland Park, Kansas 66223
> Tel.: 913-681-0380 or toll-free 888-70-FSMTB
> Fax: 913-681-0391
> E-mail: info@fsmtb.org
> *Provider of the Massage & Bodywork Licensing Examination* (MBLEX)

National Certification Board for Massage Therapy and Bodywork (NCBTMB): www.ncbtmb.com

> 1901 South Meyers Road, Suite 240
> Oakbrook Terrace, IL 60181
> Tel.: 630-627-8000 or toll-free 1-800-296-0664
> E-mail: info@ncbtmb.co
> *Provider of the National Exam for State Licensure*

ACCREDITATION

Accrediting Bureau of Health Education Schools (ABHES): www.abhes.org

> 7777 Leesburg Pike, Suite 314 N., Falls Church, VA 22043
> Tel.: 703-917-9503
> Fax 703-917-41009
> E-mail: info@abhes.org

Accrediting Commission of Career Schools and Colleges of Technology (ACCSCT): www.accsct.org

> 2101 Wilson Boulevard, Suite 302, Arlington, VA 22201
> Tel.: 703-247-4212
> Fax: 703-247-4533
> E-mail: info@accsct.org

Accrediting Council for Continuing Education & Training (ACCET): www.accet.org
> 1722 N. Street NW, Washington, DC 20036
> Tel.: 202-955-1113
> Fax: 202-955-1118
> E-mail: info@accet.org

Commission on Massage Therapy Accreditation (COMTA): www.comta.org
   1007 Church Street, Suite 302, Evanston, IL 60201
   Tel.: 847-869-5039
   Fax: 847-869-6739
   E-mail: info@comta.org

National Accrediting Commission of Cosmetology Arts and Sciences (NACCAS): www.naccas.org
   4401 Ford Avenue, Suite 1300, Alexandria, VA 22302
   Tel. 703-600-7600
   E-mail: webinfo@naccas.org

PROFESSIONAL ORGANIZATIONS

American Massage Therapy Association (AMTA): www.amtamassage.org
   900 Davis Street, Suite 400, Evanston, IL 60201-4695
   Tel.: 847-864-0123 or toll-free 1-877-905-2700
   Fax: 847-864-1178
   E-mail: info@amtamassage.org

Associated Bodywork and Massage Professionals (ABMP): www.abmp.com
   1271 Sugarbush Drive, Evergreen, CO 80439-9766
   Tel.: 303-674-8478 or toll-free 1-800-458-2267
   Fax: 800-6678260
   E-mail: expectmore@abmp.com

International Massage Association (IMA): www.imagroup.com
   25 South 4th Street, Warrenton, VA 20186
   Tel.: 540-351-0800
   Fax: 540-351-0816
   E-mail: info@imagroupinc.com

SELF-EVALUATION

Earning the professional credentials you need before you can practice is essential because it makes you more marketable and more employable, and doing so is a legal requirement in most jurisdictions. You will find the entire process much easier if you take a step back and do some solid soul-searching at the beginning of your career quest. Experience has shown that people are more likely to achieve their goals if they are clear about what they want. If you have known your entire life that you want to practice sports massage in the clinical setting of athletic sports medicine, then your path is already pretty well defined. If you're like most people, however, you feel a definite attraction to some things and not others, but you haven't yet figured out what it all adds up to in terms of choosing a career direction.

Your beliefs, attitudes, and values have already influenced you in pursuing training in massage. They are derived from many sources of influence—the region where you grew up and live now, your family's traditions and beliefs about religion and spirituality, your socioeconomic background, your ethnic heritage, and your educational and work experience. The trick is to sort all these things out and figure out what they mean in terms of your career choice.

Many tools are available to help you clarify how your interests and attractions can direct you to your career goals.

SELF-ASSESSMENT TOOLS
Personality Tests and Interest Inventories

There are many tests and questionnaires that can help you better understand your interests and natural skills. The benefit of all of them is that they cause you to think about things you like and things you don't like, and in doing so to examine how your likes and dislikes fit into a career choice.

One of the best-known personality type indicators, the Myers-Briggs Type Indicator®, is based on the philosophy of Carl Jung (1875–1961), a famous Swiss psychiatrist. He proposed that all humans fit into "typology" categories that reflect their general tendencies. These typologies are: introvert/extrovert, sensing/intuitive, thinking/feeling, and judging/perceiving. The pairs of words are more or less opposite ends of the same typology, and the test measures whether you are more like one end or the other. To take the test for official purposes, the test, which is published by Consulting Psychologists Press, must be completed under the guidance of a qualified administrator. For informal purposes and for your own use, however, you may take an online test at www.humanmetrics.com (choose Jung Typology Test). Using the Myers-Briggs Indicator, you learn valuable information about yourself in the following areas:

- *Introvert/Extrovert*
  Where, primarily, do you direct your energy? Is it to the outer world, through spoken words and action? Then, you are an *extrovert*. Or do you direct your energy to the inner world of thoughts and emotions?—an *introvert*.
- *Sensing/Intuitive*
  How do you prefer to process information? Do you prefer facts and figures and objective reality? If so, you are using sensing to process information. If you prefer to rely more on gut feel, and what might be rather than what is the current status, you would fall into the intuitive classification.
- *Thinking/Feeling*
  How do you prefer to make decisions? Similar to the distinctions between sensing and intuitive, the *thinking* personality type relies on logic, scientific analysis, and objective observation in making decisions. The *feeling* type depends more on subjective inputs, and tends to integrate qualities, such as appreciation and sympathy, into the equation before making a decision.
- *Judging/Perceiving*
  How do you prefer to organize your life? If you are structured in your life organization—that is, you have a plan, you know where you stand in that plan, and you have contingencies built into your plan that address all the what-ifs life might throw at you—you're in the *judging* classification. If, on the other hand, you discover life as you go along, and you like to keep your options open rather than make hard-and-fast decisions, you fall into the *perceiving* category.

Clarifying your preferences and aversions can help you make better career decisions for the long run.

Knowing where you fall in any of these classifications gives you information about yourself that is neither good nor bad, it just *is*. Knowing your personality indicators can help you understand how to work effectively with others, and what type of practice environment you will be most comfortable.

Other personality and interest inventories are the Keirsey Temperament Sorter and the Enneagram. There are Web-based versions of personality and interest questionnaires; be sure to respect the copyrights of these tools and take them only as directed. Some of these tests are available in abbreviated form for individuals to take if the tests are not being sold for commercial use.

The important thing about any personality test or career preference test is not necessarily what one test instrument says about you. It's the process you go through as you consider your attraction to some things and not to others that pushes you to think carefully about how those preferences and aversions might influence your career direction.

Friends and Mentors
Don't limit yourself to just studying and practicing massage skills and reading about career

options. Get specifics by building professional relationships. Talk to practicing therapists to learn what they experience in their work situations. In addition, find at least one mentor, a more experienced massage therapist who is willing to share his or her wisdom with you in an ongoing professional relationship. A mentor doesn't necessarily have to be another massage therapist. He or she might work in a related field and is familiar with the organization with which you want to work or with being an independent contractor or owner of a business. A particularly rich source of would-be mentors is at your professional association's chapter meeting.

Meet with your mentor regularly to talk and listen. As in any career, you are bound to have ups and downs; a wise mentor can help you navigate them successfully. A successful career is a continual learning process.

PERFORMING A SELF-EVALUATION

Take some time to reflect on how you would describe the career you want. Compare your image of yourself as a massage therapist with the actual opportunities in the field, which are described in the next section of this chapter. The time you spend reading, talking with others, and reflecting on insights about yourself, will help you plan a career that meets your professional, personal, and financial goals. As you answer the questions in the self-evaluation worksheet (Figure 1.6), remember that you are most likely to achieve personal, professional, and financial success if your career goals are compatible with your personal abilities, interests, character, and values.

If you are not sure about your strengths, ask people who know you well what they think your strengths are. It is important to be as honest as you can in self-evaluation, so you choose a career path that is realistic and satisfying.

After you have completed the worksheet, look over your answers. Can you begin to see the kind of work setting that would suit you best? For example, if you want to devote yourself to a particular kind of massage and minimize administrative activities, probably you would be happier as an employee than as an individual owner. If you are self-motivated and comfortable with risk, you would more likely enjoy being self-employed. Being self-employed, you can plan on spending 5 to 10 hours a week on recordkeeping, and another 5 hours a week on marketing. Your self-knowledge is the key to determining which career path is best for you.

CAREER TRANSITIONS

It's hardly fair to talk about expanding or enriching your career when you maybe haven't even started this one yet. But it's worth discussing just so you have it in the back of your mind as the first phase in your massage career starts to take form. If you know what you might like to do next, as you are experiencing the "first phase" of your career, you will recognize certain factors along the way—activities, events, mentors, role models—that will help solidify your direction or that will impel you in another direction. Most practitioners who have practiced massage therapy for many years have seen their practices evolve from one type of business emphasis to another.

This could happen for a variety of reasons. Maybe as a result of taking continuing education you have discovered a specialty area that interests you, and you would like to change the focus of your practice. Maybe your partner was transferred to a different city, or the community around you has changed.

Once you have refined your skills as a massage therapist and have developed the stamina to handle a reasonable client load as an employee, you have the confidence to branch out. Once you are no longer as completely consumed with learning to refine your skills, you have the luxury to invest in learning new areas—maybe the business aspects of operating your own practice, or learning to become a doula (someone who provides delivery and postpartum support during and after pregnancy), an acupuncturist, a researcher, an educator. Career enhancements and transitions are often the result of your allowing

FIGURE 1.6 Self-Evaluation Worksheet

You are most likely to achieve personal, professional, and financial success if your career goals are comaptible with your personal abilities, interests, character, and values. It is important to be as honest as you can in the self-evaluation, to enable you to choose a career parth that will be realistic and personally satisfying.

1 Why do you work? _____
_____
_____

2 What's important to you? (peace and quiet? intellectual stimulation? helping others? job security? expressing yourself creatively? spending time with your family? being independent?) _____
_____
_____

3 What types of activities give you satisfaction? (reading? balancing your checkbook? organizing an event? talking with a close friend? going to parties?) _____
_____
_____

4 What strengths (physical, mental, character, spiritual) do you have that can help you as a massage therapist? ___
_____
_____
_____

5 What are your goals as an individual? _____
_____
_____

6 If you're part of a couple, what are your goals together? _____
_____
_____

7 What are your ambitions? _____
_____
_____

8 Describe the jobs you've enjoyed the most (before you became a massage therapist). _____
_____
_____

9 Describe the jobs you've enjoyed the least (before you became a massage therapist). _____
_____
_____
_____

10 Do you prefer to work around other people or alone? _____
_____

11 Are you comfortable reporting to someone? If so, does it matter whether the person is a massage therapist or a non–massage-therapist manager? _____
_____
_____

12 What workplace values are essential to you? _____
_____
_____

FIGURE 1.6 (continued)

13 Do you like to structure your own use of time, or do you prefer to let someone else set priorities and arrange schedules? _____

14 Would you enjoy setting up the physical environment in which to provide massage, or would you prefer having this handled by someone else? _____

15 Will massage therapy be your main or only source of income? (right away? in time?) _____

16 With what kinds of clients would you enjoy working? (babies? children? athletes? people with illnesses or special needs such as trauma or abuse victims? animals?) _____

17 Do you like telling people about the benefits of massage and encouraging them to try it? _____

18 Do you enjoy paperwork? Avoid it? _____

19 Do you like performing a variety of business tasks each day and each week, or would you prefer to focus only on massage itself? _____

20 How many hours do you want to work each week? _____

21 How many of your work hours do you want to spend providing massages? (Consider your physical limitations as well as your financial goals.) _____

22 How many of your work hours do you want to spend on paperwork, phone calls and marketing? _____

23 Do you like working the same hours each week, or do you prefer variety and/or flexibility? _____

24 What modalities of massage are you trained to offer? _____

25 Do you enjoy speaking before a group? _____

26 What additional skills, techniques, and/or modalities do you want to learn? _____

27 How many hours of continuous education per year do you plan to take? _____

28 Do you enjoy the theories behind massage therapy? _____

29 Would you enjoy researching or teaching? _____

30 Who has given you career guidance already and might be a mentor for you? _____

31 Do your family and friends support your career goals? _____

yourself to open up to possibilities that have never seemed attainable in the past, which are now within reach because you have built a strong foundation.

All of these possibilities keep your future outlook on the profession of massage therapy as exciting as your present one. No two individual career paths are the same.

A vital massage career continues to change and grow as you do.

SUMMARY

As a new massage therapist, you are about to embark on a profession that offers a broad variety of career options. Many experienced practitioners recommend that you work as an employee for several years before opening your own business, although certainly examples abound of individuals who were successful in operating their own businesses as soon as they became licensed as massage therapists.

Significant trends that affect your career opportunities include: growth in consumer acceptance and visibility of massage therapy; more and better quality research on the effects of massage therapy; corporate franchises offering owner and employment opportunities; and greater consumer interest in alternative and complementary health care.

Career opportunities exist in the fields of wellness, integrative health care, sports/fitness, spa, corporate/franchise, and specialty settings such as pregnancy/infant, equine/animal, and massage for people who are elderly.

The credentials you will need before you can practice massage differ from state to state. It is important to understand the terminology of credentials, as it sets you apart as a professional to use such terms as *certified licensed, registered, member,* and *accredited* accurately.

The better you understand how your values, beliefs, and interests play a part in the career choices you make, the better your career satisfaction will be. Spending ample time up-front to do a thorough self-evaluation will pay off in better career decisions.

No matter what you decide when you first enter the profession of massage therapy, you may be sure that your career will continue to grow and to change. The profession offers an abundance of career opportunities for experienced practitioners to expand their careers, just as it offers many opportunities to the beginning professional.

REVIEW QUESTIONS

1 What is the definition of a massage therapist?
2 What are significant trends that affect career opportunities in the profession of massage therapy?
3 How does increased research of complementary and alternative therapies affect the profession of massage therapy?
4 What are primary areas of opportunity for working in the massage therapy profession?
5 To you, what are the pros and cons of three different career settings? (Choose three.)
6 What credentials are required in the location where you want to work?
7 What credentials will you have by the time you complete your massage training?
8 What credentials do you plan to get after you finish your training?
9 What tools can you use to help identify your needs, behaviors, beliefs and attitudes as they relate to your choice of career path?
10 How do your personal and cultural values, attitudes, and ethics influence your choice of career path?

ENDNOTES

1   2005 Massage Therapy Consumer Survey Fact Sheet. Evanston, IL: American Massage Therapy Association.

2   Knaup, A. (2005) BLS statistics quoted in Survival and Longevity in the Business Employment Dynamics data. *Monthly Labor Review,* May 2005, 50–56.

3   History overview abstracted from Tappan, F. M. & P. J. Benjamin. *Tappan's Handbook of Healing Massage Techniques: Classic, Holistic and Emerging Methods.* (2004). Upper Saddle River, NJ: Prentice Hall..

4   AMTA, 2007 Massage Therapy Consumer Survey Fact Sheet, conducted by CARAVAN® Opinion Research Corporation International during July 2007, among a national probability sample of 1,008 adults (502 men and 506 women) ages 18 and older, living in private households in the continental United States. The survey has a confidence level of plus or minus 3 percent. Commissioned by AMTA, this is the eleventh annual massage therapy survey of American consumers.

5   AMTA (2006) *Massage Therapy: Not Just a Trend.* Evanston, IL: American Massage Therapy Association.

6   NCCAM funding information can be found at www.nccam.nih.gov/research.

7   *Source:* http://preventdisease.com/worksite_wellness/worksite_wellness.html

8   Hettler, Bill, cofounder and president of the National Wellness Institute (1979) The Six Dimensional Wellness Model, available at www.nationalwellness.org.

9   Chapman, Larry, Meta-Evaluation of Worksite Health Promotion Economic Return Studies: 2005 Update, *American Journal of Health Promotion,* Jul/Aug 2005.

10 ISPA 2008 Spa Industry Study, 5th ed., conducted jointly by the International Spa Association and the Association Resource Centre Inc., available at www.experienceispa.com.

11 Ives, Jean (Spring 2004) "Massage Is in Business," *Massage Therapy Journal.*

12 AMTA (2006) *Massage Therapy: Not Just a Trend.* Evanston, IL: American Massage Therapy Association.

13 AMTA (2006) *Massage Therapy: Not Just a Trend.* Evanston, IL: American Massage Therapy Association.

14 2005 Massage Therapy Consumer Survey Fact Sheet, Evanston, IL: American Massage Therapy Association.

15 Jean Wible and René Evers, Medical Massage Program, Baltimore School of Massage, Baltimore, Maryland. (Reprinted from *Business of Massage* original edition.)

16 University of Virginia; Temple University. Authors: Joseph M. Hart; C. Buz Swanik; Ryan T. Tierney. Originally published in *Journal of Athletic Training,* 40(3), Sept. 2005, pp. 181–185.

17 ISPA 2008 Spa Industry Study, 5th ed., conducted jointly by the International Spa Association and the Association Resource Centre Inc., available at www.experienceispa.com.

18 *2007 Massage Therapy Industry Evaluation Trend Report,* November 2007, conducted by North Star Research on behalf of American Massage Therapy Foundation.

19 The Great American Back Rub: http://www.backrub.ca/home.html

20 Hand and Stone Massage Spa, available at www.handandstonemassage.com.

21 "Therapeutic Massage Franchise Fills Demand," Franchise Business Opportunities Weblog, Aug. 25, 2006, available at: www.franchise.business-opportunities.biz.

22 *Source:* Boulder College of Massage Therapy canine massage certification program.

23 *65+ in the United States,* Current Population Reports, Special Study. U.S. Census Bureau, Dec. 2005, available at http://www.census.gov/prod/2006pubs/p23-209.pdf.

Chapter 2

Creating a Therapeutic Relationship

Extend the skill of your hands even further by acknowledging and nurturing the whole person who is your client.

CHAPTER OVERVIEW

- The Therapeutic Relationship
- Ethics
- Boundaries
- Client Communication
- Role of Client Records
- Referring Clients to Others
- Client Self-Care
- Massage Session Start to Finish

CHAPTER OBJECTIVES

1 Distinguish between the wellness model and the allopathic medical model.
2 Identify the commonalities among the ethical codes of all health care professions.
3 Identify therapist behaviors that are consistent with confidentiality of client identification, personal disclosure, files, and treatment information.
4 Describe the process for establishing and maintaining professional boundaries and relationships with clients and peers in the workplace.
5 Identify examples of boundary violations
6 Identify the effect of language usage, vocabulary, style of speech, dress, posture, hygiene, and conduct on effective practitioner-client communication.
7 Describe techniques for eliciting client feedback.
8 Describe the importance of instructing the client in self-care.
9 Describe techniques for ending a client session.

Healthy therapeutic relationships are good not only for the bodies, minds, and spirits of you and your clients, but for your business as well. This chapter examines factors that contribute to or detract from a therapeutic relationship.

THE THERAPEUTIC RELATIONSHIP

In the context of your massage career, "therapeutic" describes an environment that promotes physical, mental, emotional, and spiritual health for both you and your clients. In a therapeutic environment, both you and your clients emerge healthier as a result of your session together than you were before the session. The effects of a therapeutic relationship are cumulative, and thus the benefits of your massages can increase with each visit.

The essential quality of the interpersonal contact between client and practitioner is integral to determining the effectiveness of your massage work. In *The Educated Heart*, author Nina McIntosh writes, "Your relationship with the client is what will make or break your practice, much more than your knowledge of anatomy." As a professional, it is your responsibility to set the tone and the boundaries for ethical and compassionate care of your clients. If you are too businesslike and clinical, your clients will feel like units of profit. If you have fuzzy boundaries, your clients could think of themselves more as your friends than your clients. In either case, you could inadvertently make it virtually impossible for your clients to derive the full benefits of massage that are possible when a therapeutic relationship exists.

Common threads woven throughout the therapeutic relationship include adherence to ethical behaviors and codes of conduct, sincerity and sensitivity in interpersonal communication skills, and techniques for conducting a massage session from start to finish that reflect these elements.

If you view your career within the context of a wellness model, you will see how a good therapeutic relationship between you and your clients can promote well-being of body, mind, and spirit for both of you.

WELLNESS MODEL

Most massage therapists work within the wellness model, which means that health is viewed as the sum total of a person's environment—mind, spirit, and body. This is in contrast to the allopathic, or medical, model, which is based on the concept that health is achieved primarily through the removal of disease. It would certainly be unfair to suggest that medical practitioners totally exclude the influences of mind and spirit on a person's health—or that massage therapists disregard physical symptoms. Many massage therapists, especially those who work in clinical settings, recognize when it is beneficial to focus particular attention on the physical body to promote relief of pain or discomfort. All competent massage therapists recommend that their clients seek professional health services from a qualified practitioner for symptoms that are outside the scope of practice for massage therapy. By the same token, physicians are increasingly including massage therapy among their tools of choice when referring their patients for additional therapy.

Many wellness models exist. The simplest models look at a balance between mind, body, and spirit. Some models include the components of emotional, physical, spiritual, occupational, intellectual, and social. All models are based on the premise that it is necessary for an individual to achieve balance in his or her life in order to promote optimal health and well-being. All models capture the idea that all human factors and environments

Your knowledge of how to build a therapeutic relationship with clients is as important to your practice as your knowledge of anatomy.

are interrelated. Rather than focusing on the part of the body that appears to be ailing, the wellness approach focuses first on prevention and on examining the balance of all related components. For more detail on wellness models, see the "Wellness Settings" section in Chapter 1.

Throughout the course of your career, as you develop referral networks with other health care practitioners, it will be helpful for you to identify practitioners who have an appreciation for holistic wellness approaches. Many aspects contained within the wellness model—for instance, living each day consistent with your values, and identifying problems and choosing appropriate courses of action—are integral to the ethics of the massage therapy profession, as described in the following section.

All wellness models are based on seeking balance among the different needs in one's life.

ETHICS

A PROFESSIONAL COMMITMENT

Taken together with the manual skills you learn as a massage therapist, your practice of ethics makes up the sum total of what you do as a massage therapist. This may sound far-reaching, but a complete understanding of this topic will enable you to understand that ethical behaviors and attitudes pervade your communication and your actions with clients, peers, and other health professionals.

Many people think of the words "honesty," "fairness," and "integrity" when they think of ethics. These are essential components of ethics. The opportunity to cultivate attitudes and practices that reflect these values exists in everything you do and say as a massage therapist.

Adherence to ethical standards requires that practitioners perform only those services that are sanctioned within the scope of their practice, as defined by their profession and by law. Therefore, it is critical that you understand your state's definition of the scope of practice for massage therapists, because violation of that scope would constitute breaking the law. Many states equate the functions of *diagnosing, prescribing,* and *treating* with practicing medicine, and they prohibit massage therapists from using such terms to describe their services. For example, if you were to develop a marketing brochure and state that you "treat" stress through massage therapy, you could be in violation of some states' laws. In states that do not regulate the practice of massage, adherence to your professional association's code of ethics constitutes an ethical practice. For more detailed coverage of this topic, see "Scope of Practice" in Chapter 5.

Most professions develop and publish guidelines that help guide members of their profession in ethical behaviors specific to that profession. In massage therapy, those guidelines are the code of ethics and performance standards (sometimes called standards of practice), as described next.

CODE OF ETHICS

Many professional organizations publish a code of ethics for their members to follow.

Codes of ethics differ in the level of detail in which they describe ethical practices, but they all basically adhere to these common attributes: providing high quality, respecting privacy and confidentiality, not discriminating, upholding the law, and doing no harm.

For the massage therapy profession, at least three professional organizations have published a code of ethics for their members to follow: American Massage Therapy Association, Associated Bodywork and Massage Professionals, and National Certification Board of Therapeutic Massage and Bodywork (ethics are incorporated within NCBTMB Standards of Practice). In addition, some regulatory agencies or schools of massage therapy publish their own codes of ethics.

All of these codes of ethics have the following principles in common:

All health professions' codes of ethics have these values in common:

providing high quality

respecting privacy and confidentiality

not discriminating

upholding the law

doing no harm

1 Provide the highest quality massage therapy and serve the best interests of those who seek their professional services.
2 Respect each client's right to privacy and confidentiality.
3 Acknowledge individuals' inherent worth by not discriminating or behaving in any prejudicial manner with clients and/or colleagues.
4 Conduct all business activities within their scope of practice and the law.
5 Accept responsibility to do no harm to the physical, mental, and emotional well-being of self, clients, and associates.
6 Refrain from engaging in or tolerating any sexual conduct involving their clients.
7 Respect the rights of all ethical practitioners and cooperate with all health care professionals in a friendly and professional manner.

Some codes of ethics also specify continuing education as an ethical obligation, because it helps improve massage therapists' knowledge and competency, and therefore affects the quality of massage they provide. Others specify the client's right to refuse, modify, or terminate treatment, and the massage therapist's right to refuse treatment to any person for reasonable and just cause. If you are nationally certified NCTMB, you are required to complete 6 hours of ethics training every 4 years. Many state regulatory agencies require periodic ethics training as a condition of maintaining licensure. A thorough understanding of your own professional association's code of ethics and that of your regulatory jurisdiction, if any, will help you set the tone of your practice.

RESOURCES FOR MASSAGE THERAPY CODES OF ETHICS

NATIONAL

American Massage Therapy Association: www.amtamassage.org/about/codeofethics.html

Associated Bodywork and Massage Professionals: www.abmp.com/about/codeofethics.html

National Certification Board for Therapeutic Massage and Bodywork: www.ncbtmb.com/about_standards_of_practice.php

STATE/PROVINCE EXAMPLES

Alabama Board of Massage Therapy: www.alabamaadministrativecode.state.al.us/docs/mass/7mass.htm

College of Massage Therapy of Ontario: www.cmto.com/PDFs/CodeEthics.pdf

---

Whereas a code of ethics is geared more to values, performance standards are geared more to actions.

PERFORMANCE STANDARDS

Similar to a code of ethics, but fashioned more specifically to actions and behaviors, are performance standards, sometimes called standards of practice. It might be said that a code of ethics speaks more to values, and performance standards speak more to actions.

Published performance standards help practitioners communicate clear guidelines to clients, which in turn help clients understand and trust practitioners' boundaries. According to the American Massage Therapy Association, standards serve the following purposes:

- To provide safe, consistent care
- To determine the quality of care provided
- To provide a common base to develop a practice
- To support/preserve the basic rights of the client and professional massage therapist

- To assist the public to understand what to expect from a professional massage therapist

Because these standards are specific, they are helpful to practitioners in determining appropriate professional boundaries. A few examples are shown in Figure 2.1.

Many performance standards, as you might note, suggest *boundaries* that you, as an ethical massage therapist, should stay within. Specific boundary areas are discussed in the next section.

FIGURE 2.1
Guidelines Associated with
Performance Standards

PERFORMANCE STANDARD	EXAMPLE OF GUIDELINE
Conduct of the practitioner	The practitioner seeks professional supervision or consultation consistent with promoting and maintaining appropriate application of skills and knowledge.
Sanitation, Hygiene, and Safety	The practitioner maintains current knowledge and skills of pathophysiology and the appropriate application of massage.
Professional Relationships with Clients	The practitioner maintains appropriate professional standards of confidentiality.
Professional Relationships with Other Professionals	The practitioner's referrals to other professionals are only made in the interest of the client.
Records	The practitioner establishes and maintains appropriate client records.
Marketing	The practitioner markets his/her practice in an accurate, truthful, and ethical manner.
Legal Practice	The practitioner collaborates with all others practicing massage in a manner that is in compliance with national, state, or local municipal laws pertaining to the practice of professional massage.
Research	The practitioner doing research avoids financial or political relationships that may limit objectivity or create conflict of interest.

BOUNDARIES

Establishing clear boundaries in the work setting concerns your ethical, legal, and professional responsibilities as a massage therapist. Boundaries refer to clear definitions of what you will do, what you will not do, and what you will accept and not accept in client behavior. Both you and your clients will ultimately be most comfortable if you set and clearly communicate appropriate boundaries.

Boundaries are clear definitions of what you will do, what you will not do, and what you will accept and not accept in client behavior.

CONFIDENTIALITY

Confidentiality is required not only by the code of ethics but by law. Specifically, HIPAA guidelines require strict adherence to rules for protecting clients' confidentiality. A client must feel assured that the information he or she shares with you will be kept in confidence unless the client expressly gives permission for that information to be shared with a designated other party, or if the client's health is immediately compromised.

A confidentiality policy defines types of information that may not be disclosed to others without prior consent. The primary purpose of confidentiality policies is to protect your clients. You will be asking clients to share personal information with you when you ask them to fill out the client intake form (discussed in Chapter 6). Information about care should be shared—if the client signs a statement authorizing it—only with other professionals involved in the care and, if applicable, the insurance company paying the bill. Again, HIPAA regulations include strict guidelines for sharing client information. (See more about release of information agreements in Chapter 6.) Any other personal information a client chooses to disclose during care should be strictly confidential (unless failure to disclose it would endanger someone). If you believe you must disclose information, be sure to discuss the situation with the appropriate authority, such as your supervisor.

You can prevent some problems related to confidentiality by encouraging clients to disclose deeply personal matters to a trained counselor or psychologist, rather than to you. Professional counseling is not within the massage therapist's scope of practice. Know your limits and be prepared to make referrals. Most clients will appreciate your caring and will respect the referral. Making referrals to appropriate specialists will be discussed later in this chapter.

DRAPING

The fact that the client is fully or partially unclothed during a massage implies an intimacy that must be matched with an equal level of trust.

The reason draping is an important topic within a discussion of ethics and boundaries has to do with more than just physical modesty. Massage creates a situation in which the client feels dependent on the massage therapist for enjoyment, relaxation, pain relief, or all three. Because of the close contact between client and therapist, and the fact that the client is partially or fully unclothed, an innate degree of intimacy exists that distinguishes massage therapy from most other professions. This level of intimacy must be matched with an equal level of trust. Setting boundaries includes protecting the client's privacy with proper draping procedures, which strengthens the trust factor between client and practitioner.

Most first-time clients express some degree of anxiety about whether they should be fully unclothed to receive their first massage. For this reason, it is important that you explain draping during client intake, before the client goes into the session room. Let the client know that you will undrape only one part of the body at a time, and only as you are working on it. Let the client know that the genitals and female breasts will always be draped.

For long-time massage therapy clients, draping remains an essential principle of ethical practice. Complete and professional draping at every massage session not only conveys respect for the client's emotional well-being, but his or her physical protection from drafts as well. A skilled massage therapist moves seamlessly from one phase of the massage session to the next, while covering and uncovering different sections of the client's body in one fluid motion.

It is not within the scope of this book to describe techniques of draping. However, as you practice the techniques taught in your massage training, pay particular attention to these phases of the massage session for heightened draping sensitivity:

- Before the client goes to the session room, let him or her know how to signal to you that he or she is ready and is covered by the sheet/blanket provided so you won't enter the room before he or she is ready.
- If the client has not covered himself or herself entirely, reposition the sheet for complete coverage (such as up around the shoulders).
- As you move from one part of the body to another, immediately cover the area you are leaving.
- As you perform the massage, be alert to any slippage of the sheet/blanket so you may move it back into place as appropriate.

- When you ask the client to roll from his or her back to front, or vice versa, hold the draping in such a way to assure ample privacy. For a first-time client, say something to the effect of, "I will hold the sheet up high enough that you have complete privacy as you roll over on your other side. Let me know when you're comfortable so I may adjust the sheet around you again."
- Be careful as you perform some of the draping techniques, such as tucking the sheet under the client's left thigh so you can work on his or her right thigh, that you don't inadvertently touch or come close to the upper thigh in such a way that might concern the client about inappropriate touch.

Comfort and trust are essential to your client relationships. Clients feel vulnerable under that sheet, and it's your job to ensure that they can relax completely because of their trust in your every movement.

PERSONAL SAFETY AND SECURITY

Safety issues compound boundary issues when a massage therapist practices alone in an office. As a professional, you are responsible for establishing a safe environment for both yourself and the client. Establishing such an environment involves three phases:

1 *Screening clients.* Whenever a new client calls for an appointment, request the person's name, day and evening phone numbers, referral source, and reason for calling. Take a minute to explain the technique you use and what is expected of the client. This helps you identify callers who misunderstand the nature of massage. (If someone has misunderstood, remain calm and use this opportunity to educate the caller about the nature of the profession.) Some practices have a policy of accepting only clients referred by a source they know. Others choose to clearly state to new clients before accepting an appointment that this is "nonsexual, therapeutic massage," to avoid possible misunderstanding.

2 *After the client arrives:* Have clients sign in and complete an intake form when they arrive. Take a few moments before beginning the session to establish why the client is there and what the client expects from the session. Then describe how you may be able to help the client. Before going into the session, call someone to say where you are and when you will be finished and that you will call him or her back when the session is over. Preprogram that person's number into your cell phone and take it (with its ringer muted) into the session room with you in case you need to call for help.

3 *After the session begins:* If the client is uncomfortable with the therapy after a brief time, you may choose to stop the session and not charge the client, depending on your policy regarding such a situation. If you are uncomfortable with the client's behavior, or if the client makes an inappropriate remark, state that it was inappropriate and end the session immediately. Cancel the session and request your fee. If the client refuses to pay, you are better off safe than compensated.

WORKING IN CLIENTS' HOMES

If you provide massage to clients in their homes, you will face boundary issues not always found in office-based practices. In an office environment, you set or abide by policies that are consistent for every client visit. When you go into clients' homes, you must determine a set of practices and policies that will always be followed, as well as be flexible enough to adapt to each client's different environment. At no time should you alter your adherence to the code of ethics and performance standards. The same standards of confidentiality, draping, hygiene, and client recordkeeping should always be observed regardless of where the session takes place.

Beyond these core practices, you need to decide how you want to handle certain etiquette issues of being in someone else's home. Some practical considerations include the following:

- Ask the client where you should hang your coat or put your boots.
- Remove your shoes at the door.
- Request permission before using the bathroom.
- Do not make comments on a client's furnishings or décor. You will be in the homes of clients who have more or less material goods, and any notice of their possessions could detract from the sense of therapeutic relationship you both desire.

When going to a client's home, sometimes called out-calls, you must be especially aware of security safeguards for personal safety. See the previous section "Personal Safety and Security."

DUAL RELATIONSHIPS

Within the context of performing massage therapy, the term "dual relationship" refers to situations in which two people have a personal connection that goes beyond that of practitioner and client. This could pertain to spouses, siblings, close friends, boyfriends/girlfriends, teachers or clergy, neighbors—the list is extensive. The potential for blurred boundaries exists because of possibly different expectations these clients might have due to the context in which they know you. For instance, if a good friend were chatty while receiving a massage, it might be more difficult for you to tell her that this is her time to totally relax and allow the benefits of the massage to be the focus of her attentions—in short, to be quiet—than if she were another client. Possible areas of difficulty include:

- Collecting payment after a session
- Being "on call" 24–7 because of family's or friends' expectations
- Enforcement of late or no-show policies
- Untimely chatter
- Your own concentration on massage as the focal point

> A dual relationship is one in which the massage therapist knows the client in more than one context. The most therapeutic and ethical relationships are those that allow the massage therapist to focus on the client as a client only.

The best way to avoid dual relationships is to prevent them from developing. You should not encourage clients to discuss unrelated personal matters beyond light conversation. If, in spite of these precautions, you and the client decide you are drawn toward developing a personal relationship, you should refer the person to another practitioner. This helps keep the boundary clear for your professional and personal life and allows you to maintain your ethical integrity.

ADVISING AND COUNSELING CLIENTS

Staying within boundaries also applies to giving advice to clients. Practitioners would readily agree that giving advice on topics not related to massage therapy is strictly off-limits. The temptation to give advice in other areas, however, such as health care or spirituality—topics you might perceive as related to massage—might not be as easy to resist. Wanting to help others is intrinsic to the profession of massage therapy, and therefore it can be difficult to refrain from sharing with clients information you feel would improve their lives. Examples in which giving advice to clients exceeds a practitioner's scope of practice include:

- A client tells you he is planning to have back surgery, and you advise him that massage is less invasive and that he should at least try it for 6 more months to see if he can avoid having surgery.
- A client tells you she is taking antidepressants, and you suggest that she try an herbal remedy that a trusted friend of yours has said is very effective.
- A client tells you he has a persistent pain in his low back, and you share with him your opinion that the pain might be a manifestation of the grief he feels over the recent breakup with his partner.

- Because you find your own spiritual beliefs to be a source of joy and well-being—and you believe your beliefs are generic to all faiths and would therefore not offend anyone—you encourage your clients to try your meditation techniques.

In all these examples, the practitioner's intentions are to be helpful. But in all these examples, the practitioner went beyond the scope of practice and gave advice in areas for which he or she was not qualified or which were unrelated to the professional practice of massage therapy. Referring a client to another type of health professional is not the same as giving advice. Suggesting that a client see a professional who is qualified in a way that might benefit your client is strongly recommended when you observe an area of possible need that is outside the scope of massage therapy.

BOUNDARY VIOLATIONS

Not everyone—not even all massage therapists who conduct themselves according to professional ethics—agrees on all ethical issues. Some of the best discussions you'll ever have with other respected massage therapists will center on whether a particular action is ethical of not. For instance:

- Is it ethical to date a person who is a massage client?
- Is it ethical to accept tips?
- Is it ethical to sell herbal or nutritional supplements?
- Is it ethical to accept a cup of tea from a client after an outcall session at his or her home? a glass of wine?

RESOURCES FOR ETHICS AND BOUNDARIES

CONTINUING EDUCATION

AMTA Learn'N Earn continuing education courses: www.amtamassage.org/cont_edu.html

NCBTMB list of continuing education approved providers (type "ethics" into "Course name or key words" field): www.ncbtmb.com/ceproviders_find_providers.php

BOOKS AND ARTICLES

Andrade, Carla-Krystin, & Paul Clifford. (2008). Outcome-Based Massage (2nd ed.). Lippincott Williams & Wilkins. See Chapter 4, "Preparation and Positioning for Treatment," for extensive draping descriptions.

Ashley, M. (2006). *Massage: A Career at Your Fingertips* (5th ed.). Carmel, NY: Enterprise. See Section III, "Sex, Gender and Touch."

Benjamin, Ben E., & Cherie M. Sohnen-Moe. (2004). The Ethics of Touch. Lippincott Williams & Wilkins.

McIntosh, N. (2005). *The Educated Heart* (2nd ed.) Lippincott Williams & Wilkins.

Fritz, Sandy. (2004). Mosby's Fundamentals of Therapeutic Massage (3rd ed.) Mosby.

Polseno, Diane. "Ethically Speaking" columns in mtj.

Redleaf, Angelica, & Susan Baird. (1998). Behind Closed Doors: Gender, Sexuality, and Touch in the Doctor/Patient Relationship. Westport, CT: Auburn House.

Taylor, Kylea. (1995). The Ethics of Caring. Santa Cruz, CA: Hanford Mead Publishers.

Yardley-nohr, Terrie. (2006). Ethics for Massage Therapists. Lippincott Williams & Wilkins.

Massage therapists are responsible for understanding the fine points and controversial areas within ethics, and being sensitive to others' views on the same issues.

Some of these questions may seem to have such obvious answers that you would assume unanimous agreement from other massage therapists. However, each of the questions just listed has those in favor and those against. Discussing these issues, understanding the fine points and gray areas, and being sensitive to what others might deem an ethical violation are all important responsibilities of a massage therapist.

Some professional associations provide a formal grievance process for members. Through this process, members can cite instances of alleged violation of the code of ethics, policy, or bylaws of the association. Violations could include such things as sexual misconduct, improper draping, and actions outside the massage therapist's scope of practice. The result of such a grievance, if the ensuing investigation proves that the violation did in fact occur, could be probation or suspension from the association's membership or expulsion from membership. The National Certification Board for Therapeutic Massage and Bodywork and many state regulatory agencies also have grievance processes.

Some boundary violations are punishable by law. (See the section "Failure to Comply" in Chapter 5.) Any violation of an ethical or boundary issue is a matter of professional concern. Some violations occur because of a practitioner's inexperience in the profession or lack of appropriate judgment, and not because of intent to do harm. Several ways to become fully informed of and sensitive to the implications of your behavior are to take continuing education seminars in ethics and boundaries, to participate actively in your professional chapter organization, and to meet with a supervisor or another trusted massage therapist to discuss such matters. With experience, you will become a model in ethical behavior for new massage therapists entering the profession.

CLIENT COMMUNICATION

Many elements of a therapeutic relationship highlight the importance of effective communication skills. The fact that the therapeutic relationship is dependent not only on the practitioner's intuition but also on skills that can be learned, encourages practitioners to hone their communication skills. This section identifies ways you can better understand how your verbal and nonverbal actions contribute to helping or harming your therapeutic relationship with a client.

LISTENING

Listening skills are as powerful, effective, and varied as the skills of communicating orally. The two main goals of good listening skills are: 1) to improve listening acuity so the practitioner hears the client accurately; and 2) to ascertain what a client has heard the practitioner communicate.

Inability to listen effectively can be caused by several factors. The following factors are described to help you recognize when they apply to your own listening effectiveness, and also to acknowledge possible reasons why your client doesn't always hear the message you thought you delivered.

- *Mindset*—The listener's past experiences or cultural background have created a particular mindset, or belief, about a topic. Such a belief might be, "It's not all right to have a stranger touch me." The client might not be consciously aware of this mindset and might communicate it in nonverbal ways, such as creating conflict or arriving late for appointments. A caution to be aware of here is, unless you are a trained psychologist, do not attempt to interpret the client's responses in clinical terms. Simply being aware that what the client says and what the client believes might be two different things is sufficient to your maintaining a healthy relationship with the client. Listening with a compassionate ear and striving for optimum well-being of both you and your client— not psychoanalyzing the client—is the goal.

- *Unrealistic expectations*—If the client expects a certain result that is not likely to happen, the anticipation of that result could cloud the client's understanding of your words. For instance, if the client believed that the first session of a particular modality would totally remove a painful condition—and it didn't—that client might attribute that failure to your skills rather than realize that he or she was operating under unrealistic expectations. Further, if you did not determine that the client had these expectations, you would not even be aware that they should be addressed.
- *Sensory overload*—The rate at which a listener can process incoming information depends on whether the listener is distracted by competing demands for his or her attention and by the rate at which the information is being conveyed. For instance, communicating effectively with a single parent who sandwiches in a massage for relaxation between childcare activities and a job might require extra sensitivity on your part to the client's distractions. When trying to cut through layers of distraction, your choice of vocabulary as well as your rate of speaking can help you convey information more effectively. Your awareness of a client's cultural background can also give you clues to whether the client is accustomed to such things as a fast or a slow rate of speaking and to physical proximity during normal conversation.

TALKING

Oral communication skills are essential for every massage therapist to develop. They are one of the most obvious tools to use in establishing relationships with clients. Most clients will not know the technical language of the massage therapy profession, and therefore, good, general communication skills are required in order to put the client at ease.

When a client does not follow the practitioner's instructions, it could be due to the practitioner's inability to communicate clearly and skillfully. The success of oral communication depends on your ability to present information in a way that is understood accurately by the client, in facts as well as intent. The skills of conveying information, as well as listening, affect this success.

> An effective communicator is responsible not only to say the right words but to communicate in a way that helps ensure that the listener understands the message clearly.

Choice of Words

Because your client probably will not know the technical vocabulary of massage, it is important that you learn to communicate using vocabulary that is clearly understood by the client. You have become accustomed during your training to communicate with others who speak the language of massage, and it will take practice to convert this to language clients will understand.

This doesn't mean that you should be condescending in your explanations or that you should oversimplify them—after all, it is your role to help educate clients about the role and efficacy of massage. Mastery of appropriate vocabulary means knowing when and how to use professional jargon and translate it into everyday terms.

The goal of choosing appropriate vocabulary is to achieve desired results of the session, and to convey to the client that you are sincere in your desire to form a productive working client/therapist relationship with him or her.

Voice Clarity, Tone, and Volume

You know the adage "It's not what you say, it's how you say it." A highly organized, technically correct and meaningful sentence loses its impact when poorly delivered. Clients are often initially hesitant or sometimes intimidated in the presence of health care professionals. Your clarity of voice helps convey that you feel confident of the benefits you are about to impart, sincere in welcoming the client, and professional in how you conduct your practice. Lack of voice clarity means you mumble or slur your words rather than clearly enunciate them. Lack of clarity suggests to the client that you are not confident of what you're saying. Clarity inspires trust.

Tone is a voice quality that can either reinforce or communicate exactly the opposite of the spoken words. A flat tone can convey indifference. A too-warm and soft tone can be misinterpreted as suggesting intimacy. A too-jovial tone might detract from a relaxation atmosphere.

It is important to be cognizant of tone not only when speaking but when listening. When a client's response is not clear or is surprising to you, be alert to the tone in which the client communicates or reacts to something you say. His or her tone might give you more clues to the actual meaning of the communication than words alone convey.

Volume can be used to control distance between people. A soft whisper can make the listener move closer. It can also be used in a manipulative way, to control the listener's behavior by compelling him or her to lean toward you. Loud volume conveys aggression, or it can be an attention-getting device. You could send the wrong impression to your client if your voice were meek and faltering, or at the opposite extreme, if your voice were inappropriately loud.

If you are unclear about what the client means to say, simply ask for clarification. For instance, if you think the client has pain but hasn't said so, ask if he or she is having pain in any area.

Flow of Ideas

The rambling practitioner confuses clients by jumping from one topic to the next, inserting last-minute ideas, and then failing to summarize. Inability to progress from one step to the next and thereby reach a logical conclusion is usually due to a lack of understanding of the topic or the steps in a procedure, or a too-thorough knowledge of the topic or procedure.

The first instance—lack of understanding—would cause you to either grope for words or be at a loss for words since you're not sure what you want to say in the first place. The second instance—too-thorough knowledge—could either cause you to give too much information to the client by assuming that the client has a need or interest to know more than is appropriate, or to give too little information to the client by assuming that he or she already knows this information.

If you are communicating new information to a client, practice ahead of time how you will organize your thoughts and then your communication. Provide written instructions and diagrams whenever possible, to add to the clarity of your oral communication.

Sense of Humor

Injecting a sense of humor into the client-therapist relationship can help build rapport and trust quickly, but it also has its pitfalls. Whether you can use humor effectively with your client depends on your ability to accurately read your client's acceptance of humor. It also depends on the compatibility of your sense of humor and your client's. There is no one right or wrong way to use humor, because each instance is dependent upon the situation and the client and your own comfort with humor.

Effective uses of humor might include:

- Reducing tension when it exists unnecessarily: "If something tickles you, you're allowed to laugh."
- Coaching for self-care: "I have a policy that limits me to one ski accident client a week, so be careful on the slopes this weekend."

Guard against destructive uses of humor, such as verbal fencing or sarcasm. It introduces animosity to the client-therapist relationship, and makes it difficult to enter into a healing atmosphere based on trust and comfort. If you find that you're tempted to use humor in order to avoid an uncomfortable confrontation, take a moment to think about a constructive way to communicate necessary information.

NONVERBAL COMMUNICATION

Nonverbal cues, such as dress, posture, hygiene, and facial expression, sometimes communicate more clearly than words. While everyone would probably agree that a massage therapist should dress and act professionally, opinions of what "professional" would look like are as diverse as practitioners.

Dress and Hygiene

Good hygiene and proper attire are essential for anyone who works closely with others. Attire can range from surgical scrubs to shirts and ties, from flip-flops to heels—but appropriate attire has a narrower range. If a client is put off by your appearance, everything you say and do will be tainted by the client's perception of how you look.

Similarly, posture, hygiene, and facial expression convey how you feel about yourself. They flavor the ambience of your practice as strongly as your words, policies, and techniques do. See Chapter 4 for information about how self-care can add to your therapeutic relationship with the client.

One style will not attract or deter everyone. The issue of what is appropriate for you is dependent upon how well you know your clients and which clients you want to attract to your business. What you wear and how you present yourself reflects your personal values and self-perception. Sometimes individuals undergo personal growth, maturity, and transformation over a period of years but still dress the same or react in the same ways they had in the past, purely out of habit. If you conduct a personal self-assessment regarding your own nonverbal image, you will have the opportunity to evaluate whether or not it is in keeping with your values and with your intended communication to clients. See Figure 2.2 for areas you might use as your checklist for maintaining dress and hygiene appropriate to a massage therapist.

From *Council Communicator*, July 2001, artist Beverly Ransom. Reprinted with permission.

FIGURE 2.2
Hygiene and Attire Tips

Use warm water and antibacterial soap to wash your hands before and after every massage.

Maintain appropriate dental hygiene for clean teeth and clean breath.

Keep your hair clean. If you have long hair, avoid letting it touch the client during a massage.

Keep your hands well groomed and your fingernails trimmed short. Long fingernails detract from a hygienic look, and they also could be a hazard during the massage.

Avoid massaging any areas of a client's body where there is broken skin or a rash.

Avoid client contact if you are coughing or sneezing.

Wear comfortable clothing that is neither too tight nor too sloppy looking.

Do not wear anything that might be sexually suggestive, such as low-cut necklines or hip-slung jeans. Be sure you are well covered when bending over. Avoid sleeveless outfits and short shorts.

Shoes should provide support and be comfortable and neat. If you wear sandals, be sure your feet are clean and well groomed.

Avoid wearing perfume or cologne.

Avoid sharp, noisy, or dangling jewelry.

WHOLE PRESENCE

The most gifted practitioners are present with the client in a way that is the very essence of good communication skills. Their whole selves are focused on the client and on the massage. To be totally present requires that you have a deep sense of self, of the client's mental and emotional state, and of the therapeutic connection between you and the client. For one method to help you experience whole presence, see Spotlight on Business, "An Exercise to Help You Be Present with the Client."

Ways of being fully present with the client include:

- Being on time for appointments
- Having the session room ready
- Listening with all your senses
- Maintaining eye contact
- Slowing down
- Single-pointed attention
- Attending exclusively to the client's needs

In *The Educated Heart*, author Nina McIntosh writes about the ways practitioners may inadvertently burden the client with issues that detract from the client's needs:

Practitioners with good intentions can be misled by the notion that it's helpful to clients to be open with them about our personal issues. Actually, it can be a distraction in what is their time. What is really helpful to clients is giving them our full attention, and not dragging our personal lives into the session, or asking people who are paying us to also give us emotional support or free advice.

McIntosh writes that a remark as subtle as "I can't stand this hot weather," makes it sound to the client as though you're not up to par on a given day. Such a remark might interfere with the client's ability to trust the practitioner and fully derive benefit from that day's massage. To be fully present with the client is a skill that transcends minor errors of judgment or skill in other areas of communicating.

SPOTLIGHT ON BUSINESS

An Exercise to Help You Be Present with the Client

The following exercise can be helpful to you in learning to be aware of your stroke speed while staying present and mindful at the same time. Do this exercise[1] with another practitioner who can give you knowledgeable feedback.

1 Warm up the back normally and get a good sense of the skin's warmth, texture, and color.
2 Increase your speed to a much faster than usual pace. Massage as quickly as you can without making your volunteer uncomfortable.
3 Note how you feel and sense how the client must feel. Go through similar observations detailed in step one.
4 Slow down. Go so slowly that you can barely see your hands move. Notice what is happening to the client's experience. What is happening to the space around you? How do you feel?
5 Stop. Stop right where you are and feel the skin beneath your hands. Go deeper. Feel the muscle tissue, the bones, and the viscera. Feel the blood moving and cells working to keep this body alive. Notice your fingers, palms, and the lubrication between the two surfaces. What does stopping feel like?
6 Come to a point between normal and fast, between normal and slow. Notice how the skin feels.
7 Return to your "normal" massage strokes, but this time experiment with different speeds. Know the difference between too fast and too slow.

> **RESOURCES FOR THERAPEUTIC COMMUNICATIONS**
>
> Dunn, Teri, & Marian Williams. (2001). Massage Therapy Guidelines for Hospital and Home Care (4th ed.). Information for People, Inc.
>
> McIntosh, N. (2005). *The Educated Heart* (2nd ed.). Lippincott Williams & Wilkins.
>
> Nhat Hanh, Thich. (1992) Peace Is Every Step: The Path of Mindfulness in Everyday Life. New York: Bantam.

MULTICULTURAL CONTEXTS

Almost every massage therapist will experience working with multicultural aspects of therapeutic relationships with clients. In addition to cultural differences of clients from different countries, religions, and ethnicities, multicultural might also be construed to mean differences in: age; attitudes (e.g., openness to alternative therapies); sexual orientation; language, physical attributes, and economic health; and victims of domestic violence, sexual abuse, or other trauma.

While it is outside the scope of this book to provide detailed information about working with each of the multicultural opportunities you might encounter, it will serve you well in all cases to let sensitivity to diversity be your guide. A sincere appreciation of all persons and a particular appreciation of differences are the main tools you need to excel in this area.

> **RESOURCES FOR SUPPORT OF CLIENTS WITH PARTICULAR NEEDS**
>
> Briere, John. (1992). Child Abuse Trauma: Theory and Treatment of the Lasting Effects. California: Sage.
>
> Fitch, Pamela, & Trish Dryden. (2000). "Recovering Body and Soul from Post-Traumatic Stress Disorder." mtj, Spring 2000, pages 41–62.
>
> Gift from Within, an international, nonprofit organization for survivors of trauma and victimization: www.giftfromwithin.org.
>
> Matsakis, Aphrodite. (1996). I Cannot Get Over It: A Handbook for Trauma Survivors. California: Harbinger Press.
>
> McIntosh, N. (2005). *The Educated Heart* (2nd ed.). Lippincott Williams & Wilkins.
>
> Redleaf, Angelica, & Susan Baird. (1998). Behind Closed Doors: Gender, Sexuality, and Touch in the Doctor/Patient Relationship. Westport, CT: Auburn House.
>
> Skogrand, Linda. (2007). *Surviving and Transcending a Traumatic Childhood: The Dark Thread*. Binghamton, NY: Haworth Press.

CONFLICT RESOLUTION

Although "conflict" might sound like a negative term, it is in fact a normal occurrence in everyone's life and in everyday circumstances. It becomes negatively charged with emotion only when our response to it is ineffective. When conflict occurs, it offers an opportunity for the practitioner and the client to gain a clearer understanding of whatever topic is at issue. Conflict does not need to carry negative connotations; it holds the potential of illuminating information in such a way that leads to growth for all parties involved.

An important source of information is feedback from clients. How you will respond to the feedback determines whether it will help you. Here are some suggestions:

• First, be thankful for negative feedback. Most unhappy clients do not say anything; they just do not return. If you want to grow your practice, you will need to learn from your clients.

- Choose words that encourage the other person to tell you about the issue: "Tell me about that." "Tell me more." "Go on." "Is there something you'd like to talk about?" "Is there something on your mind?"
- Listen not only to words but to the meaning behind the words. "That was an interesting massage!" can mean a lot of things. Ask specific questions to find out what the words mean.
- Do not interrupt.
- Stay centered. Focus on the needs of your client and your practice, instead of on your own disappointment with negative words, on your need for praise, or on making excuses.
- When a client stops talking, use a process of reflecting, validating, and empathizing. Indicate your understanding with words such as "I see" or "You have a right to feel that way."
- Do not make excuses; they will not help you reach a solution.
- Discuss solutions with the client. Rather than telling the client what you cannot do, you will need to talk with him or her about what you can do to make things right.
- Tell the client what to expect, and then follow through on your promises.
- Thank the client for sharing constructive criticism or suggestions with you. If you learn from the experience and use it to help you grow your practice, your thanks will be sincere.

ROLE OF CLIENT RECORDS

When used properly, creating and maintaining client records can be a useful tool in establishing healthy therapeutic relationships with clients. They are used to elicit client expectations, as well as to communicate your own expectations and what the client should expect from your practice. They formalize responsibility, for example, in establishing that it's the client's responsibility to pay for services received and that it's your responsibility to keep the client's information confidential and private. In many states, maintaining client records is a legal requirement.

The different types of client records can be confusing to clients, so it's important to explain the purpose of each. Consolidating some records together on one form can help cut down on what might otherwise seem like a mountain of paperwork. For instance, you could add the authorization to release information to the end of the client intake form rather than having a separate form.

The purpose and content of each form are explained in the "Client Records Management" section of Chapter 6. The forms covered there include:

- Client intake
- Informed consent
- Authorization to release information
- SOAP notes
- Financial responsibility
- Authorization to pay provider

REFERRING CLIENTS TO OTHERS

At some time during your professional career, you may encounter a circumstance when it makes sense to suggest that a client change to another massage practitioner. For instance, your practice might be so busy that you cannot provide the level of customer service you'd like to. Or you may run across a client who is, for some reason, just difficult for you to work with. Or your situation might be related to a type of boundary issue discussed earlier, such as if you are attracted to a client and believe the ethical choice is to refer him or her to another massage therapist. If you are unable to resolve the difficulty, the success of your practice and your own well-being may require you to encourage clients to see other massage therapists or professionals.

Building networks that help you build a larger client base by working with other massage practitioners and colleagues in allied professions is discussed in Chapter 8. Building networks is an excellent marketing tool, and it is a strategy that serves a much broader purpose than encouraging clients to see others due to specific circumstances.

The following signs suggest it may be appropriate to ask the client to see another professional:

- The client (in the health history or other communication) alludes to a problem that is outside your scope of practice or beyond your skills. Suggest someone with the appropriate qualifications and experience.
- Despite your best efforts, the client always seems to be displeased with some aspect of the massage you provide.
- You find it difficult to maintain appropriate boundaries with the client; for example, a mutual attraction is developing.
- You instinctively have a bad feeling (fear, anger, revulsion) about providing a massage to the client. This person may need help from someone other than a massage therapist.
- Part of your professional responsibility will include recognizing clients who have health problems that may affect whether or how you provide a massage. That's why it will be essential to obtain a health history when you see a client for the first time. An extensive discussion of these conditions is beyond the scope of this book.

Whatever the cause, when you determine that you should suggest that the client see someone else, you should politely but clearly explain to the client the reason. If you choose, you may also provide suggestions about how the client may find another professional, such as recommending online search directories such as AMTA's Find a Massage Therapist or names of specific specialists whose work you trust.

CLIENT SELF-CARE

Given the importance of a client taking responsibility for his or her own health, one of the most helpful things a practitioner can do for a client is to provide instruction on self-care. Encouraging clients to practice good self-care, you are becoming a valued partner in helping them achieve maximum well-being. It is important to honor the boundaries of the scope of practice for massage therapy within your state when you provide instruction on self-care to clients.

A program or routine of self-care may be focused on a particular goal, such as increasing range of motion, or more general, such as stress relief, personal growth, and general well-being. Self-care instruction to the client should incorporate awareness that established behavior patterns are difficult to change. Until self-care behavior becomes integrated into the client's daily routine, its benefits will not be fully achieved.

The most instructive action you can take is to be a role model of self-care behavior yourself. When a client observes you incorporating healthy practices in body mechanics, eating habits, attitude, exercise, and balance, your example serves as a much more potent lesson than oral or written instructions could ever be.

The most effective instruction you can give a client in self-care is the example you set.

Techniques that can enhance the practitioner's effectiveness in encouraging clients toward self-care include the following:[2]

1 *Use simplicity and repetition in spoken and written communication.* Speak to a client about no more than three new pieces of information per session, and write brief instructions in simple terms. Include illustrations when possible. Accompany with demonstrations when applicable, such as with a self-foot-massage. Ask the client to repeat the instructions back to you, to ensure that the explanation you gave was clear. This is

especially important when working with clients for whom language, learning, or hearing impairments present challenges.

2 *Use demonstration, practice, feedback, and review.* Effective feedback involves auditory (rephrase or repeat the instructions), visual (demonstrate or show illustration), and kinesthetic (use hands-on corrective guidance) senses. At each session, acknowledge that learning new habits and ways of being in our bodies takes time and patience.

3 *Use social modeling to enhance learning.* The practitioner can be a powerful model to the client of the behaviors and level of body awareness needed. For areas of expertise outside the massage practitioner's scope of practice, refer the client to good-quality instructional tapes or to reputable specialists.

4 *Gradually introduce new behaviors.* A common mistake in providing client instruction is for the practitioner to forget that what seems commonplace to him or her may seem complex to the client. Clients are more successful in learning and continuing self-care practices if they are introduced to them gradually, increasing the number and complexity of actions as the client masters the previous ones. Clients are also more apt to stick with a program that is easily integrated into his or her daily routine.

5 *Give the client suggestions for creating environmental cues and modifications.* Cueing is the simple technique of adding reminders to the everyday environment, such as strategically placed reminders on notes placed on the bathroom mirror or the car's dashboard. Audio cues, such as clock set to chime at certain intervals, can also be helpful. Modifications a practitioner might suggest include installing an ergonomic mouse for the computer, buying an adjustable office chair, or turning off the television before the late-evening news.

6 *Encourage the client to use self-observation.* Self-observation entails taking the time to be focused and mindful of nonproductive or self-defeating behaviors. Many people find keeping a journal helpful, as long as the recordkeeping itself does not become a source of stress or anxiety. Heightened attention through self-observation sheds light on habitual behaviors that were hidden from conscious awareness.

7 *Help the client create goals while focusing on the process.* After self-observation, the client may wish to write a goal or an action he or she will take to reach the goal. People who write down their goals, plans, and visions are significantly more likely to make progress toward achieving them. An important point to keep in mind is that a person's attention is best focused on the process of change and on removing the obstacles to change, rather than straining for an immediate outcome.

8 *Help the client evaluate progress.* The practitioner can check in with the client periodically to help focus on how closely the client's behaviors match his or her intentions and how the client feels about the progress he or she is making.

9 *Provide positive reinforcement.* Self-care behaviors that involve a relatively long lag time between initiation and results put the client at risk for giving up. Creating external reinforcement to keep the client motivated until the intrinsic reinforcement (e.g., pain reduction) manifests itself is useful. The practitioner may provide positive comments and encouragement, and the client may ask a spouse, friend, or coworker to help provide supportive comments as well. Some clients enjoy making a contract with themselves to gain small rewards at milestones they set for themselves.

10 *Encourage behavior maintenance and social support.* At times of emotional stress, or when the client has an inadequate network of supportive people, he or she may relapse to old behaviors. If clients lack positive coping skills and a supportive social network, they may seek a level of emotional support from the practitioner that goes beyond professional boundaries. It may be appropriate to refer the client to specialized support groups, such as those for fibromyalgia, chronic fatigue, or cancer survivors. Massage therapists will find it helpful to maintain a community resource directory and a referral list of competent professionals and organizations.

11 *Offer additional resources.* Provide information such as articles or magazine subscription

recommendations, names and addresses alternative health centers, or upcoming educational opportunities that the client might find helpful.

MASSAGE SESSION START TO FINISH

CUSTOMER SERVICE TOTAL EXPERIENCE

Fortunately, most clients are delighted with massage and its many benefits, so you will be able to focus on the most important aspect of managing a practice: ensuring a high level of customer service. Simple things like how to greet a client, how to respond to a client's inquiries, and how quickly you return a client's calls all reflect your attitude toward customer service.

Customer service is as simple yet as complicated as knowing what your clients want and then providing it—plus a little more. Doing so requires a real commitment to listening to them and caring about them. Consider every step of the sequence you go through in providing a massage from beginning to end as an opportunity to establish a strong and caring therapeutic relationship with your client. Some of these steps are as follows:

1 *Client inquiry*—When a client calls, ask about his or her needs. Ask if there's anything you can do to prepare for the session that is different from routine. For instance, you might say, "The temperatures are supposed to be really cold on Wednesday. I'll make sure to warm the sheets before you arrive."

2 *Intake interview*—When a client arrives, ask him or her to complete an intake form. Review it carefully and ask yourself, "Would this client benefit from modifications to my usual approach? Is there anything in this information that would alert me to symptoms that should be seen by another type of specialist?"

3 *Intake interview discussion*—Review the intake form and plan care with the client. Ask whether there are any areas the client does not want massaged. If the client has been referred to you by another health professional, such as a physician or a chiropractor, ask if the client has specific expectations regarding your therapy. If you know of the referral in advance of the appointment, you would have already conferred with the health professional about his or her reasons for the referral. Review your policies with a first-time client.

4 *During the session*—Encourage the client to tell you what feels right and what does not during the session. Ask about positioning, discomfort, and use of oil or cream. Adjust your approach accordingly. Many therapists ask the client to use a scale of 1 to 5 in describing pain levels.

5 *Care after the session*—At the end of the session, ask the client, "How do you feel?" Summarize the session. Give appropriate suggestions, such as advice to drink plenty of water, stretch, rest, and move. Also schedule the next session. A day later, call the client to ask how he or she is feeling, especially if the client had reported any pain.

6 *Referrals*—When a client has a condition requiring medical care, encourage him or her to see a doctor. If your assessment indicates the condition could require skeletal alignment, you might suggest an appointment with a chiropractor.

7 *Suggestion box*—Provide a suggestion box and/or cards for client feedback prominently in your reception waiting area. Regularly review suggestions, especially looking for related suggestions from several clients.

Be aware of the need to provide different kinds of support to first-time clients than to regularly established clients (see Figure 2.3). You will want to spend an extra 15 minutes or so educating first-time clients on what to expect and on client intake information. If the client has had a massage before, but this is the first time with you, focus on how you can convert him or her to a loyal client. Regular monthly clients require an extra investment of your time as well, because they are the mainstay of your business.

You can enhance customer satisfaction by educating your clients about massage before, during, and after the session. Let them know what it can do. Likewise, be sure they understand what it cannot do. Massage provides many wonderful benefits, but it does not cure the common cold.

FIGURE 2.3
Explaining Massage
to a Client

1 When a new client arrives for his or her appointment, introduce yourself with a firm, friendly handshake. Briefly describe your credentials as a qualified practitioner.

2 Be aware of why the client is seeking massage. Ask the client at the beginning of each session his or her goal for the session. Meet expectations if possible, or when it is not possible, explain why.

3 Ask your client to complete the informed consent form and the client intake form (see Chapter 6 for details). Explain that the informed consent form describes what to expect from the massage, and that the client intake form is for him or her to inform you of health issues and concerns.

4 Assume nothing. Even if a client has received massage before, you do not know what that experience entailed. Tell the client what to expect during the session, such as:

- That most sessions are an hour in length, which means I will provide massage for 50 minutes and allow 10 minutes for undressing and dressing.
- Remove as much clothing as you feel comfortable with.
- I will use a high quality oil [or lotion], but let me know if you are allergic to anything.
- I will play music or work in silence. Which would you prefer?
- To respect personal privacy, and for adequate warmth, I will cover or drape you with a sheet or towel so that only the part of the body being worked on is exposed at any given time.
- If you are uncomfortable, or curious about what I am doing, at any point during the massage, please feel free to say something. You are in total control of this session.
- Whether you want to talk or not depends on your need at the time. Again, you are in charge of the session at all times.

5 During the massage, tell the client when you are moving to more vulnerable areas, such as the anterior neck, medial thigh, or abdomen.

6 Tell, or ask permission from, the client when you are about to rest your own body on the table, get up onto the table to assist your body mechanics, or to assist with stretches.

7 Tell the client when your work gets deeper, and check in to see if the pressure is tolerable.

8 Inform the client 5 minutes before the massage is to end, and ask him or her if you should move your focus to an area that may need more attention.

9 Don't surprise the client. The client who is in a vulnerable, relaxed state trusts you.

10 Inform the client about what to expect after the massage. For example, if applicable, tell the client that soreness or tenderness may be experienced the next day.

When you give the extras of good suggestions for care and responsiveness to concerns, you will find that your clients will return and will recommend you to their friends and colleagues. Satisfied clients will tell others about how your massage has helped them. To read about the opposite experience, see Spotlight on Business, "Profile of a Bad Massage."

Profile of a Bad Massage

Sometimes it's instructive to look at what you *shouldn't* do in your massage practice in order to more clearly understand what you should do. When you read the list of these true-life experiences, reflect on whether you have ever been guilty (even inadvertently) of inflicting similar experiences on any of your clients.

- When the client calls to make an appointment, answer your cell phone while you are giving a massage to another client. You don't want to miss a chance to make an appointment.
- Arrive at your office at the same time as the client arrives.
- Remove the clutter from a chair so your client can sit down to fill out the client intake form. Don't give the client a pencil.
- Ask the client if she would like a heated pad on her back during the session. If she says yes, tell her it will take 30 minutes to heat up because you haven't had a chance to plug it in yet.
- Dribble cold oil onto your client's skin, and laugh when she is startled by it.
- Keep up a continual flow of chatter. Tell the client how you are working through your challenges with having been abused as a child.
- Use scented oils without asking the client if she prefers them or is allergic to them.
- If the client tells you she is chilly, tell her, "Well, I'll be done in just a minute."
- Set a timer to ring 10 minutes before the end of the massage so both you and the client will be aware of the time.
- With 2 minutes left until the session ends, say, "Oh, rats, I know you said your feet and scalp were your favorite parts of a massage, but I don't have time now to do your scalp."
- Send the client an e-mail later in the day asking if she felt an energy drain, because you sure did, and you wonder if she might be dealing with negative feelings. Ask when she wants to schedule her next appointment.

Striking a balance between encouraging clients to luxuriate for a few minutes after the session has ended—and making sure they leave in time for the next client's appointment—is a skill all massage therapists must learn.

ENDING THE MASSAGE SESSION

Occasionally, a massage therapist may find it difficult to get a client to leave a session room after the massage has ended. Sometimes the client falls asleep after the massage therapist leaves the room, and other times clients just seem to feel that luxuriating a few minutes longer is part of the experience they are paying for. In part, they are right—a leisurely transition from the massage into the "real world" is something you hope to promote. However, you don't want a client to still be in your session room when the next client's session is scheduled to begin. Here are several techniques you might use.

A massage should have a beginning, a middle, and an end. The end could be signaled by one of several approaches:

- You say, "We're reaching the close of our session. Is there anything else you would like me to address before we finish?"
- You say, "As I rest my hands on your back [or whatever technique you prefer to finish with], I thank you for allowing me to share my energy with you today, and I send you positive energy that will stay in your life as you leave here today."
- You don't say anything, but you convey through sweeping and light strokes, that the session is at an end, and you conclude by silently enfolding the client's feet for several seconds.

- Any of these techniques puts you in a position to end the session by gently removing any bolsters or other accessories that might jeopardize the client's safety as he or she gets up from the massage table.
- Before you exit the room, instruct the client what to do next, such as: "Please take your time getting up and dressed. Sit at the edge of the massage table for a minute to regain your balance before putting your feet on the floor. I will have a bottle of water waiting for you when you come out of the room."

ENDING THE MASSAGE APPOINTMENT

When the client emerges from the session room, you will first want to ask how he or she is feeling, and whether the massage met expectations. You will also want to elicit the client's feedback. You may say something like, "If you have any suggestions for me that would help me provide a better experience for you in the future, or for other clients, I'd really appreciate hearing them." Or you can point out a suggestion box and paper on which the client could write feedback.

If it feels appropriate, you could ask the client when he or she would like to schedule the next appointment. If you have any specials or promotions, this is the time to point them out.

If all has gone smoothly, you will book your next appointment, at which time you will start the cycle over again—providing the best therapeutic environment and improving your practice with each client visit.

SUMMARY

The importance of establishing a therapeutic relationship with clients cannot be overstated. The term "therapeutic relationship" refers to a connection between you and the client that reflects ethical behaviors and codes of conduct, and sincerity and sensitivity in interpersonal communication skills. Even if your technical skills and your business skills are excellent, your business will suffer if you do not develop the ability to foster healthy, therapeutic relationships with your clients.

An understanding of the wellness model gives you a solid foundation on which to base your client relationships. The wellness model views health as the sum total of a person's environment, which includes body, mind, and spirit. Rather than focusing on the part of the body that appears to be ailing, the wellness approach focuses first on examining the balance of all related components.

Professional tools, such as a code of ethics and performance standards, provide massage therapists with specific guidelines on which to base their values and behavior. Letting your clients know the fundamental aspects of ethics and standards on which your practice is based helps establish immediate trust. These aspects include a broad range of confidentiality and boundary issues.

Conveying to clients that you are supportive of their body, mind, and spiritual health requires that you use good interpersonal communications skills. Good communication requires attention to verbal and nonverbal skills. Verbal skills include your choice of vocabulary and how you organize your thoughts, as well as your voice clarity, tone, and volume. Listening to clients and hearing what they mean as well as what they say is as important as delivering information to them. Nonverbal factors that affect your communication with the client include your dress and hygiene, as well as the strength of your total presence with the client. Presence includes such things as eye contact, slowing down, listening with all your senses, and giving all your attention to the client.

Adhering to ethical practices, being sensitive to boundary issues, and communicating effectively can be performed at every stage of your interaction with clients. In the long run, building relationships on trust and good communication will promote your practice's growth while it yields the highest level of health and well-being to you and your clients.

REVIEW QUESTIONS

1 What is the wellness model, and how is it different from the allopathic model?
2 What behaviors may a massage therapist demonstrate that are consistent with values common to all health care professional ethics?
3 Name at least three areas in which adherence to boundaries is important to a massage therapist.
4 Discuss the pros and cons of three ethical issues in the profession of massage therapy.
5 Why is proper draping essential to the trust between a client and massage therapist?
6 Name at least three language skills that affect the quality of communicating with your clients.
7 What factors can cause a practitioner or a client to not listen effectively?
8 What nonverbal factors affect the quality of communicating with your clients?
9 In what instances might you find it necessary to suggest that a client see a different practitioner?
10 At what points in the client-therapist connection do you have an opportunity to provide customer service?
11 Why is it important to instruct clients in self-care?
12 Describe two techniques you could use to end a massage therapy session.

ENDNOTES

1   Excerpted from Elizabeth Cornell, "How to Become a Better Therapist," *mtj*, Summer 2001, 88–90, 92.
2   Adapted from Patricia A. Sharp, "Strategies to Help Clients Practice Self-Care," *mtj*, Summer 2001, 50–62.

Chapter 3
Creating a Sense of Place

Your touch of the client begins long before you apply your hands. Understand the messages you send and how they affect your relationship with clients.

CHAPTER OVERVIEW

- Physical Space
- The Clients' Perspective
- Your Perspective as a Business Owner
- Equipping Your Space
- Green Practices
- Office Space Variations
- Reevaluating Your Space
- Summary

CHAPTER OBJECTIVES

1 Identify the physical components of a session space.
2 Describe the factors that make a session space appropriate to the client.
3 Identify rules and regulations that might apply to your office space.
4 Make decisions related to the therapeutic environment, considering client preferences.
5 Identify environmentally sustainable practices.
6 Identify ways to compensate for session space that is not ideal.

The physical environment in which you practice communicates messages to your clients on multiple levels. In this chapter, we look at the components that make up your physical practice space, and how those components create the image you want them to.

PHYSICAL SPACE

HOME, AWAY, OR NEITHER?

Where you plan to work depends primarily on how you plan to operate your practice. The choices are generally: your own home; your own business location; your employer's business location; or an outcall business, where your place of practice is wherever the client is (corporate or home). Figure 3.1 summarizes where AMTA members, on average, spend most of their work time.[1]

If you choose to operate your own business, deciding whether to locate a practice at home, in a separate space, or having an outcall business combines practical considerations with subjective issues of values and feelings. As you review the options, consider your own situation, values, and comfort level.

FIGURE 3.1
Locations Where Massage
Therapists Work*

Massage therapist's home	33%
Spa/salon	29%
Massage therapist's office	28%
Health care setting	24%
Health club/athletic facility	7%
Massage therapy-only franchise or chain	5%
Other	5%

*Percentages do not add up to 100% due to multiple mentions.

A home-based practice allows you to keep costs down and be near your children's schools and activities—but also be aware of drawbacks.

Home-Based Practice

Primary reasons massage therapists cite for choosing to have a business at home include keeping costs down and being near their children's schools and activities. They value having less of a division between their work lives and their family lives. For others, the distinction of working in or maintaining an office separate from their home helps them maintain a professional focus. Some massage therapists choose to start out at home and eventually rent office space so they can hire others and expand their practice.

Another attraction of a home-based practice is the ability to write off some costs related to home expenses as business expenses. If you use, say, 15 percent of your home's square footage, you might be able to deduct 15 percent of your home expenses. Ask an accountant for professional advice regarding whether your home office qualifies for deductions. Some possibilities for deductions include:

- A share of the mortgage interest or rent payment
- A share of the property taxes and property insurance (if you deduct a share for business expenses, you may not also deduct the full amount as personal expenses)

- A share of the utilities (electricity, gas, water, garbage collection)
- A share of maintenance costs (for example, repairing the furnace, buying cleaning supplies)
- Phone services devoted to the business (either a separate phone line or the share of the home's phone bill exceeding the basic cost of the phone service and attributable to the business)

Of course, writing off these business expenses, even if and when your accountant advises you that they are qualified, does not make them free. If you are planning on a home-based massage therapy practice, you will need to occupy a home with adequate and appropriate space for the business, and you will have to forego using this space for family activities if you want to claim it as a business expense. See Figure 3.2 for a summary of the pros and cons of having a home-based practice.

Legal Considerations of a Home-Based Practice

In deciding whether to set up your practice at home, you must weigh some legal issues as well. Under the Americans with Disabilities Act, the federal government requires that most businesses serving the public be accessible to people with disabilities. This means that for legal as well as service reasons, you will need to evaluate the accessibility of your home. Can people get in and out easily, even if they use a walker, crutches, or a wheelchair? Where can they use bathroom facilities? Door handles and faucets that are lever-shaped are easier to manipulate than round knobs. Will you have to modify your home for clients?

Many cities and towns have zoning ordinances that specify whether home offices are permitted, or the circumstances under which they are permitted. For example, you might be able to set up a home office if you limit the number of clients who come each week. Or you might be able to do paperwork at home but be required to do all your massage therapy at another location.

PROS

Easy to set up, assuming existing home has enough room.

Ability to write off portion of home expenses as business expenses.

No commuting time (saves time, money, and pollution).

Possibly the least expensive way to set up a practice.

Convenient; close to family.

Control over environment, including noise, heat, air, odors.

"Homier" image.

CONS

May take space away from family and recreational activities.

May require buying or renting a larger home than otherwise needed.

Less separation from work demands at home and from family demands at work.

Layout possibly not suitable for business space or for targeted clients (for example, no separate entrance to keep clients from your living area).

Safety and security challenges of working alone in a home.

Potential for conveying less than professional image if you have to lead clients to the "bedroom area" of your home for sessions.

Clients may feel awkward about coming to your home.

Americans with Disabilities Act requirements must be met even in a home office.

Neighbors might feel uneasy about having people they don't know (your clients) come into your neighborhood.

You will work alone versus working with colleagues.

Zoning or other legal matters may require additional time and expense.

FIGURE 3.2
Pros and Cons of a Home-based Practice

FIGURE 3.3
Home Office Zoning Regulation
Provisions

If you need to file with your municipality for a home-office variance, check your local zoning ordinances to find out what is required. The following descriptions might be helpful in making your case.

- The home office or business is clearly secondary to the use of the dwelling as a residence and does not change the residential character of the dwelling or the lot in any visible manner.

- The work done in the home office or business creates no objectionable odor, noticeable vibration, or offensive noise that increases the level of ambient sound at the property lines.

- The home office or business does not cause unsightly conditions or waste visible off the property.

- The home office or business does not cause interference with radio or television reception in the vicinity.

- The home office or business has no more than two full-time employees who are not residents of the household. Special permits may be granted to allow more employees.

- The home office or business has no signs visible from the street that are inconsistent with signs allowed elsewhere in the zoning regulations.

- The home office or business sells no articles at retail on the premises that are not made or grown on the premises.

- The home office or business occupies less than half the floor areas of the dwelling.

- The home office or business has sufficient off-street parking for both the residential and business uses of the dwelling.

- The home office or business does not create a volume of passenger or commercial traffic that is inconsistent with the normal level of traffic on the street on which the dwelling is located.

Source: Kiné-Concept Business Success Workbook, as adapted from a model ordinance developed by the National Alliance of Home Businesswomen, an organization that supports the working-from-home movement.

Contact your city's business development or economic development office, or visit the public library and look up your community's zoning ordinances. If you find it difficult to learn whether zoning ordinances affect you, you may want to have an attorney help. Keep in mind that zoning restrictions on home businesses often are stricter than those for businesses in commercial zones. Figure 3.3 lists some of the zoning regulations you might encounter.

Be neighborly. Rather than merely learning what the law permits, consider the impact of your practice on your neighbors. If clients will come to your home, where will they park? Will the number of clients affect the traffic or noise level of your neighborhood? Tell your neighbors why people are visiting you several days a week. Such courtesy could pay off for your practice: your neighbors could become your clients.[2]

Practice at an Independent Location

The benefits of having an office away from home in many cases outweigh the advantages of having a home-based practice. Clients might perceive you as having a "real" business if

PROS	CONS
Parking may be more available than in a residential area.	Requires commuting to work (time consuming, expensive, and polluting).
Helps set boundaries between work and personal.	Separation from family.
Building may already be in compliance with Americans with Disabilities Act requirements and zoned for business.	Less control over the environment, including noise, heat, and smells.
	Requires negotiating a lease and paying rent.
Presence of others in an office building a possible asset in terms of safety and security.	Building management may not be responsive to your concerns about such things as security and noise.
May be more convenient for a massage therapist with a relatively small home.	May require expenses (such as phone and computer connections, washer and dryer, office equipment) for items you already have at home but are standing idle during working hours.
Neighboring businesses may offer opportunities for joint marketing.	

FIGURE 3.4
Pros and Cons of a Separate Business Location

you have a separate office location. In addition, the separation between home and business may be an advantage, particularly if you have children or a work-at-home spouse who could pose business interruptions. As shown in Figure 3.4, there are also drawbacks to having a separate office—you'll probably have less control over such things as heating and cooling, and, of course, your expenses will be higher.

Factors to consider in choosing an office space separate from your home are covered in more detail further in this chapter.

Outcall-Based Practice

Or you can skip the decision about where to practice altogether and just go where your clients are. In an outcall business, you go to another place, such as a client's home or a workplace. In either case, you don't have the same overhead expenses that are associated with owning and maintaining physical space, but neither do you have as much control over the space in which you will be giving massages.

The greater concerns about an outcall business lie with going to clients' homes or hotel rooms than going to workplaces. Those concerns revolve primarily around security issues.

Concern for your safety requires that you be vigilant in your screening process and that you always inform someone else—a friend, a colleague, the front desk staff—where you are going, whom you are seeing, and how long you plan to be gone.

Workplace massage has its own sets of pros and cons, and is covered in Chapter 1. Pros and cons that are location-related are shown in Figure 3.5.

Minimum Office

If you intend to provide all massages on-site, at the locations where your clients live or work, it might seem simplest not to set up any office. Where, then, will you keep business records, make phone calls, and store supplies? If you have a place set aside for these needs, you can manage your business in a more organized manner than if you didn't have a designated "office space." Also, you may be able to write off the costs of this space to offset your revenues and lower your income taxes. For these reasons, you may be better off setting up an office—even one as modest as a small desk in a corner of your home—that you dedicate exclusively to your practice.

FIGURE 3.5
Pros and Cons of Outcall Business Related to Location

PROS

Convenient for the client.

Little or no fixed overhead costs.

No office to maintain.

CONS

Security issues are more pronounced in any situation in which you don't know the client.

No control over environment (client's children, lack of privacy, small work area, noise from TV or office environment, etc.).

Physical demands of carrying your office with you (massage table, oils, pads, bolsters, music, etc.).

Possibility of forgetting something you'll need.

BUYING VS. CREATING A PRACTICE

A massage therapy practice may feel more like a way of life than a business, but in fact it is also a collection of assets and liabilities that can be bought and sold. Because buying any kind of business is a complex transaction, be sure to get qualified legal and financial advice before you consider buying a massage therapy practice.

The reasons you might decide to buy a massage therapy practice, rather than start your own include:

- You may be able to earn a profit faster if the practice is already established.
- You would start out using a practice name that has already acquired a good reputation and client base. However, if one massage therapist sells a practice to another, it is important for the therapist making the purchase to consider whether clients will see it as the same practice, or just someone else operating under the same name. In other words, you might pay extra for an established practice, only to lose most of the clients after the purchase is complete.
- A "package deal" may be simpler than hunting for each item needed to set up an office. However, make sure that among the benefits you enjoy is an ongoing client base. Otherwise, it might be cheaper to offer to buy the used massage tables and some equipment, rather than the practice itself. Also, be sure before you buy that each element of the practice meets your standards for quality.

If you decide to purchase a massage therapy practice, you must consider all the issues that arise when you start a practice. Find out why the practice owner wants to sell. Consider the office space and where it is located. Go over all the business records with your attorney. Examine all the financial records with your accountant, asking questions about anything you do not understand. Finally, before you buy, get answers to the following questions:

- Does the practice generate enough earnings every month to meet your financial goals?
- How many one-hour massage sessions does the practice provide each month? How many are to repeat customers?
- Has the practice been operating according to all the applicable laws and regulations?
- Will you be committed to the lease agreement that is already in place? If so, for how long?
- If you had set up the office yourself, would you have done it the same way? Will making changes be harder or more costly than setting it up your way in the first place?
- Are the practice's standards, goals, and philosophy compatible with your own?
- If there are employees, are they planning on staying?

If your examination of the practice still supports your belief that purchasing it is a good move, determine whether you have the necessary funding to complete the purchase. Will you have enough left to live on until you can begin collecting revenue from the practice? It is probably wise to assume that some faithful clients will stop coming when ownership changes hands, but you should also be ready to identify sources of new clients. Also, be sure the sales agreement includes a noncompete clause, in case the owner later wants to continue practicing in the area. Another option is purchasing a franchise massage business. This is a relatively new area of business opportunity in the massage profession. Finally, be sure to follow the same good business practices as you would if you were setting up a new practice. See "Buying a Practice" in Chapter 5 for additional information.

> Buying an existing practice could also mean buying a franchise, where the operating systems and marketing plan are readymade, so you don't have to create these yourself.

THE CLIENTS' PERSPECTIVE

When you begin the process of choosing the physical space where you will practice, look at space from your potential clients' point of view and consider how your choice of space will affect their perception of your practice. At every point of client contact, consider all the senses—what the client will see, hear, smell, and touch. Consider, too, the physical and mental ease with which the client will encounter your business—will it seem professional? welcoming? intimidating? safe? awkward? competent?

> When you choose your practice space, consider all the senses—sounds, smells, visual appearance, and touch.

AS A POTENTIAL CLIENT DRIVES OR WALKS BY YOUR WORKPLACE:
- Is your signage visible from the street?
- What image does your signage convey—clinical, luxurious, modern, holistic?
- Is the entrance into the building welcoming? into your office space (if not the same as the building's entry)?
- Are neighborhood smells apparent, such as a chocolate factory or a pig farm?
- Is it on a busy thoroughfare, or on a quiet, tree-lined lane?
- Is it easy to get to with public transportation?
- Do neighboring businesses attract the same type of client you want to attract?

AS A CLIENT ARRIVES AT YOUR WORKPLACE:
- Is your workplace easy to find?
- Is parking available?
- Are the walkways and entry safe?
- Are entries to your building and to your workplace free of obstruction?
- Is the entry to your building and to your workplace space well-lit?
- Once in the lobby of the building, does a directory or sign easily identify which workplace is yours?

AS A CLIENT ENTERS AND WAITS IN YOUR RECEPTION AREA:
- Is the area well-lit?
- Is the area clean?

- Is the entry to your workplace accessible by a person in a wheelchair?
- Is there a convenient area to leave outerwear, boots, and umbrellas?
- Are any fragrances apparent? (This could be perceived as positive by some clients and as a drawback by others.)
- What sounds are heard in the reception area? music? voices from session rooms?
- Is the area free of area rugs or other obstacles that might cause slip and falls?
- Could candles cause a fire hazard?
- When the phone rings, is there an audible ring? Is it answered by a receptionist, or an answering machine? If an answering machine, is the caller's voice heard?
- If the client needs to fill out paperwork, are pens and writing surfaces handy?
- If the client has a question, does the office layout make it easy for him or her to ask it privately before the session begins?
- Does ventilation provide healthy air quality and movement?
- Are all obstructions removed for the client's safe exit from the space?
- What does the client see on your workplace walls? art? professional association member certificate? credentials? code of conduct? standards of practice? credos? building safety instructions?
- Is the waiting area furniture comfortable?
- Are products on display?
- What reading materials are available to clients as they wait?
- Are water or other beverages available?
- If you sell products, are they displayed attractively where clients can see them and pick them up?
- Are locations of rest rooms clearly marked?

AS A CLIENT ENTERS YOUR SESSION SPACE:
- Is music playing?
- Is the temperature in the room comfortable for the client?
- Is a screen available for client privacy?
- Is the massage table already made up attractively with clean linens?
- Is lighting indirect but sufficient for the client to undress and dress?
- Are there hooks on the walls and surface areas for the client to put his or her clothes and accessories?
- Is a chair available for the client's comfort and safety in removing shoes, etc.?
- If candles are in use, are they in safe containers and placed at a safe distance from you and clients?
- Is there noticeable scent or aroma in the session room?
- Are tissues and a wastebasket handy for the client's convenience?
- If there's a window in the room, does it offer privacy from outsiders seeing in?
- Is the décor of the space restful or otherwise appropriate?
- Can voices or other noises from outside the practice space be heard?

AS A CLIENT LEAVES YOUR SESSION SPACE:
- Is water available if your client wants it?
- Is lighting sufficient to help the client move around safely?
- Is a basin of warm water and washcloth and towel available?
- Is a mirror available?
- Are all obstructions removed for the client's safe exit from the space?
- Is there a space for the client to sit and relax for a while after the massage?

AS A CLIENT LEAVES YOUR WORKPLACE OR BUILDING:
- Is there a convenient area in which the client can make payment for the massage and to book the next appointment?
- Is a monthly calendar available to make it easy for the client to re-book?

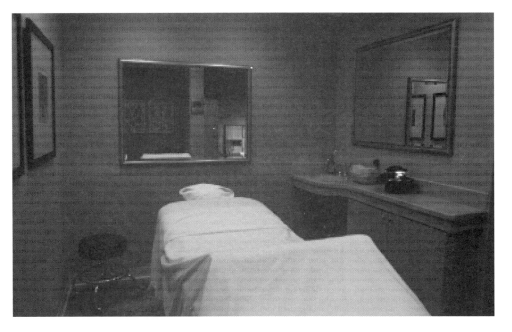

This massage room offers many conveniences to the client, such as a sink, mirrors, and tissues. (*Photo courtesy of Baptist Hospital of South Florida.*)

- Are your business cards visible for the client's convenience in passing your name along to a friend?
- If other clients are waiting in the lobby, is there adequate seating for everyone to be comfortable?

If your answer to any of these questions indicates that the location is not appropriate as it currently exists for a good massage therapy practice, can you identify strategies that would neutralize your concern? The later section "Office Space Variations" in this chapter discusses possible approaches for adapting less-than-ideal office space to your needs.

YOUR PERSPECTIVE AS A BUSINESS OWNER

In the first part of this chapter, you considered potential workplace space from your clients' perspective. It is equally important to ask questions from the perspective of a business owner. Your clients' perspective is, naturally, a major factor in the decisions you make as a business owner, but there are many other factors to consider also.

CHOOSING YOUR LOCATION

Considerations for choosing space are important to you whether you are viewing space from the perspective of a business owner or as an employee. Space options include:

- renting or leasing space for your own business
- outcall massage at clients' homes
- an employer's location
- shared space with an existing massage therapy practice

Start your search for practice space by identifying the general area in which you want to work. Once you have selected an area, you will need to determine whether it is suitable for your practice. Consider business and regulatory issues as well as your own comfort level and general appeal of the neighborhood. You will spend many hours at your workplace, and your satisfaction with your space will help you provide an optimum environment for your clients.

If you are opening your own business, contact the area's economic development office and ask for information about starting a business there. Ask such questions as:

- What are the zoning regulations? (Have an expert, such as a zoning officer or real estate attorney, determine whether your practice would be compatible with the zoning ordinances. Even a minor zoning change can take weeks or months. Also, zoning ordinances change, so even if a similar practice is in the same space or nearby, it does not mean you can set up a new practice there.)
- What will you need in the way of business licenses and permits?
- Are there tax considerations you need to be aware of?
- Is census or population demographic information available that would help you identify client demand?
- How many other massage practitioners have businesses that serve this area's population? (For a more detailed discussion of calculating supply and demand, see "Estimating Supply and Demand" in Chapter 5.)
- Is there a local business association that charges dues or a government requirement for additional taxes to operate in this area?
- Are businesses in this area expected to be open (or closed) during certain hours?
- Is the location near services you need or would enjoy? For example, is there somewhere to do your laundry if your washer breaks down? Is there somewhere pleasant where you can go for a juice or coffee break?
- Will you feel safe working in this neighborhood?
- Will your commute to and from home be convenient?

CHOOSING YOUR OFFICE SPACE

To choose a specific office building within the area, you can either visit locations that might work for you and jot down the names of leasing agents on signs advertising vacancies, or you could find a real estate agent first and let him or her identify available locations. Ask your mentor, colleagues, and other small-business owners to recommend a helpful agent (preferably one who knows what massage therapy is about). Before you use that person's services, ask about his or her fee.

Also consider using the services of an attorney. Commercial leases may lack the consumer protection of a residential lease. Find an attorney who is familiar with the practice of leasing space for a business. This person can review your lease agreement and educate you about your options, such as whether utilities should be included in the rent, whether the lease will allow cost increases, the length of time of the lease, and other expenses associated with the lease. The savings and peace of mind you achieve with a well-drafted lease agreement may more than make up for the attorney's fee.

When you identify a space that interests you, get to know it. Visit the area two or three times during the hours you plan to operate your practice. Each time, stay thirty or forty minutes and observe the environment (light, air, noise, drafts, smells, traffic).

As you narrow your selection to a particular office site, ask such questions as:

- Are nonsmoking ordinances in effect for all or part of the building?
- Are high-speed Internet connections available, and at what cost?
- Does the landlord provide recycling services?
- Are the terms of the lease acceptable and in line with standard practice for the area? For example, the landlord should be able to tell you not only the length of the lease but how much you will have to spend for rent (per square foot), utilities, and parking or other fees, including breaking the lease (opting out of the space before the lease expires).
- Will the landlord allow or build out bathroom facilities, a wash basin with hot and cold running water, and hookups for your washer and dryer?
- What will it cost to maintain the space? Include carpet cleaning, garbage pickup, and snow removal, if these apply.
- Is construction of other space within the building planned that would be disruptive to your sessions?

Signing a lease for space is no time to skimp on professional advice. Secure the services of an attorney to review your lease before you sign it.

- What provisions has the landlord made for safety and security?

You must also consider the interior space of your prospective office, including its amenities. As you review the space, evaluate space for giving massages and handling business activities, and evaluate the reception area. Ask questions such as the following:

- Are you able to control the temperature adequately? (Remember, massage clients will have greater needs for warmth than, say, customers of a store.)
- What security features and services does the building owner provide? For security issues that could affect your business, see Figure 3.6 later in this chapter.
- Are there adequate electrical outlets and wiring for your needs? Will you be able to operate your computer, clothes dryer, or any other electrical equipment?
- Is there a sink or adequate plumbing to install one?
- Is there a bathroom available for you and your clients?
- Is the space compatible with the Americans with Disabilities Act? (See Figure 3.7 later in this chapter.)
- Will the landlord make changes you need (e.g., building out plumbing)? Who will pay for them? (Often costs are shared between landlord and tenant.)
- If there were ever a loss to report, what would the landlord's insurance cover?
- Does the office space meet accessibility standards?

In addition, your state might have rules that apply to your physical practice space. See Figure 3.5 for the Florida Board of Massage rule that applies to massage establishments. As you read each rule, think of the different session rooms and offices you have been in and whether that space would be compliant.

Some of the regulations apply to areas over which you control (such as changing the linens after each use and maintain a supply to clean draping material), and others are under the control of your landlord (such as rodent and vermin control and maintenance of bathroom facilities). If your state or municipality has regulations that apply to your office space, give your potential landlord a copy of them so he or she is aware of the rules. You might ask the landlord to add a line in the lease that agrees to maintain the space in a way that keeps the space compliant with the state's or municipality's regulations for your business.

Whatever you do, wait to sign a lease until you learn these important facts. Review all the facts you have gathered with your attorney or with a trusted mentor before making a final decision.

PHYSICAL SAFETY PRECAUTIONS

Especially for a home office, but also applicable to any office environment, you must be prepared for unpredictable situations and emergencies. Before you invite any clients to your office, complete the checklist shown in Figure 3.6. This is also a good checklist to review periodically.

A critical safety concern is also for your own personal security. This requires good knowledge of your surrounding environment and careful screening of clients. For more information about personal security, see the "Boundaries" section in Chapter 2.

Another important consideration in choosing office space is whether or not it complies with the Americans with Disabilities Act. Since this is a federal law, it is likely that leased space has already been made to comply, but you need to verify this for each location.

Congress passed the Americans with Disabilities Act (ADA) in 1990, which requires businesses serving the public to make their facilities accessible to people with disabilities (also discussed in Chapter 5). In addition, if you hire employees, the workplace must be accessible to them. See Figure 3.7 for tips for making your space accessible to your clients.

A person with a disability may not be in a wheelchair but may have another disability such as heart disease, arthritis, or another condition that isn't visible—and must be accommodated.

FIGURE 3.5 Example of State Regulation of Physical Office Space

FLORIDA BOARD OF MASSAGE

64B7-26.003 Massage Establishment Operations.

(1) Facilities, Each establishment shall meet the following facility requirements:

(a) Comply with all local building code requirements.

(b) Provide for the use of clients a bathroom with at least one toilet and one sink with running water. Such facilities shall be equipped with toilet tissue, soap dispenser with soap or other hand cleaning materials, sanitary towels or other hand-drying device such as a wall-mounted electric blow dryer, and waste receptacle.

(c) Maintain toilet facilities in a common area of the establishment. Establishments located in buildings housing multiple businesses under one roof such as arcades, shopping malls, terminals, hotels, etc., may substitute centralized toilet facilities. Such central facilities shall be within three hundred (300) feet of the massage establishment.

(d) If equipped with a whirlpool bath, sauna, steam cabinet and/or steam room, maintain clean shower facilities on the premises.

(2) Personnel. A licensed massage therapist must be on the premises of the establishment if a client is in a treatment room for the purpose of receiving massage therapy.

(3) Safety and sanitary requirements. Each establishment shall:

(a) Provide for safe and unobstructed human passage in the public areas of the premises; provide for removal of garbage and refuse; and provide for safe storage or removal of flammable materials.

(b) Maintain a fire extinguisher in good working condition on the premises. As used herein "good working condition" means meeting the standards for approval by the State Fire Marshal. Such standards are presently contained in Chapter 69A-21, F.A.C.

(c) Exterminate all vermin, insects, termites, and rodents on the premises.

(d) Maintain all equipment used to perform massage services on the premises in a safe and sanitary condition, including the regular application of cleansers and bactericidal agents to the massage table. Unless clean sheets, towels, or other coverings are used to cover the massage table for each client, "regular application," as used herein, means after the massage of each client. If clean coverings are used for each client, then "regular application" shall mean at least one time a day and also whenever oils or other substances visibly accumulate on the massage table surface.

(e) Maintain a sufficient supply of clean drapes for the purpose of draping each client while the client is being massaged, and launder before reuse all materials furnished for the personal use of the client, such as drapes, towels and linens. As used herein "drapes" means towels, gowns, or sheets.

(f) Maintain lavatories for hand cleansing and/or a chemical germicidal designed to disinfect and cleanse hands without the use of a lavatory in the treatment room itself or within 20 feet of the treatment area.

(g) Maintain all bathroom and shower facilities and fixtures in good repair, well-lighted and ventilated.

(4) Financial responsibility and insurance coverage. Each establishment shall maintain property damage and bodily injury liability insurance coverage. The original or a copy of such policy shall be available on the premises of the establishment.

FIGURE 3.6 Security and Safety Considerations

PHYSICAL SAFETY FEATURES

☐ I have checked the sidewalk and entrance to my office for obstacles and toe catches.

☐ I assure that all ice and snow is cleared prior to my first appointment.

☐ I have seen and approved the building maintenance and cleaning plan (if managed by an independent building supervisor).

☐ I keep stairways and hallways free of clutter.

☐ I have checked the stability of railings.

☐ I keep throw rugs to a minimum, and make sure the ones I have do not present safety risks. (I do not use throw rugs if I practice massage on elderly or clients with physical disabilities.)

☐ If I use candles, I ensure that they are in safe containers and are placed at a distance that neither the client nor I is likely to knock them over.

☐ I properly heat thermal applications.

☐ My massage table is stable and in good repair.

☐ I maintain a log book of equipment inspections.

MEDICAL PREPAREDNESS

☐ I use client intake forms and consistently ask clients to update them.

☐ I have learned to administer first aid, including CPR.

☐ I have a first-aid kit easily available in my office.

☐ I remind clients to dispose of candy or gum before they get on the massage table.

☐ I practice universal precautions as standard procedure in my office.

PERSONAL SECURITY

☐ I have had an emergency buzzer or other system installed in case I need to call for help.

☐ I screen my clients and verify that they are clear about the nature of the service I provide. (Seasoned massage therapists recommend accepting new clients only when referred by someone else.)

☐ I have a plan for handling inappropriate comments or behavior by clients.

☐ I follow a procedure for letting someone know who I am scheduled to see and when.

FIGURE 3.7
Complying with the Americans with
Disabilities Act

Get standards from the U.S. Department of Justice (1-800-514-0301 or www.ada.gov).

Remember that disability does not just mean "in a wheelchair." Other disabilities include sight or hearing impairment, arthritis, and heart conditions.

Think about the client types you are targeting. Will certain physical limitations be more likely among this group? Are you prepared to accommodate clients with such conditions?

Plan how a person with a physical disability will enter your office, pass through doorways, and move on and off the massage table. Are there steps? Are doorknobs easy to turn? (Use levers rather than knobs if you can.)

Make sure it is easy to move around the space. Are chairs easy to get in and out of? Are floors easy to walk on? Avoid slippery, shiny surfaces (causing glare), or those covered with obstacles, such as electrical cords or small rugs.

EQUIPPING YOUR SPACE

When we consider physical components, we mean more than just the building your workplace is housed in and the equipment and furniture that fill your workplace and session space. We are talking about all the tangible attributes that make up your practice. As your client enters your space, it conveys to him or her certain expectations of the quality of massage or bodywork to follow.

Your decisions about the image of your practice will depend largely on the type of client you are serving. If your practice specializes in rehabilitative or sports massage, its décor will differ from a practice whose clients are mostly interested in relaxation and stress reduction. A clinical atmosphere might be conveyed through such effects as white walls and stainless steel fixtures, whereas pastels and crystals convey a more holistic atmosphere. As your clients walk through your doors, you want them to feel an immediate sense of confidence that your practice suits their needs and expectations.

> The style of your space should convey an immediate sense of welcome to the type of client you choose.

FURNITURE AND EQUIPMENT

Massage therapists need two kinds of furniture and equipment for the practice: 1) items for providing massage, and 2) items for office work. Figure 3.8 identifies furniture, equipment, and supplies that a typical practice needs.

You do not have to spend a fortune on office equipment. You could find a perfectly appropriate desk at a garage sale or flea market, and used-equipment suppliers may have just the items you need. However, do consider your comfort and that of anyone else who will be using the equipment. Take into account ergonomic principles and how they can help you in a profession that is physically demanding already. Realize that you do not have to outfit the ideal office from day one. Make a list of the things that are essential to your practice and which ones will enhance it further, and plan your budget accordingly.

SUPPLIES

Besides the big items of furniture and equipment, you also will have to stock the necessary supplies. Figure 3.8 details many of the supplies needed by a typical massage therapy practice. If you will practice from an office, probably you will need most of these. If you will provide on-site massages, you must provide more than one or two items to be recognized as an independent contractor.

Over the course of several years, you will buy many office and massage supplies, so it is worthwhile to identify one or more reliable sources of items you prefer to use. Office and massage supply businesses are very competitive, and not all retailers are the same. Spend

FIGURE 3.8 Equipping Your Massage Therapy Practice for Office Use

FOR OFFICE USE

FURNITURE / EQUIPMENT

☐ Desk

☐ Desk chair

☐ File cabinets

☐ Bookshelves

☐ Lamps

☐ Enclosed cabinet for linens and towels

☐ Storage cabinet for supplies

☐ Phones with automated answering system

☐ Waiting roon furniture (chairs, tables, lamps, coat rack)

☐ Sink with hot and cold water

☐ Accessible toilet

☐ Electric hand dryer

☐ Soap dispenser

☐ Smoke detectors

☐ Fire extinguisher

☐ Carbon monoxide detector

☐ Computer and printer

☐ Copier

☐ Fax

☐ Display cases

☐ Step stool

☐ Small refrigerator

☐ Water cooler

Note: refer to local zoning ordinances for additional needs

SUPPLIES

☐ Charts, forms, file folders (hardcopy or software)

☐ Appointment book (hardcopy or software)

☐ General ledger book (hardcopy or software)

☐ Receipt books (hardcopy or software)

☐ Message pads (hardcopy or software)

☐ Follow-up folder (hardcopy or software)

☐ Calculator

☐ Pens and pencils

☐ Paper (computer paper, copier paper)

☐ Stapler, staples, and staple remover

☐ Tape and tape dispenser

☐ Paper clips

☐ Ceramic or disposable beverage cups

☐ Tea bags, nonperishable food items

☐ Ink, toner for printer, fax, copier

☐ External memory storage for computer

☐ Paper towels, toilet paper, antibacterial soap

☐ Cleaning supplies—window/mirror cleaner, cleanser for bathroom

☐ Disinfectant of fungicide for cleaning floors and other surfaces

☐ Oil-removing detergent (if you do not use a laundry service)

☐ First-aid kit

FOR MASSAGE THERAPY USE

EQUIPMENT

☐ Massage tables

☐ Linens, bolserts, pillows

☐ Heated blankets and mattress pads

☐ Massage chair

☐ Linen bin with lid

☐ Washer and dryer (if you do not use a laundry service)

☐ Stereo/CD/DVD player

☐ Cabinet for lotions and oils

☐ Space heater for session room

☐ Massage accessories/equipment

SUPPLIES

☐ CDs, DVDs

☐ Lubricants and essential oils

☐ Clothing hooks and hangers

☐ Waist pack that holds massage oils or lotions

☐ Candles

☐ Aromatherapy

Developing a relationship with a supplier of office and massage supplies is well worth the time, considering the volume of purchases you will be making over a period of time.

some time calling stores, going online, and meeting with exhibitors at massage meetings and conventions. Request a catalog. You may find that the largest chains have the most limited variety of items, and a smaller retailer that specializes in service may offer a much wider selection at about the same price. Buying in bulk can save you money in the long run, but be sure you have the space to store the supplies and that nothing will expire before you use it.

RESOURCES ▸ FOR FINDING EQUIPMENT AND SUPPLY SOURCES

Online search

Exhibitors at massage therapy conventions and meetings

Ads in professional magazines (such as *mtj* and *Massage Magazine*)

Professional association conventions and online shopping malls

Professional association chapters' newsletters

Massage schools

Books such as Martin Ashley (2006), *Massage: A Career at Your Fingertips* (5th ed.), Somers, NY: Enterprise Publishing (Ashley's contains an extensive appendix of equipment and supplies.)

STYLE AND LAYOUT OF FURNISHINGS

Another important aspect of setting up your space is to decorate for aesthetics and to convey the desired image of your practice. There is no one design approach that is right for every massage business. Some practitioners prefer clean and crisp lines and a modern silhouette to their reception area and session rooms. They might choose chrome and glass for the image they want to project. Others might gravitate toward a softer décor, in which they use wood furnishings and quilted coverlets. The only requirements for interior space are that it be safe and clean. As Nina McIntosh writes in *The Educated Heart*, "We want a balance between a room that smells antiseptic and a room that looks like germs may be lurking in every corner."

Aesthetic image of space is influenced by your choices of colors, textures, shapes, sounds, lighting, room layout, and art. Check each of the following features that are important to you, and indicate at least one way your décor can contribute to providing the image you want:

- Professionalism—provided with:

- Beauty—provided with:

- Relaxation—provided with:

- Health—provided with:

- Spirituality—provided with:

- Cleanliness—provided with:

- Safety—provided with:

- Other: _____—provided with:

Cleanliness and safety can be provided regardless of budget. More luxurious surroundings, such as the one shown in the photograph of the massage room at Baptist Hospital of South Florida, require more

Image of clouds in skylight over massage table at Baptist Hospital of South Florida lends a feeling of tranquility. (*Photo courtesy of Baptist Hospital of South Florida.*)

money. Most massage therapy business owners must compensate for a limited budget with unlimited creativity—and the results can be marvelous.

Display Your Credentials

Some of the things you display may be required by law or ordinance. For example, if you are required to obtain a license, probably you will have to display it. Health laws or ordinances might specify signs or notices you must post in the restrooms. Displaying your license and other professional credentials such as your National Certification and professional association membership certificate are a simple but effective way to add to your professional image. Put professional credentials and the code of ethics in attractive frames and display them proudly. See the professional credentials section of Chapter 1 for more information about credentials and their proper use.

Make a Floor Plan

Before committing to a particular office space, it's helpful to draw out a model floor plan. Draw your massage table, a chair, and whatever other furniture you might have in the session room to scale on graph paper (or computer), and place them in different room layouts. Judge whether you will have ample space when moving around the massage table and standing at the sides or either end.

COST OF OFFICE SPACE

When you consider leasing a space, know all the costs involved. The cost of office space could be one of your largest expenses. Before you sign a lease, decide whether you can afford it by identifying the initial and monthly expenses of space, as follows:

ONE-TIME INITIAL COSTS

Cost to prepare space (painting, decorating, bringing into
  compliance with ADA, upgrading plumbing or electricity) $
Fees for real estate agent $
Fees for attorney $_____
Total initial cost to find and prepare leased space $

MONTHLY COSTS

Monthly rent $
Monthly utilities not included in rent $
Monthly taxes or fees for using space $
Shared monthly or seasonal costs of maintaining common space
  (such as snow removal or janitorial services) $_____
Monthly cost of space: $

GREEN PRACTICES

Massage therapy is intrinsically associated with environmental concern. The practice of massage therapy does not rely extensively on automation or toxic chemicals. Environmentalism is a value, not a marketing scheme. Many are drawn to the profession because of its association with simplicity and tranquility.

Some massage practices are deliberately based on principles of sustainability. The areas in which a business may employ sustainable practices include:

- Using organic oils
- Buying organic linens
- Using laundry methods and products that are easy on the environment (see Real Touch 4.1)
- Recycling everything possible
- Using biodegradable, nontoxic cleaning products

Draw your office space and furnishings to scale so you can easily try different layouts and see which one allows you the most ease of movement around the massage table.

- Buy massage tables that are made from sustainably harvested wood
- Furnish with natural fiber upholstery and area rugs
- Use compact fluorescent lighting
- Use paper with at least 30 percent postconsumer recycled content—and reuse one-sided documents as scratch paper

These are only a few things you can do—having a conservation mindset will lead you to discover many others.

Real Touch 4.1 **One Massage Practice's Laundry & Other Greenery**

Joan Knockel owns Therapeutic Massage, a six-person massage therapy business that has operated in Dubuque, Iowa, for more than 12 years. She says she has always followed environmental practices as a natural outgrowth of her holistic health beliefs, and in 2007 she decided she could do more. She says, "I don't even know if any of this makes a difference, but it does make me feel better. I'm probably not doing all I can do, but I feel good knowing I'm doing something."

Here she describes some of the green practices her business follows:

Reuse envelopes—"If a client brings in a gift certificate in an envelope and it doesn't have a coffee stain on it, I reuse it to pay bills."

Recycling—"The landlord used to provide recycling for businesses in this center, but he quit doing that, so we do it ourselves now. The recycling center is about 4 miles from here."

Laundry—"This is *huge.* The business does 3 to 4 full loads a day. First, I bought a high-efficiency front-load washer and dryer, which use less water and dry clothes faster. Then I invested in a unit that uses UV light rays and silver ions to filter cold water for washing, using no detergent, leaving fabrics 99.9999% bacteria free. The unit hangs above the washing machine, and cold water is filtered through it. *No soap is required.* Fabrics are softer because there's no soap residue, and linens last longer because hot water and soap don't wear them down. Best, we're not putting pollutants into the ground. Also, we shake out the linens so they're not wadded up when they're put in the dryer. They dry faster."

Message pads—"We convert all used paper to scratch paper and use it mostly for taking messages."

All organic lotions and oils—"They cost more, but so far we haven't raised our rates. I consider it a gift to our clients."

Sheets—"Eventually I would like to go to organic sheets, but they're more expensive than other sheets, and I consider that as our next step. We're not quite there yet."

OFFICE SPACE VARIATIONS

If money is no object, you will not have to worry about designing office space that fits your needs perfectly. However, most practitioners find that they must compensate for a gap between their ideal physical practice environment and reality. If you share space with another business, say a chiropractic office, a physical therapy clinic, or a beauty salon, you will work cooperatively with that business's personnel and policies. The same is true if you are employed by a spa, a fitness center, or a private practice, or if you practice on-site massage at a corporate location.

> An unlimited budget is not a requirement for space that is welcoming and nurturing to your clients.

The physical space in which you practice might meet many of your requirements but lack others. The room or rooms in which you have your sessions might be smaller than ideal or might not have suitable lighting. You might not have control over the room's thermostat. The room's décor might not be appropriate to a massage setting.

As you consider how to furnish your space in a way that meets your goals, take into account the people who will be using the space. If you are setting up a small office area for your use only, you can include anything that helps you work and leave out any distractions.

Be considerate of others. If you will invite clients into this space, you must think about your clients' tastes and needs. A roomful of roses or incense may lift your spirits but may not be so appealing to someone with asthma or allergies. The same goes for scented oils. Whenever you can, provide choices in music so clients receive the nurturing they need.

One of the ways to naturally create your own identity is through your choice of linens, blankets, oils, bolsters, music, and other massage accessories. You might also consider taking your own space heater if you are concerned that the room's temperature will be too chilly for the client. To reinforce a professional atmosphere, your credentials should be displayed in a visible area. You might want to provide your own lamp that casts a soft light rather than use the overhead light already in the room. If privacy is a concern, you can devise a screen to cover a window.

If you work as an on-site massage therapist at another company's site, you might have less influence over the massage environment, but there are still some things you can do to make sure the room is clean and inviting.

REEVALUATING YOUR SPACE

You will carefully analyze every aspect of your physical space requirements when you set up a business. It's important to review your space decisions on a regular basis to assure that they are still appropriate. When your lease expires is a good time to consider major changes, such as room layout, amenities that need to be added, or changes to the heating, air conditioning, and ventilation systems. These become negotiable items when you renew your lease.

Other design considerations you will want to review more frequently, such as every six months. Has your client focus changed in such a way that your décor no longer reflects their preferences and expectations? Are your framed credentials up to date? Is there a problem with traffic flow pattern that can be remedied without tearing down walls? Can you rearrange furniture in your reception area to make it more welcoming to clients? Do you need to revise your magazine subscriptions or brochures for client interest and education? Consider asking your mentor or a regular client if he or she would be willing to give you feedback on what things work and don't work as far as your physical environment. If you have a client who has a specialty in space planning, who is accustomed to being compensated for this type of consultation, maybe you could barter for an exchange of services.

The key to having a physical environment that attracts clients is understanding your clients' needs and viewing your environment from their perspective. Taking the time to review those needs on a regular basis will pay off in client loyalty and in your own renewed commitment to operating a vital and healthy practice.

Negotiate changes to your space before signing or re-upping your lease.

SUMMARY

Whether you will be designing your own workspace or will be sharing space at an existing workplace, your choices about your physical surroundings will affect the success of your practice. When making decisions about office space, it is important to consider your clients' perspective as well as your own perspective as manager of your own practice. Factors that will influence your selection of space include location, regulatory rules, zoning ordinances, convenience, appearance, amenities, design, and cost.

Unless you have an unlimited budget, you will probably have to compromise on some of the features of your office space that fall short of your ideal. There are many ways to compensate for limitations in your practice space, while still accommodating the personnel and policies of the office in which you work. Areas in which you can make a difference are in décor, comfort, and privacy for your clients. If you are an owner or renter of office space, it is important to be thorough in identifying all potential benefits, limitations and costs—initial as well as monthly—before signing a lease.

Another aspect that makes up the physical components of your office is your selection of equipment and supplies for business and for massage use. As you calculate your costs, you will decide how much and which equipment is essential to the start-up of your business, and which you may delay purchasing until later.

As long as you operate a profitable business, you will have the opportunity to continually improve and refine your physical space to your clients' and your own satisfaction.

REVIEW QUESTIONS

1 Name three physical features of your office location or space that would influence a client positively or negatively.

2 What are three primary areas of security and safety considerations you must consider when establishing a massage therapy practice?

3 What kinds of decisions about your physical environment are related to the type of clients targeted by your business? (Targeted clients might be fitness, sports, medical, spa, wellness)

4 What are some of the practices you could use to make your business environmentally sustainable?

5 What working environments could cause you to work in a session space that is less than ideal?

6 In what ways can you compensate for less-than-ideal space?

ENDNOTES

1 2007 Massage Therapy Industry Evaluation Trend Report. Conducted by North Star Research on behalf of American Massage Therapy Association.

2 Cherie Sohnen-Moe, "Zoning: Your Rights and Responsibilities." Massage Therapy Journal, Spring 1999, pages 70–71, 74, 76.

Chapter 4
Practicing Self-Care

You accomplish three things when you learn to take care of yourself—you feel great, you extend the life of your practice, and you give your clients a terrific role model. It's like insurance and free advertising rolled into one!

CHAPTER PREVIEW

- Practitioner as Client Model
- Effects of Stress
- Self-Care Techniques
  - Center Yourself
  - Exercise Your Body
  - Exercise Your Mind
  - Get a Regular Massage
  - Biomechanical Skills
- Personal Self-Care Management Strategy
- Summary

CHAPTER OBJECTIVES

1 Identify physiological and psychological effects of stress.
2 Identify various stress reduction techniques and their benefits.
3 Describe at least two ways to get physical exercise.
4 Describe at least two ways to get mental exercise.
5 Identify strategies for stress management.
6 Identify strategies to prevent self-injury through the use of proper body mechanics and holistic methods.

Taking care of yourself is not only a critical requirement to operating your business, but also to establishing and maintaining healthy relationships with your clients. The content presented in this chapter is intended not as detailed instruction, but only to highlight the importance of self-care and to describe different approaches to integrating it into your business and daily life.

If you limit the extent of your self-care practices, you also limit the longevity of your career as a massage therapist.

Acute stress is an immediate reaction to danger or aggravation; chronic stress is the accumulation of stress over time. The benefits of a self-care plan are aimed at preventing or managing chronic stress.

PRACTITIONER AS CLIENT MODEL

When a client observes you incorporating healthy practices in body mechanics, eating habits, attitude, exercise, and balance, your instructions to the client are much more influential than spoken instructions could ever be.

The principles of the wellness model (also discussed in Chapters 1 and 2) carry over into business practices as well as health practices. While most of this textbook concentrates on business skills and knowledge where the mind seems to be the most important focus—for instance, learning about licenses, taxes, and bookkeeping—the body and spirit aspects of running a business will equally influence the success of your business. If you don't take good care of your body, your longevity in the profession of massage therapy will be limited. And if you allow the daily challenges and frustrations of running a business to deplete your spiritual resources, you will diminish your creativity and your ability to communicate compassionately and clearly with clients and peers.

EFFECTS OF STRESS

Massage practitioners are faced with not only the stress of running a business or managing a career, but they have the added stress of strenuous physical effort. Stress isn't necessarily a bad thing. It can motivate high levels of performance during peak periods of activity or during times of crisis. But if stress is prolonged and low level, many parts of the mind, body, and spirit are affected negatively.

There are two kinds of stress: acute and chronic. Acute stress is your body's immediate reaction to danger, change, or surprise. For example, let's say you scheduled a mover to carry a desk, your desktop computer and printer, and two massage tables up to your new second-floor massage office today. An hour after the movers were due to arrive, you finally tracked them down and discovered they thought they were scheduled for next week. To help you out in a pinch, your brother helps you carry the furniture and equipment up to your new office space. When you are finished, you are exhausted and angry. Your heart rate is up, you're gritting your teeth, and your muscles are tensed. This is acute stress.

Chronic stress happens when a certain level of stress occurs over a long period of time. You don't book enough time to take breaks between appointments because you worry that you have to cram your schedule if you want to make enough money. Out of long-standing habit, you use poor body mechanics when you perform deep massage. You smile and "talk nice" to a client who always complains about your massage, even though you have tried everything to satisfy his requests. Your every-other-Wednesday-at-2:00 appointment arrives at 2:15, as usual, and you give her the full hour massage even though you have told her in the past that this backs up the rest of your appointments for the day. And your next-to-last appointment of the day cancels at the last minute. This is the third time she has done that, and you have told her you will have to charge her for the appointment the next time it happens. But now you're wondering if you really should do that. What if she never comes back? And those are just your *work*-related problems. That's chronic stress.

Physiological effects of chronic stress include high blood pressure (associated with heart disease and strokes), digestive problems, weakened immune system, stomach and intestinal problems, weight loss or gain, sleep disturbances, memory or concentration problems. Psychologically, chronic stress may take the form of anxiety or depression. The effects of stress also diminish your general quality of life by reducing feelings of pleasure and accomplishment. It's little wonder that with even some of these outcomes, a person under chronic stress suffers from lowered self-confidence.

On the job, any of these stress-related outcomes will detract from the immediate pleasure of your massage career and also its long-term viability. Any steps you can take to diminish stress in your life will pay off in terms of satisfaction and effectiveness in your personal and business life.

You can't always predict stress, but fortunately there are proven techniques for preventing it to some degree and coping with it to another degree.

RESOURCES FOR STRESS MANAGEMENT

About Stress: http://stress.about.com (includes links to many helpful resources about stress management)

Comfort Queen: A Place to Be Kind to Yourself: www.comfortqueen.com (see Jennifer Louden, below)

Green Cross Academy of Traumatology: http://www.traumatologyacademy.org/ SelfCareStandards.htmSelf-Care . Although this website is for those who work with trauma victims primarily, its self-care guidelines are generally applicable.

Ferguson, Thomas, MD. "Ten Guidelines for Developing a Personal Self-Care Plan." Available at Health World: www.healthy.net.

Louden, Jennifer. *The Life Organizer: A Woman's Guide to a Mindful Year* and *The Woman's Comfort Book: A Self-Nurturing Guide for Restoring Balance in Your Life:* www.thelifeorganizer.com

Stress Management Tips and Resources: www.stresstips.com

Stress Management Tips.com: www.stressmanagementtips.com

SELF-CARE TECHNIQUES

Scheduling time for self-care helps you center yourself and reduce stress. Being centered or grounded means you feel a sense of purpose and are focused on that purpose. A sense of purpose can help you feel calm even in a stressful situation and competent even in a demanding situation. For many people, being centered also includes a feeling of being connected to a higher power. If this is a part of your belief system, it can be an enormous source of strength.

CENTER YOURSELF

Centering is the act of grounding oneself in the present. It requires stilling or quieting the mind, through whatever technique works best for you. There are many ways to center oneself. The following methods have worked for others and may be helpful for you. Try these before, after, or during your working hours:

- Meditating or praying
- Using relaxation techniques
- Walking quietly—a kind of meditation
- Spending quiet time in a beautiful setting
- Practicing breathwork
- Practicing yoga

Try these outside your work:

- Religion (attending a religion's worship services and practicing its teachings)
- Reading books with spiritual messages
- Support groups with people interested in spiritual development or related growth
- Exercise
- Sacred ritual (in a context you choose)
- Keeping a spiritual journal, such as a dream journal or a gratitude journal (recording what you are thankful for each day)
- Counseling with a spiritual adviser

The ability to center oneself requires many months and years of practice. If you feel totally unable to quiet your mind after several attempts, keep trying. Eventually you will see some progress.

Whichever techniques you choose, it is important to appreciate that the condition of being centered is not something you just decide to turn on like a light switch. Rather, it comes through ongoing spiritual and mental renewal, in a maturing process that continues over one's lifetime. If you are not accustomed to tending to your mental and spiritual health, you may find that these methods seem awkward at first, and that the results come slowly. Working with an instructor and within a group of others can be very beneficial, both for the instruction and discipline as well as the social support of others who are also trying to achieve balance. Continued practice of these techniques will help you make your career personally fulfilling as well as beneficial to your clients.

RESOURCES FOR MEDITATION AND SPIRITUAL GROWTH

Your religion or spiritual organization

Adams, Douglas. (1979). *The Hitchhiker's Guide to the Galaxy.* Pan Books.

Cameron, Julia. (2002). *The Artist's Way: A Spiritual Path to Higher Creativity.* Tarcher/Perigree.

Crum, Thomas F. (1997). *Journey to Center: Lessons in Unifying Body, Mind, and Spirit.* New York: Simon & Schuster.

Easwaran, Eknath. (1991). *Meditation.* Tomales, CA: Nilgiri Press; *www.easwaran.org*

Myss, Caroline. (1997). *Anatomy of the Spirit.* New York: Harmony Books.

Self-Realization.com: www.self-realization.com

Smith, Huston. (1994). *The Illustrated World's Religions: A Guide to Our Wisdom Traditions.* Harper Collins.

NOURISH YOUR BODY

The most centered and mentally and physically active practitioner still needs to give the body necessary fuel to maintain a vigorous and demanding physical practice. Just as life in earlier times was more physically active, eating nutritious foods was also a more common practice. People ate more raw foods with fewer preservatives. The tradeoff for today's convenience and busy lifestyles is poorer nutrition for most people.

The U.S. Department of Health and Human Services and the U.S. Department of Agriculture jointly introduced new *Dietary Guidelines* in 2005. The study that led to publishing new guidelines was motivated by concern about overwhelming evidence of obesity and morbidity (sickness and disease) among Americans that were the result of sedentary lifestyles and poor nutrition. The upshot of the study was to recommend that Americans eat fewer calories, be more active, and make wiser food choices. One of the recommendations of these guidelines was that "nutrient needs be met primarily through consuming foods." Although that may seem obvious, apparently many people in the study were trying to use dietary supplements to take the place of good eating habits—and that wasn't working well.

Key recommendations of the *Dietary Guidelines* are:

- Consume a sufficient amount of fruits and vegetables while staying within energy needs. Two cups of fruit and 2½ cups of vegetables per day are recommended for a reference 2,000-calorie intake, with higher or lower amounts depending on the calorie level.
- Choose a variety of fruits and vegetables each day. In particular, select from all five vegetable subgroups (dark green, orange, legumes, starchy vegetables, and other vegetables) several times a week.
- Consume 3 or more ounce-equivalents of whole-grain products per day, with the rest of the recommended grains coming from enriched or whole-grain products. In general, at least half the grains should come from whole grains.
- Consume 3 cups per day of fat-free or low-fat milk or equivalent milk products.

Even with a busy schedule, simple changes in your habits can make a big difference. Read food labels. Knowing the nutritional contents will motivate you to choose an apple instead of a so-called "nutrition bar" the next time you grab a snack to take to the office.

EXERCISE YOUR BODY

Another key ingredient to self-care is physical exercise. It might sound counterproductive to say you need to add physical exercise to your daily routine when you already perform the physically demanding work of performing massages. But the fact is, massage is a culprit in causing repetitive stress injuries. To counteract the effects of massage, you also need large-movement exercise, weight-bearing exercise, and cardiovascular exercise of some type.

Historically, exercise was a natural part of people's lives. Walking was a form of transportation. Cooking and cleaning—and the associated reaching, bending, kneading, lifting—could consume an entire day. Mowing the lawn required muscles to push the lawn mower. Today, we have to make a conscious effort to seek exercise. The options are almost endless, depending on your preferences and needs, and include such choices as weight lifting, Pilates, yoga, aerobic dance, walking, running, martial arts, tai chi, and elliptical/treadmills/stationary bikes.

The President's Council on Physical Fitness and Sports states, "It's important to remember that fitness is an individual quality that varies from person to person. It is influenced by age, sex, heredity, personal habits, exercise, and eating practices. You can't do anything about the first three factors. However, it is within your power to change and improve the others where needed." The council describes the basic components of exercise as follows:

- *Cardiorespiratory Endurance*—the ability to deliver oxygen and nutrients to tissues, and to remove wastes, over sustained periods of time. Long runs and swims are among the methods employed in measuring this component.
- *Muscular Strength*—the ability of a muscle to exert force for a brief period of time. Upper-body strength, for example, can be measured by various weight-lifting exercises.
- *Muscular Endurance*—the ability of a muscle, or a group of muscles, to sustain repeated contractions or to continue applying force against a fixed object. Pushups are often used to test endurance of arm and shoulder muscles.
- *Flexibility*—the ability to move joints and use muscles through their full range of motion. The sit-and-reach test is a good measure of flexibility of the lower back and backs of the upper legs.
- *Body Composition* is often considered a component of fitness. It refers to the makeup of the body in terms of lean mass (muscle, bone, vital tissue and organs) and fat mass. An optimal ratio of fat to lean mass is an indication of fitness, and the right types of exercise will help you decrease body fat and increase or maintain muscle mass.

> The primary nutrition recommendations are to eat fewer calories, be more active, and make wiser food choices.

> The days when physical exercise was a natural part of everyday existence for most people are long gone, and now we have to make an extra effort to add exercise to our daily routines.

Two keys to maintaining a consistent exercise programs are: 1) establish a routine, and 2) choose a type of exercise you enjoy doing. Followers of Iyengar yoga, which requires holding poses for long periods, are not likely to equally prefer Power Yoga (Vinyasa style), where the emphasis is on flow and movement. It's one thing to try an exercise type you've never tried before, just to see if you like it. It's quite another to think you're going to be disciplined enough to stick with a type of exercise you don't enjoy at all. If you have trouble sticking to a routine, ask a friend if he or she would be willing to join you. Having a buddy system can be a very real motivator.

The payoff is in the following results: increased efficiency of heart and lungs; reduced cholesterol levels; increased muscle strength; reduced blood pressure; reduced risk of major illnesses such as diabetes and heart disease; and weight loss.

EXERCISE YOUR MIND

Good self-care also requires exercising your mind. Study of brain chemistry reveals that the brain has a neuromuscular junction, the structure in which brain chemicals make a connection with skeletal muscles. The brain neurotransmits a chemical called acetylcholine for the purpose of maintaining memory and attention, and dopamine to help regulate fine motor movement. It is this neuromuscular connection that may be the reason why deep massage can trigger the release of powerful and long-held emotional memories.[1]

Lawrence C. Katz, Ph.D., has developed a system of brain exercises called Neurobics™.[2] This system requires the use of all five body senses to stimulate and shake up your normal patterns of thinking. The exercises are designed to help your brain produce new nutrients that strengthen, preserve, and grow brain cells. Neurobics recommends the following types of exercises:

INCLUDE ONE OF MORE OF YOUR SENSES IN AN EVERYDAY TASK.
- Get dressed with your eyes closed.
- Wash your hair with your eyes closed.
- Share a meal and use only visual cues to communicate. No talking.

COMBINE TWO SENSES.
- Listen to music and smell flowers.
- Listen to the rain and tap your fingers.
- Watch clouds and play with modeling clay at the same time.

BREAK ROUTINES.
- Go to work on a new route.
- Eat with your opposite hand.
- Shop at a new grocery store.

Brain research also shows that almost any type of mental stimulation—reading, doing crossword puzzles, playing Scrabble—increases mental acuity and memory. On the other hand, extensive research has shown that watching TV shifts the brain into neutral.[3,4,5,6]

Research shows that watching TV is not an effective tool for promoting healthy mental exercise.

GET A MASSAGE REGULARLY

As you tell your clients and the public, massage can help both your body and your attitude. It can relieve stress and recharge your batteries. If it is such a good thing, why do some massage therapists get so busy that they do not receive massages regularly themselves?

A central part of your self-care should be scheduling regular massages for yourself. This can be a great opportunity for barter. If you do not have enough cash to pay for a massage, you can possibly trade services with another massage therapist.

Receiving a regular massage can also help with your professional development. Everyone has different areas of expertise, and you may pick up some techniques from the practitioner who provides your massage. In addition, you will be reminded of what it feels

THE BUSINESS OF MASSAGE

like to be the client. What can you learn about how you want to treat your clients? Indeed, there are several important reasons to regularly schedule time for your massage.

RESOURCES FOR EXERCISING YOUR BRAIN

General: crossword puzzles, Sudoku puzzles, Scrabble, brainteasers, riddles.

The Franklin Institute, Resources for Science Learning: www.fi.edu/learn/brain/exercise.html#mentalexercise

Braingle.com, a website of mental stimulation games such as brainteasers, optical illusions, riddles, trivia: www.braingle.com

Brain Matrix: Train the Brain: www.brainmatrix.com

Neurobics™, by Lawrence C. Katz and Manning Rubin: www.neurobics.com

---

BIOMECHANICAL SKILLS

Besides receiving massages regularly, you should take care of your body in other ways. Apply what you learned in your massage therapy training about body mechanics. Set aside time each day to rest your body. Take breaks to stretch your muscles. Get regular exercise, such as walking, yoga, tai chi, or aerobics. Drink plenty of water and eat a healthy diet. Invest in office furniture that is designed ergonomically to be healthy for your body's comfort. These recommendations are wise for anyone; for someone in as physically demanding a career as massage therapy, they are essential.

Of particular concern to the massage therapist is repetitive strain injuries to the hands, wrists, arms, shoulders, and back. Most people have heard of the type of repetitive strain injury called carpal tunnel syndrome. This syndrome results from repeatedly putting too much pressure on a nerve that passes through the wrist, and symptoms include pain, tingling, numbness, and weakness of the wrist and hand.

Just as you advise your clients, if you begin to experience pain, numbness, and other

---

RESOURCES FOR BODY MECHANICS

BOOKS

Butler, Sharon J. (1996). *Conquering Carpal Tunnel Syndrome and Other Repetitive Strain Injuries.* Oakland: New Harbinger.

Fritz, Sandy. (2005). *Mosby's Fundamentals of Therapeutic Massage* (3rd ed.). Mosby.

Frye. (2004). *Body Mechanics for Manual Therapists: A Functional Approach to Self-care* (2nd ed.). Lippincott Williams & Wilkins.

Green, Lauriann. (2000). *Save Your Hands! Injury Prevention for Massage Therapists.* Seattle: Infinity Press.

Wolfe, Marian. (2001). *Body Mechanics and Self-Care Manual.* Upper Saddle River, NJ: Prentice-Hall.

WEBSITES

Mayo Clinic: http://www.mayoclinic.com/health/carpal-tunnel-syndrome/DS00326

National Institute of Neurological Disorders and Stroke, Carpal Tunnel Syndrome Fact Sheet, http://www.ninds.nih.gov/disorders/carpal_tunnel/detail_carpal_tunnel.htm

---

possible symptoms of a repetitive strain injury, see your doctor and get a diagnosis. Follow the recommendations for treatment, which may include resting the affected area, stretching and flexing your muscles, ice therapy, massaging the affected area, and other means of physical rehabilitation. It is a good practice to pay attention to the way you work and to follow methods for preventing such problems. See the Spotlight on Business, "Avoiding Repetitive Strain Injuries."

SPOTLIGHT ♀♀♀♀♀ON BUSINESS

Avoiding Repetitive Strain Injuries

- Warm up your body before you get started.
- Use the weight of your whole body; do not let your arms and shoulders do all the work.
- Use body mechanics principles, as well as stools and chairs that work for your body, allowing you to stay relaxed and comfortable.
- Keep the massage table at a comfortable height for your proper body mechanics. Your fingertips should reach the top of the table when hanging at your side.
- Your feet should follow the direction of force you are using.
- When a technique compromises your health, choose another way.
- Do not wear yourself out. Schedule breaks, vary your activities, and limit your massage hours to what your body tells you it can handle.
- Use ice baths for your hands between massages.
- Receive massage yourself on a regular basis.

PERSONAL SELF-CARE MANAGEMENT STRATEGY

Before you integrate self-care into your daily routine, it can be helpful to create a plan. In creating the plan, give careful thought to what you're hoping to accomplish. Are your goals focused on getting more exercise, watching less TV, losing weight? A tool you might use to help you come up with a personal self-care plan is shown in Figure 4.1. Some of the activities you might include in such a plan are shown in Figure 4.2.

Scheduling your day is an essential work-related activity. A schedule becomes a tool for time management when you use it for all the activities you consider important. Some people are more comfortable adhering to a very well-defined schedule, such as one that says they will do 50 sit-ups every morning at 7:00 a.m. Others prefer a more loosely defined schedule, such as one that says they'll do 30 minutes of aerobic exercise three times a week. The point of building a schedule that includes work-related activities as well as self-care activities is that you consciously allocate time to a healthy balance of activities that help you and your business thrive.

Your schedule of integrated work and self-care practices might include time for many of the activities shown in Figure 4.2. Any items you check on this list should show up on your calendar. At first, it may seem odd to write "meditation" or "dinner with family" on your schedule, but aren't those activities as important to your life as the 60-minute massage you have scheduled to give this afternoon?

SUMMARY

Practicing self-care is as important to your business success as your client and business skills are. A healthy self-care routine keeps your mind, body, and spirit prepared to do the demanding yet satisfying work required of massage therapists. Not only will your focus on self-care assist your own well-being, but it is a powerful tool as a role model to your clients.

Handling stress is one of the most significant self-care benefits. By learning processes to reduce or manage stress, you will minimize physiological effects such as high blood

FIGURE 4.1
Worksheet for Developing a Personal
Self-Care Plan

1   My main area of interest (eating, exercise, learning to deal with common illness problems, etc.): _____

2   My main personal strengths and resources in this area: _____
_____

3   The best resources for me in this area (people, groups, classes, books, etc.): ____
_____

4   Some activities and goals I might choose to help me explore this area (Brainstorm!): _____
_____
_____

5   I would like to choose an initial activity that I could complete in about _____ days/weeks/months.

6   Within this time limit, the goal I'd most like to set for myself is: _____
_____

7   Some small rewards I will give myself for making progress toward this goal are:
_____
_____

8   A big reward I will give myself for reaching my goal is _____

9   I will ask _____ to be my support person in working toward this goal.

10 I will contact my support person on _____ (date) to bring him/her up to date on my explorations in this area.

11 My commitment, again, is to accomplish the following activities: _____
_____
between now and _____ (date).

On that date I will give my support person a report on my explorations in this area.

Other: _____

SIGNATURE:_____

TODAY'S DATE:_____

Source: Tom Ferguson, MD (1943-2006), available at HealthWorld Online, www.healthy.net

FIGURE 4.2
Practitioner Self-Care Checklist

A schedule that regularly integrates self-care includes most of the following activities:

☐ Conduct massage sessions, including time to set up and get centered.

☐ Keep up with the paperwork of the practice.

☐ Meet regularly with your mentor.

☐ Plan and track the progress of your practice.

☐ Think of new ideas to market your practice.

☐ Keep your life fresh and interesting.

☐ Continue your education and training.

☐ Network.

☐ Spend time with your family and friends.

☐ Spend time with your pets.

☐ Spend time alone with your spouse, partner, or significant other.

☐ Exercise.

☐ Participate in sports.

☐ Rest.

☐ Take vacations; travel.

☐ Meditate, read, pray.

☐ Participate in hobbies, cultural activities, or other types of entertainment.

☐ Do volunteer work.

☐ Other: _____

pressure and sleep disturbances, and psychological effects such as anxiety and depression. Techniques that can help you manage stress include meditation, spiritual/religious practices, physical exercise, mind exercise, proper nutrition, regular massages, and practicing effective biomechanics.

By creating a personal self-care plan and scheduling these self-care techniques into your daily routine just as regularly as you schedule client appointments, you are taking care of yourself and your business at the same time.

REVIEW QUESTIONS

1 What are some of the physiological and psychological effects of stress?
2 Identify various stress reduction techniques and their benefits.
3 Identify strategies for stress management.
4 Describe the basics of good nutrition.
5 Describe at least two ways to exercise your body.
6 Describe at least two ways to exercise your mind.
7 Describe whether or not watching television is a productive self-care technique.
8 Describe the recommended ways of achieving better nutrition.
9 Describe strategies that will help you incorporate self-care into your daily routine.

ENDNOTES

1 The Franklin Institute, Resources for Science Learning, at http://www.fi.edu/learn/ brain/exercise.html#mentalexercise
2 Keep Your Brain Alive, Lawrence C. Katz, Ph.D. http://www.neurobics.com/exercise. html
3 American Academy of Pediatrics, http://www.aap.org/family/tv1.htm
4 Brainy Child.com, http://www.brainy-child.com/article/tvonbrain.html
5 Joyce Nelson, *The Perfect Machine*; New Society Pub. (p. 82), 1992, 800-253-3605; ISBN 0-86571-235-2, as cited at Dieoff.org, http://dieoff.org/page24.htm
6 International Child and Youth Care Network, http://www.cyc-net.org/today2001/ today010907.html

Chapter 5

Launching a Successful Practice

When you give your first massage for pay, you're in business. By developing a solid business plan, you allow your business to grow by design, not by default.

CHAPTER OUTLINE

- Career Decisions
- Employment Options
- Business Structures
- Business Plan
- Goals and Objectives
- Laws and Regulations
- Insurance Requirements
- Market Need
- Services and Products
- Pricing
- Business Policies and Procedures
- Professional Assistance
- Hiring Others
- Financial
- Buying, Selling, and Closing a Practice
- Evaluation of Your Plan

CHAPTER OBJECTIVES

1 Identify an appropriate sequence of steps for launching your massage career.
2 Create effective strategy and tools for job hunting.
3 Identify the components of a business plan.
4 Set appropriate goals and objectives for starting your career.
5 Describe different types of business structures.
6 Identify legal and regulatory issues that you need to know when opening your practice.
7 Estimate the size of your market.
8 Determine the services and products your business will offer.
9 Determine the policies that will govern your business.
10 Evaluate whether or in what areas you will hire professional assistance.
11 Describe the basics of selling, buying, or closing a business.
12 Construct a financial plan.

From the previous chapters you have gained a flavor of what it means to embark on a massage therapy career, what types of credentials and qualifications you will need, and how your relationship to clients and to your work environment will affect your everyday experiences. You learned different ways to look introspectively and evaluate which choices will make you happiest in the long run. In this chapter you will learn about the business skills required to bring to fruition the type of practice you want to have.

CAREER DECISIONS

In addition to basic career choices about the type of massage you want to provide, you need to decide how you are going to make a living at it. One of those decisions is choosing whether you will be an employee or will own your business. For some, a career in massage therapy answers a long-awaited wish to be out on their own. For others, this kind of liberty is not at all appealing. They prefer to work as employees of an organization in which others handle most of the paperwork, marketing, building maintenance, and other important support details.

The choices in employment (full-time or part-time) and business ownership (independent contractor, sole proprietorship, partnership, or corporation) come in many varieties. There are pros and cons to each choice, and you are the only one who knows which one is better suited to you.

EMPLOYMENT OPTIONS

For some people, at certain stages of their career—maybe at the beginning, maybe after a number of years—the responsibilities of owning a practice are simply too overwhelming, or they just are not interested in doing it. They prefer working for someone else, maybe because they can gain expertise from others early in their careers. Many therapists are able to arrange jobs, working for someone else, that meet their personal needs for work hours, type of practice, and other criteria. They appreciate being in a situation in which someone else handles marketing, bookkeeping, and the many other responsibilities of running a business. They like getting a regular paycheck, with all the tax deductions properly made on their behalf. They may also appreciate the opportunity to watch more- experienced massage therapists and to learn the details of running a practice.

One downside of being an employee is that you give up some degree of control. Though many employers promote a collaborative spirit, at the end of the day, the employer is the boss and he or she is responsible for the profit and loss of the business. Even if the employer's vote isn't the only one, it is the biggest one. If you work on Tuesday evenings, you may not be able to get that evening off to celebrate your child's birthday. If you would like to expand the types of services you offer, you probably will have to obtain permission first from your employer. If you think the facilities could use an upgrade, you will have to sell your ideas to someone else. And sometimes an employer overschedules massage therapists, leaving them too little time between appointments for proper self-care. The pros and cons are summarized in Figure 5.1.

FINDING A JOB

Finding employment as a massage therapist could be as simple as answering an ad in the classified section of your local newspaper, interviewing for the position, and starting to work. However, if you want a satisfying career, not just a job, you'll want to devote careful thought to what your ideal job would be before you apply to any ads.

Often, the people who plan their job searches as an exercise in self-knowledge and self-marketing are those who land the best jobs. Before you create your résumé, know what

THE BUSINESS OF MASSAGE

PROS

You can learn from others, some of whom might be more experienced than you.

You can be a model for others, some of whom might be less experienced than you.

You can earn a steady paycheck.

You can avoid most of the responsibilities of running a business, including paperwork and security.

You can take advantage of employee benefits, such as paid vacation and health insurance.

You don't have to pay self-employment tax.

Your employer pays half of your social security tax withholding.

You can learn what your strengths are relative to your coworkers.

You can leave the job without the hassles of closing or selling your business.

All business expenses and risks are your employer's, not yours.

CONS

You'll receive only a portion of whatever rate the client pays for massage.

There will be some things you don't like about how the business is run, and you might not have much voice in changing it.

Your work hours might not be flexible.

You will be expected to help your employer's business be profitable, and you might feel resentful that you aren't getting your fair share.

FIGURE 5.1
Employment Pros and Cons

your career goals are. When it comes to money, for instance, there's probably a minimum amount that you must earn to cover your expenses. The more elusive goals, such as what you want for yourself in the future—your long-term goals—might be harder to describe. These are the goals that will probably add the most satisfaction to your job hunt. If you make the mental and emotional commitment now to explore how you want your massage therapy training to make a difference to you and to others long term, chances are you will be more selective in targeting a job.

Knowing your long-term goals allows you the flexibility to choose even those jobs that are not your ideal choices, because you can appreciate how certain aspects of the job are helping you reach long-term goals even if the job isn't all you hoped for. For instance, let's say your career dream is to open a private practice that employs four massage therapists and specializes in providing massage therapy to hospice patients and their families. But let's say the only job opportunity available right now is as a spa employee whose clients want primarily relaxation massage. As an employee of the spa, keeping your long-term goal in mind allows you to appreciate the spa because you are learning skills there that are transferable to your dream job in these ways:

1 You learn how to communicate with clients in a way that puts them at ease even if they are having a bad day.
2 You develop self-care skills within the context of performing a job that is sometimes stressful.
3 You observe from your employer the things you will do the same when you are an employer, and things you will do differently.
4 You welcome the opportunity to represent your employer as a provider of volunteer massage at events that benefit the types of organizations you want to support.
5 You volunteer to speak to community groups about the benefits of massage, because you know that public speaking skills will benefit you now and in the future.
6 You invest your continuing education time and money in courses that help you reach your long-term goals.

Focusing on long-term goals helps you see how everyday experiences support your growth for the future.

Sources of Job Leads

Sources of job leads could come from just about anywhere. Here are some of the more common ones:

- Classified ads in local newspapers
- Mentors and friends
- Newsletters from professional organizations and their regional chapters
- Online search: type *massage therapist jobs* into search window
- Other massage therapists
- Professional publications such as *mtj* and *Massage Magazine*
- Schools with massage training programs—many have job placement support

Be choosy about selecting potential employers. You want your first work experience to be a positive one. It can be helpful to complete the Potential Employer Profile (Figure 5.2) as you make your job-hunting decisions. If you are considering more than one employer, complete a profile for each one and compare the pros and cons.

Create Your Résumé

The purpose of your résumé is to let prospective employers know your qualifications for employment. In most cases, the employer will see your résumé before he or she has had the opportunity to meet you in person. Naturally, you want to make sure that your résumé and cover letter create the impression you want to create, while taking care to keep all information factual.

The categories of information that are generally included on a résumé (see Figure 5.3) are:

- Your name, address, telephone, and e-mail address
- Summary of who you are and what you are seeking—This can be stated either under a Profile header, which summarizes your strengths and skills, or under an Objective header, which states the type of position you are seeking.
- Qualifications—List your credentials (such as NCTMB certified or state licensed, professional memberships) and describe the modalities you are qualified to practice. Graduates of 500-hour programs are usually qualified to practice Swedish techniques. Many other modalities require additional training and additional certificates of completion. Describe licensing and registration as required by the area in which you will practice. For information on credentials, see the section "Professional Credentials" in Chapter 1.
- Education—List schools you have attended, number of hours/credits, and any workshops or seminars that are relevant to the type of position you are seeking.
- Employment history—Name and location of employer, dates of employment, short description of job, and anything about your experience there that applies to the type of position you are seeking.
- Awards and Affiliations—Here is where you would list your membership in a professional association and any awards or professional-related affiliations that a prospective employer might be interested in. For instance, as a student, did you ever give a presentation about the benefits of massage to fitness club members at the YMCA? While you are a student is a good time to do things that will help you on your résumé.

Many job ads specify "previous experience required." But what if you are just graduating from massage therapy training and you don't have previous massage therapy job experience? Learn how to translate previous job experiences or volunteer experiences into skills that will help you in your job search. Even if you've never before held a job as a massage therapist, consider how the following experiences would sound to a potential employer:

> While you are a student is a good time to do things that will help your résumé—such as volunteering at a community event or making a presentation about massage training at a local job fair.

POTENTIAL EMPLOYER PROFILE WORKSHEET

Number, in order of preference, the types of business you would most enjoy being associated with as a massage therapist (1 = first choice, 8 = last choice)

____ Fitness/Sports ____ Chiropractic practice ____ Hospital

____ Massage therapy practice ____ Physical therapy practice ____ Other

____ Wellness center ____ Spa/Resort/Salon

For each business you choose to consider, complete the following information.

POTENTIAL EMPLOYER

Name of business: _____

Address: _____

Phone/E-mail: _____

Name of owner/manager: _____

Type of business: ☐ Private ☐ Franchise ☐ Branch office ☐ Other

Number years in business: _____

Type(s) of massage offered: _____
_____

Reputation in the community: _____
_____

Target markets for this business:

   Age range: _____ Gender: _____

   Occupations: _____ Income: _____

   Education level: _____ Openness to alternative therapies: yes/no

   Social/cultural environment: _____
   _____

1 How could this business benefit from incorporating your services? (For example, would you attract a younger clientele? Do you have particular qualifications that would be helpful to a certain type of client?) _____
   _____
   _____

2 What suggestions could you present to the owner of this business that would convince him or her that you are interested in the growth of this business? _____
   _____
   _____

3 What do you anticipate your compensation would be from this business?
   Pay range: _____
   Benefits (medical insurance, paid time off, flexible hours, etc.): _____
   _____

4 Other than income, what value would you seek from this working relationship?____
   _____
   _____

FIGURE 5.2
Potential Employer Profile Worksheet

FIGURE 5.3
Sample Résumé

JAN A. SANGER, LMT, NCTMB
1234 Anystreet Boulevard
Health City, USA
jsanger@email.com

OBJECTIVE

To develop a professional, client-centered therapeutic massage career.

QUALIFICATIONS

- Education from COMTA accredited massage therapy school
- Effective and ethical delivery of massage therapy
- Proficiency in SOAP charting and documentation
- Knowledge of massage indications and contraindications
- Understanding of physiological developmental stages
- Current Red Cross certification in CPR and First Aid Safety

EXPERIENCE

SCHOOL OF NATURAL THERAPEUTICS, City, State
Student – September 2009 to July 2011

- 750 hours classroom/coursework
- 250 hours clinical practice in student clinic

MUTUAL INSURANCE COMPANY, City, State
Commercial Policy Processing Technician – March 2007 to December 2009

- Reviewed and prepared commercial policies and set up yearly renewal files.
- Coordinated underwriting information & processed new business applications.

LIFE INSURANCE COMPANY OF AMERICA, City, State
Sales Support Representative – April 2005 to March 2007

- Prepared underwriting data (financial and medical).
- Ordered medical exams, blood tests, and physician statements.
- Supported brokers with product information, customer feedback, and new business leads.
- *Selected for special assignment:* Designed office personnel grid for use in field offices.

Customer Service Billing Representative – January 2004 to April 2005

- Maintained accounts and premium payment records.
- Processed reconciliation of client accounts and responded to client requests.
- Served as backup supervisor within work region.
- *Selected for special assignment:* Managed biweekly schedule for flextime employees.

EDUCATION/CREDENTIALS

- Licensed Massage Therapist (LMT), state of _____
- Nationally Certified in Therapeutic Massage & Bodywork (NCTMB), 2011
- Therapeutic Massage Certificate, School of Natural Therapeutics, City, State, 1,000 hour Massage Therapy Program, July 2011
- B.A. in Business Administration/Marketing, State College, City, State, 2004

AWARDS AND AFFILIATIONS

- Professional Member, American Massage Therapy Association (AMTA)
- Chapter Member, AMTA State Chapter
- Co-coordinator of chair massage booth at Paws for a Cause, August 2010
- Awarded 1995 "Support Rep of the Year" based on increased territory sales

- As a student intern, I provided more than 175 massages to clients through supervised student clinic. I developed a 20% rate of return clients, which was higher than the class average.
- My previous job as veterinary technician taught me the importance of customer service skills and putting people at ease who are under stress.

Select your examples carefully, so you can limit your résumé to one page (or two, if you have extensive experience that is applicable). Note in Figure 5.3 that the individual's résumé does not show employment experience as a massage therapist. Consider the ways in which this person's experience in the insurance industry can be applied to a future career as a massage therapist.

Many businesses are now equipped to recruit employees via online applications. Some require you to use an online form or to e-mail them your résumé.

Although writing and snail-mailing paper documents is almost a thing of the past, many businesses still operate under some combination of traditional and online means. E-mail communication is usually briefer and more informal than letters that are sent through the mail, but be sure to keep your tone professional in either type of communication.

Create Cover Letters

Letters to potential employers are one of the most important tools you can use in your job search. They should always accompany your résumé when you apply for a job. You will direct letters to advertised job ads as well as to contacts that you hope have jobs or job-search suggestions that might help you. Your cover letter reflects your personality and allows you to attract the prospective employer's interest. You will tailor your cover letter to fit each opportunity.

THREE PARTS OF A COVER LETTER

Every cover letter includes an introduction, a body, and a close.

- The *introduction* is where you introduce yourself and catch the reader's interest.
- The *body* of the letter describes how you are suited to the job. Motivate the reader to want to meet you by describing how your skills can help the prospective employer's business.
- The *close* is your final paragraph. The end of the letter expresses your appreciation for the reader's time and interest, and promises future contact.

If your letter sounds like a form letter, the prospective employer might not finish reading it. Personalize your introduction to the particular place of business or person to whom you're writing. If a friend or associate referred you, include this information in the first paragraph. Or write something like, "Your business attracted my interest because I saw that your business sponsored a chair massage at the Special Olympics last month."

A cover letter does not take the place of personal contact. In your final paragraph, tell the prospective employer that you will call next week to request an appointment for an interview—and then be sure to write this commitment on your calendar so you don't forget.

Communication Strategies for Interviewing

When you interview for a job, be prepared to present your qualifications and to answer questions about your career goals. Practice your responses with a friend or your mentor. Review your résumé, and anticipate questions your potential employer might ask. Think through how your previous job experience, if not as a massage therapist, gave you skills that are transferable to a massage therapy job. (See Spotlight on Business, "Tips for Pre-interview Preparation.")

Practicing your responses with a friend might seem awkward, but it is well worth the time. Even if you are confident of your qualifications, speaking about them out loud isn't always as easy as it seemed in your head. And if you are not sure how you would answer questions where you don't feel confident—a lack of experience, previous long or numerous periods as unemployed, responding to a question you know a potential employer is not allowed by law to ask—it will help you tremendously to practice before you are in the actual interview.

FOR INSTANCE:

Situation	Possible response
• Lack of experience	"Even though this will be my first paid employment as a massage therapist, our student internships were very comprehensive in giving me actual experience with clients and with business practices such as scheduling appointments and collecting payments."—or—"My previous employment as […] gave me good experience in providing customer satisfaction, plus I learned good work habits that make me even more valuable as a massage therapist—things like punctuality, reliability and knowing how to work efficiently in an office environment."
• Periods of unemployment	Be open about the reason for unemployment and explain that the condition for previous unemployment has now changed. "Now that my education, skills and schedule put me in a good position to work full-time as a massage therapist, I'm eager to participate in a practice where I can benefit people."
• If asked an inappropriate or illegal question	Be direct and firm, but not antagonistic, in rephrasing the interviewer's question to you in appropriate terms, such as saying to an interviewer who asked if you have children: "I believe that, in asking that question, you are trying to understand whether I can be relied upon to work the hours required. You will find that I am very reliable because I place a high priority on getting repeat business, and I want clients to know they can depend on me to keep my appointments." If the interviewer persists in asking inappropriate questions, you should feel free to say, "Maybe you are not aware that the question you are asking me is not allowed by law. If I can answer other questions that pertain to the job you advertised, I would be happy to do so."

Every life experience can work to your advantage if you can express it in a way that relates to your value as an employee.

SPOTLIGHT ON BUSINESS

Tips for Pre-interview Preparation

- Be confident of your career goals, and understand how this prospective job helps you achieve those goals. For instance, "I want to become the manager of a destination spa" differs vastly from "I want to become an experienced massage therapist so I can one day open my own practice." The entry job might be the same, but how it helps you achieve your goals will be different.
- Look at your résumé with fresh eyes. Anticipate the questions a prospective employer might ask you based on your résumé.
- Become comfortable in answering the most challenging questions by anticipating them and practicing in advance. Ask a friend to practice with you. The responses you have in your head frequently sound different when you hear yourself say them aloud.

- Learn as much as you can about the company you're interviewing with. Your questions will reflect your knowledge and can't help but impress the interviewer that you took the initiative to learn about them in advance.

Be ready to ask the prospective employer questions to determine whether the job for which you are interviewing will help you achieve your career goals, such as:

- What kinds of clients do you have?
- How does massage therapy fit into your organization's mission?
- What responsibilities does the job include? (Request a job description, if the organization has prepared one.)
- What are your policies for scheduling and tips?
- How many massages are scheduled in a row, and how long are breaks between massages?
- How many of the clients are insurance clients?
- What types of massages are advertised to clients? (For example, if deep tissue massage is advertised, how many of those massages could you be asked to give in a row?)
- How many hours are considered part-time and full-time, and what bearing does that have on employee benefits?
- If business is seasonal, what are the expectations regarding in-season and off-season?
- What expectations would the business have of me? For example, would I be expected to:
  - bring my own massage table to the workplace?
  - provide my own oils/lotions or music?
  - perform office duties?
  - fold towels?
  - sell products or non-massage services?

It is not unusual for a prospective employer to request a massage from the practitioner/ job candidate. When you go to the interview, dress appropriately to allow for the potential of giving a massage. If appropriate, you may even volunteer to demonstrate your skills by offering a complimentary massage. Customize the massage to the type of job for which you're applying, such as whether it's sports/fitness or relaxation. Inquire about the interviewer's preferences in massage, as you would with a real client. See the Spotlight on Business, "Criteria for Interview Demo Massage," as a guide to criteria a prospective employer might use in evaluating the effectiveness of your massage.

SPOTLIGHT ON BUSINESS

Criteria for Interview Demo Massage

1. Pressure (too light or too heavy?)
2. Temperature (too cold or too warm?)
3. Comfort of headrest and bolster placements
4. Draping (insufficient or awkward?)
5. Practitioner talking (too much or not enough?)
6. Practitioner listening (wasn't responsive to questions?)
7. Smooth transition between strokes

Eventually, but perhaps not in the first interview, if you think the organization might be a good fit, you will want to know whether the job meets your earnings objectives. Therefore, you need to have an idea how much money you need to earn. You will want to inquire among friends and associates to find out what customary fees are, as well as what percentage of fees employers customarily retain, in your locale. When you think about income, be realistic about understanding how much money will be taken out for taxes, and what your expenses will be (such as commuting or any supplies you might have to provide yourself).

Consider whether you want to be paid a flat rate or a percentage of what the business charges for each massage session, if this is negotiable. Also ask about benefits such as health insurance, paid vacation time, option to take time off without pay, and reimbursement of continuing education expenses. Review your potential employer's benefits package to see what kinds of insurance are included and whether you will be responsible for a portion of the premiums.

Always send a thank you letter to the person who interviewed you within 24 hours after the interview. An e-mail is also appropriate but not quite as memorable.

Job hunting can be educational because you can learn about the different settings that employ massage therapists and about the different modalities that tend to be used in various settings. Even if you do not think a particular interview will turn into a job offer, you can ask for a chance to meet with a person you think will have insights to share about a massage therapy career.

Once you have accepted a position, you might consider sending a note to individuals who gave you advice while you were job hunting, and always to those who gave you referrals. Even if a person's referral did not lead to your new job, you will want to express

---

RESOURCES FOR JOB HUNTING AND RÉSUMÉ PREPARATION

Talk to practicing massage therapists to find out what they like and don't like about their practices. Find out what other jobs they have had as massage therapists, and what they did and didn't like about other jobs.

Find a mentor who is willing to help you build your professional skills. Participate in professional associations and organizations, and take advantage of opportunities to build relationships where you can learn from someone who has more experience than you do.

CAREER GUIDANCE AND RÉSUMÉ PREPARATION

Ashley, Martin, & Deborah Fay. (2006). *Massage: A Career at Your Fingertips* student workbook. Carmel, NY: Enterprise Publishing.

Bolles, Richard N. (2003). *The 1999 What Color is Your Parachute? A Practical Manual for Job-Hunters and Career-Changers*. Berkeley: Ten Speed Press.

Career Builder: www.careerbuilder.com, enter *massage therapist* in keywords box

Quest Career Services: www.questcareer.com

Sohnen-Moe, Cherie (2008) *Business Mastery³*. (4th ed.). Tucson, AZ: SMA.

JOB HUNTING WEBSITES

AMTA Job Bank: www.amtamassage.org/jobbank

Employment Spot.com: www.employmentspot.com, enter *massage therapist* in keywords box

FlipDog.com: www.flipdog.com, enter *massage therapist* in keywords box

Indeed.com: www.indeed.com, enter *massage therapist* in keywords box

JuJu Job Board: www.juju.com, enter *massage therapist* in keywords box

MassageJobs.com: www.massagejobs.com, no need to enter key word

Salary.com Career Advancement Tools and Resources: www.salary.com/careers

FIGURE 5.4
Types of Businesses

Sole Proprietorship

SOLE PROPRIETORSHIP
One person has ownership and liability

Partnership

GENERAL PARTNERSHIP
Partners share ownership and liability

LIMITED PARTNERSHIP
There are two types of partners in a limited partnership

General partners play an active role and have unlimited liability

Limited partners invest in the partnership, do not play an active role, and have liability only up to the amount of their investment

Corporation

LIMITED LIABILITY COMPANY (LLC)
Permitted in most states; generally must have at least two owners

Taxed as a partnership

Owners' liability limited as in a corporation

CORPORATION (SOMETIMES CALLED C CORPORATION)
Separate entity from its owner, or stockholders, formed in accordance with state regulations

Business pays income tax, and owners pay tax on any dividends

S CORPORATION (OR SUBCHAPTER S CORPORATION)
Corporation that meets IRS size and stock ownership requirements (if the corporation is small enough, a shareholder with at least 50% of the stock may request S corporation status)

Pays taxes as a partnership

Retains liability advantages of corporations

PROFESSIONAL CORPORATION
Separate entity from individual owners

Taxed at higher rate than other corporations

Limited liability for owners

your appreciation for the help, and to inform the person what job you selected. Maybe even enclose a few business cards if the person could be a source for referring clients to you at your new practice.

BUSINESS STRUCTURES

If you have decided on self-employment, whether as an independent contractor who travels to a few clients, the co-owner of a large practice, or something in between, you will have additional decisions to make about how to structure the ownership of your practice. What you choose depends partly on whether you will work as the sole owner of your practice or will share ownership with others.

In the United States, your primary business structure choices are sole proprietorship, partnership, corporation (a variety of corporate types exist), and limited liability company (see Figure 5.4). In Canada, the four types of business structures are sole proprietorship, partnership, corporation, and cooperative. Figure 5.5 summarizes what many people view as the pros and cons of each type of structure.

SELF-EMPLOYMENT OPTIONS

Self-employment has some obvious attractions. For example, you can set your own work standards and hours. You decide where to work and the kinds of services you offer. You can emphasize the kinds of therapy and benefits that you consider the most worthwhile. The business you establish is your own practice. Your income potential is almost as unlimited as your potential to attract and meet the needs of clients. At the same time, you can use the expenses of operating your practice to reduce your taxable income. For example, if you buy office equipment you can deduct the expense. If you make a house call, you might be able to write off a portion of the travel expense. And if you operate your practice out of your home, you can deduct a variety of business costs.

Self-employment also has a downside. Your income varies according to the number of clients you see and the number of days you work, and it is often hard to predict what you will earn from month to month. Also, you will have start-up expenses, so you might need another source of funds while you are waiting for your first payments from clients. If you start out smaller than anticipated, your income may be disappointing. Yet even if you provide massages only a few hours a month, you are legally considered a business, so you have all the responsibilities of any business owner.

As a business owner, you must determine what taxes you owe, so you have to maintain careful records of your earnings and expenses. Additionally, self-employed people are responsible for paying the share of taxes that employers pay on behalf of their employees, which is known as self-employment tax.

Running a practice involves other responsibilities as well. Finding and keeping clients can be a challenge. You must be sure that you or someone you trust is collecting your fees. If you maintain a space in which to practice, you must be sure it looks professional, feels comfortable, and meets building codes. Even if you hire people to handle some of these tasks, you, as the owner of the practice, are responsible for ensuring that the work is done properly. All this can be especially challenging when you are just starting out as a massage therapist.

Self-employment also has financial implications. Being able to write off expenses is nice, but you have to spend your own money first. Also, any benefits, such as time off and health insurance, will reduce your business earnings. See Figure 5.6 for a list of pros and cons of self-employment.

Owning your own private practice has many rewards but also many risks.

FIGURE 5.5 Pros and Cons of Business Structure Types

BUSINESS STRUCTURE/ IRS DESIGNATION	PROS	CONS
SOLE PROPRIETORSHIP (IRS 1040)	Simplest form of business structure. All business decisions may be made without consulting others. Paperwork requirements are minimal, compared to other business structures (no annual reports or minutes are required).	Owner is personally liable for all actions of the business. Some may find working alone to be an isolating experience. May be more difficult (than for a different type of business) to borrow money from a lending institution.
PARTNERSHIP (IRS 1065)	An association of two or more owners offers more resources to the business in terms of money and different talents. In a simple partnership, ownership is 50-50. Tax filing is the same as for an individual and sole proprietorship.	Partners are personally liable for the debts and actions of the business. Joint decision making can be challenging.
CORPORATION		
S CORPORATION (IRS 1120S)	Business is taxed at the individual (sole proprietorship) level, not at the corporate level. Individual liability is limited; however, the actions of the owner are still subject to liability. Tax advantages might apply to start-up losses and to taxable gains when you sell the business.	Paperwork required to set up and operate an S Corp is less than for a corporation but more than for a limited liability company (LLC) or partnership. If you withdraw income for your work, you are considered an employee and must file payroll returns with the IRS. Annual meetings and minutes are required.
LIMITED LIABILITY COMPANY (LLC) (SAME IRS DESIGNATION AS SOLE PROPRIETORSHIP, 1040)	Distribution of profits may be allocated proportionately rather than 50-50.	No annual meetings or minutes are required. An LLC requires more paperwork than a sole proprietorship or partnership but less than a corporation.
COOPERATIVE (MORE COMMON IN CANADA THAN IN THE UNITED STATES)	Liability is limited to the value of the shares held by each member. Each member of a cooperative has one vote in any decision regarding the cooperative. (This may be a pro or a con.)	Each member of a cooperative has one vote in any decision regarding the cooperative. (This may be a pro or a con.)

Sole Proprietor

If you are self-employed, you are mostly likely a sole proprietor or an independent contractor. If you work by yourself, providing massage in exchange for payment and you are not an employee, you are an independent contractor *and* a sole proprietor. *Independent contractor* describes your relationship to the party who pays you. It means you have (formally or informally) contracted to provide particular services, rather than to become an employee. *Sole proprietor* describes ownership; it means you are the only owner of your business—and you are in fact a business owner, even if your business consists only of you, a massage table, and a box of business cards.

The simplicity of forming and operating a business is the main reason so many massage therapists operate sole proprietorships. As a sole proprietor, you can practice under your

FIGURE 5.6
Pros and Cons of
Self-Employment

PROS

You choose the name of your business.

You set up your own work hours.

You choose where you want to work.

You choose what services you offer.

You choose whether to sell merchandise, and what to sell.

Your business is part of your identity.

Your income potential is not limited by someone else's control.

Many of your expenses are tax deductible.

CONS

Until you have developed a stable client base, you will have unpredictable income.

You have to pay start-up and ongoing expenses.

You are responsible for knowing the laws and regulations that apply to your business.

You must develop, implement, and pay for marketing and promotions.

You are responsible for the administrative operation of your business (computer support, telephone, website, billing, taxes, etc.)

You have to pay taxes, including self-employment tax.

If you work alone, you might get lonely.

own name or select a name for your practice. You can set up a practice in a home office (assuming local laws permit it) or in an office space that you rent alone, with a staff, or with other professionals. Or you can be an independent contractor who travels to other facilities where you have contracted to perform services.

A sole proprietorship has disadvantages, too. Working alone can feel isolating, and, compared to other forms of business, you may find it relatively difficult or expensive to borrow money, especially if you have not kept meticulous records. In a legal sense, a sole proprietorship is not separate from the individual owner. Therefore, a massage therapist who sets up an office but fails to pay all the related bills will be personally liable. That is, creditors can seek payment from the therapist's personal assets. Similarly, if someone falls and breaks a hip in a therapist's office, and the therapist lacks general liability insurance to cover the person's injury-related expenses, the person could sue the therapist, and the therapist could be required to pay from personal assets.

If this level of liability concerns you, seek advice from a legal professional who can counsel you on protecting yourself legally in your particular situation. Also, cultivate relationships with experienced massage therapists, who can act as mentors. They may be able to allay many of your concerns.

Independent Contractor

An independent contractor is an individual who performs services for another person or business under an implied or written agreement and who is not subject to the other's control, as he or she would be as an employee. The business that hires an independent contractor is not liable for the contractor's actions. As an independent contractor, you have the benefit of writing off your expenses *and* letting someone else run the business. If you want to be an independent contractor, understand that, for tax purposes, the IRS has guidelines—Form SS-8—for distinguishing an independent contractor from an employee. See Figure 5.7 for the comparison between Employee and Independent Contractor, and Figure 5.8 for IRS distinctions.

EMPLOYEE	INDEPENDENT CONTRACTOR
Can be instructed to follow your business's rules and procedures.	Must be free to determine how and when to complete a project.
Ongoing working relationship (this can be either a pro or a con, depending on the situation).	Relationship limited to scope of project(s) contracted for.
Paid a wage or salary, with taxes withheld.	Paid a fee, from which no taxes are withheld.
Share of social security taxes are paid by employer.	Responsible for paying his or her own self-employment tax.
Benefits are typically part of employment compensation package.	Must charge a fee large enough to provide self with benefits.
Employment relationship is covered by antidiscrimination and labor laws.	Contracting relationship is covered by contract law.
Works agreed-upon business hours.	May not be available at times needed (unless contract specifies certain hours).

FIGURE 5.7
Employee vs. Independent Contractor

PARTNERSHIPS AND CORPORATIONS

For the therapist eager to build a large practice, a sole proprietorship (described earlier in this chapter) may be too limiting. This massage therapist might instead share ownership with others by forming some type of partnership or corporation.

- A partnership is an association of two or more people in which they agree to operate a business as co-owners. To start the business, they sign a partnership agreement, register the business's name with the proper state authorities, and obtain a business license if required by law. As with a sole proprietorship, the partners are personally liable for debts of the practice.
- A corporation is a legal organization whose assets and liabilities are separate from those of its owners. Each state has laws spelling out the requirements for setting up a corporation. These requirements will include filling out papers called articles of incorporation, electing at least a minimum number of officers, and obtaining an Employer Identification Number from the IRS.
- The federal government recognizes several types of partnerships and corporations: sole proprietorships, general partnerships, limited partnerships, and several types of corporations. If you are interested in forming any type of partnership or corporation, seek qualified legal and financial advice. Your advisers can help ensure that you satisfy all the legal requirements and structure the organization in a way that meets the objectives of all participants.
- An S Corporation is specifically designed for small businesses. It may have tax advantages, such as paying taxes as an individual rather than as a corporation. If you withdraw income for yourself, you pay yourself as an employee and must file a payroll tax return with the IRS. Another advantage of an S Corp may be reduced capital gains tax if or when you sell your business.
- A limited liability company (LLC) combines some aspects of a partnership with some aspects of a corporation. Its participants are called members, not stockholders. It enjoys the same liability protection as a corporation; that is, the assets held by the LLC are at risk rather than the personal assets of its members. Single-owner LLCs pay taxes as though they are a sole proprietorship (using IRS Form 1040), and multiple-owner LLCs pay taxes as though they are a partnership (using IRS Form 1065).

FIGURE 5.8
IRS Distinction between Employee
and Independent Contractor

The IRS can determine that you are an employee, for tax purposes, even if you have signed an independent contractor agreement. To be sure of your distinction, file IRS Form SS-8.

EMPLOYEE OR INDEPENDENT CONTRACTOR

Check each of the statements that describes your work.

☐ You describe how, when, and where you will perform your work.

☐ You know how to provide the services; the company that contracted with you did not train you in its procedures.

☐ Your services are not something the company has made part of its operations.

☐ You do not personally provide some of the massages or other services for which you are paid. (For example, you hire an assistant to do some of the work.)

☐ Any assistants you use work for you, not for the company.

☐ You do not have an ongoing, continuing relationship with the company.

☐ You set your own work hours.

☐ You can work less than full-time if you prefer.

☐ You do not have to work at the company's facilities.

☐ You are not required to follow a sequence of procedures established by the company.

☐ You do not have to submit progress reports on your work.

☐ You are paid by the job (number of massages), rather than by the hour, week, or month.

☐ You have to bear the cost of any travel or other expenses required to carry out the work.

☐ You use your own supplies and equipment; the company does not pay for them.

☐ You have paid for any equipment or facilities you use.

☐ You assume a risk of loss if something goes wrong.

☐ You work for more than one company.

☐ You offer massages to the general public.

☐ The company cannot fire you; it can only decide whether to contract with you again in the future.

☐ If you fail to perform the services contracted for, the company could hold you legally liable.

The more boxes you checked, the more likely the IRS will agree that you are an independent contractor, meaning you are self-employed. If only a few of these statements apply to you, however, you may not meet the legal standard for being an independent contractor, *even if you have signed a contract that says you are not an employee.* Because the IRS considers you to be an employee, you should either change your work arrangements or have the organization with which you have a contract withhold employment taxes.

For more information, go to the Internal Revenue Service at www.irs.gov/tax. To request a ruling from the IRS, file IRS Form SS-8, which can be downloaded from the website, or call 1-800-829-3676.

- The success of any partnership or corporation will depend on the talent and commitment of all the owners. Remember, the time to evaluate your partners is before you sign the partnership agreement or articles of incorporation.
- To assess whether this relationship will benefit you, answer these questions:
  - What talents and other resources will this person contribute to the practice?
  - What characteristics of this person will make him or her hard for me to get along with? Am I willing to work with the things I do not like?
  - Does the person really have access to the financial resources he or she has promised to contribute?
  - Will this person work the hours necessary to make the practice a success?
  - Does this person have a good track record of honoring promises and commitments?
  - Are this person's goals for the practice consistent with my own?
  - Does this person live up to my own standards professionally, ethically, and in terms of business sense?
  - What could be the potential reasons for ending the partnership at a later date, and how would we do that?

Only when you are satisfied with your answers to all these questions should you form a partnership or corporation. It is much more difficult and costly to change your mind after you have entered into an agreement. For more details on setting up a particular kind of business, see the resources listed here as well as the Spotlight on Business, "Get to Know Your SBA Business Development Center."

RESOURCES FOR FORMING A CORPORATION OR PARTNERSHIP

- your accountant or attorney

- the office of your state's secretary of state or corporate commission (see the state government listings in your phone book or on their Web sites)

- Small Business Administration (1-800-8-ASK-SBA or www.sba.gov)

Get to Know Your SBA Business Development Center

The Small Business Administration offers a full range of tools to help entrepreneurs set up a new business. Four types of assistance are available, as shown below:

SMALL BUSINESS PLANNER

Write a business plan
Find a mentor
Finance start-up
Buy a business or franchise
Name your business
Choose a structure
Protect your ideas
Get licenses and permits
Pick a location
Lease equipment

SERVICES

Financial assistance
Contract opportunities
Disaster assistance
Online training
Counseling and assistance

Special audiences (women, veterans, Native Americans, en Espanol, etc.)
Laws and regulations
Compliance

TOOLS
Library and resources
Audio/video
Monthly Web chat
Forms

LOCAL RESOURCES
Click on your own state to see an extensive listing of local SBA resources and how to access them.

BUSINESS PLAN

Creating a business plan is your first step toward earning a living as a massage therapist. Just as you wouldn't drive from Burlington, Vermont, to San Antonio, Texas, without looking at a map, neither would it be wise to launch a business without first creating a business plan. Putting your career goals and operational plans into writing is important if you plan to be an employee, but it is essential if you plan to be self-employed. A business plan helps you define your goals and evaluate realistically whether or how those goals can be achieved. It helps you look at the immediate and near-term future as well as plan ahead for where you want to be in five years. If you plan to borrow money to fund your business's start-up, your lending institution will require a written business plan.

DUAL PROFESSIONS: MASSAGE AND MANAGEMENT

To operate a successful massage therapy practice, you must be both a skilled massage therapist and a good business manager. It's likely that your skills are stronger in one area or the other at this point, and your challenge will be to strengthen your skills where they're weaker or hire someone who can take on these responsibilities.

> Performing the best massage in the world but not being good at collecting fees and paying estimated taxes on time—and vice versa—will ruin your chances of having a healthy business.

The massage therapist who loves performing massages but is not careful about setting his or her fees appropriately, not collecting payment when it is due, or doesn't pay estimated taxes on time runs the risk of not being in business for very long. Likewise, the business manager who loves setting up spreadsheets and negotiating leases but is distracted about other issues when he or she should be giving his or her full attention to the client will also have disastrous business results.

Many clients expect massage therapists to offer a wide array of modalities and services—not just Swedish massage, but hot stone, shiatsu, and Esalen as well, and not just a telephone answering machine for taking reservations but an online reservation system where the client receives immediate confirmation.

By looking over the topics shown on the Career and Practice Planning Worksheet, you get an idea of how many areas a massage therapist must be knowledgeable about. The worksheet is not meant to overwhelm you but to organize your planning such that when you do launch your career, you will do so from a firm foundation.

Building from the ground up, you'll start with setting goals and objectives.

CAREER AND PRACTICE PLANNING WORKSHEET

This chapter is built around the topics that are typical of most business plans, and which are seen in Figure 5.9, the Career and Practice Planning Worksheet. Many other business-building tools are available from sources such as the Small Business Administration and other resources listed in this chapter.

A written business plan will be important to you for two reasons:

1 You will need the documentation if you are going to request assistance from external sources, such as applying for a business loan.
2 There is more financial investment and risk associated with starting your own business than in being an employee, so you want to be as thorough as possible in laying the groundwork before you open your doors.

Even if you do not plan to open a private practice immediately, the exercise of writing a business plan is still helpful because it makes you think about many aspects of your practice from the viewpoint of the owner. As an employee, your ability to wear the hat of the business owner will make you a strong asset.

RESOURCES FOR BUSINESS-BUILDING TOOLS

BOOKS

Abrams, Rhonda. (2004). *The Successful Business Plan: Secrets and Strategies* (4th ed.). Better Business Bureau Books.

Tiffany, Paul, & Steven D. Peterson. (2004). *Business Plans for Dummies* (2nd ed.). Wiley.

ORGANIZATIONS AND WEBSITES

bplan.com: www.bplan.com; contains templates, samples, articles, and helpful links.

Canada Small Business BC Resource Centre: www.sb.gov.bc.ca/smallbus/workshop/busplan.html

Home BizNet, a Web site specializing in resources for home businesses: www.homebiznet.net

Inc.com is a resource for entrepreneurs, and it contains a variety of tools for start-up businesses. Subscribe to Inc. magazine either online at www.inc.com or by calling 1-800-234-0999.

NOLO Law for All: www.nolo.com/encyclopedia. By going to the Business tab and choosing Small Business, you'll find a wealth of information that's helpful and straightforward.

Service Corps of Retired Executives (SCORE), a free consulting service provided by the SBA: see the government listings in your phone book for the local office or visit www.score.org

SBA Business Plan Outline: www.sba.gov/starting/indexbusplans.html

Small Business Administration (SBA), a federal agency that offers many publications and loan guarantee programs: 1-800-8-ASK-SBA or www.sba.gov

SoYouWanna.com: Website www.soyouwanna.com presents serious business plan writing in a humorous manner.

GOALS AND OBJECTIVES

Yogi Berra, a famous baseball player and coach who is equally famous for his comic wisdom, offered sage advice regarding the practice of setting goals and objectives when he said, "You've got to be very careful if you don't know where you're going, because you might not end up there." The beauty of setting goals and objectives is that they give you a roadmap that clearly marks the beginning, planned route, and final destination of your business journey. Setting goals helps you plan where you want to end up.

In determining what you want to achieve over the course of your career, you will create goals and objectives:

1 Goals are broad statements that express values or mission
2 Objectives are more specific business-oriented statements in support of your goals. They are time-bound and measurable. That is, they are stated in terms of specifically what will happen and when.

FIGURE 5.9 Career Planning and Practice Planning Worksheet

I.   PRACTICE GOALS AND OBJECTIVES

(See Marketing Plan for goals and objectives specific to marketing.)

1   What type of job are you seeking, or what type of practice do you want to set up?_____
_____

2   What are your desired working hours and number of massages per week?

Working hours _____

Number of massages per week _____

3   What are your objectives for income?

Weekly   _____

Monthly   _____

Annually   _____

4   In what time frame do you want to achieve these objectives? _____

II.   LAWS AND REGULATIONS

1   What state laws and licensing requirements, if any, govern massage therapy and bodywork?

Hours of school required	_____	_____
Practicum required	Yes	No
State licensing exam required	Yes	No
NCTMB certification required	Yes	No
FSMTB exam (MBLEX) required	Yes	No
Hours of continuing education (CE) required	_____	_____
How often CE requirements must be met	Annually	_____
	Every 24 months	_____
	Other	_____

2   What is the scope of practice for massage therapy in your state?_____
_____
_____
_____

3   What restrictions, if any, does your state place on the practice of massage therapy? (List. Use an additional sheet if necessary.)_____
_____
_____
_____
_____

4   What county or municipal laws and licensing requirements are required?_____
_____
_____
_____
_____

FIGURE 5.9 (continued)

5 What fees are required?

State registration/certification/licensing

Application fee   _____

Certification fee   _____

Renewal fee   _____

County or municipal

Business license or permit   _____

Renewal   _____

III.   INSURANCE

What insurance will you buy?

Type of Insurance	*Provider*	*Cost*
Professional liability	_____	_____
General liability	_____	_____
Property	_____	_____
Business interruption	_____	_____
Disability	_____	_____
Workers' Compensation	_____	_____
Health (medical)	_____	_____

IV.   MARKET NEED – SUPPLY & DEMAND

1 How large is the total consumer demand for massage in your market?_____
_____
_____
_____

2 What massage services are being provided already in your area?_____
_____
_____
_____

3 Describe the categories of potential clients you plan to serve._____
_____
_____
_____

4 What experience, skills, and credentials do you have that will enable you to meet the needs of this market?_____
_____
_____
_____

5 How large is the market you plan to serve?_____
_____
_____
_____

FIGURE 5.9 (continued)

6 Is the total number of clients in these categories large enough to meet your income objectives?

Yes _____   No _____

7 If not, what other client category can you target, or in what other communities or settings will you work?_____
_____
_____
_____

8 Are there other client categories that might also seek your services? If so, who, and how many?_____
_____
_____
_____

9 What other experience, skills, and credentials will you need to meet these needs?_____
_____
_____
_____

10 If you'll be working with others, how will their experience and skills complement yours in meeting the needs you have defined?_____
_____
_____
_____

V.   SERVICES AND PRODUCTS

1 What massage modalities do you plan to offer?_____
_____
_____

2 What, if any, other services do you plan to offer (such as aromatherapy, yoga, training seminars, specialty retreats, etc.)?_____
_____
_____
_____

3 What, if any, products do you plan to sell (such as lotions, vitamins, CDs, T-shirts, etc.)?_____
_____
_____
_____

4 How do the additional products and services fit in with your main practice of massage therapy?_____
_____
_____
_____

FIGURE 5.9 (continued)

VI. PRICING

1 What price do you plan to charge for each type of service or product? For each, indicate the price charged by other local sources of similar services or products.

	Your Price	Local Price
_____	_____	_____
_____	_____	_____
_____	_____	_____
_____	_____	_____

2 If your prices are different from others', explain how you will justify the difference to your clients. _____
_____
_____
_____

3 Do you plan to offer discounts? If so, for what reasons and by how much? _____
_____
_____
_____

VII. MARKETING PLAN (SEE CHAPTER 7, "SPREADING THE WORD")

1 Marketing Goals, Strategies, Objectives, Tactics

	Goals	Strategies	Objectives	Tactics
New Clients	_____	_____	_____	_____
	_____	_____	_____	_____
	_____	_____	_____	_____
	_____	_____	_____	_____
	_____	_____	_____	_____
Client retention	_____	_____	_____	_____
	_____	_____	_____	_____
	_____	_____	_____	_____
	_____	_____	_____	_____
Winning back clients	_____	_____	_____	_____
	_____	_____	_____	_____
	_____	_____	_____	_____
	_____	_____	_____	_____

2 Practice Identity

Practice name: _____

Description of targeted client type: _____

Description of practice décor:

   Exterior (signage, etc.): _____

   Interior: _____

FIGURE 5.9 (continued)

3 Advertising – Check the types you will use.

☐ Billboards ☐ Directory listings

☐ Brochure that tells about your business ☐ Links to other websites

☐ Bulletin boards at local businesses ☐ Newsletters to clients

☐ Business cards ☐ Print ads (newspaper, magazines)

☐ Cable TV ☐ Radio

☐ Direct mail ☐ Website

☐ Other: _____

Provide details of how you will use advertising to market your practice. _____
_____
_____

4 Promotions – Check the types you will use.

☐ Cross-promotions with other businesses

☐ Gift certificates

☐ Giveaways (branded/unbranded)

☐ Other: _____

☐ Other: _____

☐ Other: _____

Provide details of how you will use promotions to market your practice. _____
_____
_____
_____

5 Public Relations – Check the types you will use

☐ Presentations at local organizations

☐ Media releases

☐ Volunteer at community events

☐ Other: _____

☐ Other: _____

Provide details of how you will use public relations to market your practice. _____
_____
_____

6 Networking

List names of organizations with whose members you will network. _____
_____
_____

List other ways in which you will network. _____
_____
_____

FIGURE 5.9 (continued)

VIII.   PHYSICAL SPACE (SEE CHAPTER 3, "CREATING A SENSE OF PLACE")

1 Where do you plan to practice?

☐ Home-based practice

☐ Clients' homes (outcall)

☐ Rented or leased office space

☐ Other business location (hospital, fitness center, etc.)

☐ Corporate workplace

☐ Retail setting

☐ Other: _____   ☐ Other: _____

2 What furnishings will you need to provide in order to create the desired environment for your practice? (Enter cost under expense chart in Financial section.)_____
_____
_____

3 Will anyone else be working with you? Yes ____ No ____

If so, where will they work? _____
_____
_____

IX.   BUSINESS POLICIES

Relationship Policies

Client Related

1 State your customer service philosophy. _____

2 Specify the code of ethics your business follows. _____

3 Specify the standards of practice your business follows. _____

4 What procedures will you follow to protect our clients' confidentiality? _____

5 Your cancellation policy: _____

6 Your late arrival policy: _____

7 Your no-show policy: _____

8 Your business hours: _____

9 Your rates for services: _____

10 Your fees are: _____

11 In what instances will you offer discounts? _____

12 Under what circumstances will you provide complimentary massage? _____

13 Your policy for accepting/not accepting credit cards (and which ones):_____

14 Your policy regarding requiring payment in advance. _____
Exceptions:_____

15 Your policy regarding tips. _____

FIGURE 5.9 (continued)

16 Your policies regarding safety and security: _____

17 Your intake form includes: *Yes*   *No*

    a   informed consent   _____   _____

    b   insurance information   _____   _____

    c   assignment of benefits   _____   _____

    d   release of medical records   _____   _____

    e   contract for care   _____   _____

    f   SOAP notes   _____   _____

    g   financial responsibility   _____   _____

    h   authorization to pay provider   _____   _____

18 What is your policy about boundaries between personal and professional relationships? _____

19 What is your policy about draping? _____

20 What is your about making referrals? _____

21 What is your policy about accepting referrals? _____

22 What is your policy about accepting insurance reimbursement clients? _____

Employee Related

1 Employee work hours and days: _____

2 Employee benefits include: _____

3 What is your policy for pay increases for employees? _____

4 What are your dress and hygiene requirements? _____

5 What is your policy about employees accepting tips? _____

6 How will you protect confidentiality in communicating with employees? _____

7 What is your policy regarding employees accepting clients outside of employer's business? _____
_____
_____
_____

8 What is your requirement regarding employees signing a noncompete or nonsolicitation agreement? _____
_____.
_____
_____

9 What is your policy about reasonable causes for dismissing an employee? _____
_____

10 What is your method of conflict resolution? _____
_____

Internal Structure Policies

1 What is your plan for computer back-up and security? _____

2 How will you protect client and employee records? _____

FIGURE 5.9 (continued)

3 What is your supplier relations policy? _____

4 What is your equipment maintenance policy? _____

5 Maintenance and updating of financial records

Record	Update Frequency
Checking account	_____
Budget	_____
Ledger sheet	_____
Balance sheet	_____
Income statement	_____
Cash flow statement	_____

6 Tax return filing

Tax Form	Filing Schedule
Form 1040-ES Estimated Tax for Individuals	_____
Form 1040 U.S. Individual Income Tax Return	_____
Form 1040 Schedule C Profit or Loss from Business	_____
Form 1040 Schedule SE Self-Employment Tax	_____
Form 1065 Schedule K1 Partner's Share of Income	_____
Form W-2 Wage and Tax Statement	_____
Form 1099-MISC (report payments of $600 or more to independent contractors)	_____
Form 2106 Employee Business Expenses	_____

Other:

_____   _____

_____   _____

X.   PROFESSIONAL ASSISTANCE

For what areas will you hire professional assistance?

☐   Business consulting

☐   Contract negotiation

☐   Accounting/bookkeeping

☐   Taxes

☐   Legal

☐   Graphic design

☐   Marketing

FIGURE 5.9 (continued)

XI.   HIRING

1   Do you plan to bring others into your business?

☐   Clerical support

☐   Administrative support

☐   Massage therapists

☐   Other: _____

2   These individuals will be

☐   Employees

☐   Independent contractors

3   How do you plan to recruit individuals for these positions?_____
_____
_____

4   What training and expenses will be required?_____
_____
_____

XII.   FINANCIAL

Job Hunting Expenses   *Estimated Costs*

Printing résumés   _____

Travel to and from interviews   _____

Correspondence with interviewers and other
networking contacts   _____

Other

_____   _____

Total: $_____

Self-employed Expenses

1   How much do you need to spend on each of the following?

Expense	One-time Expense	Annual Expense	Monthly Expense
Office/practice space			
Office furnishings			
Office equipment			
Office supplies			
Massage therapy equipment			
Massage therapy supplies			
Laundry			
Utilities (heat, water, etc.)			
Business licenses/permits			
Health insurance			
Liability insurance			

FIGURE 5.9 (continued)

Property insurance	
Accountant's or bookkeeper's fees	
Attorney's fees	
Printing business cards, stationery, brochures	
Fees for professional license	
Fees for professional membership(s)	
Dues for chamber of commerce or other business/ community organizations	
Directory listings: print and online	
Digital communications (voice cell or landline, Internet connection, PDA)	
Website (designer/ maintenance)	
Property taxes (if you own your business space)	
Estimated taxes	
Continuing education	
Other	
Other	
Other	
Other	
Other	
Totals	

2 Where you will obtain the funds you need?

☐   Personal assets

☐   Partnership with others

☐   Borrow Clerical support

3 How much income do you expect to earn each month?

From massage sessions $_____

From sales of merchandise $_____

From room rental to other practitioners $_____

From other sources $_____

Total: $_____

FIGURE 5.9 (continued)

4 Does your expected level of income exceed your estimated monthly expenses?

☐ Yes

☐ No

5 If not, where will you obtain additional funds to operate your practice while you are in the development phase? (How will you support yourself until you are meeting your income needs?) _____
_____

6 At your expected level of earnings and expenses, how long will it take before you have paid your start-up costs and have begun to meet your income needs? (Consider your local cost of living and the needs of yourself and family members, if any.) _____
_____

XIII.   PROFESSIONAL DEVELOPMENT (SEE "PROFESSIONAL DEVELOPMENT BUSINESS PLAN" IN CHAPTER 8)

Professional Advocacy

Issue of importance to the profession   *How you plan to become involved with this issue.*

_____   _____

_____   _____

What is your plan for educating consumers about the profession of massage? _____
_____
_____

Allied Professions

List the allied professions with whom you plan to develop professional relationships. _____
_____
_____

What is your plan for developing professional relationships with allied professions? _____
_____
_____

What is your plan for maintaining these relationships? _____
_____
_____
_____

Continuing Education

Formal Training

1 List the continuing education requirements for renewal of your credentials. _____
_____

2 What courses or training classes do you plan to take over the next three years?

	Name of course	*Cost*	*Location*
Year one	_____	_____	_____
Year two	_____	_____	_____
Year three	_____	_____	_____

FIGURE 5.9 (continued)

Informal Training

How do you plan to continue your education through informal methods? _____
_____
_____
_____

Research

1 What is your plan for becoming research literate? _____
_____
_____
_____

2 What is your plan for becoming involved in massage therapy research? _____
_____
_____
_____

3 What is your plan for incorporating massage therapy research into your practice for client education? _____
_____
_____
_____

Supervision

1 What is your plan for incorporating professional supervision into your practice development? _____
_____
_____
_____

2 What is your plan for providing supervision to a colleague for his or her practice development? _____
_____
_____
_____

XIV. EVALUATION OF PLAN

1 What challenges do you need to address before you can implement this career plan? _____
_____
_____
_____

2 What is your plan for addressing those challenges? _____
_____
_____
_____

3 What is your time frame for addressing those challenges? _____
_____
_____
_____

GOALS

Goals—broad statements that express your business values or mission—can include both philosophical and practical statements. One way to develop goals is to answer questions such as the following:

- What kind of work do you want to do?
- Do you want to work alone or with others?
- What kind of business relationship do you want with others (as employer/employee or as partners)?
- What level of income do you want?
- For what do you want to be known?

Goals are broad statements that express your business values or mission; objectives are specific business-oriented statements that support your goals.

Your goals might be stated in several different subject areas. Examples of different types of goals include:

TYPE OF GOAL	EXAMPLE
• Short-term	Build up stamina to provide six massage sessions in one day
• Long-term (five years)	Develop a specialty in infant massage
• Financial	Pay back school loans
• Personal	Flexibility to take up to 6 weeks off per year without pay
• Client Profile	Wellness clients who are interested in learning how to optimize their health
• Employer Profile	Massage practice in an integrative health care setting that has excellent reputation among oncology practitioners

OBJECTIVES

To develop objectives—specific business-oriented statements in support of your goals—you would answer questions like the following:

- What steps do I need to take to achieve my goals?
- In what time frame do I need or want to do certain things?
- How will I know if I have met my goals? This refers to putting measurements in place so you can keep track of how close you are to reaching your goals.

Objectives that would support the first goal shown previously might be as follows:

GOAL

- Build up stamina to provide six massage sessions in one day.

OBJECTIVES

- Within one month of graduation, get a job with a business that does a high volume of massage business.
- Supplement my paid massages with two volunteer massages per week.

Very clear goals and objectives become your lighthouse when your business enters rough waters. Goals shine a light on your intended course, and objectives are the ship's rudder—they guide your way to achieving certain milestones. If either your goals or objectives become disconnected from the actual practice of your business, it's time to either rewrite the goals and objectives, or to steer your business practices closer to the intended path.

Regardless of what your specific goals and objectives are, all need to be carried out within the framework of your state and local laws and regulations.

LAWS AND REGULATIONS

In the United States, the responsibility to regulate professions that have an impact on the health, safety and welfare of the public rests with the states. Laws and regulations apply to two areas of your business. The first is those that apply to the profession of massage, such as the qualifications you must prove before you are allowed to practice massage, and the scope of practice for massage in your state. The second is the laws and regulations that apply to all businesses that operate in your state and municipality, such as business permits, health laws, and so forth.

PROFESSIONAL LAWS AND REGULATIONS

As of this writing, 38 states regulate the practice of massage therapy. In states that are regulated, you are required to hold a valid license or other form of registration/certification from the state in order to practice, or advertise to the public that you practice, massage therapy. Professional licensure laws establish a minimum level of competency necessary to safely and effectively practice.

The qualifications for licensure vary from state to state, and usually are expressed in terms of education requirements, type of exam required, and continuing education requirements. Education requirements also vary from state to state, with all requiring a minimum of 500 hours. Two states, Nebraska and New York, require 1,000 hours. Most states require passing the MBLEX (FSMTB) or the NCTMB exam, and some states have their own exam.

Requirements for continuing education range from 3 hours annually to 25 hours biennially (every two years). Some states have no continuing education requirements. Some states require annual CPR certification.

Fees for licensure also vary from state to state; some have a separate fee for the application and another for the license, and some combine them; some have a renewal fee and a fee for a duplicate license. Fees range from $20 to $300 for initial licensure.

Some states require a criminal background check and fingerprints. On the surface this might seem like an unfair practice that implies less-than-upstanding motives on the part of those who wish to become licensed. However, this law, where it is practiced, is for the purpose of screening out any individuals who have been found guilty of criminal conduct in the past and who might be intending to get a massage therapy license for the purpose of misusing it. Individuals in other health-care professions are subject to the same requirement.

For a handy reference that lists regulations by state, go to http://www.amtamassage.org/about/lawstate.html.

Similarly, many counties and municipalities also have regulations and ordinances that apply to the practice of massage.

Scope of Practice

States that regulate the profession of massage develop a specific scope of practice for the profession. A scope of practice defines the parameters of what a massage therapist is allowed to do and not to do. For instance, some states' scopes of practice say massage therapists may "treat" but may not "diagnose." Some say you may treat certain conditions if a physician has referred a patient in writing. Some states only allow those who are licensed medical professionals to use terms such as "treatment" or "medical," restricting massage therapists from using those terms for their practice. For specific examples, see Figure 5.10. Knowing your state's scope of practice is essential, not only because it is your professional responsibility to know it, but also because *not* knowing it carries the potential for significant penalties.

Failure to Comply

Most state regulatory agencies have a grievance process through which action can be taken to suspend or revoke a professional license. Reasons for such actions, as well as procedures

FIGURE 5.10
EXAMPLES OF STATE
MASSAGE LAWS

The following excerpts are partial. To see a complete document of your state's regulations, go to the state regulatory body's website or call them.

STATE MEDICAL BOARD OF OHIO

4731-1-05 Limited Practitioner: Scope of practice: massage therapy.

(A) Massage therapy is the treatment of disorders of the human body by the manipulation of soft tissue through the systematic external application of massage techniques including touch, stroking, friction, vibration, percussion, kneading, stretching, compression, and joint movements within the normal physiologic range of motion; and adjunctive thereto, the external application of water, heat, cold, topical preparations, and mechanical devices.

(B) A massage therapist shall not diagnose a patient's condition. ... In determining whether the application of massage therapy is advisable, a massage therapist shall be limited to taking a written or verbal inquiry, visual inspection including observation of range of motion, touch, and the taking of a pulse, temperature and blood pressure.

(C) [intentionally excluded here]

(D) A massage therapist may treat temporomandibular joint dysfunction provided that the patient has been directly referred in writing for such treatment to the massage therapist by a physician currently licensed pursuant to Chapter 4731 of the Revised Code, by a chiropractor currently licensed pursuant to Chapter 4734 of the Revised Code, or a dentist currently licensed pursuant to Chapter 4715 of the Revised Code. ...

(E) [intentionally excluded here]

(F) Massage therapy does not include:

(1) The application of ultrasound, diathermy, and electrical neuromuscular stimulation or substantially similar modalities; and

(2) Colonic irrigation;

(3) The practice of chiropractic, including the application of a high velocity-low amplitude thrusting force to any articulation of the human body;

(4) The use of graded force applied across specific joint surfaces for the purpose of breaking capsular adhesions;

(5) The prescription of therapeutic exercise for the purpose of rehabilitation or remediation of a disorder of the human body;

(6) The treatment of infectious, contagious or venereal diseases;

(7) The prescribing or administering of drugs; and

(8) The performing of surgery.

STATE OF WISCONSIN DEPARTMENT OF REGULATION AND LICENSING

460.13 Advertising. A certificate holder may not advertise that he or she practices massage therapy or bodywork unless the advertisement includes his or her certificate number and a statement that the certificate holder is a "certified massage therapist and bodyworker" or "certified massage therapist" or "certified bodyworker."

FIGURE 5.10
(continued)

WASHINGTON STATE DEPARTMENT OF HEALTH

RCW (Revised Code of Washington) 18.108.230

Animal massage practitioner

(1) A massage practitioner licensed under this chapter may apply for an endorsement as a small or large animal massage practitioner upon completion of one hundred hours of training in either large or small animal massage. Training must include animal massage techniques, kinesiology, anatomy, physiology, first aid care, and proper handling techniques.

(2) An applicant who applies for an endorsement within the first year following July 22, 2001, may submit documentation of a minimum of fifty hours of training with up to fifty hours of practical experience or continuing education, or a combination thereof, to fulfill the requirements of this section.

(3) Massage therapy of animals does not include diagnosis, prognosis, or all treatment of diseases, deformities, defects, wounds, or injuries of animals. For the purposes of this section, massage for therapeutic purposes may be performed solely for purposes of patient well-being.

Most regulatory agencies specify a grievance process and take action if any person or business fails to comply with the regulations.

for how to file a grievance, are detailed in the state's published regulations, and generally have to do with ethics or license validity violations.

The following are actual cases taken from Washington, Tennessee, and Ohio official state records. The names of individuals have been removed here, but the names did appear in the official records and are available to the public.

WASHINGTON STATE DEPARTMENT OF HEALTH

In November 2005 the Massage Program entered an Agreed Order with [name], licensed to practice massage [license number]. He agrees to surrender his license on allegations of inappropriate touching and disclosure of confidential information.

In October 2005 the Unlicensed Practice Program issued a Cease and Desist Order against [name]. She continued to practice massage, including treating and billing patients, after her license was expired.

In September 2005 the Massage Program charged massage practitioner [name] with unprofessional conduct [license number]. She allegedly knowingly allowed unlicensed people to perform massage on clients at the spa she owned.

STATE OF TENNESSEE BOARD OF HEALTH, BOARD OF MASSAGE LICENSURE, AUGUST 2005

- Licensee: [name of business]
  - Violation: Operating as a massage establishment without a license
  - Action: Assessed $1,400 in civil penalties and $170.00 in case costs
- Licensee: [name of individual], Unlicensed, [name of town], TN
  - Violation: Advertising using the word massage without a license
  - Action: Assessed $100 in civil penalties
- Licensee: [name of individual], LMT, [name of town], TN
  - Violation: Practicing in an unlicensed facility
  - Action: Assessed $3,400 in civil penalties

- [name, license number, and town]—Massage therapy license granted, then suspended for 90 days; interim terms and conditions established; probationary terms established, effective upon reinstatement of license. Based on massage therapist's admission of failing to provide full and accurate information to the Board on licensure application. Agreement effective 10/12/06; agreement to remain in effect for at least five years prior to any request for termination.
- [name, license number, and town]—Permanent surrender of massage therapy license accepted by Board in lieu of formal investigation by the Board related to alleged violation of the code of ethics. Effective 10/12/06.

As the previous examples show, laws that govern the profession of massage are enforceable, and you are individually responsible for knowing them and following them. If you are unlicensed or have allowed your license to lapse, if you work in a facility that is unlicensed, if you violate any code of ethics standards, if you provide inaccurate information, or if you share clients' confidential information, you run the risk of facing serious penalties. Not only do you risk doing serious, possibly irreversible, damage to your career, but to the massage profession as a whole.

Working in an Unregulated State

Many, perhaps most, massage therapists who work in states that do not regulate the profession of massage choose to follow the same practices as if they were regulated. So, some take the NCTMB exam because they want to show *Nationally Certified* after their name on a business card.

Even in states that do not regulate massage, many cities within them do. For instance, the application for a license to operate a massage practice in the city of Denver (Colorado is not regulated) requires verification that a massage therapist has taken a minimum 500 hours of training. Similarly, in Valdez, Alaska (also an unregulated state), the application for a business permit asks you to provide proof of one of the following:

- Graduate of a post-secondary education school of massage therapy which requires the successful completion of at least 500 hours of supervised instruction and which is approved by any state. *(Supply diploma or certificate of graduation)*
- Hold current, valid license as a massage practitioner from another state/city with substantially the same requirements as the City of Valdez. *(Please supply copy of license)*
- Hold current certification as a massage therapist from a national certification board or program. *(Please supply copy of certificate)*

BUSINESS LICENSES AND PERMITS

In addition to regulations that govern your professional license, state and local governments also have requirements for business licenses and permit. As just described, some of those requirements could include professional criteria, particularly in places that don't regulate massage at the state level.

Fees for business licenses and permits are not the same as fees charged by your state for a massage therapy license, which is a professional license. For instance, in Wisconsin, the Title Protection Act says you can't call yourself a massage therapist until you are licensed, or you become state registered, or become nationally certified.

As you gather information, you may discover other requirements for starting your practice, such as zoning regulations. Check with your state departments of revenue and consumer affairs, county clerk, and city hall about the following:

- State, county, and/or city massage therapist license
- City and/or county business license
- City and/or county certificate of occupancy for an office

- State and/or county dba ("doing business as") permit for operating your practice under a name other than your own
- Building permits for building or remodeling space
- Permits from your local fire, health, or police department
- Seller's permit for your state, city, or county (if you are required to charge a sales tax for selling products)
- Employer identification number (EIN) from the IRS (if you are a partnership or corporation or if you hire employees)

Even if you don't have a *place* of business—that is, you take your business off-site to such places as corporate workplaces or client's homes—you probably still need to have a business license. See the example of Salina, California, in the Spotlight on Business, "Selected Business License/Permit Fees."

To find out about local requirements for business licenses and permits, check with your state departments of revenue and consumer affairs, county clerk, and city hall.

SPOTLIGHT
ON
BUSINESS

Selected Business License/Permit Fees

Local governments may require a business license, permit, or registration. The fee may vary according to the type of business and where it is located. Here are some examples of annual fees and one-time start-up business license fees owed by massage therapists in several locations.

CITY	FEES
Lancaster, California	$125 to file, $125 annually, plus $125 per "massage technician"
Salinas, California	$225 annually for an off-premise massage business license
Denver, Colorado	$35 to file, $125 annually
Overland Park, Kansas	$300 for application
Raleigh, North Carolina	$125 to file, $50 annually
Marysville, Washington	$25 for city massage practitioner license + $50 for general business license + one-time $5 for trade name (doing business as [dba] name)
Cheyenne, Wyoming	$130 annually

Another area to research is whether you will be subject to some form of business tax by your city, county, or state. To find the requirements of your own city, contact your local government office that handles business services. You might find it listed under such names as *city clerk, tax and licensing division,* or *business license division.*

PROPERTY TAXES

If you own the property on which your practice is located, you may have to pay a state property tax. If you operate out of your home, and if you own (rather than rent) your home, the portion of property taxes you attribute to your home office would be considered an expense of your practice. For example, suppose you have set up an office that you use exclusively for your practice, and it occupies one-fifth of the square footage of your home. Usually you then can deduct one-fifth of your property taxes as a business expense; however, be sure that you do not also deduct that portion as a personal expense on your personal tax return. It is best to consult an accountant about a property tax deduction such as this.

INSURANCE REQUIREMENTS

PROTECTING YOURSELF FROM LOSS

Along with other key business concerns such as retirement planning, setting up an office, and preparing marketing materials, you should plan to use insurance to protect yourself from work time losses such as being hospitalized or losing your home in a fire. When you set up a massage therapy practice, your coverage needs increase. The following types of insurance are appropriate to massage businesses:

1 *Professional liability (also known as malpractice or personal injury) insurance.*
This coverage protects you against claims by clients that they were injured because of the work you did. It is essential for every massage therapist, and is included in most memberships to professional associations. Professional liability insurance protects the policyholder from wrongful advice or errors on the practitioner's behalf, which allegedly lead to some kind of harm to the client. It also covers claims that are related to the "scope of practice," that is, the services you provide in your capacity as a professional massage therapist.

Professional liability rates are affordable in the massage therapy profession, largely because there haven't been many claims against your peers in the profession. This absence of claims is to some degree attributable to the ethical standards massage therapists follow, and the care with which services are rendered. In order to maintain the excellent record in the profession, practitioners must abide by these guidelines:
- Do not use terms that imply that you are offering diagnoses for ailments, or treatment that addresses any ailment. Massage therapists do not have the authority to prescribe medical solutions, diagnose conditions, or offer specific treatment for cures.
- Get a second opinion from a physician if the client complains of symptoms that may suggest contraindications for massage.

2 *General Liability ("slip and fall") insurance*
This coverage protects you against claims that a person or his or her property was injured on your property or because of something you did outside your capacity as a professional (for example, spilling coffee on a client's computer). Whereas professional liability protects you from claims made due to "things you do" as a practitioner, general liability protects you from claims made due to "where you work." Since personal injury can be the basis for this type of claim, and personal injury claims can be extremely expensive, be sure your general liability insurance is in full effect when you start your practice.

> All massage therapists are required to carry general liability insurance. This coverage is usually included as part of your professional association membership.

Some issues to be aware of include:
- If you rent commercial space, the area you individually occupy will be covered by your general liability policy. Common areas, such as hallways and parking lots, will be the landlord's responsibility. You may want to verify the physical areas each policy covers with your office's rental or leasing manager.
- If you plan to work from your home, check with your homeowner agent on your general liability options and property insurance. Some residential policies make allowances for business use of property, and some don't. Some homeowners' policies have an optional "rider" that can extend coverage for business use. In unusual instances, homeowners' policies become void when there is commercial use of the property. Be diligent in checking into your specific situation.

3 *Property insurance*
This coverage pays for the loss of property as a result of specified hazards such as fire, windstorm, or theft. If you work out of your home, check your homeowners' insurance coverage. If you rent, lease, or own a separate business space, find out what kind of

property insurance you will need to cover such things as loss of equipment and supplies in the event of property damage.

4 *Business interruption insurance*
This type of coverage pays you for income lost when specified hazards prevent your practice from operating.

5 *Disability insurance*
This type of insurance provides benefits to offset some of the income you lose if you become disabled. For most massage therapists, no work means no income. Massage therapists engage in physically demanding work – work that is often interrupted due to physical illness or injury. Disability income insurance is the type of policy that provides the disabled worker with some income when he or she can't work. Variables that affect the price include:

- Term: How long will the policy pay benefits once benefits have begun?
- Waiting period: How long does the beneficiary need to wait from the point of disablement until the policy starts paying benefits? The waiting period can range from 30 days to six months.
- Benefit amount: How much of the beneficiary's income will be covered? This can range from 25 to 70 percent. Benefits are not taxable, so a 65 percent benefit is very close to actual take-home pay.
- Type of occupation: The more likely a person's income will be disrupted due to injury, the more expensive the premium will be.
- Age of the insured: The older the insured, the higher the premium.

6 *Workers' Compensation*
If you employ others, you need to be aware that the government requires all businesses with at least one employee to have workers compensation coverage. It provides comprehensive coverage to any employee who is injured on the job. Workers' compensation provides:

- Payment of medical bills related to an on-the-job injury
- Payment of rehabilitation services resulting from the injury
- Payment of lost income while the employee convalesces
You have the option to purchase workers' compensation coverage that covers yourself, but you do not need to do so. You do need to purchase coverage as soon as you employ someone.

Many people mistakenly believe that workers compensation is a government-backed form of insurance. In fact, workers compensation policies are issues by private insurance carriers in compliance with government regulations. Rates are based on occupational ratings. The more dangerous a job, the higher the premium. The classification of your employee and their annual earnings will determine the annual premiums.

7 *Health (medical) insurance*
Health, or medical, insurance covers the cost of personal injury or illness. Personal medical insurance is in effect regardless of your activity that leads to the injury or illness, whereas workers' compensation covers only issues directly related to work.

Medical insurance plans vary tremendously in cost, from low-deductible, all-inclusive (very expensive), to high-deductible, "catastrophe" plans (more affordable). As opposed to liability policies in which the insurance covers injury to others, medical insurance covers injury to the policyholder. Since injuries can be very expensive to address, purchasing medical insurance should be a very important component of your business planning.

As a small business owner, here are some issues to be aware of:

- You may be able to purchase personal medical insurance under a group plan. This usually means a better price but fewer options.

- If you have workers' compensation coverage for yourself, you are only partially protected. If you break a leg skiing, you are not covered by workers' compensation.
- Check with your accountant to see if you can claim the cost of medical insurance as a pre-tax expense in your business.
- Medical insurance addresses your medical bills but not your lost income due to an inability to work. Only workers' compensation and disability insurance cover lost income.

Source: Insurance section adapted from Barry Antoniow. *Kiné-Concept Institute Business Success Workbook.* Fredericton, New Brunswick, Canada: Kiné-Concept Institute Maritimes. Used with permission.

Although accidents aren't always preventable, avoiding risk is your best course of action. See Figure 5.11 for tips on how to minimize your loss in the event you do encounter disaster.

RESOURCES FOR DISASTER PREVENTION/RECOVERY

Emergency Management Guide for Business & Industry:

www.fema.gov/business/guide

General overview of emergency planning: www.ready.gov/business/plan/index.html

Firsthand accounts of how business owners successfully prepared for the unexpected:

www.disastersafety.org

FIGURE 5.11
Disaster Preparation Tips

CUT YOUR RISK

BACK IT UP. Keep copies of important computer and paper-based files, and store them in another location away from your office, preferably in another building. Preparing now prevents frustration later when you have to scramble to replace lost paperwork and then retype or refile what you find.

CREATE A RESOURCE LIST. Finding trustworthy, experienced contractors to help restore your office is more likely to happen when you have the time to check references and comparison shop. Have the names and contact information for important resources, such as electricians, plumbers, painters, and carpenters, ready before you need them.

PLAN YOUR BACKUP OFFICE. Identify possibilities for continuing your practice in the event that you suddenly lose access to your office. Keep a list of clients who could receive care at home. Stockpile supplies such as lotions and towels off-site, where they will be easily accessible.

CREATE A MUST-CALL LIST. An emergency call list with phone numbers and addresses for key contacts will make it easier to spread the word about your disaster and get your recovery plan under way. Include information on employees, local and state emergency management agencies, clients, suppliers, realtors, financial institutions, insurance agents, and claims representatives.

INFORM YOUR CLIENTS. Let your clients know what's happening, where and how to continue treatment, and when you expect to be back in operation. Such consideration makes it easier to maintain the relationships you've worked hard to build.

Source: Insurance Information Institute, in Julie Monahan, "Business Insurance for Better or Worse," *mtj,* Spring 2004. Used with permission.

WHERE TO FIND INSURANCE COVERAGE

Ask your professional association about professional and general liability coverage, plus a variety of other optional business, health, disability, term life insurance, medical and accident insurance, and business equipment and overhead insurance. You should seriously consider purchasing the optional types of insurance to protect yourself. After all, if you cannot work, you cannot practice.

MARKET NEED

BACKGROUND

In the next part of your business planning, you will address the environment in which you plan to work, defining the needs that exist and how you hope to meet the needs you have identified. A key to success in establishing the level of market need, also known as demand, in your area is striking a healthy balance between your enthusiasm about the growth of massage therapy, and fear of too few clients. You want to be realistic—neither too optimistic nor pessimistic—about how many clients you can attract to your business. Reasons for enthusiasm include the increasing acceptance of alternative health therapies, increased third-party insurance reimbursement for massage services (see Chapter 6, section "Client Insurance Billing and Reimbursment"), and more research to prove the efficacy of massage (see Chapter 8, section "Research").

In addition, you will describe your qualifications, and the qualifications of others working with you, to meet those needs. As you start planning for your practice, this section will help you describe to others why they should choose you as a provider of massage. How do you differ from other practitioners in your area? What will attract clients to your business?

> The concept of supply and demand is that you want to find out how many people might get massage (demand) and how many massage therapists are working in your area (supply). Creating demand is the challenge of good marketing.

ESTIMATING SUPPLY AND DEMAND

At the local level, your success as a massage therapist requires that your services meet a need in the market or community where you practice. Whether they will or not depends on the demand for massage and how well that demand is met already by other massage therapists. If the existing demand is less than the supply, consider how you can educate people about the benefits of massage and thus increase the demand for it, such as volunteering at community outreach events. See Chapter 7 for strategies and tips on increasing demand and visibility.

By getting to know the local market in your community and surrounding areas, you identify the potential for your practice. This is a three-step process:

1 *Estimate current supply*: Estimate the number of practitioners already offering massage and whether they practice full-time or part-time. This tells you how much existing supply already exists in your community.
2 *Estimate total demand*: Estimate the demand for massage in your market—that is, the number of clients (massage consumers) in your area times the number of massage sessions you estimate they will get per year.
3 *Calculate unmet demand*: Subtract the current supply from the total demand. The remainder is the unmet demand. If the unmet demand is large enough to support your career goals, there is a good opportunity for you in the community you have chosen.

See the section "Career Trends in Massage Therapy" in Chapter 1 for data about consumer growth trends in our profession, or view the latest survey results at the American Massage Therapy Association website (www.amtamassage.org and click on News Room). This site contains the latest consumer survey information as well as recent statistics regarding the demand for massage.

Estimating Supply

Look at the number of massage therapists currently serving your market's need for massage. Other massage therapists can help you build awareness of massage's benefits, but, of course, clients of theirs might not be clients of yours. You should be aware of all sources of massage in your community. Related professions might be considered secondary competition, such as chiropractors, physical therapists, or estheticians. In some cases you might collaborate with them to expand your mutual client bases, and in other cases their clients would not see a massage therapist in addition to seeing them. Figure 5.12 shows a process for doing this. It makes a few assumptions:

- Half of the massage therapists work full-time, giving an average of 24 hours of massage sessions per week. (More than 19 hours of massage sessions a week is considered full-time.)
- The other half give an average of 10 hours of massage sessions per week.
- All the massage therapists work 50 weeks per year.
- Clients receive eight massage sessions per year.

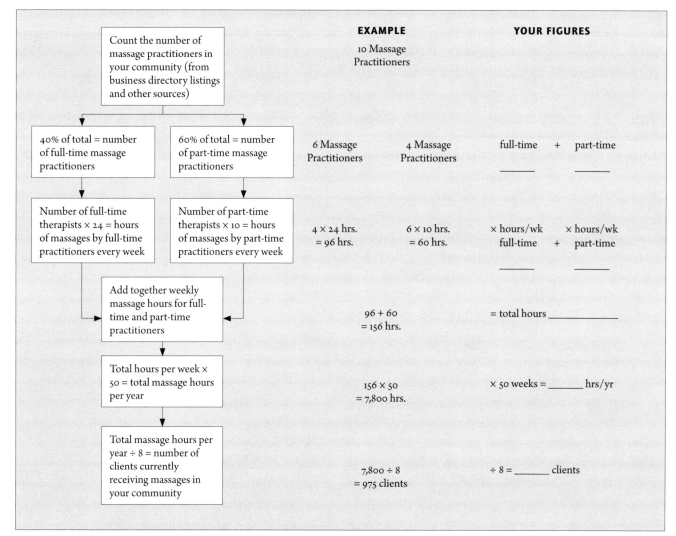

FIGURE 5.12
Estimating Supply

If you can estimate in which ways your community is different from the national average, you can adjust the numbers accordingly.

ESTIMATING DEMAND

If you know general or national patterns, you can begin to investigate the demand in your area, and how well that demand is being met already. For help in identifying national patterns, see Chapter 1, section "Career Trends in Massage Therapy." The survey information is based on adult Americans living in private households. To estimate the number of people in that category where you live, you might ask your local library, city hall, chamber of commerce, or business development to help you.

Do you expect local demand to be typical of the national average? If so, use an estimate of about 17 percent of the local adult population who live in private households to predict the number of potential clients of all the massage therapists in the area over a one-year period.

Using survey information and knowing national patterns can be helpful when you are trying to make estimates. Keep in mind that this is not an exact science, and there is no one formula that is going to give you the "right" answer. In addition to making a quantitative estimate, you will want to factor in anecdotal information, such as:

- How many people do you know personally who might be clients?
- How interested are your community's residents in alternative health methods?
- Do you intend to open your business in an area that has a massage therapy school? (The assumption here would be that the supply of trained massage therapists could be higher than average in a town with a massage training school, versus in a town that does not have such a school.)

Use your estimates to calculate demand, as shown in Figure 5.13.

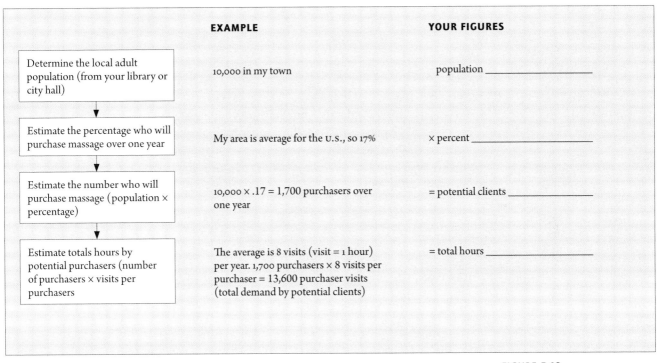

FIGURE 5.13
Estimating Demand

ESTIMATING UNMET DEMAND

The potential for your practice is high if you estimate that the total demand for massage therapy is much greater than the number of clients already being served by practicing massage therapists. There should be enough unserved clients to keep you busy for the number of hours you want to spend giving massages. Here is how to determine the potential for your market (Figure 5.14):

1 *Supply:* Show your community's supply of total massage hours now provided by massage practitioners
2 *Minus Demand:* Subtract the demand for massage hours from the number of supply hours
3 *Unmet Demand in Hours:* The difference gives you the number of unmet demand hours.

4 *Unmet Demand in Number of Clients:* Divide unmet demand hours by eight (if you think the number of clients visits per year in your community is the same as the national average) to get the number of potential clients in your community.

	EXAMPLE	YOUR FIGURES
Supply: Show your community's supply of total massage hours now provided by massage practitioners	7,800 hours supply	supply: _____ hours
Minus Demand: Subtract the demand for massage hours (demand) from the number of supply hours	Minus 13,600 hours demand	– demand: _____ hours
Unmet Demand in Hours: This gives you unmet demand, stated in massage hours	Equals 5,800 unmet demand hours	= _____ unmet demand in hours
Unmet Demand in Number of Clients: If divided by eight, it gives you unmet demand stated in number of clients	5,800 divided by 8 = 725 potential clients	÷ 8 = _____ unmet demand in number of clients

FIGURE 5.14
Estimating Unmet Demand

YOUR POTENTIAL

The next step is determining how many of those potential clients you want to attract to your business. This is estimating your individual supply of hours, as shown in "Estimating Your Potential" (Figure 5.15). To do this, you would calculate how many massage hours you want to provide each week. Keep in mind that your work hours will be longer than your massage hours because of the time it takes to perform all the non-massage duties required to operate your business.

1 Hours you want to work each week
2 Times weeks you want to work each year
3 Divided by eight visits per client per year
4 Equals number of clients you need
5 Your Potential—Compare your supply to the unmet demand. If your supply is less than or equal to the unmet demand, your potential is promising. If your supply exceeds the unmet demand, you will have to expand the area you serve, choose a less-served area, or develop marketing and education strategies to increase the demand in your area. See Chapter 7 for marketing strategies that can help you develop a plan.

If you live in an area where you feel confident that you will have enough clients to support your business as you need, or that you will be able to increase the number of clients through your marketing efforts, you are ready to develop the rest of your plan.

SERVICES AND PRODUCTS

Determining the services and products you want to make available to your clients requires more than a casual decision. Some massage therapists like to focus on a particular modality of massage they enjoy performing. Others see massage as part of a wider range of related services they want to offer clients. (If so, they may have to meet additional qualifications to provide those services.) Yet others seek professional growth and enjoyment from teaching, research, and public education. If you want to do several of these, you will need

	EXAMPLE	YOUR FIGURES
Work Hours per Week: How many hours do you want to work (giving massgaes)?	20 hours per week	_____ hours per week
Work Weeks per Year: Multiply times weeks you want to work each year	× 50 weeks = 1,000 hours per year	× _____ weeks per year = _____ hours per year
How Many Clients: Divide by eight visits per year (at one hour each) to estimate how many clients you need	1,000 ÷ 8 = 125 clients	÷ 8 clients visits per year = _____ number of clients
Your Potential: If your individual supply is less than or equal to the unmet demand, potential is promising. If your supply exceeds the unmet demand, you will have to expand the area you serve or develop marketing and education strategies to increase the demand.		

FIGURE 5.15
Estimating Your Potential

to plan carefully the number of hours you will spend on giving massage sessions and other income-related activities, allowing enough time for your other professional activities.

Some practitioners also sell merchandise. The products most frequently sold are oils, body lotions, aromatherapy products, and vitamins. Others sell CDs, books, jewelry, magnetic and crystal products, and apparel. If you want to do this, first consider how well the products fit within the scope of your practice. Do they support and further your image as a professional?

Before deciding to sell products, consider the drawbacks as well as the potential for profit. Liability issues might arise if a client is allergic to a particular oil or lotion, or if a client misuses a movement aid. Individuals can order products so inexpensively off the Internet that many product vendors are finding it difficult to make a profit unless they can order in bulk. Bulk requires additional storage space and more inventory control. On the other hand, if you buy a small quantity and keep your prices low, your profit disappears. Some practitioners feel that selling products detracts from their main focus, providing massage.

In some states, licensure for massage therapists prohibits the sale of products. Find out whether your state imposes such restrictions. If product sales are permitted, and the products you want to offer are a good fit, plan for the expense and time of ordering the products, keeping them in stock, and maintaining adequate records of inventory and sales, including the collection of any sales tax.

PRICING

Whatever array of services and products you offer, you will need to make pricing decisions. The guideline most often heard is about $1 per minute, which can be higher in urban and tourist areas, lower in rural areas, and higher for specialty types of massage, such as hot stone massage.

Keep in mind that what you charge per hour for massage times the number of hours you work is the total *gross* income from your practice, before all taxes and expenses. For example, if you charge $60 for a 1-hour massage session, with 20 hours of actual massage sessions per week, your gross practice income (before expenses) would be $1,200, and for 50 weeks would be $60,000.

In setting your fees, consider your costs, as well as prices for comparable products and services from other sources. In general, conform to local pricing custom. If you charge more, clients may conclude you are too expensive. If you charge less, they may not value your services as highly. By charging less than the going rate, you will also soften the local market and thus make it more difficult long-term for you and your peers to charge fees that cover your expenses. Either way, your pricing should support your business objectives, which could be: a) to provide low-cost massage by focusing on high volume and minimal expenses, or b) to provide premium-priced massage by offering specialty modalities and customized services to a targeted client group. Your pricing objective should be supported by your marketing plan (see Chapter 7), which effectively communicates to your targeted clients either why your prices are a value (if they are lower than average) or are worth more (if they are higher than average) than similar services.

Whether or not to discount services has long been a matter of discussion among massage therapists. Professional and ethical guidelines do not take a specific stance on discounting. Many experienced massage therapists express strong opinions, pro and con, about the practice of discounting their services. Those in favor of it view it as a good promotional technique. They offer discounts to attract clients who see massage as a luxury they cannot afford but who might become regular clients once they experience the benefits of one. They offer volume discounts as a way of expressing gratitude to clients who get regular massages from them.

The other view of discounts is that massage therapy is a health benefit, and health professionals do not offer their services at a discounted rate. Some massage therapists feel that the practice of discounting diminishes the professionalism of massage therapy. Offering a free massage to a client who has referred other clients to you, however, might be viewed as a thank-you or as a payment in lieu of advertising expenses.

Yet another aspect of discounting concerns whether you are willing to discount your fees in order to be included in insurance companies' or HMOs' list of approved providers. The pros and cons of participating in these programs are extensive, and there is no clear "best practice" among massage therapists regarding participation. See Chapter 6 for more information regarding becoming an approved health care provider for purposes of insurance reimbursement.

See Spotlight on Business, "Is Discounting a Good Tactic?" for more discussion points.

Whether or not to discount your prices is seen by some as a professional issue.

SPOTLIGHT
ﾘﾘﾘﾘﾘON
BUSINESS

Is Discounting a Good Tactic?

Most experienced massage therapists have strong opinions regarding whether discounting their services is a good marketing tactic or not. Both sides of the issue are shown below. Except in provinces that prohibit discounting, you will have to decide for yourself whether to include it among your marketing practices.

PROS

A good promotional technique that could attract someone who has never tried massage before

Might attract clients who see massage as a luxury they cannot afford but who might become regular clients if they experience the benefits of one

An expression of gratitude to regular clients, as in volume discounting

Might be considered a type of advertising expense if you use it to thank a client for referring a new client to you

Might be required as a condition of participating in an insurance company's or HMO's list of preferred providers

Could be valuable in promoting the profession in support of a cause, such as attracting attention to Breast Cancer Awareness Month or AMTA's National Massage Therapy Awareness Week™

CONS

Massage is a health benefit, and health professionals do not offer their services at a discounted rate

Detracts from professionalism; for example, dentists do not offer a bonus card for every 10th cleaning free

An option to discounting that would not detract from professionalism is a sliding scale of fees to those in reduced financial circumstances

Some Canadian provinces prohibit discounting

Clients might come to expect discounts if they are offered too easily

BUSINESS POLICIES AND PROCEDURES

Business policies and procedures are the nitty-gritty of how you will conduct your business on a day-to-day basis. Internal structure policies and procedures concern areas such as bookkeeping, purchasing, office administration, and filing taxes. Relationship policies concern how you interact with clients, employees, and coworkers.

This section describes the policies a practitioner needs to set up prior to opening the doors of a practice. Whether as an employee, a sole proprietor, or in a practice that requires managing personnel, it is best to have policies to follow. Policies are statements of what is and is not acceptable; they help you set boundaries. When you encounter a situation governed by a policy, it gives you a basis for handling the situation. For example, if your practice has a policy not to accept tips, whenever a client offers a tip you can simply reply, "Thank you, but our policy is not to accept tips."

When you establish your business, you will want to have policies in place from the beginning. Policies not only help standardize your treatment of clients in ways that promote excellent service, but they also help decrease your business risk. You might want to ask your legal advisor for input regarding areas in which policies should be written—such as protocol if someone should be injured while at your premises, access for clients with disabilities, or expectations of employees.

You may find that you will change your policies over time, often based on client feedback, employee feedback, and your own changes in opinion about what works and what feels right. Your annual planning calendar should indicate a time each year, or more frequently if appropriate, to review your policies and determine whether they need to be modified.

If you have your own office, you will have wide latitude in setting policies. If you work at client sites, you will be influenced by your clients' policies, but as an independent contractor you still will have some latitude in governing what is acceptable. Establish your policies before you look for work and discuss them when you interview. Be sure that your policies are compatible with those of the organizations at which you consider working.

Examples of where you might want to create policies are shown in Figure 5.16. The purpose of developing policies in each of these areas is not to become "policy heavy" in your business. Rather, considering each of these areas for potential policy development gives you the opportunity to decide whether a particular policy could help you set a solid foundation that could support a therapeutic relationship with your clients and help you reduce your business risk.

When you have finished developing your policies, prepare printed versions in a

Having a policy in place doesn't mean that your business is inflexible. Be aware that one policy does not fit all situations, and judge the appropriate enforcement of them.

FIGURE 5.16
Policy Categories

RELATIONSHIP POLICIES

CLIENT RELATED

Customer service philosophy

Code of ethics

Standards of practice

Clients' confidentiality

Appointment cancellation

Late arrival/No-show

Business hours

Fee structure

Discounts

Complimentary massage

Credit cards (if and which ones)

Payment in advance (and exceptions)

Acceptance of tips

Safety and security

Injury protocol in event of injury or illness

Client intake form (inclusion of possible options: informed consent, insurance information, assignment of benefits, release of medical records, contract for care, SOAP notes, financial responsibility, authorization to pay provider)

Boundaries between personal and professional relationships

Draping

Making referrals

Accepting referrals

Accepting insurance reimbursement clients

EMPLOYEE RELATED

Employee work hours and days

Employee benefits

Pay increases for employees

Dress and hygiene

Employees accepting tips

Confidentiality in communicating with employees

Employees accepting clients outside of employer's business

Employee noncompete or nonsolicitation agreement

Reasons for employee dismissal

Method of conflict resolution

INTERNAL STRUCTURE POLICIES

Procedure for opening the office

Computer back-up and security

Protection of client and employee records

Update schedule for financial records: checking account, budget, ledger sheets, balance sheet, income statement, cash flow statement

Tax returns forms and schedule

Supplier relations

Equipment maintenance

manual for you and each of your employees, if any. Post important policies such as your professional association's code of ethics and your cancellation police where you and clients can easily refer to it. During your employee meetings, review and discuss policies periodically. You should request that your employees sign a statement acknowledging that they have read and that they understand the policies of your business.

PROFESSIONAL ASSISTANCE

As you think about the policies you want to help govern your business operations, there might be a few areas where you realize you could use a little help. When it comes to getting professional assistance from business experts, this is a great time to start a massage therapy practice. Not only is the demand for massage growing, but so has society's appreciation of the importance of small businesses. As a result, experts in a variety of fields stand ready to help you with the technicalities of setting up and operating your practice.

Most people who start a massage therapy practice do so because they want to help others feel better through massage. However, working for yourself, either alone or in a practice with others, imposes additional responsibilities. Indeed, when you are self-employed you have to wear more than one hat. Sometimes you will wear your massage therapist's hat; at other times you will don your administrator's hat and deal with issues such as legal requirements, money, taxes, insurance, and office space.

You must become knowledgeable about many regulations and procedures in order to set up your massage therapy practice. The information is available if you spend hours in the library, on the Internet, or on the phone. However, unless you have a law degree and an accounting degree, it may be more efficient—and wiser—to call in experts in fields such as law, accounting, marketing, and graphic design.

As you plan how to set up your practice, and even after you get started, be aware of the knowledge and expertise you have, the areas you can learn quickly, and those aspects that might better be given to someone with professional training in relevant areas. To get a sense of the areas in which you will want to seek out professional assistance, take a look at the checklist in Figure 5.17. It helps you identify where you want to draw upon professional assistance, and where you want to handle the business on your own.

> The types of professional assistance you might want to hire include attorneys, accountants, tax consultants, financial consultants, marketing specialists, and graphic designers.

WHERE TO FIND PROFESSIONAL ASSISTANCE

You can get the most help and advice from someone who understands your situation if you work with professionals who specialize in small businesses and in the health care field. Try to find professionals who already have experience with other massage therapy practices. To identify such people, talk to your mentors and to other massage therapists. Ask questions such as:

- Do you do your own _____ or hire it done?
- Who is your accountant (or attorney, marketing professional, etc.)?
- How long have you used this person's services?
- In what ways has this person been helpful to you?
- Did you have any difficulty in working with this person?
- How has using this person benefited you, as opposed to doing the same work yourself?
- Do you think this person would be helpful to me? How? (Or why not?)

When you have gathered two to three recommendations that sound promising, set up appointments to meet with these professionals. When you call, ask questions such as:

- Have you worked for other massage therapists?
- Have you worked for other businesses my size?
- Will there be a charge to have an initial meeting? If so, how much?

In your meeting, ask about the professional's experience in relevant areas, such as home offices or lease negotiations. As you listen, consider whether you have good rapport with this person. If a problem occurred, would you feel comfortable calling on this person for help? After you find someone who seems well qualified and able to communicate with you, you can move on to establishing a professional relationship with him or her.

Sometimes there is a fee for an initial consultation, because the time of a skilled professional is valuable. Be sure to clarify this point before agreeing to an appointment.

FIGURE 5.17
Do It Yourself or Hire Someone?

For each item, check whether you can and want to do it, want to learn it, or want to hire professional assistance.

	CAN DO IT	WILL LEARN IT	HIRE SOMEONE
1 Find out what licenses I need	☐	☐	☐
and what papers to file.	☐	☐	☐
2 Learn the zoning laws.	☐	☐	☐
3 Negotiate a lease.	☐	☐	☐
4 Set up financial recordkeeping system.	☐	☐	☐
5 Keep financial records up to date.	☐	☐	☐
6 Prepare tax returns.	☐	☐	☐
7 Design logo, brochures, business cards.	☐	☐	☐
8 Develop marketing plan.	☐	☐	☐
9 Write a newsletter.	☐	☐	☐

IF YOU WANT SOMEONE TO DO:

Items 1–3, contact an attorney

Items 4–6, contact an accountant

Item 7, contact a graphic designer

Items 8–9, contact a marketing communications specialist

COMMUNICATION STRATEGIES FOR ESTABLISHING PROFESSIONAL RELATIONSHIPS

Consider whether you will want professional advice on an ongoing basis. Most massage therapists have sole proprietorships (that is, they have no partners or shareholders), so their businesses are fairly simple, and they don't need constant or frequent advice. More than likely, they simply want help getting started, preparing tax returns, finding a new location, or developing marketing materials. Thus, probably you will want to be billed only for specific tasks you request the person to do. In that case, you need to agree on what the scope of the services will be and what the professional will charge you. Be sure to agree to the services in writing before the professional begins any work for you.

Sometimes the fee for a professional service may seem high. Suppose your accountant says preparing your year-end taxes will cost $250, and you think, "But that's only for routine paperwork! I did all the bookkeeping myself." Instead of jumping to the conclusion that the accountant's fee is too expensive, compare the fee to doing the work yourself. How long would it take you to prepare the same tax return? If you have a variety of expenses related to an office, equipment, and employees, you will need days to be sure you have prepared your returns correctly. Could you earn as much as the accountant's fee by providing massage during that same time period? And which task would you rather be doing?

NEGOTIATING A GOOD RATE

Before you contact any professional to discuss your needs, you will want to be clear about what you want that individual to do for you. If you decide to interview more than one person for the same assignment, presenting a clear list of what you need will help you compare different individuals' proposals on and apples-to-apples basis.

Professional negotiators recommend getting a few written quotes for the service you request, and then comparing the quotes. This gives you some negotiating power if you want to bargain. Be sure that the person charging less is offering you services of acceptable quality and scope. Before you decide to interview and request quotes from several professionals, however, reflect on how you like to be treated by your clients and whether you find price comparisons the best way to choose a professional. You might decide to favor one professional, based on the recommendation of friends and associates, and see first whether you can negotiate an acceptable fee with that person.

Compared to the real cost of doing everything yourself, a professional's fees may look like a bargain. However, if the professional you want to work with charges fees that seem high, negotiate with him or her for something you can both accept. Explain that the fee quoted is a lot of money for your practice to afford but that the professional was recommended highly, that you had hoped the fees would be less, and that you want to work out a reduced fee with him or her. The professional may be willing to be flexible about the fee, especially if you mention that as your practice grows, you will renegotiate your arrangements.

If you do not have the money to pay a professional's fee, an alternative is to explore whether the person is willing to consider a barter arrangement. With barter, you exchange services or goods that you agree are of more or less equal value. Tax requirements for bartered business are somewhat complex, so if you do participate in a barter system, be sure to consult with your accountant about any tax-related issues.

VALUED ADVISORS

Some people are reluctant to hire an accountant or attorney because they believe they can handle the paperwork of tax returns, financial statements, and contracts themselves. That may be true, but accountants and attorneys with small-business experience do not do only paperwork; they can be valuable advisers, as well.

If you establish a relationship with professionals you trust, you can consult them whenever you make a significant move, such as setting up a new location, buying a big piece of equipment, or considering an ongoing business relationship with a spa. The professionals may be aware of financial or legal implications that had not occurred to you, or they may suggest ways to protect yourself or to get the most out of your efforts.

HIRING OTHERS

MAKING THE DECISION TO HIRE OR NOT

You might decide, even when you first open your practice, that you want to work with others, in either an employer/employee or a client/independent contractor relationship. Information regarding the hiring process is contained in this section.

Hiring employees improves the capacity of your practice to serve clients. It also greatly increases your responsibilities as a business owner. Therefore, before you take that step, review the pros and cons listed in Figure 5.18, and then answer these questions:

- Am I thinking about hiring someone because I know or anticipate that I cannot complete the workload myself? If so, do I want to manage a larger practice? Would I be more satisfied if I consider other ways to keep up with my workload (such as reducing the number of clients I serve or contracting with an accountant to do my taxes)?

- Am I thinking about hiring someone because I don't want to work alone? If so, would I be more satisfied with a partner, or with becoming an employee myself?
- Would I obtain the same benefits more easily by subleasing space (if my lease permits), charging therapists a share of the rent or a percentage of their fees?
- Am I thinking about hiring someone because I would like to focus on the administrative and marketing aspects of the practice and let someone else handle the massage sessions? If so, do I have the necessary skills?
- Will I have enough work for the person I hire to do year-round? Or am I anticipating being too busy during a peak period that will later level off?

It is crucial to be confident about your decision to hire someone. That person will depend on you for a livelihood. You may want to start with a trial period to decide whether you and the employee are compatible, during which time you can pay the person as an independent contractor and there are no promises of an employment offer. Otherwise, if you decide a few months later that you cannot afford or really do not want this person to work for you, your hiring decision was ultimately harmful to the employee.

Despite the complexity and expense of hiring employees, they can be valuable assets of your practice. When you hire the right people, you establish ongoing ties with them and have the right to expect them to meet your guidelines. Entering into an independent contractor arrangement is simpler in some ways. However, you have less control over what the contractor does. The samples of an employment agreement (Figure 5.19) and independent contractor agreement (Figure 5.20) illustrate the issues to consider when setting up both types of arrangements.

If you determine that you want to hire an employee, you must begin advertising the position and selecting candidates. Ask for leads from people who might know someone

FIGURE 5.18
Pros and Cons of Hiring Others

PROS

More people can get more work done.

A qualified employee can be expected to follow your work systems and policies.

An employee can expand the range of skills and talents available in your practice.

A greater number of people can increase scheduling flexibility.

Another person builds teamwork and can make you feel less isolated.

CONS

You must spend time training and supervising each employee.

You must learn and comply with a host of labor and tax laws.

You must have a consistent source of funds to pay your employee (and the withholding taxes).

Your practice could be liable for harm done by an employee in the course of his or her employment.

You must cover for an ill employee, which can require double work or rescheduling clients.

You might have to address issues related to absenteeism or unsatisfactory performance.

with the desired background. You can also look in job banks and place advertisements in local and trade publications. Many people advise against hiring friends and family for the obvious reason that, if the employment situation doesn't work out for one or both of you, you don't want to have harmed an ongoing family or personal relationship.

Decide ahead of time qualifications that are important to you. How will you measure those qualifications in an employee? Will you need advice from a mentor or someone else with experience in making employment decisions? Be sure to check the references provided by each applicant, especially when hiring someone who will work with your money or your clients.

Several important laws affect how you will go about the process of screening candidates and selecting an employee. To avoid costly lawsuits, be sure to learn what you can and cannot ask. Some of the laws to become familiar with are as follows:

- Antidiscrimination laws such as the Civil Rights Act prohibit you from selecting employees on the basis of race, color, religion, sex, national origin, age (for adults under age 70), or marital status.
- The Americans with Disabilities Act (ADA), passed by Congress in 1990, forbids discrimination based on disability (assuming the person can do the essential tasks of the job). It requires that employers make reasonable accommodations to permit disabled employees to do their work. It also requires that businesses serving the public make their facilities accessible to people with disabilities. (See Chapter 3, "Creating a Sense of Place," for more information about ADA requirements.)
- The Federal Immigration Reform and Control Act of 1986 requires that employers verify that they hire only people who are eligible to work in the United States. However, it also prohibits employers from discriminating against eligible foreign workers.

FIGURE 5.21
Questions to Ask and Avoid
During an Interview

QUESTIONS TO ASK A POTENTIAL EMPLOYEE

"What have you learned during your experience as a massage therapist?"

"Our office is open on evenings and weekends. Will you be able to work those hours?" (to learn whether a person will be available on evenings and weekends)

"Some of the potential clients in our area speak Spanish, Portuguese, and possibly other languages. What languages do you speak fluently?"

QUESTIONS TO AVOID ASKING A POTENTIAL EMPLOYEE

"How old are you?"

"What is your religion?"

"Do you have young children?" (to learn whether a person will be available on evenings and weekends)

"What country are you from?"

"What kind of an accent do you have?"

FIGURE 5.19 Sample Employment Agreement

EMPLOYMENT AGREEMENT

This Agreement is hereby made this _____ day of _____ between
_____ and _____ , located
(NAME OF MASSAGE THERAPY PRACTICE)   (NAME OF EMPLOYER)
at _____ , and _____ , residing
(STREET, CITY, STATE, ZIP)   (NAME OF MASSAGE THERAPIST)
at _____ , for the performance of massage therapy services according to the
(STREET, CITY, STATE, ZIP)
following terms and conditions.

TASKS TO BE PERFORMED, EQUIPMENT, AND SUPPLIES

In the source of his/her employment, Employee shall primarily be required to perform massage therapy. However, when not engaged in treatments, Employee shall be required to assist other practitioners with clients, perform clerical duties when requested, and participate in the cleaning and organizing of Employer's place of business.

Employee shall provide massage therapy services only within the limits and scope of his/her knowledge and/or licensure, if applicable, and is responsible for maintaining appropriate certification and licensure (including all costs thereof unless otherwise agreed).

Employee shall dress in a style consistent with Employer's image, possibly including uniforms, the purchase of which may or may not be the responsibility of Employee.

Employee shall maintain client records in the manner prescribed by Employer, the same to be and remain the property of the Employer.

Employer shall supply, at its sole expense, all equipment, tools, materials, and/or supplies necessary for Employee to perform the tasks set forth in this Section 1, including but not limited to (list all equipment and supplies that will be supplied, such as room, table, draping linens, lotions, music, marketing materials, etc.).

Employee shall be required to work _____ hours per week according to a schedule set forth by Employer.

COMPENSATION

Employer shall pay Employee twice monthly at a rate of $_____ per hour worked, plus an additional $_____ per half-hour massage performed and $_____ per one-hour massage performed.

Employer shall be responsible for paying all required federal, state, and local withholding, Social Security, and Medicare taxes.

Employee may participate in any Employer benefit programs as Employee becomes eligible.

Employer shall provide/maintain insurance coverage for workers' compensation, unemployment, general liability, fire, and theft.

FIGURE 5.19 (continued)

TERMS AND TERMINATION

This Employment Agreement is effective as of the date first written and shall continue in effect until terminated by either party, given reasonable cause, or upon thirty (30) days written notice to the other party of the intention to terminate.

The following are considered reasonable cause:

Failure of either party to perform the obligations under the Agreement;

Action by either party exposing the other to liability for property damage or personal injury;

Violation of applicable ethical standards and/or loss of licensure for services provided;

Failure of Employee to maintain the standard of service deemed appropriate by Employer; or

Employee's engagement in any pattern or course of conduct on a continuing basis that adversely affects Employee's, Employer's, or other employees' ability to perform services.

Termination of this Agreement shall not relieve Employer of its obligation to pay Employee any monies due and owing even if such monies are not due until after the date of termination.

ADDITIONAL PROVISIONS

Employee has the right to perform similar services for others during the term of this Agreement; however, such services may not be performed on Employer's premises.

During the term of this Agreement and for six (6) months after termination, Employee shall not solicit Employer's clients or employees for private practice.

Any of the Employee's independent marketing materials must be approved in advance prior to the materials' display or distribution to Employers' clients.

The provisions of this Agreement shall be interpreted and enforced in accordance with the laws of the State of _____. All unresolved disputes arising out of this Agreement shall be finally settled by Arbitration.

This document represents the entire agreement of the parties with regard to the employment of Employee and supersedes any and all prior written or verbal agreements. Any amendments to this Agreement must be in writing and signed by both parties. Should any provisions of this Agreement be deemed unenforceable, the remainder of the Agreement shall continue in effect.

_____   _____
Employer Signature   Employee Signature

_____   _____
Employer Name   Employee Name

FIGURE 5.20 Sample Independent Contractor Agreement

INDEPENDENT CONTRACTOR AGREEMENT

This Agreement is hereby made this _____ day of _____
                                                              (MONTH/YEAR)
between _____, a provider of massage therapy services with its
        (NAME OF MASSAGE THERAPIST / MASSGAE THERAPY BUSINESS)
principal office located at _____ ("Independent Contractor")
                           (STREET, CITY, STATE, ZIP—CAN BE THERAPIST'S RESIDENCE)
and _____, with its principal place of business at
    (NAME OF CLINIC / BUSINESS / HIRER OF SERVICES)
_____ ("Client"), for massage therapy services at Client's place
(STREET, CITY, STATE, ZIP)
of business according to the following terms and conditions:

1. SERVICES TO BE PROVIDED, EQUIPMENT AND SUPPLIES

1.1 Independent Contractor agrees to provide Massage Therapy Services ("Services") at Client's place of business to patrons of Client within the limits and scope of its knowledge and/or licensure, if applicable. (A specific description of the massage therapy services that will be made available can be included.)

1.2 Independent Contractor shall supply, at its sole expense, all equipment, tools, materials, and/or supplies necessary to provide the Services except for the following: (List any equipment, etc. provided by Client, e.g., massage table or chair, towel cart, room with sink and countertop, appointment scheduling for Client's patrons, insurance billing).

1.3 Independent Contractor shall set his/her own hours, but agrees to be available to patrons of Client a minimum of hours per week. For scheduling purposes, Independent Contractor shall attempt to be available on a consistent basis, and agrees to notify Client if his/her availability will change.

2. FEES AND TERMS OF PAYMENT

2.1 Independent Contractor shall set the fee charged to patrons of Client for Services.

2.2 Client shall collect said fees on behalf of Independent Contractor and shall remit the same to Independent Contractor, less 30% to cover operating expenses, room rental, and equipment usage, within five (5) days of receipt.

2.3 No federal, state, or local income tax or payroll tax of any kind shall be withheld or paid by Client on behalf of Independent Contractor. Independent Contractor shall be solely responsible for all tax liability.

3. EXPENSE REIMBURSEMENT, FRINGE BENEFITS, INSURANCE

3.1 Client shall not be liable to Independent Contractor for any expenses paid or incurred by Independent Contractor unless otherwise agreed to in writing.

3.2 Independent Contractor acknowledges that because it is not an employee of Client, it is not eligible for and shall not participate in any employer benefits of the Client, including pension, health, or other fringe benefits.

3.3 No worker's compensation or unemployment insurance shall be obtained by Client concerning Independent Contractor or employees thereof. Independent Contractor agrees to comply with all workers' compensation laws concerning its business, and if a corporation, shall provide Client a certificate of workers' compensation insurance.

3.4 Independent Contractor shall furnish Client with current certificates of coverage and proof of payment for all applicable insurance, including, but not limited to liability insurance with minimum coverage of $_____ aggregate annual and $ per occurrence.

4. TERM AND TERMINATION

4.1 This Contract for Massage Therapy Services is effective as of the date first written above and shall continue in effect until terminated by either party upon thirty (30) days written notice to the other party.

4.2 Termination of this Contract shall not relieve Client of its obligation to pay Independent Contractor any monies due and owing even if such monies are not due until after the date of termination.

FIGURE 5.20 (continued)

4.3 This notice required by this Section shall be sent to the respective addresses set forth above via (I) certified mail, return receipt requested, (II) overnight or second-day courier delivery, or (III) facsimile message if a confirmation copy is sent by one of the methods set forth in subsection (I) or (II). Notice shall be deemed given when received by the other party.

4.4 During the term of this Contract and for six months after termination, Independent Contractor shall not solicit patrons or employees for any purposes.

5. ADDITIONAL PROVISIONS

5.1 By Independent Contractor. Independent Contractor agrees and acknowledges:

a. that it will dress in a style consistent with the Client's image;

b. that it will maintain patron records in a mutually agreed manner;

c. that all patron records remain the property of Client unless otherwise agreed;

d. that it has no authority to enter into contracts or agreements on behalf of Client;

e. that it has complied with all applicable laws regarding business permits, certificates, and/or licenses that may be required to carry out the Services to be performed under this Contract;

f. that it will indemnify and hold Client harmless from any and all loss or liability arising out of or incurred as a result of the performance of Services under this Contract.

5.2 By Client. Client agrees and acknowledges:

a. that Independent Contractor may perform similar services for others during the term of this Contract;

b. that it has no control over the means, manners, and method by which the Services are provided;

c. that it has no authority to enter into contracts or agreements on behalf of Independent Contractor.

5.3 Assignment. This Contract may not be assigned, in whole or in part, by either party without the express written consent of the other party.

5.4 Choice of Law. Any dispute under this Contract or related to this Contract shall be decided in accordance with the laws of the State of _____.

5.5 Entire Agreement. This document represents the entire agreement of the parties with regard to the provision of Services and supersedes any and all prior written or verbal agreements. Any amendments to this Contract must be in writing and signed by both parties. Should any provision of this Contract be deemed unenforceable, the remainder of the Contract shall continue in effect.

_____   _____
Independent Contractor Signature   Client Signature

_____   _____
Independent Contractor Name   Client Name

To help you comply with these laws, Figure 5.21 gives a few examples of questions to ask and questions to avoid during an employment interview. Be sure you are fully knowledgeable about what is and isn't acceptable to ask.

COMPLYING WITH EMPLOYMENT LAWS

Many employers do not understand all of the employment laws. Fortunately, common sense and fairness go a long way toward preventing problems:

- To comply with antidiscrimination laws, be very specific about the qualifications for which you are looking. Think in terms of abilities, education, and experience. When you interview candidates, focus on those qualities, rather than other attributes that may not be relevant. For example, wrongfully assuming that the gender, age, or race of a potential employee will make clients uncomfortable is discriminatory. Further, it prevents you from seriously considering candidates who may be well qualified and skilled in client relations.
- The same advice holds for complying with ADA. Focus on qualifications. If you wonder how a person with a disability could perform a particular task, you can ask the applicant to perform it so you can see if he or she is able to accomplish the task. You might have to make some accommodations, but if you have made your practice accessible to clients already, chances are it will be accessible to most employees.
- To comply with the Immigration Reform and Control Act, you must be sure everyone you hire provides proof of citizenship or authorization to work in the United States. Have each person complete Form I-9, Employment Eligibility Verification, available from the U.S. Immigration and Naturalization Service. The INS also publishes an information handbook titled "Handbook for Employers: Instructions for Completing Form I-9." To ensure compliance or to get answers to any questions about these laws, obtain advice from an attorney familiar with employment matters.

Weigh the advantages and disadvantages of hiring an employee or bringing in an independent contractor before you make a decision about working with others in your practice.

USING INDEPENDENT CONTRACTORS

Given the many requirements involved with hiring employees, many massage therapists prefer to get help in the form of independent contractors. An independent contractor provides a service, but not as an employee. From the employer's perspective, the main differences are summarized in Figure 5.22. To avoid the obligations of an employer by contracting with people instead of hiring them, be sure to treat them as independent. In other words, you cannot tell independent contractors how to go about the work they do

FIGURE 5.22
Employee vs. Independent Contractor

EMPLOYEE	INDEPENDENT CONTRACTOR
Can be instructed to follow specific rules and procedures	Must be free to determine how and when to complete a project
Has an ongoing work relationship	Relationship is limited to scope of project(s) contracted for
Paid a wage or salary, with taxes withheld by employer	Paid a fee, with no taxes withheld
Share of social security taxes paid by employer	
It is reasonable to expect benefits in addition to pay	Responsible for paying self-employment tax
Employment relationship is covered by labor and antidiscrimination laws	Expects a fee large enough to provide self with benefits
Expected to work agreed-upon hours	Contracting relationship is legally covered by contract law
	May not be available for projects when needed

for you—what steps to follow, what hours to be in the office, and so on. Instead, you must agree on the end result of the work, and then select people you trust to do the job in an acceptable way.

An independent contractor will charge a fee that amounts to more earnings per hour than an employee would receive. After all, independent contractors need to earn enough to provide their own benefits, such as insurance, time off from work, and so on. On the other hand, you are paying independent contractors only for the specific tasks contracted for (not for the occasional slow week or for benefits), so you may still come out ahead.

Communications Strategies for Negotiating an Independent Contractor Agreement

Whether you intend to become an independent contractor or you hire one, the issues surrounding negotiating a contract concern fair treatment of both the person who is contracted and the business that does the contracting. Both parties need to feel confident that the business arrangement will lead to mutual value and a good working relationship with each other and with your mutual clients. As you enter into contract negotiations from either side of the negotiating table, you will want to discuss the following areas:

SERVICES, EQUIPMENT AND SUPPLIES

- Will the independent contractor provide his or her massage table, linens, oils and lotions?
- Who pays for laundry?
- How much flexibility will the independent contractor have in furnishing/decorating the session room?
- What does the business offer in terms of privacy for clients, control of heat/air in the session room, restroom proximity, and other amenities?
- Will the receptionist at the business make appointments for the independent contractor? Who pays the receptionist?
- Will the independent contractor work during set hours, or only by appointment? If only by appointment, will the session room be available at all times?
- Does the independent contractor set his or her own policies regarding cancellation, tipping, appropriate dress, etc.?
- Does the independent contractor have the authority to sub-contract to another practitioner and allow that person to use the same space?

FEES AND TERMS OF PAYMENT

- Who sets the independent contractors' fees?
- Who collects payment from clients?
- Will the business do any advertising or marketing of the independent contractor's services?
- Who pays for business cards that show the business as the contact information?
- Will the independent contractor rent space from the business?
- Will the independent contractor pay the business a percentage of fees from massage sessions?
- Will the business guarantee a minimum number of clients or fees to the independent contractor per month?
- Does the independent contractor or the business have the ability to set a maximum number of appointments per week or month?
- Is the fee percentage split based on a specified number of massage appointments per week or month?
- Does the fee percentage split stay the same regardless of the number of appointments?
- If the independent contractor brings in his or her own clients, is the fee percentage split the same as when the business generates the appointment?

EXPENSE REIMBURSEMENT AND INSURANCE

- Are there any expenses of the independent contractor for which the business will be responsible?
- What documentation does the business require that shows the independent contractor's paid liability insurance coverage?

ADDITIONAL PROVISIONS

- Who owns client records?
- What credentials does the business require that show the level of training of the independent contractor?

TERMS AND TERMINATION

- What is the duration of the independent contractor agreement?
- What are the terms for ending the agreement prior to its expiration date?

WORK HOURS AND SCHEDULING

Your business plan should describe anyone who will work with or for you, as well as the number of hours you want that person to work, or the number of sessions you want per week. For a basis of comparison, see Figure 5.23, which shows that the highest number of average hours worked per week is in spas and health clubs.

SEGMENT OF MASSAGE THERAPIST TYPE	AVERAGE HOURS PER WEEK PROVIDE MASSAGE THERAPY
Sole practitioner	18
Contractor	19.1
Spa/salon	22.8
Health care	21.6
Health club	23
Full-time employee	32
Part-time employee	17.7

Source: 2007 *Massage Therapy Industry Report* (November 2007), conducted by North Star Research on behalf of American Massage Therapy Association.

FIGURE 5.23
Hours Worked Per Week

RESOURCES FOR FINDING MASSAGE THERAPISTS TO HIRE

Placement offices and job postings at schools provide relevant training referrals from friends and colleagues

Placing want ads in local newspapers

Ads for massage therapists in the AMTA Job Bank: www.amtamassage.org

Want ads in massage-related magazines and journals (e.g., *mtj*, *Massage Magazine*, *Massage Today*)

RESOURCES FOR EMPLOYMENT LAWS

U.S. Department of Labor (compliance with employment law): www.dol.gov/compliance.

Fred Steingold & Amy Delpo (2005) *The Employer's Legal Handbook* (NOLO).

Equal Employment Opportunity Commission—information about antidiscrimination laws and Americans with Disabilities Act: 1-800-669-4000 or www.eeoc.gov.

Immigration and Naturalization Service (www.ins.usdoj.gov), or get the phone number for your local office from the government pages of your phone book.

Information about the Immigration Reform and Control Act

FINANCIAL

FINANCIAL OBJECTIVES AND PLANS

The financial section of your business plans seems on the surface as though it might be the toughest part to construct. But it's really just a matter of compiling the costs associated with all the business components you've been making decisions about up to this point.

Be as specific as you can about your financial objectives and plans. You need to be sure you can afford your plans. Completing all the information in the Financial section of your business plan will help you decide whether you need to modify your plans in order to be profitable.

To complete the financial section of your career planning worksheet, you will need to estimate your start-up costs, your monthly expenses, and your revenues. This is similar to when you estimated supply and demand of your client base and the number of available massage therapists in your area, but this adds in the financial overhead not included in the supply and demand model. These are the categories to plan for:

START-UP COSTS
- Printing business cards, stationery, brochures
- Dues for professional association membership and other business organizations, such as chamber of commerce
- Correspondence with professionals and other networking contacts
- Cost of setting up office and/or practice space in home or other location
- Rent (and initial deposit) for office/practice space
- Purchase of equipment and supplies
- Fees for professional services, such as attorney, accountant, graphic designer
- Government fees, such as license, business license tax, or incorporation fees
- Liability insurance
- Other costs

ESTIMATING MONTHLY EXPENSES
- When you create your business plan, make an estimate of your monthly expenses. These expenses are likely to fall into the following categories, as shown on the Career and Practice Planning Worksheet:
- Marketing communication pieces, such as brochures, signs, and ads
- Rent/mortgage payments for your work space
- Supplies
- Merchandise to sell
- Loan payments
- Phone and utilities
- Employees' pay
- Professional services, such as attorney and accountant
- Taxes (property, business, income)
- Insurance (liability, disability, health)
- Membership fees
- Continuing education
- Professional publications
- Other expenses, such as equipment, school loans, and laundry

ESTIMATING MONTHLY REVENUES
- Your revenues are likely to fall into three primary categories:
- Revenue from massage sessions
- Revenue from product sales
- Fees from associate who shares space with you (if any)

BREAKEVEN ANALYSIS

When you estimate your revenues and expenses, you may be surprised at how long it will take you to break even. See Figure 5.24 for an example of how to calculate whether your monthly expenses and revenue will allow you to break even. If your first estimate shows that you expenses will be higher than your revenue, see if you can adjust your estimates by planning to work a few more hours each month or reducing your expenses, while still staying within a realistic framework.

When you are satisfied with your estimates, convert the estimated revenue into the number of clients you will need to meet your target for breaking even:

- Estimated monthly revenue
- Divided by your hourly fee
- Equals number of massage hours per month

FIGURE 5.24
Breakeven Analysis

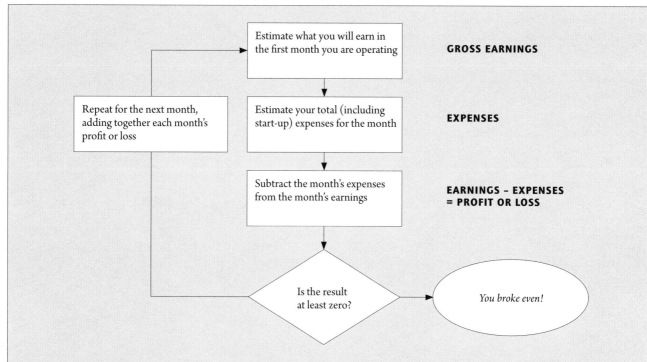

When you estimate your revenues and expenses, you may be surprised at how long it will take you to break even. To continue your breakeven analysis, adjust your estimates. For example, to break even sooner, try working a few more hours each month. Estimate the change in monthly revenues and expenses. Now redo the breakeven analysis with your new numbers.

When you are satisfied with your estimates, convert the estimated revenue into the number of clients you will need to meet your calendar for breaking even:

- Estimated monthly revenue $ _____

- Divided by your hourly fee   ÷ _____

- Equals number of massages per month   = _____

- Divided by number of massage hours   ÷ _____
  for an average client in a month

- Equals number of clients per month   = _____
  to achieve estimated revenue

As you complete your breakeven analysis and review the other ideas in this section, you may realize that you need another source of funding to pay your bills as you get started. Some people are fortunate enough to have a spouse, family member, or other person who will provide for their financial needs while they work toward financial stability.

If you need some other source of funding, can you take on a full- or part-time job to cover expenses while getting started as a massage therapist? (Be sure the job leaves you with enough energy to do your best as a therapist.) Other ways to get funding are to borrow from a bank or credit union, or to form a partnership with someone who has the money to invest. If you are starting out on your own, your credit cards are an easy source of funds … but be careful! It is easy to run up big bills without really thinking through how to make the monthly payments that must follow soon after. When you can't pay the total owed in full at the end of billing period, credit card interest rates and late fees can spiral out of control very quickly.

PLANNING FOR RETIREMENT

When you are 20 or 30 years old, retirement seems very far away. When you are in the midst of setting up a practice, you are facing many expenses, and this can hardly seem the best time to be thinking of setting money aside for later. However, the sooner you start putting some money into an IRA or other investment, the better off you will be. In Canada, the IRA-equivalent is the Registered Retirement Savings Plan, or RRSP. Compound interest makes the value of your investment rise faster over time. If you save for forty years instead of for twenty, you save for twice as long but earn far more than twice as much. Thus, the sooner you start saving, the more you can benefit from this "magic" of compound interest.

The financial protection that comes from careful recordkeeping can also result from planning for retirement. Someday you will probably want to rest from your successful career. Therefore, you will need to attend to the financial needs of retirement. The specific approaches available to you will depend somewhat on whether you are an employee or operate a business (including a sole proprietorship). Keep in mind that if you have employees but provide retirement benefits only to yourself, you probably will not be able to deduct the cost of these benefits from your business profit.

Most people try to balance risk with return by using more than one method of saving for retirement. A financial adviser can be very helpful when you are making these decisions.

By beginning now to plan for retirement, you will have a nest egg and be able to enjoy what you do even more. Each month, set aside money for taxes and for retirement savings. In later years you will reap the benefits and be glad you prepared. For this reason, it is a good habit to start your retirement plan when you start your practice. Refer to Figure 5.25 for a chart that shows how the concept of compound interest makes your money work for you.

If you get in the habit of using your credit card when you run out of cash, be aware that high interest rates and penalties can spell disaster in just a matter of weeks or months.

Having "extra money" to put into a retirement fund is a luxury few people enjoy, so make retirement savings a required and inflexible part of your financial plan even when it doesn't seem that you can afford it.

FIGURE 5.25
The Power of Compound Interest

APPLYING FOR FUNDS

If you want to get funding, whether by borrowing from a bank or by sharing ownership (as in a partnership or corporation), you will need to present your plans in an organized way. People who invest in your practice will want some assurance that you will use their money wisely. One way to demonstrate this is to prepare a business plan. To do so, use the

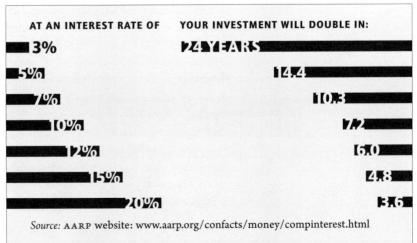

AT AN INTEREST RATE OF	YOUR INVESTMENT WILL DOUBLE IN:
3%	24 YEARS
5%	14.4
7%	10.3
10%	7.2
12%	6.0
15%	4.8
20%	3.6

Source: AARP website: www.aarp.org/confacts/money/compinterest.html

RESOURCES FOR SAVING FOR RETIREMENT

PROFESSIONALS

Accountant

Insurance agent (who may get a commission for selling you something)

Certified Financial Planner (typically will charge a fee for advice, but will not get commissions for selling you something)

Employer's (or spouse's employer's) human resources department

WEBSITES

Fidelity Retirement: http://personal.fidelity.com/planning

Quicken financial software: www.quicken.com

Yahoo! Personal Finance: http://finance.yahoo.com/retirement

BOOKS

Knight, J. (2006). *Retiring Wealthy for Dummies.* United Kingdom: Wiley.

Orman, Suze. (1999). *The Courage to Be Rich: Creating a Life of Spiritual and Material Abundance.* New York: Riverhead Press.

Orman , Suze. (2000). *The 9 Steps to Financial Freedom: Practical and Spiritual Steps So You Can Stop Worrying.* NewYork: Crown Books.

Zelinski, Ernie J. (2004). *How to Retire Happy, Wild, and Free: Retirement Wisdom that You Won't Get from Your Financial Advisor.* Berkeley, CA: Ten Speed Press.

information in the Career and Practice Planning Worksheet, to write a report with the following categories:

- Summary—your goals
- Laws and Regulations—a description of the laws and regulations that apply to your business and a statement of how these requirements will be satisfied.
- Market Need—a description of the demand already met by other massage therapy practitioners in your area, your target market (the categories of clients you plan to serve), and your qualifications to meet those needs
- Services and Products—a description of the services and products you plan to offer, their cost, and your pricing plan.
- Marketing Communications—this section identifies how you will using marketing to attract new clients and retain them, and the ways you will use marketing communications tools (business cards, brochures, etc.). (See Chapter 7.)
- Physical Space—a description of where you will practice and how that space will be furnished
- Business Operations—a description of your business policies and working operations, such as who you will work with and how you will provide for adequate staffing and training
- Financial—your needs for start-up funding and where you plan to get the funds; your projected monthly revenues and expenses, including the expense of paying off any loans; the value of your practice's assets (such as equipment you have already obtained for the practice) and liabilities (any money you owe).
- Conclusion—how your plans will enable you to meet your financial objectives

You will also need to attach relevant documents. Depending on your circumstances, these might include résumés of key people (including yourself), letters of recommendation, tax returns for the past three years, proof of liability insurance, and brochures or other marketing literature for your practice.

BUYING, SELLING, AND CLOSING A PRACTICE

BUYING A PRACTICE

Buying someone else's established practice has several advantages. In a competitive environment, buying an already-successful practice equates to eliminating some level of competition and acquiring already-established clients. This allows you to spend less time and money recruiting new clients than you would have to do if you were creating a new practice from the start. It also saves you the step of evaluating and purchasing such items as office and massage equipment, office and massage supplies, and computer systems—a time-consuming and costly step in establishing a practice.

The cost of a practice is determined by its hard assets (furniture, equipment, etc.), soft assets (projected expenses of unpaid balance of the lease, insurance premiums, etc.), and its goodwill. Goodwill is the reputation of the practice in the community, the loyalty of the practice's clients (the likelihood that they will remain as clients after the purchase), and the value of the working relationships between the practice and such businesses as suppliers, creditors, insurance companies, health care partners, and business organizations. The most challenging part of this process is appraising the value of the practice's goodwill. Business consultants generally estimate the value of goodwill to be 30 to 40 percent of the practice's annual gross income. As a buyer, you might want to negotiate a purchase price that may be based partially on client retention as measured after a stated period of time. The value of any asset is in its worth to the buyer, not to the seller. The seller might greatly value an asset of the business that you, the buyer, don't think you'll ever make use of—in which case it is of little value to you. See Figure 5.26 for tips on assessing income from the practice.

One way to enhance the value of goodwill is to negotiate a period of transition with the seller, during which the seller and buyer work together before the seller leaves the

FIGURE 5.26
Assessing Practice Income

ASSESS THE GROSS INCOME FOR EACH OF THE PRECEDING FOUR TO FIVE YEARS.

Assessing four to five years, rather than looking at just the previous year's income, shows possible cycles in the practice's income. Be wary if the seller implies there is unrecorded cash income. There is no value to unrecorded cash income because there is no way to prove or measure it. Such a statement on the part of the seller should cause the buyer to question other information being provided.

ASSESS THE NET INCOME FOR EACH OF THE PRECEDING FOUR TO FIVE YEARS.

Calculate the ratio of net income to expenses. An experienced consultant can give you a range of ratios that fall within expectations of a healthy massage business. If the business's ratio is higher in expenses and lower in income than what is advisable, determine whether this is due to something you can fix, such as poor management or ineffective scheduling systems.

IDENTIFY THE SOURCES OF THE INCOME.

What is the balance of direct-paying clients versus insurance payors (third-party reimbursement)? Of the insurance payors, what is the length of time between billing date and income receipt? Are third-party reimbursement clients a category of clients you had hoped to include in your practice? Are the direct-paying clients likely to continue doing business with the practice when the original owner has left?

practice. This helps ensure client loyalty, maintain effective referral networks, and establish important working relationships between the buyer and suppliers, and related businesses.

SELLING A PRACTICE

It might seem odd to consider the idea of selling your practice while you're just getting started in planning it, but the topic is included here because it might, at some point, be an idea you will want to consider. For the time being, you can earmark this section and come back to it when you are wildly successful and are thinking about next steps.

Whatever direction your career in massage therapy takes, you may decide at some time in the future to shift the focus of your professional life. If this happens, you may need to decide what to do with the assets of your practice. Your choices depend in part on the form of ownership you have:

- If you formed a corporation, it is most likely that you would sell the assets of the business, pay any debts owed by the business, and distribute the net proceeds of the liquidated business to the shareholders/owners.
- If you formed a partnership, you and your partners can agree to dissolve the partnership (or you can leave the partnership, in which case it dissolves). Your partnership agreement will state what share of the assets each partner owns, and you are free to dispose of your assets as you see fit. Or you can find someone else to take your place in the partnership. If the other partners agree, the partnership continues without you. Finally, you and the partners can agree to sell the partnership to someone else.
- If you are a sole proprietor, you own all of the business's assets and are responsible for all of its liabilities. You can sell the assets yourself, and use them to pay off your liabilities. Another option is to sell the practice to someone else who will then operate or liquidate.

Expect that any potential buyer will want a close look at your business records so you should have them ready before you offer your business for sale. It is wise to have prospective buyers sign a confidentiality agreement so that if they decide not to go through with the purchase, any proprietary information about your business will be protected. When selling a practice, as with starting one, getting the advice of an expert (e.g., accounting, legal) will enable you to act with full understanding of tax and other implications and help you arrive at a fair deal. See Figure 5.27 for tips on selling a practice.

Business brokers and appraisers can help you determine the value of your business. An accountant with experience in such transactions can also help you arrive at a fair selling price. A review of practice-selling and practice-buying consultants' advice yields a wide range of what a practice is worth—anywhere from 45 percent of annual gross receipts to a full year's gross receipts. So, retaining knowledgeable legal and financial advice is essential.

CLOSING A PRACTICE

If and when the time comes that you choose to close your practice, you will want to do so in such a way that you control your expenses, retain valuable assets, and maintain your goodwill with clients, suppliers, and the community. Figure 5.28 contains a checklist that may be helpful to you.

EVALUATION OF YOUR PLAN

In the final section of the Career and Practice Planning Worksheet, evaluate your plan. Do your ideas support the basic goals you recorded at the beginning of the worksheet? If not, change either your career objectives or the details of your plan. Take another look at your expenses—Can you save money on supplies? Do you need to hire an employee right away? Can you start out with used office furniture? It is better to make changes in the planning stage than to waste precious time, money, and energy on a plan that doesn't hold together solidly from the outset.

FIGURE 5.27
Six Tips on Selling
a Practice

1 Consult with knowledgeable legal, financial, and business specialists who have experience in selling massage therapy practices.

2 Don't sell in desperation. Plan to sell your practice far enough in advance that you can consult with experts, make a solid business plan, and take your time to find a good buyer whose qualifications match your business and clients' needs.

3 Set a reasonable price for your business. Remember that sellers usually overstate the value of goodwill (such as customer loyalty and reputation in the community), and buyers prefer the bulk of their purchase price to be in hard assets, which may be depreciable for taxes.

4 Get your paperwork in order, and have your accountant review your financial records prior to putting your practice up for sale.

5 Anticipate that a potential buyer will scrutinize every detail of your practice, and that the buyer probably won't be as complimentary toward your business as you think is fair. Keep in mind that this is a business transaction, not a social transaction.

6 While your business is on the market, keep your staff and your clients happy. You want to do everything you can to make the buyer feel confident that buying your business is a good and profitable decision.

FIGURE 5.28
Checklist for Closing
a Practice

Notify your clients that your practice will close on such-and-such date, thank them for their past business, and assure them that all client records will be destroyed.

Request final statements from your suppliers, and determine whether unopened merchandise may be returned for credit. Pay any balance owed or request any refund due to you.

Maintain your office insurance coverage until your office is officially vacated, and then cancel your policy and request a refund of any unused premium. Be sure to retain copies of all old policies.

Do not cancel your professional liability insurance if you plan to continue practicing massage in any capacity.

Notify utilities, including telephone and Internet access, of the date you wish service discontinued. Find out from your voice provider the options regarding how calls to your disconnected number will be handled. (You might be able to refer callers to a new number, or just notify them that the number has been disconnected and that no other number is available.)

Keep business checking account open for three months after your practice closes. This allows for any outstanding checks to clear. However, if you have any automatic debit arrangements for paying bills, be sure to get written confirmation of the date those payments will end. Keep all records. Check with your accountant regarding any other issues of which you should be aware.

File necessary final tax returns.

Leave a forwarding address with the post office.

Discontinue magazine subscriptions and asked for a refund or notify distributors of a new address.

Write "Retired—Return to Sender" on all junk mail.

Cancel or change status in professional organizations.

Send personal letters of appreciation to individuals who have helped you in your career.

Donate books and other assets/supplies you won't be using to a nonprofit organization. Retain your receipts for tax purposes.

Securely store all legal and insurance files.

Source: Adapted from Professional Management and Marketing, 3468 Piner Road, Santa Rosa, CA 95401; tel. 707-546-4433; info@practicemgmt.com; www.practicemgmt.com.

SUMMARY

Launching your practice means putting your dreams and ideas into action. Your career as a massage therapist empowers you to make many decisions about where you will work and how your workplace will look and feel. Whether you decide to provide massage as an employee or provide it through your own business, your practice will carry its own identity in terms of your technical and client-care skills.

If you seek employment as a massage therapist, you would start by creating goals and objectives, just as you would do if you were starting a business. You would learn about prospective employers in your area, create your résumé and cover letters, and practice appropriate interview strategies before going on your first interview. The result of thorough planning is getting a job that helps you build a satisfying career, even if your first job is a stepping stone to a more suitable job later.

When you first enter the profession, you will need to decide whether you will be self-employed or employed by someone else. If you choose self-employment, you will then decide whether your business will be a sole proprietorship, a partnership, or a corporation. If you are self-employed and you work at a site other than your own practice, you will probably be considered an independent contractor. The IRS makes a distinction for tax purposes between employee and independent contractor, and it's important to clarify which one you are.

Creating a business plan is important because it allows you to develop short-term and long-term goals that will direct your career, whether as an employee or self-employed. After you decide on your goals, you will develop objectives that essentially give you an action plan for achieving your goals. The sections of a business plan may include: 1) goals and objectives; 2) laws and regulations; 3) insurance; 4) the supply and demand of your market; 5) services and products; 6) your pricing plan; 7) marketing communications plan; 8) physical space; 9) business policies and procedures; 10) professional assistance; 11) your hiring plan; 12) your financial plan; and 13) your plan for professional development.

In creating your business plan, you will need to learn what is required of your business in terms of local licenses and permits, zoning requirements, and insurance. If your plan includes hiring employees, you will need to understand employment laws and hiring practices. You will also want to become familiar with professional assistance that is available to you so you can decide whether you want to learn to do specialty tasks, such as bookkeeping, yourself, or to hire someone else to do it for you.

Enjoy making all the decisions required in the initial stages of launching your career, because they enable you to practice your profession in the way you have envisioned.

REVIEW QUESTIONS

1 What skills do you need for the process of finding a job?
2 Create an effective strategy for job hunting.
3 What are the pros and cons of a sole proprietorship, a partnership, a corporation, and a limited liability company?
4 What are the components of a business plan?
5 For what purposes would you use a business plan?
6 Where would you go to find out what the scope of practice is for massage in your state?
7 If your state regulates massage, what are its qualifications for becoming licensed?
8 If your state does not regulate massage, what local qualifications apply to becoming licensed to open a massage business?
9 How can you identify the supply of and demand for massage therapy in your community?
10 What are some of the pros and cons of selling merchandise?
11 What factors influence pricing of your services?
12 In what four areas might you establish policies that will govern your business?

13 What are three important steps to consider if you want to sell your business?
14 Describe why a person might choose to buy an existing business rather than building his or her own business from the start.
15 Why is it important to evaluate your business plan before you try to implement it?

Chapter 6
Managing Your Practice

The best management system is transparent to clients—it is the underpinning of the business that facilitates your ability to extend skilled and nurturing touch to clients.

CHAPTER OVERVIEW

- Financial Management
- Taxes
- Client Records Management
- Client Insurance Billing and Reimbursement
- Time and Schedule Management
- The Automated Office
- Human Resources Management
- An Employee's Perspective: A Practice within a Business
- Chapter Summary

CHAPTER OBJECTIVES

1 Describe the pros and cons of hiring professional bookkeeping or accounting services for your business.
2 Identify four types of financial reports and their purpose.
3 Describe how to collect on an invoice if your client is slow to pay.
4 List the types of taxes for which your business is liable.
5 Identify at least five deductions that you might be able to claim on your income tax.
6 Describe the types of client records you must maintain.
7 Describe the issues for and against accepting client insurance payments.
8 Identify strategies for effective management of the work environment.
9 Identify legal considerations that affect you if you have employees.
10 Describe how your massage practice is like your own business even if you are not self-employed.

Your purpose, regardless of your specific goals and objectives, is to care for your clients, earn enough money to support your needs, and have fun while doing it. Good planning in setting up your systems, and prompt attention to maintaining them, will allow you to minimize the time you spend managing and administering them.

FINANCIAL MANAGEMENT

Good financial management is a learned skill that allows you to continue doing what you went into business for in the first place—to give massages. Once you grasp the importance of a few key financial reports, you will appreciate how helpful they are in letting you view your practice's financial health. Not only are financial records a requirement of satisfying federal, state, and sometimes local tax laws, but they are also beneficial to your business in other ways:

- They will serve as your early warning system, to alert you to trends and patterns that might need to be corrected in order to become or remain profitable.
- They can be a key input into your marketing plans, as they can help you figure out which kinds of clients are most profitable.
- They are helpful in providing information to others who need to know about the business aspects of your practice (for example, lenders or buyers of the practice).
- Your clients may want or need information about their expenses. A bill from you shows what they owe, and a receipt shows what they paid. These forms also tell what products or services they received, as well as the date of the service.
- You (and your accountant) will need a record of how much you have earned and what, if anything, your clients still owe you. The amount they owe is an asset of your practice.

The creation of these financial reports requires regular and systematic recordkeeping. Recordkeeping can become a gratifying part of your practice when you recognize how it helps you increase profits, keeps you from getting into tax trouble, saves you time at the end of every month, and enhances your value to clients. Invest a solid chunk of time before you open the doors of your practice to create a system that allows you to devote minimum time to maintaining the system. The key to good recordkeeping is consistency in keeping your records updated. Those records are much easier to maintain when you've taken the time to establish a system that makes sense to you.

Recordkeeping can make your practice run more smoothly, or it can be an endless source of frustration. To be sure you set up the right recordkeeping procedures for your practice, you may want to consult with a bookkeeper or accountant. Even a short meeting can generate a lot of helpful advice. You can also set up systems that will generate the forms of information that an accountant can easily work with (and that will enable you to meet IRS guidelines when you file your tax returns).

Recognizing the connection between good financial records and profitability makes the task of maintaining them more satisfying.

GENERAL PRINCIPLES

Keeping Financial Records

If you make a habit of careful recordkeeping, you will be better organized and more able to focus on your own needs and those of your clients. Adhering to a few basic guidelines helps you establish a firm foundation on which to build your financial system. These guidelines include:

- Devote one credit/debit card solely to business use. (The card may be in your name or the name of the practice.)

- Open a business checking account. Most financial institutions require low minimum deposits for opening an account.
- Pay only business-related expenses with your business checking account or credit/debit card; pay personal bills out of your personal account.
- Keep a record of every deposit to your account, as well as every payment.
- Make all deposits of business income to your business account. Depending on your type of business, you can either transfer money to your personal account or pay yourself a salary out of your business account.
- For every expense, keep a record of whom you paid, the amount of payment, the type of expense, and the date. You will need receipts if you claim expenses as tax deductions.
- Keep each year's appointment book or calendar with your tax records for that year. You may need to use it for backup information about business travel and related expenses.
- The Internal Revenue Service and state tax agencies expect you to keep records of your sources and amounts of income. If you are ever audited, these agencies will inspect billing records along with your practice's other financial records.

Keep receipts for all business expenses.

Back-up

If you keep records on your computer, be sure you get in the habit of saving and backing up your work. This can be accomplished in many ways; the principle is that you want the same information available in more than one place. The most common procedures are:

- Make a hard copy (on paper) and file it somewhere other than where the computer is.
- Save your work onto a flash drive or an external hard drive, which you also keep separate from where your computer is.
- Save your original receipts in a safe place. The IRS does not accept scanned or photocopied documents as verification of receipts.

In the event of fire or water damage, your work will be safe in an alternate location.

Document Retention

As you record your revenues and expenses, file all your receipts and check stubs. Sort expense receipts by category and revenue receipts by client type or date, so that you can easily find them again if you need to refer to them. Canada requires that all records be kept for 7 years. In the United States, rules for how long you must save your records varies by document. They are shown in Figure 6.1.

FIGURE 6.1
Retention Guidelines for Business Records

DOCUMENT	RETENTION
General correspondence	5 years
Bank statements	7 years
Cash receipts	7 years
Canceled checks	7 years for most (but keep canceled checks of major purchases indefinitely)
Year-end-financial statements Employee contracts Vendor contracts Licenses and permits Insurance claims Tax returns	Indefinitely

In judging how much information to keep and how much to throw away, it's helpful to understand retention guidelines for business records. As a general rule, you should keep:

- For 5 years—general correspondence
- For 7 years—all tax-related information (such as returns, receipts, and records that support tax deductions, w-2s, and 1099s)
- Indefinitely—all records related to tax deductions and all documentation regarding legal matters

USING PROFESSIONAL BOOKKEEPING SERVICES

Because not everyone who opens a massage therapy practice has the time or inclination to maintain financial records at the level of detail required, you may want to hire a bookkeeper. The considerations listed in Figure 6.2 will help you decide whether to do so. Unlike certified public accountants, bookkeepers may not be qualified to give you financial advice, but they can handle the day-to-day responsibility of recording the practice's transactions. Unless your practice is very large, you will not need a full-time bookkeeper. You can find someone with a good track record by getting referrals from other massage therapists or business owners in your area. It's a good idea to interview accountants or bookkeepers before you hire them. The interview will give you a good idea of whether you would feel comfortable working with them. Ask them if they have any other massage therapists as clients. If they don't, ask what type of small businesses they do have as clients. Explain to them the nature of your business—where your income and expenses come from, its possible fluctuations, etc. Because honesty and accuracy are essential when your livelihood is at stake, be sure to ask for references and check them carefully.

> Because your finances are your security, ask trusted sources about the honesty and accuracy of any financial specialist you are thinking of contracting with.

TYPES OF FINANCIAL ACCOUNTS

Checking Account

The simplest, safest, and most convenient place for most of your money is in a checking account—preferably a separate business account—at your local bank or credit union. Often, community banks are the friendliest toward small businesses. Make an appointment with a banker, and bring in the business plan you developed in Chapter 5. It can be helpful to get to know a banker, in case you have questions or your banking needs expand as you go along.

You can negotiate terms for your banking relationships, just as you do for other professional relationships. Ask these types of questions to find out what is the best arrangement the financial institution can offer you:

- What interest rate does this account pay on balances?
- Is there a minimum balance?
- What fees are charged if I go below the minimum balance?
- When is interest credited?
- What other fees is this account subject to?
- What fees are associated with using automated teller machines (ATMs)? Do fees differ if the ATM is not associated with my "home" bank?
- Does this account offer overdraft protection? If so, how does it work?
- If I keep more money in this account, could I arrange more favorable terms?
- Is online banking available?
- What guarantee do I have that the terms in effect when I open my account will not be affected if this bank merges with or is bought by another financial institution?

Bank Fees

When you are comparing checking accounts, consider the fees banks typically charge. Here are some examples:

- Check printing fees

FIGURE 6.2
Pros and Cons of Using a Bookkeeper

PROS	CONS
You can delegate tasks to someone whose job it is to do bookkeeping and accounting.	By delegating to someone else, you could become less familiar with the financial details of your practice than if you were maintaining the records yourself.
If the person doing the bookkeeping is a skilled professional, you will save time and reduce the potential for errors compared to doing it yourself.	You are responsible for ensuring that the bookkeeper is honest and the figures correct. For example, you should review a week's postings every month against the information provided by the bookkeeper. Even if you pay a specialist to handle the financial aspects of your business, it is essential that you are familiar enough with your business's finances that you would quickly sense if something were off-kilter. Most damage, even when caused by dishonesty, can be controlled through early detection.
You can devote your time to massage and other more productive or satisfying activities.	You must pay the bookkeeper for his or her work (in cash or through a barter arrangement). Keep in mind that barter is taxable income and you must pay taxes on the value of the service received, even if you "pay" for it with a massage.

- Credit card/debit card fees
- Credit card scanner fees (if you accept payment by credit card)
- ATM fees
- Deposit fees
- Lock box drop fees
- Insufficient funds fees
- Some banks attract customers with no-fee accounts; be sure to understand the "no fee" conditions, such as minimum deposit, length of time before fees go into effect, and what those fees will be.

Credit Accounts

The use of credit cards as standard business tools is a relatively new phenomenon. In the past, a small-business owner would go to a bank to negotiate a loan. As a small-business owner, you would have to convince the banker, based on information in the business plan, that your plans were solidly grounded (low risk to the bank) and that you would be able to pay off the loan according to the terms agreed upon. Today, financial institutions are more than happy to give you a credit card, with little justification required on your part to prove that you are a good credit risk. Not only are credit cards sent out unsolicited, but they allow $20,000 credit limits, seemingly with very little justification required—enough to encourage an inexperienced business owner to charge beyond his or her means and regret it for months, possibly years.

As many small-business owners could tell you from painful experience, credit card debt can be a fast road to big trouble. Let's say you want to buy a $600 massage table but you don't have the cash to pay for it. You could set aside $150 a month for four months, but this table has everything you want—it's easy to set up, the face cradle is easy to put on and take off, the height is easy to adjust, and the pad is 3 inches thick, much more luxurious than the old table you've been using—and you want it now. So you charge it. *If* you pay $150 a month on your credit card bill—the amount that you can afford—at 18.5% annual percent rate interest, you will end up paying a little more than $30 in interest fees for the privilege. All things considered, that's not too bad a tradeoff for getting the table 4 months earlier than you could have otherwise. However, if you ever miss a payment date, even by one day, you will pay a late fee of $35 minimum, and if you pay less than $150 a month, the interest you pay on the remaining balance will add up to more than the $30 already mentioned. The main message is, if you can avoid buying on credit, avoid it. If you can't, be prudent.

> If you can avoid buying on credit, avoid it. If you can't, be prudent.

CREATING A BUDGET

A budget is simply a plan for how you will spend, save, and invest the money you anticipate receiving, organized by category. A budget is beneficial only if you use it. There are several ways to do so:

> A budget is a plan for how you will manage the money you spend and receive.

- Create an expense and revenue budget when you are starting your practice. Review it to make sure you have enough funds to get started. If you see months when you may be short of cash, plan how you will handle that potential challenge.
- Review your budget at least once a month. Add your actual expenses for that month, as well as your total for the year so far. Are your expenses within your budget guidelines? Or, is there a need to change your spending or your budget?
- Follow a similar monthly process to evaluate whether your earnings have lived up to your expectations. If revenues have fallen short or expenses have been higher than expected, how can you improve your situation? (See section "Recovery Strategies" in Chapter 7 for more detail.) If earnings have exceeded your expectations, you have other issues to consider: is your massage practice providing a positive experience for you, or are you getting burned out? Do you want to expand your practice or limit your clients?
- Create a new budget at the end of each year to plan for the following year. Then review it before you begin your new year. Will your budget enable you to meet your goals? If not, what can you change?
- Review your budget regularly. Remember that it is a guideline you have created to help you reach your goals.

When you created your Career and Practice Planning Worksheet in Chapter 5, you developed the basics for your budget. To create an expense budget, you can use a format such as the one shown in Figure 6.3:

1 List all the expenses you think you might incur in operating your practice. To prepare a complete list, review the section "Financial" in the Career and Practice Planning Worksheet.
2 Organize the expenses on your list into categories, such as operations (providing massages or other services or selling products), marketing, administration (setting up and running your office), taxes and license fees, rent, utilities, and wages paid to employees and/or fees paid to contractors.
3 For each item in a category, estimate for each month what you will spend on that item.
4 Add the monthly amounts for each item to determine annual amounts.
5 Add the annual amounts for each item in each category to get totals for each category of expense.

Maintaining separate expense entries for items that directly affect your cost of providing massage, such as oils, sheets and laundry service, is helpful. Expenses related to production of income are considered "cost of goods," and they should be distinguishable from expenses associated with general business activity, such as office supplies, bank charges,

FIGURE 6.3 Budget Worksheet: Expenses

EXPENSE CATEGORY	JAN	FEB	MAR	APR	MAY	JUN	JUL	AUG	SEP	OCT	NOV	DEC	TOTAL YEAR
Utilities													
Rent, lease, mortgage													
Wages paid to employees													
Commissions and fees paid													
Employee benefit costs													
Taxes and licenses													
Insurance													
Computer software													
Subscriptions													
Office supplies													
Oils													
Linens													
Laundry services													
Other massage supplies													
Advertising													
Depreciation													
Travel, meals, entertainment													
Dues for professional organizations													
Continuing education													
Legal and professional services													
Interest payments													
Repairs and maintenance													
Car expenses													
Bad debts													
Other expenses													
TOTAL EXPENSES													

FIGURE 6.4 Budget Worksheet: Income

EXPENSE CATEGORY	JAN	FEB	MAR	APR	MAY	JUN	JUL	AUG	SEP	OCT	NOV	DEC	TOTAL YEAR
Relaxation massages													
Integrated health massages													
Sports/fitness massages													
On-site massages													
Client insurance massages													
Other massages:													
Other services:													
Sales of merchandise													
Rent from shared space													
Fees from contractors													
Other revenue:													
TOTAL EXPENSES													

and telephone services. Maintaining individual budget lines for specific expenses will also allow you to compare prices to previous periods or to industry averages, so you know when to search for more competitive pricing.

You can follow a similar process to estimate all your sources of income by type of account (e.g., outcall, workplace massage, third-party reimbursement). To do this, complete the worksheet shown in Figure 6.4, following the same steps as for the expense worksheet. This time, substitute the revenue categories for the expense categories. For example, you might plan to do a lot of chair (on-site) massages in stores during the December holiday shopping season, then cut back on the chair massages in January and focus on providing massages to people who received gift certificates. Estimate the total for each month and for each category of account. Then add your estimates to get totals for the year and for each category.

Many massage therapists prefer to create a budget on a computer, while others feel more comfortable using paper and pen. One advantage to using a computer is that once you have learned the basic operation of the application you use, such as Excel, it can make your work easier in many ways, including computing all your totals automatically. While specialty software is not necessary, many programs are available to help small businesses set up budgets and compare them to actual expenses. See the section "The Automated Office" later in this chapter for more details.

TYPES OF FINANCIAL REPORTS

Whereas budgets are projections you create before you provide services or sell goods, financial reports consist of data that help you keep your finger on the financial pulse of your business. They're the day-to-day recordkeeping that will be a testament to your financial prowess as a business owner. It is important to get into the habit of keeping these records up to date daily or, at the very least, weekly. If you let recordkeeping slip for any longer than a week, it is too easy to forget details or lose notes that are important to your business. This section describes the types of financial records you will want to keep and tips for maintaining them.

Four basic kinds of financial reports you might want to create for your business are: ledgers, cash flow statements, income statements, and balance sheets (see 6.5). They are important for several reasons. First, partnerships will want these statements so that all the partners can be clear about the practice's performance, and sole proprietors can benefit from preparing them to monitor their performance and identify weaknesses to correct. Second, if you incorporate, the law requires that the corporation prepare each of these statements at least once a year. Your budget and billing records are a useful starting point for preparing financial statements, which are widely used formats for recording and evaluating how well a business is doing financially. And finally, financial statements are an essential part of a loan application.

Ledger Sheet

The starting point for preparing any financial statement is to keep detailed records on ledger sheets, such as the one shown in Figure 6.6. A ledger sheet may be literally a sheet of paper in a book, or it may be a computer document with the same format. Your checking account record will provide the information for your ledger sheet, as it will show your payments and deposits in chronological order. To create the necessary financial statements for your business, you will want to categorize these expenses into types, such as office supplies, massage supplies, wages, rent, utilities, laundry, etc.

For revenues, record:

A ledger is a list of all receipts and expenses according to category.

- The date work was performed (In places where an accrual basis of accounting is required, you must record your income when the work is performed, not when payment is received. If you are billing by invoice, such as for rent from shared space, record the date of invoice.)

TYPE OF REPORT	PURPOSE OF REPORT	FREQUENCY
Ledger Sheets – the basis from which financial statements are created	Shows all income and expenses, categorized by type (supplies, wages, etc.)	Daily. Well-kept checking account records provide the same information as a ledger, but they are not categorized by type of expense.
Balance Sheet	Shows your practice's assets, liabilities and equity. This is different from the income statement because it includes capital assets such as equipment you already own and lease deposits that will be refunded to you later.	Quarterly or annually
Income Statement	Shows your practice's revenues, its expenses, and its income or profit.	Monthly and year-to-date
Cash Flow Statement	Shows your practice's existing cash on hand, as well as its income and expenses.	The most helpful cash flow statement is one you create that *projects* your income and expenses for the month so you know if you will need to borrow money or delay expenses in order to stay in the black.

FIGURE 6.5
Types of Financial Reports

- The date you received payment
- Who paid you
- The invoice number
- The amount you received
- The form of payment (cash, check, charge). It is also helpful to record the check number or reference number of the charge in the event you have to track the payment later.
- Year-to-date total
- For expenses, record in the appropriate category (i.e., supplies, equipment):
- The date you paid
- Who you paid
- What you purchased
- The check number
- The amount you paid
- The form of payment (cash, check, charge)
- Year-to-date total

At the end of each month, add the entries to find the monthly total and the year-to-date amounts (how much you earned or spent so far that year). Do this regularly, to keep the task simple.

Balance Sheet
A balance sheet is like a financial snapshot of your practice. As shown in Figure 6.7, it shows three things:

1 Your practice's assets—everything you have, from cash to furniture, that you can use to operate the practice
2 Your practice's liabilities—everything your practice owes, such as loan payments and utility bills
3 Your practice's equity—the value that remains after you subtract the total liabilities from the total assets

REVENUES

TYPE: RENT FROM SHARED SPACE

DATE BILLED	DATE PAYMENT RECEIVED	RECEIVED FROM	INVOICE #	AMOUNT	FORM OF PAYMENT	YEAR TO DATE
01-06-09	01-15-09	Chris Smith	204	$250	Check #708	$250
02-05-09	02-15-09	Chris Smith	211	$250	Check: #756	$500
03-05-09	03-15-09	Chris Smith	210	$250	Cash	$750

EXPENSES

TYPE: OFFICE SUPPLIES

DATE PAID	PAYMENT TO	ITEM PURCHASED	CHECK #	AMOUNT	FORM OF PAYMENT	YEAR TO DATE
01-10-09	Spiffy Office Supplies	3 reams paper	#704	$22.19	Check	$22.19
01-11-09	Office Warehouse Inc.	5 ink toner cartridges	#706	$124.19	Check	$146.38
02-02-09	Office Warehouse Inc.	Electric pencil sharpener	#715	$43.70	Credit card	$190.08

FIGURE 6.6
Ledger Sheet

Your balance sheet shows where your practice stands at the end of a particular time period, such as the end of the year or the end of a quarter. The concept of equity reflects an accumulation of the owner's investments, withdrawals, and the accumulated earnings of your business.

To prepare a balance sheet, you begin by listing all the assets of the business:

- *Current assets*: The first assets to list are those you can spend within the next month, such as cash and the value of your accounts receivable (the bills you have sent out).
- *Other assets*: Next, list your other assets, including the value of your inventory (if you have items for sale), supplies, and equipment.
- *Fixed assets and depreciation*: Fixed assets—generally anything over $250 in a massage practice—are said to depreciate. A fixed asset is something that has a useful life, such as a massage table, a computer, and an air purifier. You may choose to expense the item over the useful life of the asset. This means that each year you own the asset, you subtract part of its value. To do this, you would use a depreciation table. To find out about the different ways in which you could depreciate a fixed asset, consult an accountant or research IRS guidelines
- *Total assets*: Complete the top portion of the balance sheet by adding the asset values to determine total assets.

Next, prepare the bottom half of the balance sheet:

- *Liabilities:* List the practice's liabilities, which will mainly be any bills you have not paid yet.
- *Total liabilities:* Add the liability items and record the total liabilities.
- *Owner's equity:* Subtract total liabilities from total assets. The result is equal to the owners' equity. Record this amount under the total liabilities.
- *Total liabilities and owners' equity*: Finally, add the total liabilities and the owners' equity.

If you did everything correctly, the sum of the total liabilities and owners' equity equals the total assets, thus the name "balance" sheet.

In practice, many rules govern the preparation of balance sheets and other financial statements, including the calculation of depreciation. It is up to you to decide whether you want to learn these rules or to hire an accountant.

The sum of liabilities and equity will equal the business's total assets—thus the term "balance sheet."

FIGURE 6.7
Simplified Balance Sheet

ASSETS	
Cash	$4,800
Accounts Receivable	400
Inventory	700
Supplies	1,000
Equipment	3,000
Total Assets	$9,900
LIABILITIES AND OWNERS' EQUITY	
Liabilities	
Accounts Payable	$1,800
Owners' Equity	
M. Johnson, Capital	8,100
Total Liabilities and Owner's Equity	$9,900

Income Statement

Besides knowing what your practice owns, you (and your lenders) will want to know whether it is making money. An income statement is also known as a profit and loss statement, or P&L for short. For this, you prepare an income statement, such as the sample in Figure 6.8, which describes the practice's financial performance in terms of three basic measures:

An income statement shows whether your business is making a profit or not.

1 Your revenues—the payments you received (from clients, interest on bank accounts, and so on)
2 Your expenses—the payments you made
3 Your income or profit—your total revenues minus your total expenses

By preparing an income statement after the close of each year, you can compare statements from year to year to see whether you are achieving your financial goals and building your income. If your income is not growing, you may want to make some changes to achieve your financial goals.

From your ledger sheets, you will have the information to put into the format of the income statement:

- At the top, record your revenues by category (service or product).
- Add your revenue amounts to find total revenues.
- Below that number, list the expense categories and the amount for each.
- Add the expenses to find the total expenses.
- Record your gross profit: total revenues minus total expenses.
- Subtract your income taxes. The result is your net profit.

If you prepare income statements, they will be very helpful when it comes time to pay quarterly estimated taxes and prepare your tax returns. If you are a sole proprietor, the basic information on an income statement corresponds to the information you will need to provide on Schedule C with your annual federal income tax return.

Cash Flow Statement

A common problem of many new businesses is that, although they have a lot of work to do, they keep running out of the cash they need for day-to-day expenses. To head off this

FIGURE 6.8
Simplified Income Statement

REVENUES	
Revenue from massages	$34,000
Revenue from product sales	2,500
Fee from associate (who shares space)	5,000
Total revenues	$41,500
EXPENSES	
Salary (part-time bookkeeper)	$ 5,000
Rent	9,450
Purchases of products for sale	1,500
Marketing communication	2,500
Utilities	1,000
Supplies, laundry	2,000
Membership fees, continuing education, and professional publications	2,250
Total expenses	$23,700
Net Profit	$17,500
Less income tax	$2,650
NET PROFIT AFTER TAX	**$15,150**

problem, keep an eye on your practice's cash flow—the amount of cash received by the practice versus the amount it spends.

For a small practice, preparing a cash flow statement after-the-fact probably is less important than projecting your cash flow. A cash flow projection is like a month-by-month budget, but each item you record should involve receiving or spending cash (including checks and credit card receipts). For example, doing work for which you will bill an insurer will not generate immediate cash, but receiving the insurer's payment will in the month you receive it. Likewise, charging something on your credit card does not involve spending cash; paying the credit card bill (including interest) does. Look at each month's totals to see whether the business will generate enough cash to pay your bills that month. If it will not, you will need to plan to have some funds available when you need them (in savings, by borrowing, or by establishing a line of credit with your bank).

The formal way to do this is with a cash flow statement, such as the one in Figure 6.9. To prepare this statement, follow these steps:

A projected cash flow statement is one in which you list the income you expect to receive, and when, and the expenses you expect to incur, and when.

1 Record the amount of cash you received during the period.
2 Record the amount of cash (including checks) you paid out for expenses (not investments, such as buying equipment).
3 Subtract total cash paid out from total cash received to find net cash from operations.
4 Record the amount of cash you received from and spent on investments, such as interest earned, equipment purchases, and stock purchases. In this example, the massage therapist purchased equipment but did not have money coming in from investments, so the only cash flow is negative—that is, money going out of the practice.
5 Record cash flows from financing. This can include investments the owner made in the

business (positive cash flow) or draws by the owner (negative cash flow, because the owner takes money from the practice).

6   Add all the positive cash flows and subtract from that figure the total negative cash flows to find the net increase or decrease in cash.

7   Record the amount of cash the practice had at the beginning of the statement period. Add this to the net increase or decrease to find the cash at the end of the period.

Your cash flow statement should also include non-cash income and expense. An example of non-cash income would be Accounts Receivable, such as when you send an invoice to a client but have not yet received payment. An example of non-cash expense would be Accounts Payable, such as when you charge an item to your credit card but have not yet paid the credit card bill. These are "accrual" income and expenses, which means you have "accrued," or "accumulated," them, and are important to identify in your financial statements.

FIGURE 6.9
Simplified Cash Flow Statement

CASH FLOWS FROM OPERATIONS FOR PERIOD [MONTH/DATE/YEAR] TO [MONTH/DATE/YEAR]	
Cash receipts from revenues	$34,000
Cash payments for expenses	(5,100)
Net cash from operations	$28,900
CASH FLOWS FROM INVESTING	
Purchase of equipment	$(1,200)
CASH FLOWS FROM FINANCING	
Investments by owner	$ 1,000
Draws by owner	(25,000)
	$(24,000)
Net increase (or decrease) in cash	$ 3,700
Cash at beginning of period	1,800
Cash at end of period	$5,500

RESOURCES FOR PREPARING FINANCIAL STATEMENTS

BOOKS

Kamoroff, Bernard B. (2006). *Small Time Operator: How to Start Your Own Business, Keep Your Books, Pay Your Taxes, and Stay Out of Trouble* (27th ed.). Laytonville & Willits, CA: Bell Springs.

Zobel, Jan. (2005). *Minding Her Own Business* (4th ed.). Naperville, IL: Sourcebooks.

ORGANIZATIONS AND WEBSITES

Internal Revenue Service: www.irs.gov, for information about preparing statements that comply with income tax regulations

PlanWare: www.planware.org

Small Business Administration: 1-800-8-ASK-SBA; www.sba.gov. Also see Spotlight on

Business, "Get to Know Your SBA Business Development Center" in Chapter 5 for more detail on the range of support the SBA offers.

TechRepublic: www.whitepapers.techrepublic.com

U.S. Securities and Exchange Commission: www.sec.gov or check the federal government listings in your phone book, for information about preparing statements that comply with rules governing how corporations report their performance

Your Business Pal: www.yourbusinesspal.com

INVOICES

The most basic kind of billing record is a copy of your bill. A bill—also called an invoice—is a request for payment. Your bill, as shown in Figure 6.10, should include the following information:

- the name, address, and phone number of your practice (as on your letterhead)
- your registration or license number
- the invoice date and number
- the name of the client
- the date you provided services or sold goods, if different from the date of the bill
- a description of the services provided and products sold (for example, "1-hour massage" or "aromatherapy pillow")
- the cost of each item and the total amount due (indicating the amount of sales tax separately, if any applies)
- a statement of finance terms, such as "Payment due upon receipt of invoice."
- Expression of appreciation for their business.

FIGURE 6.10
Invoice

CLIENT

Name: _____   Invoice Date: _____

Address: _____   Invoice #: _____

Telephone: _____   Practitioner: _____

Social Security No. _____

DATE OF SERVICE	DESCRIPTION OF SERVICES/PRODUCTS	PRICE	QUANTITY	TAX	TOTAL DUE	PAYMENT AMOUNT	PAYMENT METHOD	BALANCE DUE

For clients who plan to submit insurance claim:

Insurance Carrier: _____

Policy/Group #: _____

CPT/Group #: _____

Payment due upon receipt of invoice.

We appreciate your business.

Referring Physician: _____

When your client pays, you can mark the bill "paid in full" and use a copy as a receipt for the client. A receipt is a document showing that the person billing has received payment.

There are some variations. If you contract with a spa, health club, health clinic, or other organization, your contract will determine whether you will bill for the number of massages, time with clients, or some other arrangement. Your bill would detail how you fulfilled the contract (for example, "10 hours at x dollars per hour"). Also, if you are billing a third-party payer, such as an insurance company, the payer will probably have some requirements about the information you provide. (Client insurance reimbursement is covered in more detail later in this chapter.)

If you are billing individual clients, you will probably bill and collect from them just after the massage. The usual way to do this is to present the bill, collect payment, and give the client a receipt in the form of the bill with a notation that you have received payment in full. If you prefer a manual method, a sales receipt book with carbon copies works great. Give the original or top copy to your client as a receipt, and keep the bottom copy as a record of payment. Computer software offers another way to keep these records. Enter the same information directly into your computer, printing out a combination bill/receipt for the client. Sales receipt books and basic software that can handle billing are available from office supply stores, or you can create your own templates and customize these forms to your business using your existing computer software.

Mailing and Collecting on Invoices

If you are working under contract with organizations, such as third-party payers or organizations that provide their clients with massages, you probably will need to send invoices (automated or snail mail). At a minimum, keep copies in an A-to-Z follow-up file folder or your automated invoice file; use a formal accounts receivable register for a large practice. When you receive a payment, make a record of when you received it. Also record the payment in your accounts receivable ledger.

Check your revenue ledger weekly to make sure your clients are paying you within about 30 days. If not, you should call the client, ask to speak with the person who handles accounts payable, and discuss the client's payment policy. If you ask questions in a professional, courteous manner, the person you talk to should be able to clarify what you can expect. If you find, for example, that insurance claims routinely take weeks to process, you can plan for the lag time or choose to focus on building a different kind of client base. Immediately after your conversation, make notes of what you learned or agreed to, so that you can refer to them the next time you review your tickler file.

If You Do Not Get Paid

If you work primarily for clients who pay you at the time of service, you may never encounter a nonpaying client. However, if you want to work in a situation in which you submit a bill and wait for payment (for instance workplace massage, where you bill a corporate client), there could be a risk of slow payment or, worst case, none at all. Most organizations want to keep current with bill payment, so a polite phone call will resolve most problems. If the client has trouble paying, however, focus on setting up a payment plan—not just on demanding payment in full.

But what if patience and a phone call do not work? Consider your options, and remember that bill collection will take time. If your bill is under $100, consider whether you would be better off financially to spend that time working for another client. (Talk to your accountant about tax deductions for bad debts and collection expenses.) If the unpaid bill is large, you can contact a collection agency, which may handle collection efforts in exchange for a percentage of the fee. You certainly want to avoid angry discussions with (soon-to-be-former) clients, and you probably will not want to take the matter to court, because that route is time consuming and usually expensive. A rule many massage

Your financial plan should incorporate the timing of when you will receive payment. If you bill a corporate account or file a claim for insurance reimbursement, your payment might be received days or weeks after you do the work, compared with individual clients, who usually pay at the time of the session.

therapists follow is that they will not reschedule a client until his or her bill is paid in full, thus limiting the amount of money owed.

Keep your perspective. Most clients will pay, and you need to focus on your ultimate goals.

TAXES

At any gathering of massage therapist business owners, the topic of taxes is sure to generate lively discussion, because there are many war stories about practitioners who got into trouble because they didn't understand the rules for paying taxes. Understanding what is required of your business for taxes and relying on a knowledgeable accountant or tax advisor is indispensable to the financial success of your business.

If you are employed, your employer withholds taxes for you, and you do not have to file quarterly estimated taxes. Your employer already withholds federal, state, FICA (Social Security), and Medicare taxes from your pay, and gives you a W-2 form at the end of the year so you can file income tax. If you are self-employed or if you are an independent contractor, and if you earn more than $400 a year, you must pay your own federal, state, FICA, Medicare and self-employment tax, and must file quarterly estimated taxes in April, June, September, and January, using a 1040 form. If your practice is incorporated, you must also file a corporate tax return. (The corporate return for quarterly report of tax withholding is IRS Form 941.)

As a general rule, IRS regulations require that you pay at least 90 percent of the amount due for that quarter, or 100 percent of the amount you paid for that quarter in the previous year. If you pay less on your estimated taxes, you will owe a penalty when you file your annual return. To avoid the penalty, either pay as much as you did the preceding year or multiply your tax rate by the gross profit on your income statement and pay that amount.

When you start your business, you will have to guess at what your total tax liability will be. Until you have an established history, err on the side of caution. A good general rule is to set aside one-third of your gross receipts for taxes, at least until you have an established record of your business's finances.

TYPES OF TAXES

FICA

FICA stands for Federal Insurance Contributions Act, and it is the mechanism establshed by the federal government to fund Social Security. When you're an employee, your employer pays half, and you pay the other half.

SELF-EMPLOYMENT TAX

When you're self-employed, you pay the entire amount of the employer's and employee's FICA tax just described. This amount constitutes a self-employment tax, and the intention is that this amount should fund your Social Security account for your later benefit. In addition to the Social Security self-employment tax at the federal level, some states also apply a surcharge to self-employed individuals.

PROFIT & LOSS

If you make a profit, you are taxed on that profit. Therefore, if you are in a position that allows you the luxury of investing profits back into your business, doing so will reduce your tax liability. For instance, if you need to buy new office furniture, it's a good idea to buy it toward the end of the tax year. Doing so enables you to invest your money for most of the year, and then to take advantage of whatever tax deductions might be allowed for business expenses in that tax year. Profit shows upon your IRS 1040 Form as income.

In some cases, if your business does not generate profit (your expenses are greater than your revenue), you will be able to deduct the loss. There are restrictions on what can be

If you are an employee, your employer funds half the amount you owe to fund FICA (Social Security) and Medicare. If you are self-employed, you pay these yourself in the form of self-employment tax.

considered a loss and time limits on how many years you can declare a loss, so check with your tax advisor.

SALES TAX

To find your state's sales tax tables, go to Federal Tax Administration: www.taxadmin.org. In Canada, go to Canada Revenue Agency: www.cra.gc.ca.

Some states have a sales tax on the sale of services, and many states tax the sale of goods. Some cities and counties also have sales taxes. You are responsible for determining whether the services or goods you sell are subject to sales tax. You must collect the tax at the time of service or sale and pay it according to the schedule set by the appropriate governmental body. You may also need to obtain a sales tax (or seller's) permit. In Canada, this is called the Goods and Services Tax (GST).

INCOME

Keep track of all income, including tips. Always issue a receipt to a client, and write "check" or "cash" on the receipt. Note the amount of tip either on the receipt or next to the client's name in the appointment book. You might need documentation at some point that shows that your income receipts equal your bank deposits.

One good reason to claim all tips—even cash—on your tax return, is because it's the law. Other good reasons are because it may affect your retirement income (by being included as income on which you have paid self-employment tax, which funds what is now Social Security), and it may help your ability to borrow.

Do not assume that it's all right to not report tips. Some industries, such as the restaurant industry, are required by the Internal Revenue Service to automatically withhold taxes on employees' wages plus 10 percent, assuming a certain level of tips.

Understand the distinction between tax avoidance and tax evasion. Tax avoidance means that you claim something as a deduction, which might be allowed or disallowed by the IRS. If the IRS disallows the deduction, you must pay the tax plus a penalty or interest for not having paid the tax initially. Tax avoidance is not illegal.

Tax evasion is illegal. It means that you have not reported all of your income to the IRS, and it could result in your going to prison. Report your tips!

If you sell products, you also pay state sales tax that you have collected on your sales, if your state has sales tax. You need a sellers' permit in order to sell products. In Canada, you may need to apply for a Goods and Services Tax (GST) permit.

DEDUCTIONS

Deductions are also known as write-offs and business expenses. In general, an expense is deductible if it meets three conditions established by the IRS:

1 You incurred the expense in connection with your practice.
2 The expense is ordinary (common or accepted as an expense of running a massage therapy practice) and necessary (appropriate or helpful for developing and maintaining your practice).
3 The deduction is based on precedent and on the reasonable belief that it is accurate.

Some deductions, such as transportation expenses and expenses for entertaining clients, are limited, however, so check with the IRS, your state tax agency, or your accountant if you are not sure about a deduction. See Figure 6.11 for a list of possible tax deductions for your business.

Figure 6.12 lists several types of deductions that could apply to your business if you travel to your clients' locations, travel to attend a professional meeting or continuing education, or work out of your home.

Although software programs can simplify recordkeeping and tax preparation, there are still instances in which manual tools can still be helpful. For instance, to keep track of mileage, you might want to secure a mileage log (Figure 6.13) with rubber bands to the underside of your car's visor and stick a pen there so you will have a recordkeeping chart handy where you can read the odometer.

It is essential to keep records of tax-related activities. Keep receipts for everything. Set up a series of file folders, either manually or in your automated system, and label them by categories such as dues, rent, utilities, etc., and file the receipts in these folders as soon as

FIGURE 6.11
Typical Tax Deductions for a Practice

Note: The inclusion of an item on this list does not mean that it is necessarily appropriate as a business tax deduction. You need to consult with your accountant, tax specialist, or the IRS on all questions regarding appropriate deductions.

☐ Office- and massage-related supplies

☐ Cost to acquire items you offer for sale (e.g., shipping)

☐ Subscriptions to magazines for office reception area

☐ Fees for accountant, attorney, graphic designer, etc.

☐ Credit card feeds

☐ Bank account fees

☐ Wages for employees and fees paid to contractors (Deduct your own salary if your business is a corporation but not if it is a sole proprietorship.)

☐ Home office expenses (if home is principal place of business)

☐ Insurance

☐ Telecommunications charges (e.g., Internet service provider, business lines)

☐ Computer services charges

☐ License fees

☐ Property tax, sales tax, business tax

☐ Depreciation of fixed assets (e.g., office property if you own it, computer)

☐ Rent/mortgage payments

☐ Utilities for office space

☐ Linen and/or cleaning service

☐ Uniforms (if a condition of employment)

☐ Gifts to clients

☐ Travel expenses and mileage related to your practice (except to and from home and your primary place of business)

☐ Meals (limited) with other professional sduring which business is discussed

☐ Membership dues in professional organizations

☐ Subscriptions to professional journals

☐ Attendance at professional conferences

☐ Continuing education to maintain credentials or expand business potential

☐ Books and resources related to health education and massage therapy

FIGURE 6.12
Special Case Tax Deductions

Note: The inclusion of an item on this list does not mean that it is necessarily appropriate as a business tax deduction. Consult with your accountant, tax specialist, or the Internal Revenue Service on all questions regarding appropriate deductions.

MILEAGE

The types of trip for which you may claim mileage as a deduction differ depending on whether you are an employee or self-employed.

An employee claims deduction on IRS 1040 Schedule A.

A self-employed person claims business expenses on IRS 1040 Schedule C.

IRS Form 2106 is used to calculate business mileage. The form specifies that you have a mileage log.

Keep a mileage log that shows when/why of mileage.

Get a receipt for tolls.

The rules about what mileage is deductible and what is not are very specific, and you are advised to consult a tax specialist.

TRAVEL

For business-related travel, including continuing education, you may deduct airfare, cab fare, hotel, registration fees, and some meals (generally 50 percent). Ask your accountant to clarify travel rules.

HOME OFFICE

Calculate percentage of square feet used solely for business.

Deduct this percentage of rent/mortgage, interest, insurance, repairs and maintenance, utility bills, and property taxes.

Be aware that claiming a deduction for a home office might be a red flag for audits. Make sure your accountant approves all deductions. Make sure your city permits and licenses are all up to date, such as city occupancy permit to use your home for business, fire inspection, and property inspection.

FIGURE 6.13
Mileage Log

AUTOMOBILE MILEAGE LOG[1]

DATE	STARTING MILEAGE	ENDING MILEAGE	TOTAL BUSI-NESS MILES	TOTAL PER-SONAL MILES	TOTAL COM-MUTE[2] MILES	FROM	TO	REASON
TOTALS								

1   Consult a tax specialist to learn when you can and cannot claim miles as a tax deduction.
2   Commute miles = roundtrip distance from home to office.

FIGURE 6.14
Tax Obligation Worksheet

Consult an accountant or tax specialist about the tax obligations of your practice. If you must pay the tax, learn the payment date or schedule.

TYPE OF TAX	WHEN PAYMENTS ARE DUE
Income Tax	
☐ Federal	_____
☐ Social Security (FICA) and Medicare (self-employment tax)	_____
☐ State/Province	_____
☐ County	_____
☐ City	_____
Sales Tax (Ask whether a sales tax permit is required)	
☐ State/Province (on services? on goods?)	_____
☐ County (on services? on goods?)	_____
☐ City (on services? on goods?)	_____
☐ GST (Goods & Services Tax, Canada only)	_____
Business Taxes and License Fees	
☐ State/Province	_____
☐ County	_____
☐ City	_____
Property Taxes (on property you own and use for business)	
☐ State/Province	_____
☐ County	_____
☐ City	_____

Note: If you incorporate and/or hire employees, you will also have to withhold (and pay) taxes from each employee's paycheck.

you pay the expense. Putting together your tax records at the end of the year will be much easier if you don't have to search for receipts.

Whenever you complete a tax return of any kind, keep a copy of it in your files. If you file amendments to the return, keep copies. If the IRS or state tax agency sends you any correspondence about your taxes, keep a copy in your files.

In general, it is prudent to store copies of your tax documents and supporting materials (such as receipts) for about seven years. This is especially significant for massage therapists with a home office. Tax returns with deductions for home office expenses are more likely to be audited than returns without this expense.

Tax preparation doesn't have to be burdensome, if you keep good records and keep track of when different taxes are due. Figure 6.14 can help you see the due dates for different types of taxes at a glance.

TAX FORMS

What forms you need to file will in some cases vary by individual, so check with your accountant, the IRS, or the state and federal taxing bodies. Listed here are some of the forms required by the U.S. Internal Revenue Service for federal income taxes:

- Form 1040-ES for paying estimated taxes
- Form 1040 for calculating the tax you owe on your earnings as the operator of your sole proprietorship, a partner in your partnership, or the employee of your corporation
- Schedule C for calculating the earnings of your sole proprietorship or Schedule K1 (Form 1065) for calculating the income of your partnership. Schedule C accompanies your personal Form 1040. The managing partner of a partnership sends Schedule K1, which instructs you where to insert amounts on your Form 1040. (If your practice is incorporated, the corporation files Form 1120 to report its income.)
- Schedule SE for calculating your self-employment tax (for Social Security and Medicare), if you have a sole proprietorship or partnership
- Form W-2 for reporting the income of any employees
- Form 1099-MISC for reporting payments of $600 or more to independent contractors
- Form 2106 for Employee Business Expenses (including Business Use of Automobile)

You may need to file other forms as well; for example, if you have property to depreciate or if you have a home office for which you are claiming deductions, the IRS requires additional documentation.

USING THE SERVICES OF A PROFESSIONAL ACCOUNTANT

Unless you are particularly knowledgeable about taxes, finances, and the rules that apply to businesses, there are many advantages to hiring a professional accountant. A good accountant can help you set up efficient financial recordkeeping systems that will ultimately increase the value of your business by highlighting areas of vulnerability so that you can take corrective action. A specialist might also help prevent your business from paying higher taxes than necessary, and reduce the chance of your being audited. The time you could spend learning and doing financial and tax-related work otherwise could be spent giving massages and bringing in revenue!

RESOURCES FOR FILING TAX RETURNS

Your accountant or tax advisor, particularly if they have other massage therapists as clients

Your state's tax agency

Internal Revenue Service: 1-800-829-1040; www.irs.gov

Revenue Canada: 1-800-267-5177; www.ccra-adrc.gc.ca

CLIENT RECORDS MANAGEMENT

You want to keep information not only about your money but about your clients as well. Client records allow you to manage your business effectively, provide some measure of legal protection, and most important, provide one of the most effective mechanisms for communicating clearly with your client within the therapeutic relationship. More information about the significance of these documents to the client-practitioner relationship is contained in the "Role of Client Records" section of Chapter 2.

Client records will help you provide appropriate care. You will need several kinds of records, as identified in Figure 6.15. It is important to keep accurate and comprehensive records on all of your clients, including types of clients, money due and received, and follow-up done with clients and insurance companies.

Some client records may be consolidated onto one form rather than on separate documents. For example, the client intake form shown in Figure 6.16 includes an informed consent statement as well as a release of medical records authorization. You may opt to exclude this section from your client intake form and offer instead a separate authorization form for these specified purposes, such as those shown in Figures 6.17 and 6.18.

Set up files, either paper or automated, to keep your important papers organized. Look through an office supply catalog to find ways to organize different kinds of records. Client records to maintain and keep in a safe place include the following:

- Client information, such as client intake form, authorization to release information, etc.
- Records of your appointments (organized by date)
- Records of products sold to clients
- Treatment notes, if required. (In some states, New York for example, the law requires massage therapists to keep treatment notes, even if they work in a spa setting. Check with your local licensing entity to find which laws pertain to your practice.)
- Copies of the receipts you issue to clients for payments, showing any sales tax you collected (organized by date)

CLIENT INTAKE FORM

Massage therapists aren't trained to diagnose conditions but still have a responsibility to do no harm. A well-designed client intake process, in which you gather information about your client's health, allows you to gain confidence and lower the risk of clients misundersanding the purpose or expected outcome of the massage therapy session,

The purposes of a client intake form are:[1]

- To minimize malpractice liability
- To clarify to the client your professional boundaries (for example, the form may state that you do not dignose or treat medical conditions)
- To find out for what purpose the client is seeking massage

At the beginning of a client's first visit, you should devote at least 10 to 15 minutes to an intake interview. During this time, ask the client to complete an intake form, which consists of the following parts:

- Contact/personal information
- Current client conditions
- Previous conditions therapists should know about
- Clarification of conditions
- Follow-up questions
- Current medications
- A disclaimer

FIGURE 6.15
Client Records

RECORD	INFORMATION ON RECORD
Informed consent	☐ Information about your approach to massage, modality, and techniques
	☐ Benefits, limitations, and contraindications
	☐ Possible outcomes (with no promises or guarantees)
	☐ The nature of a session, including the process of disrobing and draping
	☐ Scope of practice—what you can and cannot do given your credentials and jurisdictional/professional oversight
	☐ Your credentials and areas of expertise
	☐ Session duration and fees
	☐ Availability and hours of operation
	☐ Collaboration policies with other health professionals
	☐ Policies for missed appointments and late arrivals
	☐ Insurance reimbursement capabilities
	☐ Client forms to be completed
Client intake	☐ Request this information from the client:
	☐ Personal data (address, phone number, etc.)
	☐ Health history (including previous massage experience)
	☐ Desired results from massage
	☐ Informed consent (sometimes called *consent for care*—a description of the nature of massage and scope of expected benefits and risks, acknowledged by the client's signature)
	☐ Medical release authorization
	☐ Assignment of benefits (payment responsibility)
	☐ Insurance information, if necessary

FIGURE 6.15
(continued)

Client release of information	☐ If medical release authorization is not included on client intake form, you may use a separate document. Information to include:
	☐ Name of business/contact to whom client has requested information be sent
	☐ Address and telephone of business/contact
	☐ Statement requesting and authorizing release of records and/or authorizing discussion of client's information with named business/contact
	☐ Client's name, date of birth, and Social Security number
	☐ Patient's signature and date form is signed
	☐ If authorization should span a period of time, specify "good through" date.
SOAP *notes*	☐ **Subjective** complaints and functional goals, including information from intake form and pain questionnaire, a drawing showing location of symptoms, descriptions of any relevant injuries or surgeries (client may complete this section).
	☐ **Objective** information from visual observation, palpation, range-of-motion testing, and a description of the nature of the massage provided.
	☐ **Assessment,** including records of assessment by physician and massage therapist's documentation of subjective and objective changes that are an immediate result of the care provided.
	☐ **Plan** for massage: frequency, focus, modality, recommended "homework" the client might do.
Client log	☐ Client name
	☐ Comments made by the client regarding preferences and aversions (for example, client's birthday, personal interests, "I don't my ears to be massaged," etc.)
	☐ Observations made by massage therapist for future visits (for example, "Client likes warm sheets, prefers lavender scent," etc.)
Client billing record	☐ Client name
	☐ Invoice number and date
	☐ Nature of visit
	☐ Amount billed
	☐ Date and amount of payment received

FIGURE 6.16 Client Intake Form

Name:_____ Date:_____Date of Birth:_____

Phone–Work:_____ Home:_____ E-mail:_____

Address:_____ City:_____ State:_____ Zip:_____

Occupation:_____ Employer:_____

Work Responsibilities:_____

Primary Care Provider:_____ Phone:_____ Fax:_____

Address:_____ City:_____ State:_____ Zip:_____

Emergency Contact:_____ Relationship:_____

Phone–Work:_____ Home:_____ Cell/Pager:_____

CURRENT HEALTH

Have you ever received massage therapy before?   ☐ Yes   ☐ No   Frequency:_____

Reason for today's visit:_____

Desired results of today's session:_____

Today's primary concern or goal:_____ Other:_____

Classify concern   ☐ Minor   ☐ Problematic   ☐ Major

Classify type   ☐ Recurring   ☐ Getting worse   ☐ Getting better

Have you had this concern/goal before?   ☐ Yes   ☐ No   Explain:_____

Have you received treatment for this before?   ☐ Yes   ☐ No   Explain:_____

List activities affected:_____

Current medications:_____

(include over-the-counter pain relievers and herbal remedies)

Stress reduction/exercise activities:_____ Frequency:_____

Check any of the following that apply to your current health:

☐ pregnancy   ☐ heart conditions   ☐ circulatory conditions   ☐ blood clots   ☐ diabetes

☐ infections   ☐ cancer   ☐ difficulty breathing   ☐ arthritis

Comments:_____

Is there anything I should know to ensure your comfort regarding:_____

Allergies/sensitivities: ☐ oils   ☐ lotions   ☐ scents   ☐ detergents   ☐ foods   ☐ animals

☐ other:_____

Contact lenses (the face pillow may put pressure on your eyes):_____

Hearing abilities (communication is helpful during the session):_____

Hair, make-up, clothes (Will you return to work after your session?):_____

Movement abilities (i.e., getting on and off the table, pillows, etc.):_____

Comments:_____

FIGURE 6.16 (continued)

MARK ON FIGURES ALL AREAS OF:

Pain, tenderness with os

Numbness, tingling with zzs

Swelling, stiffness with xs

Scars, bruises, open wounds with HHs

RATE SEVERITY OF ALL SYMPTOM AREAS FROM 1-10:

(1 = I feel like a newborn baby, 10 = Put me out of my misery)

1   2   3   4   5   6   7   8   9   10

PREVIOUS HISTORY

(list in chronological order, give dates or ages, and treatment received)

Surgeries:_____

Accidents:_____

Major illnesses:_____

CONSENT FOR CARE

It is my choice to receive massage therapy. I am aware of the benefits and risks of massage and give my consent for massage. I understand that there is no implied or stated guarantee of success or effectiveness of individual techniques or series of appointments. I acknowledge that massage therapy is not a substitute for medical care, medical examination, or diagnosis. I have stated all medical conditions that I am aware of and will inform my practitioner of any changes in my health status.

Signature:_____ Date:_____

INSURANCE INFORMATION

Client's full name:_____ Date:_____ Ins. ID #:_____ DOI:_____

Is your condition the result of an auto accident?   ☐ Yes   ☐ No   If so, in what state did the accident occur? ___

☐ A work injury?   ☐ A health condition?   ☐ Other:_____

What type of insurance do you have that may cover you for this condition? (check all that apply)

☐ Auto   ☐ Workers' compensation/State industrial   ☐ Liability   ☐ Health

Was a police/accident report filed?   ☐ Yes   ☐ No

Client's relation to insured?   ☐ Self   ☐ Spouse   ☐ Partner   ☐ Child   ☐ Other

Insured's full name:_____ Ins. ID #:_____

Date of birth:_____   ☐ Male   ☐ Female   ☐ Single   ☐ Married   ☐ Partnered   ☐ Other

Address:_____ City:_____ State:_____ Zip:_____

Phone–Work:_____ Home:_____ Cell/Pager:_____

Employer's name/school name:_____

Address:_____ Phone:_____

FIGURE 6.16 (continued)

Primary insurance plan name:_____

Group number:_____ Plan number:_____ Phone:_____

Plan's billing address:_____ City:_____ State:_____ Zip:_____

Secondary insurance information:_____

Who is your attending physician? Name:_____

Address:_____ City:_____ State:_____ Zip:_____

Office phone:_____ Fax:_____

Permission to consult with _____ regarding _____ Your initials:_____

Has an attorney been retained? ☐ Yes ☐ No Name:_____

Address:_____ City:_____ State:_____ Zip:_____

Phone–Work:_____ Home:_____ Fax:_____

ASSIGNMENT OF BENEFITS

I am responsible for all charges for all services provided. In the unfortunate event that my insurance company denies payment, or makes a partial payment, I am responsible for any balance due. If you, my massage therapist, have contracted with my insurance company at a discount rate for services, the amount remaining will be waived and I will not be asked to pay the balance.

I authorize and direct payment of medical benefits to my massage therapist, _____ for services billed.

Signature:_____ Date:_____
              (SIGNATURE OF PARENT OR LEGAL GUARDIAN IF CLIENT IS MINOR)
Signature of parent or legal guardian (if client is a minor)

RELEASE OF MEDICAL RECORDS

I authorize the release of my medical records or other health care information, including intake forms, chart notes, reports, correspondence, billing statements, and other written information to my attorneys, healthcare providers, and insurance case managers, for the purposes of processsfng my claims.

Signature:_____ Date:_____
              (SIGNATURE OF PARENT OR LEGAL GUARDIAN IF CLIENT IS MINOR)
Signature of parent or legal guardian (if client is a minor)

(Please inform your practitioner immediately upon signing any exclusive Release of Medical Records with your attorney that may impact the above release statement.)

CONTRACT FOR CARE

I will participate fully as a member of my healthcare team. I will make sound choices regarding my sessions' plan based upon the information provided by my massage therapist. I agree to participate in my own self-care program and adhere to the plan we select. I agree to communicate with my practitioner any time I feel my well-being is being compromised. I expect my practitioner to provide safe and effective treatment to the best of his or her skill and knowledge.

Signature:_____ Date:_____
              (SIGNATURE OF PARENT OR LEGAL GUARDIAN IF CLIENT IS MINOR)
Signature of parent or legal guardian (if client is a minor)

The client intake form may also include a question about insurance information, if applicable. The client should sign the consent for care, assignment of benefits, and release of medical records, if necessary, as well as the consent for care. Also use this form to record the client's health history. Your intake form should be designed to uncover conditions that will help you plan the course of the massage therapy session or signal your need to refer the client to his or her doctor before beginning massage therapy. For example, the health history should ask about the location and intensity of any pain, as well as numbness and swelling.

The client intake form is fundamental to your business practice. The information you include could vary by the type of practice you manage.

INFORMED CONSENT AGREEMENT

The concept of informed consent originated in the 1960s, when the right of consumers to understand and agree to medical procedures became a nationally important topic known as patient's rights. Patients now must give consent for most medical care, except in emergency situations, and they also have the right to withhold or withdraw consent at any time. The concept of informed consent is now customary in many fields of health care. It holds the potential for reducing practitioner liability and litigation, because the client expressly consents to the services the massage therapist provides. But the value of informed consent is even greater if viewed as the foundation of an ethically safe experience for the client.

Informed consent agreements are basic to ethical standards within the massage therapy profession. They provide accurate information to clients regarding professional services offered, they help define the therapeutic relationship, they present the credentials of the therapist and the manner in which sessions are conducted. The information enables the client to make an informed decision about whether he or she wants to receive the services. Informed consent also serves as a protective mechanism safeguarding the therapist in the event of any liability issues that may arise during or after services are provided.

Informed consent serves the needs of both the client and the therapist who have mutual responsibility for a therapeutic partnership. The client has the right to have professional services, credentials, and products explained, as well as the responsibility to respect the business practices of the professional and to actively participate in the healing work. The therapist has the right to know information about the client in order to determine whether or not the therapeutic service will be of assistance to him or her, and the responsibility to inform the client of the benefits, limitations, contraindications, and possible outcomes of the work.

You may want to call this agreement an informed consent agreement (see Figure 6.17), or it could also be called a professional policies and procedures agreement. It could be an attachment to the client intake form, or a separate form. Make it a practice to ask the client

FIGURE 6.17
Informed Consent Simplified Form

CLIENT AGREEMENT

I, _____, understand that the massage therapy given to me by _____
is for the purposes of reducing pain and stress, pain reduction, relieving muscle tension, increasing circulation, or for other reasons noted here.

I understand that massage therapy does not diagnose illness or disease, or any other disorder, and that the massage therapist does not prescribe medical treatment or pharamceuticals, nor provide spinal manipulations.

I understand that massage therapy is not a substitute for medical examinations or medical care, and that it is recommended that I work with my primary caregiver for any condition I may have.

I have stated all my known physical conditions, medical conditions, and medications, and I will keep the massage therapist updated on any changes.

Signature:_____ Date:_____

Source: Diane Polseno, "Informed Consent." *mtj,* Spring 2001. Used with permission.

to arrive about 10 minutes before the scheduled appointment to complete standard health forms. After reviewing this form with the client, and making sure you have addressed any questions the client asks, write a couple of sentences at the bottom of the form specifying that the client understands the nature of the work and agrees to receiving services. Include a place for the client's signature and date.

For further discussion of the ethical dimensions of informed consent and its impact on your therapeutic relationship with the client, see Chapter 2.

CLIENT RELEASE OF INFORMATION AGREEMENT

Your client should sign a release of information agreement (also called *authorization to release information*) when he or she requests that you send information to another person or business, such as a physician or an insurance company. If medical release authorization is not included on client intake form, you may use a separate document. It should contain the following information:

- Name of business/clinician to whom client has requested information be sent
- Address and telephone of business/clinician
- Statement requesting and authorizing release of records and/or authorizing discussion of client's information with named business/clinician.
- Client's name, date of birth, social security number.
- Patient's signature and date form is signed
- If authorization should span a period of time, specify "good through" date.

SOAP NOTES

SOAP notes—standing for Subjective, Objective, Assessment, and Plan—are used in many health care and wellness settings. They are a common method for charting a patient's health problems and care in hospital and medical settings, as well as in private practices.

FIGURE 6.18
Client Release of Information Form

Request made to:

Name of massage practice:_____

Address:_____ City:_____ State:_____ Zip:_____

License #:_____

I authorize the release of my medical records or other health care information, including intake forms, chart notes, reports, correspondence, billing statement, and other written information to the following person or business.

Name of business/clinician:_____

Address:_____ City:_____ State:_____ Zip:_____

Telephone/Fax:_____ E-mail:_____

Signature:_____ Date:_____

Client name:_____

Date of birth:_____

Social Security number:_____

If this authorization should cover more than a single release of information, please specify dates below.

Authorization if valid until _____ .

(DATE)

(See later section "Client Insurance Billing and Reimbursement" for more details about how SOAP notes relates to client insurance documentation.) One of their purposes is to indicate progress in an objective format. SOAP notes can provide the following benefits:

1 They offer a convenient shorthand for noting and later reminding yourself of the client's condition.
2 They are commonly accepted by insurance companies as a standard form of communicating the client's condition and therefore improve the possibility of a health claim being reimbursed on its first submission.
3 They allow you to compare earlier notations so you can judge progress when reviewing a client's chart.
4 Because they are used as standard documentation in the medical community, they increase the ability to communicate care services and results with medical staff.

The SOAP format has four parts:

1 *Subjective*—The client's subjective complaints and functional goals, including symptoms, affected daily activities, and the client's goals for the session (for example, "mild shoulder pain, increases with lifting; goal: to lift child without pain").
2 *Objective*—The massage practitioner's objective findings and recommended plan (for example, "tender point—right trapezius, mild right shoulder elevation, direct pressure with active assisted movement").
3 *Assessment*—The massage practitioner's assessment (to demonstrate progress)—rating the client's subjective changes and the massage therapist's objective changes as a result of the session(s) (for example, "no shoulder pain; right shoulder elevation within normal limits"). Note that diagnosis or prognosis is not within the scope of practice for massage therapists.
4 *Plan*—The massage therapist's plan for future care and the client's self-care plan, coordinating the session frequency with a doctor's prescription as necessary (for example, "weekly massage to reduce shoulder pain; ice shoulder 8 to 10 minutes as needed")

Gathering this much information on healthy clients might be difficult. Not all clients receive massage therapy to address physical ailments. Figure 6.19 shows two methods of SOAP charting (upper portion is for relaxation massage; lower portion for medical documentation) to record information specific to the needs of relaxation and health issues.

FINANCIAL RESPONSIBILITY

If your practice includes clients with insurance reimbursement, you will also want forms that specify payment responsibilities. The financial responsibility form specifies that if insurance does not cover the entire fee shown in the claim, it is the client's responsibility to pay the remaining fee. Another form often encountered with insurance reimbursement is the authorization to pay provider form, which specifies that the insurance company should send the payment directly to the massage therapist rather than to the insured individual. See the "Client Insurance Billing and Reimbursement" section in this chapter for more information.

RECORD OF CLIENT VISITS

You will also want to keep a running client log by date (see Figure 6.20). This record of client visits should include patient name, session type and duration, total charges and adjustments, payment amount, and any amount to be billed to an insurance company. It is also useful to note telephone conversations with clients, particularly if the conversation includes more than just routine scheduling.

FIGURE 6.19 SOAP Charts

SOAP FOR RELAXATION MASSAGE

Client Name:_____

Session Type:_____ Duration:_____ Date:_____

S: Goals for Session

O: Techniques Applied

A: Comments

P: Follow-up

Provider Initials:_____

SOAP FOR MEDICAL MASSAGE

Client Name:_____ Date:_____

Insurance ID number:_____ Date of Injury:_____

Modality Type (code):_____ Duration:_____

Modality Type (code):_____ Duration:_____

Current Medications:_____

S: Functional Goals

   Symptoms: Location/lntensity/Duration/Frequency/Onset

   Activities Affected by Condition

O: Visual/Palpable Findings, Modalities

A: Resulting Subjective and Objective Changes

P: Massage Plan/Self Care Homework

× Adhesion	• Tender Point	☀ Inflammation
↻ Rotation	≡ Hypertonicity	◎ TriggerPoint
○ Pain	≈ Spasm	/ Elevation

Provider Initials:_____

RECORD OF CLIENT VISITS

DATE	NAME	SESSION TYPE	DURATION	TOTAL CHARGES	ADJUSTMENTS	PAYMENTS	INSURANCE BILLED
04/27/09	Sally Jones	Myofascial release	60 min.	$130	—————	$15 co-pay	$115
4/27/09	Jim Taylor	Esalen	60 min.	$100	10% cash discount	$90	—————

FIGURE 6.20
Record of Client Visits

RESOURCES FOR CLIENT DOCUMENTATION

BOOKS AND ARTICLES

Kettenbach, Ginge. (2004). *Writing SOAP Notes* (4th ed.). Philadelphia: Davis.

Thompson, Diana L. (2005). *Hands Heal: Communication, Documentation, and Insurance Billing for Manual Therapists* (3rd ed.). Lippincott Williams & Wilkins.

Thompson, Diana L. (2005). *Hands Heal Essentials: Documentation for Massage Therapists.* Lippincott Williams & Wilkins.

Walton, Tracy. "Taking a Health History." *mtj,* Winter 1999.

WEBSITES FOR FORMS AND SOFTWARE

Download client documentation forms free at:

AMTA Washington Chapter: http://amta-wa.org

The Bodyworker: www.thebodyworker.com

Sohnen-Moe Associates, Inc.: www.sohnen-moe.com/forms.php

SOAP notes software:

Win City Software: www.wincityinc.com

Soaper Daily SOAP Notes, version 3.0, www.bodyzone.com

CLIENT INSURANCE BILLING AND REIMBURSEMENT

As a massage practitioner, you will have the option to accept clients whose massage therapy services are paid for by insurance (sometimes referred to as third-party reimbursement). This section will help you make that decision. (For information about your own insurance needs such as professional liability coverage, see the section "Insurance—Protecting Yourself from Loss" in Chapter 5.)

CHOOSING WHETHER TO ACCEPT INSURANCE REIMBURSEMENT CLIENTS

Nearly 20 percent[2] of massage therapists balance their income between insurance reimbursement payers and out-of-pocket payers (clients who pay at the time they receive massage). Whether insurance reimbursement makes sense to you as a reasonable method for doing business will depend to a large degree on how you like to operate your business. Many practitioners who accept insurance for reimbursement say they enjoy working with clients who have health care issues that might be helped by massage. Some practitioners observe that clients who experience chronic pain or have been in an automobile accident arrive for their massage appointments with not just physical pain but emotional as well. Establishing and maintaining good client relationships could require more time and different listening skills than working with clients who come for wellness massage, and many massage therapists welcome the challenges and satisfaction of working with this group.

Another factor that massage therapists welcome is the potential to earn more income. The average rate insurance companies pay for a one-hour massage treatment is $73—an increase of more than 30 percent since 2005.[3] Processing the claims requires extra training and administrative time, but it also could yield higher pay. Additionally, clients with injuries benefit from frequent sessions. Whereas a client seeking wellness massage may schedule monthly sessions, a prescription for soft tissue injuries may recommend massage one or two times per week.

Many massage therapists who do not accept insurance for reimbursement say they prefer to be paid on a cash basis at the time of service, and not wait for payments to be processed. Some massage therapists feel that learning how to work with health care referrals and insurance providers, process claims, and staying up to date on codes and rules is too steep a learning curve to climb. However, as with learning most new skills, once you have learned how to do it, you will not only feel confident about doing it but you will neutralize many of the obstacles that you thought stood in your way initially. For example, if you know how to file a claim correctly the first time you submit it, you greatly reduce the chance that it might be denied or delayed.

The pros and cons of insurance reimbursement are summarized in Figure 6.21.

FIGURE 6.21
Pros and Cons of Seeking Insurance Reimbursement

PROS	CONS
Insurance coverage provides access to a potentially large and growing client base.	You would have to learn how to work within the medical/insurance company's system.
Medically prescribed massage may be billed at a somehwhat higher rate than relaxation massage. However, be aware that it is a federal crime to charge different rates for the same service.	Paperwork and documentation such as SOAP notes, claims filing, and recordkeeping are required.
More people could receive massage therapy, and more often, if it is a covered benefit.	You may have to meet insurance plan requirements such as timely filing, number of sessions allowed, and fee schedules, especially for workers' compensation cases. The insurance company may require you to obtain authorization prior to providing prescribed medical services.
If you work through hospitals and clinics, they may be required to do the billing and pay you as an independent contractor or employee. This might reduce your own paperwork requirements while still yielding the pay benefits of insurance reimbursement.	
	The insurance company or referring physician may define the type and/or extent of care you provide.
Working with insurance helps those to be able to receive massage therapy who may otherwise have never learned about or been able to afford it.	Denials, delays, adjustments and reductions often occur. However, these are considerably reduced or eliminated with proper prior training and adequate documentation.
By working within the health care referral community, you are educating health care providers, employers, insurance adjusters/carriers, and the general public about the benefits of massage therapy.	Working with clients who are ill and injured offers challenges that some massage therapists will welcome but others will find daunting.
Working with injured or ill clients offers you the opportunity to increase your knowledge and understanding of particular health conditions and how massage can be helpful.	

RESOURCES FOR INSURANCE BILLING AND REIMBURSEMENT

BOOKS AND PUBLICATIONS

David Kent Health Systems, www.Kenthealth.com

Mahoney, Vivian M. (2008). *Manipulate Your Future: Complete Guide to Practice Building & Massage Insurance Billing.* Available at www.massageinsurancebilling.com or vivianmadison@aol.com, 865-436-3573.

Sohnen-Moe, Cherie (2008) *Business Mastery³* (4th ed.). Tucson, AZ: SMA.

Thompson, Diana L. (2005). *Hands Heal: Communication, Documentation, and Insurance Billing for Manual Therapist* (3rd ed.). Lippincott Williams & Wilkins. Also available at www.amazon.com.

GENERAL REQUIREMENTS

Laws and regulations regarding different types of insurance coverage differ from one type to another as well as one state to another. However, two requirements that apply in all cases, with the exception of some discount plans, are:

1 the need for the massage therapist to carry professional liability insurance with specified amounts of coverage, and
2 the determination that massage is medically necessary.

Professional Liability Insurance

An insurer will require that the provider (the massage therapist) must have professional liability insurance. The standard in the massage therapy profession is $1 million per occurrence with a $3 million annual aggregate.

Medically Necessary

In all cases, in order for massage therapy to qualify for insurance reimbursement, the service must be deemed *medically necessary.* That determination is made by a treating physician who diagnoses a medical condition. When a physician refers his or her patient to a massage practitioner it must be done via written prescrition.

Because massage therapists' scope of practice does not allow them to diagnose, a written prescription by a physician designating a medical condition is necessary. There are some exceptions, in some states, where an insurer's specific plan may provide an opportunity for its subscribers/members to receive a specified number of treaments without a prescription. Medical necessity is still required with plans that permit self-referrals to massage. In these instances, medical necessity is verified through the practitioner's chart notes documenting significant injury and progress as a result of care.

TYPES OF INSURANCE COVERAGE

Massage therapy has made great progress in being accepted as a health care service covered by some insurance programs. The types of insurance or medical coverage plans covered in this chapter are:

1 Auto & Personal Injury
2 Workers' Compensation
3 Health Insurance
4 Self-Insured Employer Plans
5 Discount Plans

Medicare and Medicaid are not included in this list because they do not cover services provided and billed by a massage therapist. Understanding each type of coverage will help you know if and when to expect payment from an insurance company or if you will need to collect directly from your client. The most common forms of insurance reimbursement are from automobile insurance and workers' compensation cases, with health insurance increasingly recognizing the value and covering massage therapy service when provided and billed directly by a massage therapist. Figure 6.22 shows the types of client insurance most frequently encountered by massage therapists.

FIGURE 6.22
Insurance Types that Offer Reimbursements

Percentages indicate proportion of answers to the question, Which of the following insurance types offer reimbursement for your services?

Automobile: 74% **74%**

Workers' Compensation: 60% **60%**

Health: 48% **48%**

Personal Injury: 47% **47%**

Other: 5% **5%**

Source: 2007 *Massage Therapy Industry Evaluation Report* (November 2007). Conducted by North Star Research on behalf of American Massage Therapy Association)

Auto Insurance and Personal Injury

Someone injured in an automobile related accident may be covered for massage treatments as part of his or her insurance policy. If you agree to take this client, you may choose to obtain payment from the insurance company, rather than from the injured person. There are different levels of medical coverage through auto insurance.

Personal Injury Protection (PIP)

In no-fault states, personal injury protection (PIP) insurance is often mandatory. This policy covers costs incurred as the result of an accident but without having to determine fault. No-fault does not mean that a driver cannot be held responsible for an accident. Many no-fault states still require liability insurance (that is, bodily injury and property damage coverage) since expenses that exceed a threshold amount may require that the driver who was at fault pay additional expenses and/or be sued. One way to find out if your state allows no-fault auto insurance is to check with the Insurance Information Institute at www.iii.org/media/hottopics/insurance/nofault.

With PIP coverage, your client will either be the first party (meaning that the person who is receiving the massage is the insured) or the third party (meaning that your client is covered by the insurance of another person). In some cases, the client will pay you directly and then will submit the receipt you give him to his insurance company. In other cases, you will provide the massage and then file a claim with the insurance provider for reimbursement. In still other cases, it is possible you might agree to provide a massage, or series of massages, to a client whose insurance provider might or might not approve coverage until the time the provider and the injured party reach a settlement. In these cases, you would request a letter of protection (LOP) from the client's attorney in order to "earmark" funds for your services in the event of a favorable settlement. These cases may be profitable to you, but they can be risky. In the event settlement is unfavorable or insufficient, you may have gambled and lost. Even though the client is ultimately responsible for all treatment expenses, you may be one of many in line for back payments.

Other Personal Injury Coverage

Other personal injuries can be those injuries that are not automobile related such as in "slip and fall" cases. This could be a slip and fall in a grocery store or other place of business or an injury that took place at one's home where homeowners insurance may be responsible.

These types of policies are usually limited in dollar amounts available for medical coverage unless the injury is so severe as to involve an attorney when benefits are exhausted.

As before, any treatment or service provided that you expect insurance reimbursement for must be prescribed by a treating physician indicating the medical diagnoses to prove medical necessity. Your fees should be customary and reasonable per your geographical region.

Workers' Compensation

Workers' compensation is the benefit that covers an employee injured while on the job. Authorization must be obtained prior to beginning treatment and before payment of any claims are made to a health care provider. Most states prohibit collection of any sort from an injured worker when you have been provided with authorization either by the insurance company adjuster or the employer directly. The focus of workers' compensation is to keep the injured worker on the job if possible or to return that person to work as soon as possible. Most states have a workers' compensation fee schedule that specifies the fee you will be reimbursed regardless of what your going rates are.

Be sure to keep your documentation consistent with the physician's diagnoses. If the client complains that areas of the body are involved other than those described by the physician, and your findings are consistent with the client's complaints, immediately discuss this with the treating physician to see if those areas might be added to the diagnosis and prescription, if the physician is in agreement. This applies to all insurance cases, and it can be critical to your receiving payment as well as to your ethical responsibility to the client.

Health Insurance

Health insurance coverage for massage therapy when provided and billed by a massage practitioner has increased significantly in the past few years—however, it remains sporadic and unpredictable. Most health insurance companies do cover massage/manual therapy techniques/soft tissue manipulation as listed under the Physical Medicine Codes in the AMA CPT Code book. However, while massage therapy is a covered benefit there are often insurance rules that disallow the service to be provided and billed by a trained, licensed, or certified massage therapist. They will, however, reimburse for massage therapy services when provided by an MD, physical therapist, or chiropractor, who frequently have neither the training, time, nor desire to do the massage therapy. These sorts of rules do not apply to personal injury and workers' compensation cases. Some massage therapists are working to change the insurers' philosophy on this issue, using education and evidence-based research to reinforce their position.

Preferred Provider Organizations

A preferred provider organization (PPO) may offer coverage for massage therapy under a policy's general medical coverage, with some limitations. One of the major limitations is that often massage therapists are not allowed to be "in-network" or "participating" providers. Therefore, if massage therapy is a covered service, the client would have to pay the massage therapist as an out-of-network or as a nonparticipating provider. In this case, the client would have to pay a higher deductible and possibly a co-pay amount, but the benefit might still be to the client's advantage compared with paying the full rate to the massage therapist and not receiving any coverage benefit at all.

If a massage therapist is fortunate enough to encounter an insurance company that allows them to be an in-network or participating provider, the insurance company may limit what conditions a massage therapist may bill for, the type of massage techniques that may be used, or they may require you to negotiate fees. In all cases, be sure to thoroughly analyze the insurance contract and request the review of a lawyer if necessary.

Self-Insured Plans

While some employers choose to purchase insurance plans to cover their employees, other employers choose to self-insure. Self-insured employers use their own money, and usually employee contributions, to insure. However, you will often hear an insurance company name associated with these plans because the employers use insurance companies to administer their policies for them. As a general rule, self-insured plans do not include massage therapy as a covered service; however, there may be exceptions.

Discount Programs

Discount programs, also called affinity plans, require massage practitioners who participate in them to agree by contract to discount their fees, often about 25 percent off what is considered the usual and customary "time of service fee" in their geographical region. While this may be an opportunity for added income it is most often offered as a substitute for actual insurance coverage under the employer offered health plans. An insurance company will list all providers agreeing to offer a discount (often 25 percent) in their members/subscribers directory.

While these affinity or discount programs offer clients an opportunity to receive massage therapy at a discounted rate—*which you agree by contract to offer*— this is not to be considered reimbursement by the insurer for a prescribed medical condition. Patients/clients pay out of pocket. As with any contract, you should read it carefully and if in doubt have an attorney review it before signing it. Remember, this is not insurance coverage. It is simply a way insurers have to offer the purchasers (usually employers) of their policies more benefits to offer enrollees, members, or subscribers.

Other Insurance Options

Many insurance companies offer alternative approaches in response to consumer demand for massage. Some companies offer alternative/complementary benefits, for which the subscriber (your client) pays an added premium, often under a waiver portion of their policy. The number of massages, or other alternative health services a subscriber may receive, depends on the type of benefit he or she may have purchased.

Although still rare at this time but a growing trend, some insurance companies offer a wellness benefit. Companies that buy this benefit offer their employees access to massage therapists who are preferred providers under that specific policy requirement.

BILLING AND RECEIVING REIMBURSEMENT

When Clients Submit Bills to Their Insurance Company

When a client pays at the time of service, the massage therapist must provide an invoice to the client for the services provided. It is helpful to use the standard 1500 Insurance Claim Form, formerly referred to as HCFA and CMS 1500 Billing Forms. Be sure you are using the most current form, as shown in Figure 6.23, which went into effect July 1, 2007. If your form shows 12-90 in the lower right corner, it is the old form.

Documentation/SOAP Notes

SOAP notes were discussed earlier in this chapter (see the explanation of SOAP notes in the "Client Records Management" section). Regarding the need to keep SOAP notes for insurance documentation, it is important to know that insurance and medical cases are legal cases.

Be sure your SOAP notes are written in a timely manner (as soon as each treatment session is completed), legible, accurate, in order, and filed with your claims. Be prepared to provide copies of your documentation to the insurance company and/or attorneys working on the case. As you prepare your SOAP notes, pay particular attention to how they relate to the physician's description:

S Subjective: Chief or major complaint by clients' physical complaints and functional limitations *that pertains to physician's diagnosis or injury description*

O Objective: Your palpation findings, visual observations, and movement test results; massage techniques; location applied; duration of session

A Assessment: What benefits the patient derived from your treatment session at the time of service and in the days that follow, including functional outcomes

P Plan: For a massage therapist, your plan would be to follow the physician's orders by written prescription and any specific procedures within your scope of practice you plan to do or advise the client to do.

Work on the specific areas of injury as well as the surrounding areas. When asked for a report on the client's progress, do not diagnose or offer a prognosis. Only indicate in writing the treatment or service you provided and changes you observe that are related to the diagnoses. Remember to have clients sign an authorization to release health information form and an authorization to pay practitioner form.

SPOTLIGHT ON BUSINESS

Insurance Reimbursement Terminology

Assignment of benefits: Instructions by the client to the insurance company to remit payment to you rather than to them. This statement could be included on your client intake/initial evaluation form.

Initial Evaluation/Reevaluation Form: Initial evaluation means the same as client intake. It is the term more commonly used by physicians and insurance companies. Also used is the term *reevaluation form*.

Payment Agreement: Be sure to have your client sign an agreement that says if PIP (personal injury protection) insurance limits are reached, your services are denied, co-pays or deductibles have not been met, or other charges are due and unpaid, the client understands that it is his or her responsibility to pay you for the treatment received. This statement should be included on a form signed during your client intake/initial evaluation.

Prescription: The orders written by a treating physician indicating the patient's name, medical diagnoses, duration and frequency of treatment, physician's signature and NPI number.

Release of Records: You cannot release patient/client records without the /patient/ client's signature. This statement should be on a form signed during your client intake/ initial evaluation.

WORKING WITH HEALTH CARE PROVIDERS

If you are interested in working with insurance companies, you will also need to work with other health care providers. The client's treating provider will evaluate and diagnose the medical condition, who will, if necessary, write a prescription for their patient to seek massage therapy for his or her medical condition.

If you would like to work with health care providers, you will have to build professional relationships with them. Brief guidelines about how to become approved as a health care provider by insurance companies are included here. See the section "Networking and Referrals" in Chapter 7 for more information on building professional networks.

CARRIER

1500

HEALTH INSURANCE CLAIM FORM

APPROVED BY NATIONAL UNIFORM CLAIM COMMITTEE 08/05

▢▢ PICA   PICA ▢▢

1. MEDICARE   MEDICAID   TRICARE CHAMPUS   CHAMPVA   GROUP HEALTH PLAN   FECA BLK LUNG   OTHER   1a. INSURED'S I.D. NUMBER (For Program in Item 1)
▢ (Medicare #)   ▢ (Medicaid #)   ▢ (Sponsor's SSN)   ▢ (Member ID#)   ▢ (SSN or ID)   ▢ (SSN)   ▢ (ID)

2. PATIENT'S NAME (Last Name, First Name, Middle Initial)   3. PATIENT'S BIRTH DATE MM DD YY   SEX M▢ F▢   4. INSURED'S NAME (Last Name, First Name, Middle Initial)

5. PATIENT'S ADDRESS (No., Street)   6. PATIENT RELATIONSHIP TO INSURED   Self▢ Spouse▢ Child▢ Other▢   7. INSURED'S ADDRESS (No., Street)

CITY   STATE   8. PATIENT STATUS   Single▢ Married▢ Other▢   CITY   STATE

ZIP CODE   TELEPHONE (Include Area Code) ( )   Employed▢ Full-Time Student▢ Part-Time Student▢   ZIP CODE   TELEPHONE (Include Area Code) ( )

9. OTHER INSURED'S NAME (Last Name, First Name, Middle Initial)   10. IS PATIENT'S CONDITION RELATED TO: 11. INSURED'S POLICY GROUP OR FECA NUMBER

a. OTHER INSURED'S POLICY OR GROUP NUMBER   a. EMPLOYMENT? (Current or Previous) YES▢ NO▢   a. INSURED'S DATE OF BIRTH MM DD YY   SEX M▢ F▢

b. OTHER INSURED'S DATE OF BIRTH MM DD YY   SEX M▢ F▢   b. AUTO ACCIDENT? YES▢ NO▢ PLACE (State)   b. EMPLOYER'S NAME OR SCHOOL NAME

c. EMPLOYER'S NAME OR SCHOOL NAME   c. OTHER ACCIDENT? YES▢ NO▢   c. INSURANCE PLAN NAME OR PROGRAM NAME

d. INSURANCE PLAN NAME OR PROGRAM NAME   10d. RESERVED FOR LOCAL USE   d. IS THERE ANOTHER HEALTH BENEFIT PLAN? YES▢ NO▢ *If yes*, return to and complete item 9 a-d.

READ BACK OF FORM BEFORE COMPLETING & SIGNING THIS FORM.
12. PATIENT'S OR AUTHORIZED PERSON'S SIGNATURE I authorize the release of any medical or other information necessary to process this claim. I also request payment of government benefits either to myself or to the party who accepts assignment below.

SIGNED _____ DATE _____

13. INSURED'S OR AUTHORIZED PERSON'S SIGNATURE I authorize payment of medical benefits to the undersigned physician or supplier for services described below.

SIGNED _____

PATIENT AND INSURED INFORMATION

14. DATE OF CURRENT: MM DD YY   ILLNESS (First symptom) OR INJURY (Accident) OR PREGNANCY(LMP)   15. IF PATIENT HAS HAD SAME OR SIMILAR ILLNESS. GIVE FIRST DATE MM DD YY   16. DATES PATIENT UNABLE TO WORK IN CURRENT OCCUPATION MM DD YY FROM TO MM DD YY

17. NAME OF REFERRING PROVIDER OR OTHER SOURCE   17a.   17b. NPI   18. HOSPITALIZATION DATES RELATED TO CURRENT SERVICES MM DD YY FROM TO MM DD YY

19. RESERVED FOR LOCAL USE   20. OUTSIDE LAB? YES▢ NO▢ $ CHARGES

21. DIAGNOSIS OR NATURE OF ILLNESS OR INJURY (Relate Items 1, 2, 3 or 4 to Item 24E by Line)
1. _____ . _____   3. _____ . _____
2. _____ . _____   4. _____ . _____

22. MEDICAID RESUBMISSION CODE   ORIGINAL REF. NO.

23. PRIOR AUTHORIZATION NUMBER

24. A. DATE(S) OF SERVICE From MM DD YY To MM DD YY	B. PLACE OF SERVICE	C. EMG	D. PROCEDURES, SERVICES, OR SUPPLIES (Explain Unusual Circumstances) CPT/HCPCS MODIFIER	E. DIAGNOSIS POINTER	F. $ CHARGES	G. DAYS OR UNITS	H. EPSDT Family Plan	I. ID. QUAL.	J. RENDERING PROVIDER ID. #
1									NPI
2									NPI
3									NPI
4									NPI
5									NPI
6									NPI

25. FEDERAL TAX I.D. NUMBER   SSN EIN ▢▢   26. PATIENT'S ACCOUNT NO.   27. ACCEPT ASSIGNMENT? (For govt. claims, see back) YES▢ NO▢   28. TOTAL CHARGE $ 29. AMOUNT PAID $ 30. BALANCE DUE $

31. SIGNATURE OF PHYSICIAN OR SUPPLIER INCLUDING DEGREES OR CREDENTIALS (I certify that the statements on the reverse apply to this bill and are made a part thereof.)

SIGNED _____ DATE _____

32. SERVICE FACILITY LOCATION INFORMATION
a. NPI   b.

33. BILLING PROVIDER INFO & PH # ( )
a. NPI   b.

PHYSICIAN OR SUPPLIER INFORMATION

NUCC Instruction Manual available at: www.nucc.org   APPROVED OMB-0938-0999 FORM CMS-1500 (08-05)

- Be sure you have adequate training in the modalities that are appropriate for injuries or diseases that health care practitioners work with, including neuromuscular therapy (NMT), myofascial therapy, manual lymph drainage (MLD), and deep tissue massage. If your entry-level education did not provide enough of this training, look for relevant courses at massage schools, community colleges, or through other continuing education sources.
- Health care providers who refer patients to massage therapists include chiropractors, rheumatologists, internists, neurologists, neurosurgeons, osteopathic physicians, family practitioners, obstetricians, gynecologists, doctors of sports medicine, orthopedic surgeons, physiatrists, physical therapists, and psychiatrists.
- Note: If you are planning to be reimbursed by insurance you may want to stick to the types of providers that handle the types of cases you are most likely to be reimbursed for.
- Contact other health care providers by phone or introductory letter (see Figure 6.24). Follow up with them. Make an appointment through their secretary or front desk personnel.
- Include data that support the efficacy of massage.
- Confirm with health care providers why you should work together.
- Explain the method you will use to measure the success of your work.
- Explain your process of working with clients. Include procedures such as initial evaluation/client intake, documentation/SOAP notes, etc.
- Demonstrate your competency. You may decide to enhance your credibility by providing the health care provider, office manager, a patient or nurse with a complimentary massage, demonstrating what you do, how you do it, and why you do it. Or, write a case report describing a client interaction and share it with potential referring caregivers.
- If you are working with a referred patient, the following information should be included in your follow-up letter or report to the primary care provider:
  · Restatement of goals for client's care
  · Description of care provided and client's progress
  · Projected goals if client care is extended to more visits

Keep in mind that physicians are extremely busy and have very limited time. Make any time spent with them or their office personnel by phone or in person short and to the point. Show them how you can be of service to them and their patients.

The two most common code classifications for health insurance billing are CPT (Current Procedural Terminology) and ICD (International Classification of Diseases). The designation ICD-9 means that this code publication is in its 9th edition.

SUBMITTING CLAIMS

Massage practitioners who have experience submitting claims for insurance reimbursement offer the following advice for successful and timely receipt of payment:

- When you are seeking insurance reimbursement you must bill the insurance company according to its requirements.
- If the massage practitioner works in a doctor's office, ask that the office process the claim.
- Preapproval or verification of coverage does not guarantee payment from an insurance company. It is always the policy that rules, not necessarily what an adjuster tells you, even though contacting and communicating with an adjuster is a good start.
- If you bill electronically, you must be totally HIPAA compliant. As of May 2007, you must have a National Provider Identification number (NPI) to show on the required spaces on claim forms (a HIPAA requirement) if you are filing electronically. To obtain your own NPI go to www.nppes.com or call 1-800-465-3203.
- If you are part of a complementary/alternative medicine discount plan, that plan may have its own coding system. This should be revealed to you upon contracting with them if you should decide to take that route.

FIGURE 6.24
Introduction Letter to Request Health
Care Referrals

ABC MASSAGE THERAPY, INC.

123 Any Street

Anywhere, USA 50XX9

[date]

Dear Dr. _____:

My name is _____, and I am a licensed massage therapist. [I am new to your area/We are sharing a patient for the first time], and I wanted to tell you a little bit about myself and the kind of work I do [in the hope that we may work together]. It is my intention to support your health care plan and to provide quality care to your patients.

I have experience in actively participating with health care teams and am able to communicate through standard forms of documentation. Enclosed are sample copies of my charting and report writing style. I am committed to keeping my referring physicians apprised of their patients' progress.

My specialty is [headaches]. I have attended advanced study courses on this condition and have taken a particular interest in [headaches related to whiplash trauma]. Recently published results of research regarding the efficacy of massage on patients with headache pain report [cite research and summarize its results]. I am also highly skilled in [working with a variety of musculoskeletal dysfunctions].

I have enclosed a brochure that describes my practice and services, and the fees for various services. I have included information about the benefits of massage therapy specific to conditions your patients might experience.

Professionalism, communication, and quality health care are my strengths. Please call me if you wish to discuss any of this information in more depth, or if any of your patients have the need for an exceptional massage therapist.

I look forward to working with you.

Yours in health,

[name]

Licensed Massage Therapist (LMT)

Nationally Certified in Therapeutic Massage and Bodywork (NCTMB)

Encl.

- Only doctors are permitted to diagnose, so any diagnostic codes must come from the office of the doctor who referred the client. In cases where the client is self-referred, provide diagnosis codes for symptoms only, such as neck pain, shoulder stiffness, or ankle swelling. The adjuster will not tell you what codes to use, or what they will reimburse for each code.
- Include the appropriate CPT (Common Procedural Terminology) or ICD-9 (International Classification of Disease) codes as provided by the physician. Note: The CPT code identifies the procedure, or type of soft tissue manipulation, you are performing on the patient. The ICD code identifies what is being treated. CPT and ICD-9 codes change; be sure to verify the code before using it.
- The physician's order (also called a referral) for your client's treatment should include: the diagnosis code or codes, the frequency of treatments, total number of treatments, doctor's name and identification number (NPI), and a statement that massage is medically necessary.
- Attach the patient's prescription to the claim, indicating that massage services are medically necessary. The prescription should contain the patient's diagnosis, specify that massage is the prescribed service, and the location, frequency, and duration of the sessions. In addition to the ICD or CPT code, the claim must include the physician's license number.
- *Never send an original prescription.* Always send a copy and keep the original in the client's file.
- Contact the claims representative or insurance adjuster in advance of the claim being filed. The individual who will process the claim may have misunderstandings about massage, and it can be helpful if the massage therapist speaks directly with the underwriter to ask questions such as, "What specific documentation do you want me to provide?" (This could be a copy of your license, a copy of the prescription, a copy of the session notes, or progress reports.)
- Depending on the type of work you do, and the company you are dealing with, you may wish to describe your services as "soft-tissue mobilization," "myofascial release," or "massage therapy."
- After about 45 days with no payment, contact insurer to be sure your bill was received, and find out if there is any reason it has not yet been paid.

CPT and ICD-9 codes change regularly, so be sure to verify that the code you're using is the current one before you submit a claim.

FOLLOWING UP ON CLAIMS

- Keep copies of claim forms you file with the insurer.
- Keep any correspondence, phone notes, and forms related to inquiries about or approval or denial of claims indicating the name of the client; his or her insurance company; the invoice number, amount, and date billed; and any partial payment and date paid.
- Check reimbursement dates against dates billed. Resubmitted bills for missed payments must match insurance company payment records.

HEALTH INSURANCE PORTABILITY AND ACCOUNTABILITY ACT (HIPAA)

With the proliferation of the Internet in the 1990s, concern grew that personal health care information might not be properly protected. The result of this concern was the introduction of government regulation named the Health Insurance Portability and Accountability Act, or HIPAA. At its root is the desire to enforce confidentiality and to protect personal health information (sometimes referred to as PHI). These regulations went into effect in 2003 for providers of health care services who file insurance claims electronically. The name of this regulation is HIPAA, Health Insurance Portability and Accountability. HIPAA is a federal regulation that is intended to simplify the electronic transactions involved in administering and interacting with health care plans. The results

FIGURE 6.25
Client Insurance Log

CLIENT INSURANCE LOG

Client Name: _____ Invoice #: _____ Date of Injury: _____

Insurance Company: _____

AMOUNT BILLED

Session Date	Modalities (CPT code)	Duration (units)	Total Charges	Adjust-ments	Billing Date	Amount Billed
						TOTAL

AMOUNT PAID

Date of Payment by Client	Total Amount Paid by Client	Date of Payment by Insurance	Total Amount Paid by Insurance
	TOTAL		TOTAL

AMOUNT REBILLED

Rebilling Date to Insurance	Added Interest	New Total Billed
	TOTAL	

Notes: _____
_____
_____

are intended to streamline the processing of health care claims, reduce the volume of paperwork, and provide better service for providers, insurers and patients—and, in doing so, to reduce the national costs associated with health care.

Under the HIPAA guidelines you are considered a "covered entity" if you submit patient identifiable information by electronic means. If you are a massage practitioner who electronically submits claims to health plans as a service provider, HIPAA means that you will need to follow a set of rules in the following areas in order to be reimbursed.

Electronic Transactions

The method of filing claims online, or electronically, is known as Electronic Data Interchange (EDI). If you file electronically, you must comply with the new HIPAA standards. The reason for national standards is to make conducting these transactions simpler and less costly, by establishing a single set of rules that all health care plans, providers, and organizations must follow.

The types of EDI transactions for which HIPAA mandates standards for health plans include:

- enrollment/disenrollment
- eligibility
- payment and remittance advice
- premium payments
- claim status
- referral certification and authorization
- coordination of benefits

Keep in mind even if you file your claims through a billing service that electronically submits your claims or whether you use a clearinghouse to submit claims, you still must be HIPAA compliant.

One of the possible outcomes of HIPAA is that electronic methodology could become the standard method for transactions of health care claims in the future. If you now conduct all transactions manually, this emphasis on electronic filing might encourage you to increase your knowledge and use of technology and HIPAA rules and regulations in order to stay abreast of industry changes. Many of the massage-specific software programs have insurance billing capability built in.

Privacy of Client Information

It is imperative to always keep patient records private and confidential. HIPAA mandates stringent security standards to protect an individual's health information, sometimes called PHI, while permitting the appropriate access and use of that information by health care providers, clearinghouses, and health plans. Protection of client health information, if it is transmitted electronically, will be required in order to prevent misuse of any individually identifiable information. Some of the ways in which HIPAA assures these protections include the following:

- Providers are required to give patients a written explanation of how they use, keep, and disclose the patient's health information.
- Patients must be able to see and access copies of their records.
- Providers are required to obtain patient consent before sharing the patient's information electronically, and patients have the right to request restrictions on the uses and disclosures of their information.

If you need more information about how HIPAA requirements for security standards might impact the way in which you collect, store, or share client information, go to www. cms.hhs.gov/HIPAAGenInfo.

Penalties for Noncompliance

HIPAA requirements apply to all private sector and government health plans, all health care clearinghouses, and all health care providers who choose to submit or receive health care transactions electronically. Penalties for noncompliance start at $100 for each violation, and go up to $25,000 maximum for multiple violations of identical requirements. Penalties for wrongful disclosure of individually identifiable health information can include prison time and fines up to $250,000.

TIME AND SCHEDULE MANAGEMENT

TIME MANAGEMENT

Massage therapy is a healing profession. It enhances people's health and well-being. But for a massage therapist, it can be hard on the body. If you want to be truly successful, you must set aside time to take care of yourself, including your body, mind, and spirit. See Chapter 3 for more detail about self-care.

The word health comes from the Old English word *hāl*, meaning "whole." If we want to be healthy, we must take care of our whole selves. Managing your personal and family lives is an important part of recognizing your wholeness. Consider the time for self-care as a primary business commitment, and place a high priority on it when it comes to scheduling your day's activities. If you are well rested and clearheaded, you will provide better massages and be more attuned to your clients' wants and needs. Likewise, you will be better able to handle work-related stress if you have solid support from your family, friends, and religious or spiritual community.

Each of us has the same amount of time—24 hours in every day. Whether we are satisfied with our work and our lives depends in part on how we spend those 24 hours. Time management involves making conscious choices about time. For example, you can allow extra time between appointments for catching up with late arrivals, or you can let clients know you have a policy that when someone's late arrival interferes with another appointment, you have to shorten the late person's session.

One basic tool of time management is the to-do list. It helps you decide what tasks you need to do and which of those tasks is most important. Allowing, of course, for surprises, you focus on the most important task first. An example of a way to manage your time using a to-do list follows:

1   *Weekly activities list*—Each week, list the activities you would like to accomplish during that week. Include the tasks you must accomplish, as well as those that you simply hope to complete.
2   ABC *ranking*—Next to each item that you believe is essential to your career or personal life, write an A. Mark items that are important but not essential with a B and remaining items with a C.
3   *Scheduling*—Block out time in your schedule for the A-level items on your list. Schedule this time as early in the week as possible, in case something unexpected forces you to reschedule them.
4   *A-level tasks*—Get started on the A-level items. Try not to think about the other tasks on your list. If something comes up, see if you can work it into your list; decide whether it is more important than your current A-level project.
5   B- *and* C-*level activities*—When you cannot do an A-level activity, do something you marked B; when you cannot do a B-level activity, do something you marked C.
6   *Reevaluation*—If something remains on your to-do list for longer than four weeks, reevaluate it. Is it something you really need to do? Can someone else do it? Should you just take it off the list altogether?

When you make a to-do list and rank activities, keep your goals in mind. For example, if you want to enjoy your work and your life, you have to allow time for rest. If you do not,

Time management is concerned with more than just efficiency. Balancing the needs of your business with your personal needs requires sufficient time to handle both of them in a way that promotes wellness— yours and your clients'.

you may have to list a nap as an A-level activity. Likewise, you cannot make writing SOAP notes a C-level activity simply because you do not enjoy doing it; you have to fulfill your obligations to do the paperwork related to your work. However, you can break up some tasks that seem overwhelming. For example, if you run your own practice, you might not want to make writing a policy manual an A-level activity, but writing a particular section of it might be ranked as A-level. Some massage therapists schedule things they like *least,* or that take the most energy, during a time of day they know they are fresh. That time of day will differ for each individual. On some days, the most important thing you do will be listening to someone or taking a walk and coming up with a great idea.

Another basic tool of time management is the calendar or appointment book. Entering your activities onto a calendar can help you remember what you need to do and avoid or resolve conflicts. It will also help you put your to-do list into action.

RESOURCES FOR TIME MANAGEMENT TOOLS

Go to your office supply store for a variety of calendars and scheduling tools.

Mind Tools: www.mindtools.com

Small Business Canada has a variety of topics on its website, several pertaining to time management tips: www.sbinfocanada.about.com

10 Top Time Tamers: www.getmoredone.com

APPOINTMENT SCHEDULES

To stay organized and be ready for clients, you will need to keep a record of appointments. Depending on the complexity of your business, you might need a more formal system than a paper calendar. If using a manual system, purchase an appointment book and keep it near the telephone. Be sure to mark out the times you are not available. At the beginning of each week, take a careful look at the calendar and note when you will be available so you will not be guilty of stream-of-consciousness planning while you have a client holding on the phone. Whenever a client calls to set up, change, or cancel an appointment, record the appointment immediately.

If callers can't see you at one of your available times, you might offer to refer them to another massage therapist. Your concern for their schedule will be impressive to them, and it is possible they will be flexible enough to accept one of your available openings. You can let clients know you are willing to give them the same time slot for a standing appointment if they prefer to schedule in advance. This way, you save appointment times that are convenient for them.

One way to streamline your appointment setting and to take some measure of control over your schedule is to offer clients only two options at a time: "morning or afternoon?" "weekday or weekend?" "2 p.m. or 3 p.m.?" This helps them to quickly narrow their decisions, and helps you keep better track of your blocks of time.

Make sure your appointment book has enough space to mark changes and still be readable. For each date, time intervals such as hours or half hours usually are marked. Write the client's name and phone number in the appropriate space or spaces so that the total length of the appointment is indicated. Colored pencils are helpful to use for marking an appointment book because they allow you to associate a color with a different activity or person using the massage room. Also, for a client's first visit, be sure to schedule additional time for the intake interview.

If you have an employee who records appointments, you will need to provide him or her with guidelines for allowing time between appointments. Instruct your employee to schedule at least 30 minutes for rest, cleanup, and preparation between clients.

First-time clients require an extra 15 minutes for completing the client intake form and allowing time for you and the client to become acquainted.

Records of how you plan to use your time take the form of schedules. Schedule your time and your appointments carefully so that you will be ready for your clients when they arrive for an appointment. This is an important part of professionalism. If you will travel to appointments, allow plenty of time for traffic and to set up. Also, if you will see a series of clients at one location, be sure to allow about 30 minutes between appointments to change linens, get a drink of water, make notes about your previous client, and give your hands an ice bath.

Handling Phone Calls

Setting up appointments requires telephone skills as well as an appointment book. Of course, you cannot sit by the phone all day yourself, so you need a plan for how to handle phone calls. You could:

- Use voicemail or an answering machine to record messages. This is the easiest arrangement, but consider how your clients will react to getting a recording.
- Always smile when leaving your outgoing message, and listen to it before you save it. It must sound clear and professional.
- Always return calls within 24 hours, and several times during business hours. People are more willing to leave a message if they know you are prompt about returning calls.
- Use an answering service. This costs a little more, but it ensures that your clients will talk to a person and not a machine. A good answering service will handle calls in a professional manner. If you use one, provide appropriate information and training to ensure that the service is very familiar with your business. Just as you do when choosing other outside services, get referrals. Occasionally test the service by calling your office and letting the service answer. Do you like the way they handle your call before they know it is you calling?
- Use software or a service agency that allows clients to make reservations online.
- Carry a pager and give your clients a pager number. This may be useful if you have clients with urgent needs. However, it has the disadvantage that clients will have to reach a device rather than a person.
- Mute your phone's ringer during appointments. You should never interrupt an appointment to answer the phone—indeed, you should not be aware you have had a call until you check after an appointment.
- Hire a receptionist to answer your phone during business hours. This enables you to establish your own guidelines for quality of client service, but it is also the most costly solution. It makes the most sense for a large practice or a situation in which you are sharing space and the receptionist with other professionals.

As with most of your business decisions, your choice of answering systems should be driven by what will provide the best client satisfaction and what you can afford.

THE AUTOMATED OFFICE

Although not every office finds automation necessary (see Real Touch 6.1), software programs can be useful for automating everything you do in your massage business except actually giving the massage. You can customize your own word processing and spreadsheet applications to meet your needs, or you can buy off-the-shelf software that is specially designed to meet the needs of small businesses—even the specialized needs of massage therapy businesses.

Many software packages are available that are tailored specifically to massage therapy businesses. A few of them are:

- Customer Pro-File Massage Management Software (www.landsw.com)
- Cassowary Massage Office Management Software (www.axpistos.com)
- EasyTabs, For Independent Massage Therapists (www.easytabs.ca) (Canada)

- Edge Management Systems (www.edgemgmt.com) (Canada)
- Massage Manager (www.massagemanager.com)

Most of these software packages have the following features in common:

- *Client manager*—Includes clients' names and contact information, information from intake form, and such information as birthdays or special dates, occupation, referrals, and advertising promotions. Allows you to view client history: therapist, type of massage, medical/health occurrences, products purchased, SOAP notes, payment history, etc.
- *Calendar scheduler*—Allows you to schedule appointments, noting the name of client, type of appointment, name of therapist, and notes.
- *Expenses*—Keeps track of all expenses in categories you define.
- *Gift certificate*—Keeps track of gift certificates by number, date, who purchased it, who it is for, value, payment type, and expiration date (if your state allows an expiration date).
- *Supplier management*—Keeps track of products and suppliers, both for products you use in your business and merchandise you sell, to help with inventory control.
- *Reports*—Financial, employees, independent contractors, referrals, discounts and other information can be organized by month, year, or by specific date, client, or therapist.
- *Mailing labels*—Allows you to integrate your address book with a mailing program.

Some of the packages offer specialty features, such as:

- Support for third-party billing (billing your clients' insurance companies)
- Online appointment booking

When choosing a package that's right for you, compare software features and consider which appeals most to your knowledge, preferences, and needs. Most software packages are available for a free trial period. Before choosing, it's very helpful if you can find other massage practices that use the same software. If you don't know of one personally, don't hesitate to ask the software seller for references. Do not base your selection solely on price. Depending on how helpful the software is in designing and maintaining good systems, the price difference might be more than offset by how much time the program can save you and how much better you can serve your customers.

> Software packages are custom-designed to support massage therapy practices. Specialty features include insurance billing and online reservations capabilities.

Managing without (Much) Automation   *Real Touch 6.1*

Not everyone sees total automation as a goal to shoot for. At Therapeutic Massage, a six-person massage therapy business in its twelfth year of business in Dubuque, Iowa, owner Joan Knockel says she leaves e-mail and Internet connections at home. She uses a Quicken software program for financial information and a spreadsheet for client information, but that's the extent of automation at her business. She says, "Not being automated helps keep us laid back, and more connected to our clients."

- *Scheduling*—Six massage therapists, each of them independent contractors, use a master *paper* calendar to schedule their appointments. They pencil in the times they are available for client appointments, and they keep the schedule flexible to allow for personal needs.
- *Client Information*—Client information from the intake form is entered on a spreadsheet. The information is printed out and kept in a file folder, which therapists review before each client appointment and then update by hand after the appointment. "We don't worry about a power outage or computer problems preventing us from getting to client information," says Joan.

- *Message Taking*—The office phone is muted, so only if someone is sitting at the front desk and sees the flashing light is the phone answered in person. Otherwise the call is routed to voicemail. When messages are retrieved, the person listening to the message writes it out on paper. Joan says, "Somehow it seems that more energy flows through the physical act of writing out a client's message. I feel more connected to the client when I write it out in my own hand and not type it on a machine."
- *Gift Certificates*—Gift certificates are also written out by hand. "It would be so easy to print them," Joan says, "but we like doing them by hand so the client feels the energy in the handwriting. It's sort of like the difference between handwriting a thank-you note versus sending an e-mail."
- *Handling Payments*—Each massage therapist handles payment collection with her own client. The business does not accept credit cards. "We like to keep it simple, and I think our clients feel the difference in terms of our relaxed environment," Joan says.
- *Inventory Control*—Joan says her inventory control system is very efficient: "Whenever somebody uses the last of something, they tell me and I buy more."

HUMAN RESOURCES MANAGEMENT

If you hire employees or enter into contracts for others to provide your practice with services, managing your practice will include managing the work of those people. This process begins with selection of qualified people. In addition, you must ensure that their work meets the standards you have established for your practice. For information about the pros and cons of working with employees vs. independent contractors, see "Hiring Others" in Chapter 5.

Many problems can be avoided by clearly communicating expectations up front.

If you do hire employees, it is your responsibility to clearly communicate their duties and your policies. You must be able to identify problem situations early to assist employees in correcting them. You must also have a plan in case an employee does not perform as expected and fails to improve.

WORK HOURS AND SCHEDULING

Your business plan should describe anyone who will work with or for you, as well as the number of hours you want that person to work, or the number of sessions you want per week. For a basis of comparison, see Figure 6.26, which shows that the highest number of average hours worked per week is in spas and health clubs.

FIGURE 6.26
Hours Worked Per Week

SEGMENT OF MASSAGE THERAPIST TYPE	AVERAGE HOURS PER WEEK PROVIDE MASSAGE THERAPY
Sole practitioner	18
Contractor	19
Spa/salon	22.8
Health care	21.6
Health club	23
Full-time employee	32
Part-time employee	17

Source: 2007 Massage Therapy Industry Report (November 2007), conducted by North Star Research on behalf of American Massage Therapy Association.

PAY AND BENEFITS

Your responsibilities to the employee include compensating the employee through a combination of pay and benefits. The wage (hourly rate) or salary (weekly or monthly rate) you pay an employee is something the two of you agree on at the time you hire the employee. In addition, some portion of an employee's compensation is in the form of benefits (see Figure 6.27). When you are calculating the amount your business can afford to pay an employee, keep in mind that as much as another 80 percent of the employee's compensation could be in the form of benefits.

REQUIRED BY LAW	OPTIONAL BENEFITS
Basic wage or salary or commission	Vacation pay
Matching employee's share of social security taxes (FICA)	Sick pay
	Disability coverage
Overtime pay for work beyond 40 hours per week	Health insurance
	Life insurance
Federal and state unemployment taxes	Retirement plans
Workers' compensation insurance	Continuing education
Note: Check with your state labor department to find out which benefits are required in your state.	Child care options
	Paid massage
	Non-work-related classes

FIGURE 6.27
Employee Pay and Benefits

Withholding Taxes

Federal and state income tax laws also impose requirements for employers to withhold taxes. Your practice is considered an employer if you hire anyone or if you incorporate. (If you incorporate and draw a salary, you are an employee of your practice.) If you are an employer, you must get an employer identification number (EIN) from the IRS.

Whenever you hire employees, they should complete a W-4 form to specify their withholding allowances. Each quarter, you need to send the withholding amount to the IRS and/or state tax agency with the required form. In the case of federal income tax, you submit the check for income taxes, FICA (social security), and Medicare taxes with Form 941. The amount of income tax you withhold will depend on the tax rate and the withholding allowances claimed by the employee. For social security and Medicare taxes, the employer withholds 7.65 percent from the employee's pay and also pays another 7.65 percent as the employer's share. Self-employed individuals, including independent contractors, in contrast, pay the full 15.3 percent themselves.

RESOURCES FOR WITHHOLDING AND WAGE REPORTING

The Social Security Administration (1-800-772-6270 or www.ssa.gov) provides online information, an information kit, and a service center to answer questions about wage reporting.

IRS Publication 15, Circular E: Employer's Tax Guide, details how to meet federal regulations.

Your state's department of revenue has information about state withholding requirements.

By January 31 of the following year, you must send each employee a w-2 Form. This form shows the employee's total earnings and the amount withheld for each kind of tax. State and local withholding schedules and forms vary, so check with your state's and municipality's tax agency.

Educating yourself ahead of time is important protection from the penalties for failure to comply with tax laws and regulations.

The Work Environment

Employers must provide a safe and healthful workplace. Keeping the practice area clean and sanitary protects employees as well as clients. Employees should understand the importance of washing their hands, disinfecting equipment, and other basics of hygiene and sanitation. In addition, solvents and chemicals used in the practice must be stored properly, according to directions on the container.

A primary issue facing massage therapists is repetitive strain injuries, such as carpal tunnel syndrome. Employers should ensure that employees take such precautions. It is important for employees who spend hours at a computer each day to have ergonomically correct chairs and desks, and massage therapists to have ergonomically correct massage tables and accessories, and to regularly take breaks to avoid eye, wrist, and muscle strains.

Maintaining an office environment that's safe and healthful is a minimum requirement. If you additionally want to provide an environment that communicates that you value your employees and want to create a setting that adds satisfaction and enjoyment to their work, there are many other things you can do—and not all of them cost money. Some examples of "soft" employee benefits (benefits that don't cost hard money) are:

- a 15-minute exercise break every afternoon
- a meditation room
- a used-book sharing library

> The most authentic motivational tool is a sincere desire to include employees as part of your business team and to solicit their ideas in running the business.

Although these little extras are easy to do, a good employer has to be careful that perqs (perquisites, a little add-on or benefit) don't become meaningless add-ons. The most meaningful motivational techniques require that you share as much information as you can with employees about your business so they share with you the desire to make it successful. Include them in your decision making as much as possible, celebrate individuals and team successes, and always say thank you—in writing if you can.

As an employer, you set the tone of your practice. Let your employees know how you like to operate so they can be part of the team. This involves various aspects of motivation. Authentic motivation involves several issues related to employee needs and expectations (see Figure 6.28).

FIGURE 6.28
Motivational Impacts

EMPLOYEE NEEDS AND EXPECTATIONS

Employees expect fair compensation for their work, plus reasonably safe and pleasant working conditions.

Employees do best if they understand what is expected of them.

Employees do best if they have some control over the resources they need to achieve their goals.

EMPLOYER RESPONSIBILITIES

Employers must provide fair pay and benefits and safe working conditions.

Employers need to select people who are capable of learning the job, and they may need to provide some training as well.

Employers need to provide clear directions and to check whether employees understand them.

Employers must be sure they understand what employees need, and provide access to those resource, such as supplies, petty cash, or authority to give refunds to unhappy clients.

THE BUSINESS OF MASSAGE

Meeting these guidelines requires continuous two-way communication between you and the people who work for your business. Block out time in your schedule to meet regularly with your employees, individually and as a group. Also, schedule annual or more frequent performance appraisals. During the meetings and appraisals, be sure to listen as well as talk to your employees. Ask what they need from you in order to do their jobs better or enjoy their work more. This can be a rich source of valuable information to both of you. Use the process as a positive planning effort that is not punitive in any way.

RESOURCES FOR SUPERVISING EMPLOYEES

BOOKS

Andersen, Erika. (2006). Growing Great Employees. Proteus International. www.growinggreatemployees.com.

Belker, Loren B. (2005). The First-Time Manager (5th ed.) New York: AMACOM Books.

WEBSITES

Entrepreneur.com: www.entrepreneur.com

Free Management Library: www.managementhelp.org

Small Business Resources: http://smallbusiness.yahoo.com – This site features links to a variety of websites that specialize in small-business matters.

EMPLOYEE POLICIES

If you have employees, you can help them succeed by being clear about what you expect. You and they will need to know when they are expected to be at the office. They will also appreciate being able to refer to your practice's policy manual to see what benefits you are providing, including the schedule for performance appraisals.

The purpose of developing employee policies is not to become "policy heavy" in your business, but rather to establish a solid set of guidelines that will enable you to communicate clearly and succinctly what your business requires and expects. (This will also be true of policies you will want to create in the areas of pricing, clients, and business development.)

Employee policies will include such topics as tipping and wages, work hours and days off, benefits, dress and hygiene requirements, reasons for dismissal, and competition from other employees (see Figure 6.29). Your policy manual can be viewed as a legal document, so have your attorney review it before you distribute it.

As an employer, you perform a constant juggling act between achieving a balance between the financial health of your business, your relationship with employees, and your relationships with clients. Ultimately, if your practice follows policies that foster employee growth, those policies will help your practice grow and will benefit you financially.

If your employees or contractors include other massage therapists, you may want policies with a noncompete, or nonsolicitation, clause regarding who retains clients when an employee leaves his or her position. Many employers require their staff to sign a nonsolicitation clause in which employees agree that when they leave the practice, they will not actively solicit existing clients to go with them. An alternative is a penalty finder's fee to compensate you for any clients you lose. (A noncompete, or nonsolicitation, clause forbidding a former employee or contractor from starting a similar business within a set number of miles may not stand up in court.)

Many massage therapists believe that building professional relationships is more important than worrying about this type of competition. In any event, the client and

FIGURE 6.29
Employee Policy Setting Worksheet

therapist have formed a therapeutic relationship, so be sure to allow for closure between them. Ultimately, clients will make the final decision to see the massage therapist with whom they feel most comfortable.

EMPLOYEE POLICIES (SEE FIGURE 5.9 CAREER AND PRACTICE PLANNING WORKSHEET IN CHAPTER 5)

Employee work hours and days:_____
_____

Employee benefits include:_____
_____

What is your policy for pay increases for employees?_____
_____

What are your dress and hygiene requirements?_____
_____

What is your policy about employees accepting tips?_____
_____

How will you protect confidentiality in communicating with employees?_____
_____

What is your policy regarding employees accepting clients outside of employer's business?_____
_____

What is your requirement regarding employees signing a noncompete or nonsolicitation agreement?_____
_____

What is your policy about reasonable causes for dismissing an employee?_____
_____

What is your method of conflict resolution?_____
_____

SPOTLIGHT ON BUSINESS

Who Owns Client Records?

Related to the topic of noncompete clauses is the larger issue of who owns client records. Clients have the right to seek care from the practitioner of their choice. The client completes an intake form on his or her first visit to a practitioner. In the United States, if the practitioner is an independent contractor who rents space and maintains client records independently, the practitioner owns the client record. If the practitioner is an employee, the business owns the client record.

As a former employee, you would not be entitled to take any client records with you if you were no longer employed by that business. If you signed a noncompete or non-solicitation agreement, you could not ethically seek business from your former employer's clients. Clients are free, however, to choose the practitioners they prefer, and if one continued as your client, you would ask him or her to complete a new client intake form.

The rules are different in Canada, where by law the information on the client intake form belongs to the client. Some provinces (Ontario, for instance) require massage practitioners to retain access to client records for 10 years. This means that massage practitioners must either retain the records themselves, or must sign an agreement with the employer that allows the practitioner to have continued access to client records in accordance with the province's requirements.

AN EMPLOYEE'S PERSPECTIVE: A PRACTICE WITHIN A BUSINESS

If you are an employee at another business, you still have the opportunity to learn and practice many of the skills you would need if you owned your own business.

Of particular importance is managing your client relationships. How you keep track of your client retention rate and acquisition of new clients depends to a large extent on your employer's policy regarding how clients are assigned to you, and the employer's tracking system. If you work in an environment where you have some degree of influence over encouraging repeat business—such as a fitness center, a day spa, a chiropractor's office—you will want to track your rate of client retention (repeat business) and your acquisition of new clients. In a destination spa environment, chances are that repeat clients won't be a large part of your practice. However, you might still be able to assess your effectiveness in client relationships by using some type of feedback mechanism approved by the employer.

If you discover that many clients don't return for repeat business, it's important to assess the reason why. If other massage therapists at the same employer experience more repeat business than you do, possibly it is within your control to improve your performance. In addition to using the feedback comments clients might share with the employer, you might also request feedback from your employer and other massage therapists regarding what the problem might be. If the business as a whole experiences poor repeat business, possibly the problem is due to business operations problems, such as a flawed reservations process, uncompetitive rates, or an atmosphere that doesn't feel welcoming to clients. Out of respect for your employer/employee relationship, and possibly your future job growth, your approach in discussing these areas with your employer must be diplomatic.

For other areas that you can experience career development within your own practice, while working as an employee, consider the areas shown on the Career Practice and Planning Worksheet.

GOALS AND OBJECTIVES

Set goals and objectives that you can achieve short-term and long-term as an employee. They might apply to gaining more responsibility at your place of employment, or they might apply to someday establishing your own business.

Regarding your income goals, you might have the opportunity to negotiate a compensation plan with your employer. If your income is based on the number of clients you see, possibly you can develop a strategy jointly with your employer that would bring in more clients. If you earn a fixed percentage of the massage rate, possibly you could negotiate a higher percentage in exchange for taking on additional responsibilities. Those responsibilities could support your achieving your goals and objectives, such as an objective to "learn how to manage and control supplies inventory."

LAWS AND REGULATIONS

You know the qualifications your employer required of you to take the job there. Would you need more or different qualifications if you owned your own practice? Ask questions to learn more about the laws and regulations that apply to where you work. For example: What certificates, permits, or licenses are displayed in the office reception area and session rooms? When do they expire, and what steps are involved in renewing them? Does a State health inspector ever visit the business, or is that a possibility? In what areas is compliance with health laws monitored by the employer, and how do employees help ensure that compliance is being met? If the employer hires a massage therapist who just moved to your area from another state, are the hiring considerations different than for those who received their training in your state?

One way to become very familiar with laws and regulations that affect the profession of massage therapy is to become involved with your professional association's local chapter. Chapters are frequently engaged in helping to develop and pass legislation, or sometimes trying to defeat certain legislation, that would affect the massage therapy profession in each state.

BUSINESS STRUCTURE

What is your employer's business structure? A corporation? A sole proprietorship? What do you observe about the business structure that would lead you to form an opinion about whether it best fits the needs of the business? You might note that in a partnership, one partner handles the marketing and customer-care aspects of the business while the other one handles the financial and accounting aspects—or you might note that differences of opinion between the partners actually detracts from the smooth running of the business. As you observe areas of challenge or problems, you can always ask yourself how you would handle a similar situation if you owned the business or if you managed the office.

SERVICES AND PRODUCTS

If you have an interest in merchandising, taking on responsibility in managing services and products is an excellent way to learn this aspect of a business. Learn all that you can about the services and products your business offers. Learn about what other services and products are available that might complement what the business offers, or that might satisfy requests that clients have been making. By staying abreast of trends in the profession, you will anticipate new business opportunities before consumer demand occurs.

Other ways in which you can become more knowledgeable about services and products is to ask suppliers questions about their products and their business operations. For example, you might learn about the options for laundry services, an important area of every massage therapy business. Propose to your employer that you explore alternatives to how the business currently handles its laundry. You might discover that the business is already getting the best quality and service for what it spends, or you might arrive at a different conclusion and be able to make a recommendation.

PRICING AND MARKETING

As an employee, you might not have a lot of influence on pricing, as that is generally set by the employer. But that doesn't mean you can't observe what works well and what doesn't. For instance, do clients seem to respond better to volume discounts ("Buy four massages and get the fifth one free"), to joint-marketing discounts ("Get a free 60-minute massage when you renew your fitness club membership"), or to seasonal advertising ("Escape the aches of snow shoveling, and come in for a massage")?

PHYSICAL SPACE

Since the location and interior of your employer's place of business are a given, you might still have an opportunity to put your own imprint on the session room where you practice. Are you allowed to bring in your own artwork, furnishings, or decorative accessories? You will spend a good part of your working day in your session room, so not only do you want it to feel good to your clients, but you also want it to feel good to you.

BUSINESS POLICIES AND PROCEDURES

Similar to your opportunities to learn about supplies and services, you will also develop opinions about what you think works or doesn't work in the area of business operations. It is your responsibility as an employee to adhere to the employer's business policies and procedures, and you will learn from experience which policies you would choose for your own practice and which ones you would change.

HIRING

If you become a manager or assistant manager of your employer's business, you might have the opportunity to become involved in the hiring process. Your employer might ask you to interview a job candidate, in which case you will need to understand appropriate interview questions and techniques.

You might take advantage of another opportunity to learn new business skills by volunteering to mentor a new employee. Depending on the job training tools that might already be in place where you work, this could be a golden opportunity to offer to develop a training checklist for new hires. It would include such things as a review of work policies and code of ethics, explanation of work processes (for example, "When you use the last of a supply, here is the form where you write down the date and the supply," "Our process when asking a new client to complete an intake form is …"), a tour of the facilities, and an introduction to co-workers.

FINANCIAL

Every business can offer stable employment to others only to the extent that it is profitable. Therefore, every business must rely on its employees to contribute to rather than detract from its profitability. That is why some businesses include information regarding their financial operation as a part of new employee orientation. As a massage therapist, you should know how many massages per week you must perform in order for the business to make money (or break even, or lose money). You should be aware whether the business suffers from problems with "shrinkage"—employees illegally helping themselves to supplies that belong to the business, and what can be done to control the problem.

Professional publications often publish readers' viewpoints in favor or against the practice of employers requiring that massage therapists sell merchandise or additional services as part of their opportunity to earn commissions or bonuses. This is a relatively common practice at spas, and the overall atmosphere within which employees are asked to sell merchandise is usually key to whether or not it is seen as a positive or a negative. If an employee understands the things that contribute to profitability, and if the primary focus of the business is on its clients' well-being, then many massage therapists feel entirely comfortable telling clients about products and services that can improve some aspect of their life. If, on the other hand, the emphasis of the business owners is purely on selling merchandise for the sake of profitability, the clients as well as other employees will not respond well to such an environment.

At the core of being a professional and an employee is the commitment to practice to the very best of your ability, improve your skills and your knowledge with each new day, and share with your employer a strong dedication to each client. With such a commitment, you help strengthen the business you work for, you help enhance the impact of massage on your clients, and you grow as a professional.

SUMMARY

Learning to operate a business that serves its clients well and also yields a profit requires good skills in financial management, client records management, time and scheduling management, and human resources management.

Keys to good financial management include keeping accurate records that allow you to create financial statements that help you see the health of your business in terms of how much money you're receiving and how much you're expending. Good financial control systems can alert you to danger signs and allow you to take corrective action, such as cutting back on expenses or seeking more paying clients.

Gaining the advice of an accountant or tax specialist is especially important if you are self-employed. A specialist can help you determine how much you owe in quarterly estimated tax payments, and can help you identify allowable business tax deductions.

Equally important to financial management is your management of client records. Client records include: client intake form, informed consent statement, release of information approval, SOAP charts, client follow-up, and client visits and billing record. This information allows you to provide responsible health care to the client, and also gives you an opportunity to educate the client about what to expect in your massage sessions.

Keeping accurate client records also allows you to see trends in your growth or decline of client visits so that you can modify your marketing tactics to fit your business needs.

If you choose to accept client insurance reimbursement, you will need to set up an administrative system that helps you operate a referral system with other health care providers. You will also need to submit claim forms to insurance companies and track receipt of insurance reimbursement payments.

Other administrative tasks necessary to running your business include good time management and scheduling skills.

If you choose to hire employees, your minimum responsibility as an employer is to pay payroll taxes, comply with other state and national employment laws, and provide a safe and healthy work environment. Going beyond the minimum means valuing employees' inclusion as an integral part of the work team and providing benefits that are meaningful to them. If you work as an employee for another business, you are still managing a practice within that setting and will need the same management business skills as the massage therapist who owns his or her own business.

Once your management systems are in place and your method of recordkeeping is organized, you may find that the paperwork requirements of running your business produce a type of satisfaction that is different from but equal to the satisfaction you derive from your client care duties.

REVIEW QUESTIONS

1 What basic financial business records and statements are relevant to the management of a massage therapy practice?
2 How could you handle collecting a bill from a client who is overdue in paying you?
3 What types of taxes does your business have to pay and when are they due?
4 What are five business-related tax deductions you might be able to claim on your income tax return?
5 Name three advantages to hiring a professional accountant to assist you with financial and tax management.
6 What client records are necessary to your massage practice?
7 What communications strategies are appropriate for networking effectively and building relationships with other health care professionals in the care of shared
8 What are the pros and cons of accepting client insurance reimbursement?
9 What factors should you consider when choosing the best method for clients to make appointments?
10 What legal considerations affect your business if you have employees?
11 How is managing a business you own similar to managing your massage practice as an employee of another company?

ENDNOTES

1 Born, Bryan, DC. (2007) "Fundamentals of New Client Intake." *mtj* (Fall 2007).
2 *2007 Massage Therapy Industry Evaluation Trend Report,* November 2007, conducted by North Star Research on behalf of American Massage Therapy Association.
3 *2007 Massage Therapy Industry Evaluation Trend Report,* November 2007, conducted by North Star Research on behalf of American Massage Therapy Association.

Chapter 7
Spreading the Word

Knowing how to attract and keep clients is—next to your hands-on skills—the most important skill you will need to run a profitable massage therapy practice.

CHAPTER OVERVIEW

- Importance of Marketing
- How to Create a Marketing Plan
- Marketing Tools
- Advertising
- Promotions
- Public Relations
- Networking and Referrals
- Stages of Business
- Recovery Strategies
- Reevaluating Your Plan
- Summary

CHAPTER OBJECTIVES

1 Name the four primary parts of a marketing plan and the purpose of each part.
2 Name at least three marketing strategies you can use to develop and maintain a client base.
3 Describe the pros and cons of different marketing strategies.
4 Describe at least one tactic that would be appropriate for each type of marketing strategy.
5 Describe the difference between a feature and a benefit.
6 Name two warning signals that your practice is experiencing a downturn.
7 Describe recovery strategies that could help your business if you experience a downturn.

The best technical and therapeutic skills in the world won't do you or others much good until you have clients coming through your door on a regular and repeated basis.

IMPORTANCE OF MARKETING

This is the essence of good marketing: to find ways to attract clients to your business and to keep them coming back. Your skills as a massage therapist are essential to retaining clients, but you can't show them your skills until you get them to your practice for their first visit. Whether you enjoy the marketing aspect of developing your practice or you see marketing as a necessary evil, you will find that the right mix of effective tools is the engine of your business.

Finding and keeping enough clients to make your practice successful is as simple—and as complex—as offering what people want, even exceeding their expectations, and making sure they know about it. You can reach people through marketing, which is the sum total of all the activities that go into developing, pricing, and distributing services and products and informing people about their benefits. Let your imagination run free, and have fun. Marketing thrives on creativity.

MARKETING BASICS

Some people equate marketing with advertising; however, marketing is much more than advertising. In its simplest form, it requires planning that allows you to satisfy your clients' needs and wants. Its basic steps are:

- Determine your market opportunities.
- Select your target client categories.
- Determine what services and/or products to offer.
- Set prices.
- Decide where and when to offer services.
- Plan how to communicate with your potential and current clients.

An effective mix of these marketing activities will give you a good return on your marketing expenses. In other words, you will see an increase in income that more than offsets the cost of marketing. As you make marketing decisions concerning your practice, you may find it helpful to consider that marketing has long been used for many services.

Indeed, history is a great teacher and can help you. To draw on experience, ask for help from your mentor and others with a massage therapy practice. Also do some basic research to read about others' marketing decisions. There are a variety of sources that can be helpful to you:

- The Small Business Administration publishes a variety of materials, including standard costs for types of marketing communications materials.
- Professional publications, such as mtj and Massage Magazine, include success stories in every issue. You can also pick up good tips and lessons from the letters to the editor departments in these publications. Take note of the marketing decisions other successful therapists have made.
- Check the marketing books in your local library to find case studies of successful companies.

- Take advantage of networking opportunities at professional association chapter meetings where you can gain excellent marketing guidance from your peers.
- Other excellent sources of marketing ideas are your local chamber of commerce and business development organizations, which typically conduct marketing seminars and workshops for the benefit of local entrepreneurs.

With a little imagination and creativity, you'll find that the same marketing ideas that work for other small businesses can work for a massage therapy business as well.

RESOURCES FOR SMALL BUSINESS MARKETING

ORGANIZATIONS AND CONFERENCES

Professional associations' national, chapter, and regional meetings and conferences

Courses at your community college or at professional conferences

BOOKS AND PUBLICATIONS

Ashley, M. (2006). *Massage: A Career at Your Fingertips* (5th ed.). Carmel, NY: Enterprise.

Holloway, Colleen S., LMT, "Success Beyond Work—What Prosperous Massage Therapists Know: Minimum Work, Maximum Profits, and a Sellable Business." Available at 1-888-748-5167; www.successbeyondwork.com.

Levinson, Jay Conrad (1998). Guerrilla Marketing: Secrets for Making Big Profits from Your Small Business (3rd ed.). Boston: Houghton Mifflin.

Lonier, Terri (1998). Working Solo: The Real Guide to Freedom & Financial Success with Your Own Business (2nd ed.). New York: Wiley.

Massage Magazine: Massage Magazine, Inc., 5150 Palm Valley Rd., Ste. 103, Ponte Vedra Beach, FL 32082; 1-888-883-3801; www.massagemag.com

mtj: AMTA, 1-877-905-2700; 500 Davis St., Suite 900, Evanston, IL 60201-4695; www.amtamassage.org/mtj

Peterson, S. D., Findlay Schenk, B., Jaret, P. E. (2005). *Small Business Marketing for Dummies.* Wiley.

Sohnen-Moe, Cherie (2008) *Business Mastery³* (4th ed.). Tucson, AZ: SMA.

WEBSITES

Idea Café, The Small Business Gathering Place®: www.ideacafe.com

Working Solo: www.workingsolo.com.

Guerrilla Marketing: www.gmarketing.com

Marketing Best Practices: www.marketingbestpractices.com

HOW TO CREATE A MARKETING PLAN

Chapter 5 introduced the Career Practice and Planning Worksheet, which included a section called "Marketing Plan." As with all good business plans, a marketing plan begins with goals, objectives, and tactics.

MARKETING GOALS, STRATEGIES, OBJECTIVES, AND TACTICS

Applying marketing principles to your business efforts will help you reach your goals and objectives as a massage therapist. When you create a marketing plan, you will include four basic parts: 1) meaningful goals, 2) effective strategies, 3) reasonable objectives, and 4) working tactics. Recall from Chapter 5 that goals state your overall values and mission for your practice. Objectives are more specific, measurable statements of your goals. And tactics are actions that help you carry out your strategy. For each objective, you identify tactics, or actions, for reaching the goal. The following example illustrates these levels of planning:

- *Goal*—overall values and mission
  - Build a full-time practice.
- *Objective*—specific and measurable statement of your goals
  - Add 5 new wellness clients a month for 10 months, until I am working more than half time.
- *Strategies*—the approach, or method, you will use in meeting your objective
  - Give demo chair massages at alternative health care sites.
  - Write educational articles and give presentations to community organizations.
  - Participate in community events.
- *Tactics*—actions that help carry out your strategy
  - Offer seated chair massage demos at local health-food store, at which I will distribute 100 new-customer discount coupons.
  - Write an article about the benefits of massage for pain reduction, to be printed in my local fitness club's monthly newsletter.
  - Give an educational presentation at my local fitness center.
  - Volunteer at local athletic and health fund-raiser events at which I will distribute informative brochures and cards.

The reason goal-setting is your first step in making your marketing plan is that all other elements of the plan should be focused on achieving those goals.

The four basic parts of a marketing plan are your goals, objectives, strategies, and tactics.

SETTING YOUR GOALS

The goals you set when you begin your practice will focus primarily on generating a base of clients. Determining the total number of clients you intend to develop should balance with the number of hours you work per week, the demand for massage in your area, and your breakeven analysis. (See the section "Estimating Supply and Demand" in Chapter 5.) In addition, you should consider the modalities these clients will want. Typically, an established full-time practice requires about 105 total clients: 90 who make monthly appointments, 8 to 10 to come in twice a month, and 4 or 5 who come in every week. Most massage therapists need two to three years to build a client base that size.

CHOOSING YOUR STRATEGIES

When you are starting your practice, reaching your goals will require marketing communication strategies for attracting clients. Most of these strategies involve learning what clients want and educating them about your services and how you can meet their needs. Your strategies will influence the types of marketing communications you will use. For instance, if you understand that referral networks are the major source of clients for massage, you will focus on developing them as one of your strongest marketing tools. Your strategy will also describe the appropriate balance of advertising and public relations tools. The following list contains brief descriptions of the types of marketing strategies you might choose for your business:

- *Advertising*: A paid form of communication in which the advertiser seeks to inform its audience and/or persuade the audience to act (for example, to buy something). Advertising may use a variety of media, including newspapers, magazines, yellow pages, radio, television, and the World Wide Web.

- *Promotions*: Motivating offers to stimulate trial or increase demand. Examples include the use of gift certificates, discounts, and premiums.
- *Public relations*: Nonpaid communication to influence opinions and beliefs. Methods of public relations include issuing media releases, holding news conferences and other public events, participating in events likely to be covered by the news media, and participating in community events.
- *Networking*: Developing an active system for generating opportunities for referrals to your practice through word of mouth.

Comparative Strengths of Marketing Strategies

To carry out a strategy of, say, announcing the opening of your practice, you can combine advertising, promotions, public relations, and networking tactics. Be aware of the type of response most likely to result from the following methods:

- Advertising may be used for general awareness or to advertise a specific event.
- Promotions provide incentives for people to make an appointment.
- Public relations builds general awareness of your practice.
- Networking and referrals build specific awareness of your practice.

Thus, to encourage action as well as awareness, you need to create a variety of marketing communications tools. As you combine these tools, also keep in mind that they have different advantages and drawbacks:

- Advertising costs more than other forms of communication, but it allows you to control the words used, as well as the placement and timing of the message.
- Promotions are intended to work quickly. They typically carry an expiration date (if expiration dates are allowed in the state or province in which you practice).
- Public relations costs less than other marketing communications, but the news media—not you—control the final delivery of the message.
- Referrals tend to take a long time to generate business. However, they will probably provide more clients than other marketing tools.

Once you have chosen your strategies, you will need to define your objectives, or what specifically you expect to achieve.

CHOOSING YOUR OBJECTIVES

Your objectives will state in what time frame you want to achieve a specified and quantified result. Your goals will probably refer in some way to attracting and retaining clients. The more specific your objectives are, the easier it will be to create tactics that support them. For instance, the following examples refer to different ways to build your client base. By developing a separate objective in each category, it will be much easier to decide which tactics will work best than if your objective is too general.

- *Generating clients*: How many new clients do I need or want (number and/or percentage growth)?
- *Cash versus insurance reimbursement*: How many do I want as cash clients (who pay me directly), and how many who pay me through insurance reimbursement?
- *Focus of practice*: Do I want new categories of clients?
- *Retaining clients*: What percentage do I expect to retain as repeat clients? Of course, you want most or all to come back, but 100 percent client retention is not realistic. What percentage do you actually retain, and do you want it to increase? If so, by how much?

Understanding the best use of different types of marketing strategies makes the most of your limited time and advertising dollars.

- *Increasing visit frequency*: Are there clients who have expressed the desire to come on a regular basis, but don't? How many? How can you help them maintain a regularly scheduled massage appointment? What is the average increase of scheduled appointments by client per year? (A general rule is that clients should come monthly.) Be sensitive to clients' budgets and preferences.
- *Recovering clients*: If my goal is to expand my client base, how many former clients (number and/or percentage) do I want to bring back?

Once you have created your goals and your objectives, you have a good foundation on which to make decisions about how you will go about fulfilling them. Your next step is to choose tactics that will help you do that.

CHOOSING YOUR TACTICS

The type of tactics you choose will depend on what you're trying to achieve (your goals and objectives), and on your strategy for achieving them. Tactics are the actions you will take in order to achieve your goals and objectives. They refer to the different ways in which you can gain visibility with your target market.

Examples of tactics include:

- Buy a mailing list of fitness club members and send them a coupon to try their first massage at a discount.
- Rent a booth at a community event and give 5-minute chair massages in return for prospective clients' names, addresses, and e-mail addresses.
- Give each of your clients a nondisposable water bottle on which is printed "Refresh Yourself with Massage," and your practice's name and number.

As discussed in more detail later in this chapter, it is important to keep detailed records about the results of your marketing efforts so you know which of them gives you the best results for the cost.

MARKETING TOOLS

YOUR PRACTICE IDENTITY

Every practice has a unique identity. In Chapter 2, you explored the therapeutic relationship that only you can establish with your clients. In Chapter 3, you considered various physical attributes (such as signage and convenient parking) that would attract clients to your business. In Chapter 5, you read about ways in which you could imprint an identity on your practice as an employee or as a business owner. In Chapter 6, you read about building relationships with health care providers, particularly if you choose to accept insurance reimbursement clients. Now we take all these things that, combined, make up your practice identity, and learn how to communicate them effectively to attract and retain clients. This is the essence of marketing.

At the core of marketing is the concept being visible—easy to find and easy to reach. Visibility applies not just to clients being able to find you when they have come for their first appointment but also to your general visibility to all prospective clients. You must decide how you will bring your practice to the attention of potential clients.

Most massage therapists build their client base through a combination of referrals and a wide variety of marketing communication tactics and tools. For example, you can advertise in local newspapers and the business pages of a telephone directory, send a news release to the local paper, post signs where your target clients will see them, or make presentations to community groups. Being listed in a print or online directory of massage therapists can be an excellent way for prospective clients to find you.

> The more you can quantify your objectives, the better you can design tactics that will help achieve your goals.

TYPES OF MARKETING PRACTICES

Many massage therapists use print, electronic, or broadcast media, or a variety of all types to tell potential clients about their products and services. Figure 7.1 lists the types of marketing practices used by AMTA members. All of these practices can be effective, and it is your strategy that determines to what extent and at what time you want to employ any or all of them.

MARKETING PRACTICE	
Advertise services in some way	72%
Print Advertising	
Advertise in yellow pages	26%
Advertise in local newspapers	21%
Flyers/brochures/newsletters	5%
Signs/posters	2%
Online (Internet) (compared to 21% in 2005)	32%
Community Events (compared to 15% in 2005)	33%
Local events	28%
Local coupon books/mailers	12%
Local business/networking groups	4%
Events/fairs/expos	1%
Other	
Radio	5%
Business cards	4%

Source: 2007 Massage Therapy Industry Evaluation Trend Report, November 2007, conducted by North Star Research on behalf of American Massage Therapy Association.

FIGURE 7.1
Marketing Practices Used by AMTA Members

Once you have selected the appropriate balance of marketing practices that fit your goals and your budget, you are ready to create the actual piece of advertising, or speech, or direct mail coupon that meets your needs. When you get to this stage, you will want to think in terms of which benefits are most likely to attract clients to your business. This is the concept of features and benefits.

FEATURES AND BENEFITS

When you are communicating with people about massage or about your practice, speaking in terms of their features and benefits helps your audience understand how you can help them:

- Features are descriptions of the service itself—for example, how long is a session and what techniques does it involve?
- Benefits describe the positive effects of receiving the service. They answer the question, What will it do for me? The benefits of your massage might be stated in terms of reduced stress or lessened pain. In general, when you want to get someone's interest or persuade someone to try something, you have to communicate the benefits along with the features.

Figure 7.2 provides examples of features and benefits related to a massage therapy practice. As you develop features and benefits for your own marketing communications, you will want to tie them back to your goals and objectives. Keeping a mental picture of your target market in mind as you work on features and benefits will be helpful.

FIGURE 7.2
Sample Features and Benefits for a
Massage Therapy Practice

FEATURES (INFORM)	BENEFITS (ATTRACT & PERSUADE)
Choose from 60- or 30-minute table massage or 15-minute chair massage.	Flexibility in scheduling sessions that fit your schedule.
Swedish massage.	Relief of stress and muscle tension.
CDs and books on meditation available for sale.	Resources to help you relax between appointments.
Massage therapist is member of a professional association.	Assurance of quality care because therapist follows a professional code of ethics and standards of practice.
All therapists are licensed and nationally certified.	Confidence that care is provided by fully qualified professionals that have been specially trained to care for clients' needs

When you describe benefits that could attract targeted clients to your business, it will be helpful to be aware of the types of benefits that your clients might find appealing. Figure 7.3 describes why Americans most often choose to get a massage.

FIGURE 7.3
Why People Get a Massage

Medical purposes (such as muscle soreness and spasm, injury recovery and rehabilitation, and pain relief)	37%
Relaxation and stress relief	26%
As a result of receiving a gift certificate or because it was free	26%

Source: AMTA 2005 Consumer Survey

A Caveat

It is important that you take special care in your oral and written communications with clients and other professionals that you accept the full responsibility of your professional status as a massage practitioner. This means adhering to the scope of practice, the code of ethics, and all regulations that apply to you in your state or province. Make sure you have a client's signed release of information (see Chapter 6) before sending client records to another practitioner or clinician who has been specified by name on the client's release form.

Also be especially sensitive to your use of terminology in communicating in writing and orally. Since "treatment" is outside the scope of practice for massage practitioners in many states, be careful not to use the term even in ways that seem generic to you, such as "treating" a client for stress.

PRINTED LITERATURE

Well-designed letterhead, envelopes, business cards, and postcards are excellent ways to communicate the benefits of your business. Types of print literature you might want to develop include the following:

- a brochure about the services your practice offers

- brochures about the benefits of massage, perhaps different brochures about different modalities or different client needs
- business cards on which one side contains your business information and the other can be used to note the date and time of the client's next appointment
- a price list
- notice of special offers or events
- notice offering gift certificates for special occasions
- cards requesting client feedback and suggestions

You may want to simply arrange these items on tables where clients will wait. Or you can place them in literature racks to keep them organized yet accessible.

ELECTRONIC PRESENCE

When consumers are seeking a massage therapist, they can ask friends for recommendations, call a professional association to get the names and numbers of local practitioners, look in the business pages of their local phone directory—and many are increasingly searching the Internet. Many practices, even very small ones, open an online storefront in addition to their physical office. See the resources box for a list of helpful tools for building a website, advertising on the Internet, and electronic directories specific to qualified massage therapists. If clients go online, you want to be there!

Creating a Website

Your first decision is whether to hire a website designer to create your website or to do it yourself. Website design software is now available that makes it possible for non-techies to create their own website without having to know HTML programming language and other technical details that you used to have to know. Before you select software, it's a good idea to talk with others who have set up their own websites, to find out what they liked and didn't like about the software they used. You can also get references for website designers that others have used and liked.

You can be present on the Internet in many different ways. You can have your own website, where you determine the extent of information and services you want to provide. Some practices simply have a home page that provides information about how to contact them. Others have extensive websites that allow them to schedule appointments electronically, order products online, take virtual tours of their practices, and access educational information. The choice of how much or how little information you choose to provide on your website will be determined by how much time you want to spend creating and updating the site, and how much money you want to spend. The more complex the online features you offer, the more expertise and/or money you will need to maintain the site.

If you offer clients the opportunity to book appointments online, check at least weekly to verify that the feature is working. If a prospective client tries to make an appointment by clicking but goes nowhere, he or she will either call for an appointment instead, will try another massage practice's website, or will decide making an appointment is more trouble than it's worth. If you offer the feature, make sure it works.

You can extend your presence further by linking your site to other related sites, and to listing your practice with massage therapy directories.

> If your website offers an advanced feature such as online appointment booking, check regularly to make sure it works. A feature that doesn't work properly is worse than not having the feature at all.

Tips for a Do-It-Yourself Website[1]

When websites were first becoming popular, you either had to hire a Web designer or you needed to know HTML programming to create your own. That's no longer the case. Software has now become available that can make the most basic novice look like a savvy technophile. A few basics to follow include:

- Keep it simple. A five-page Website is sufficient for including the most important information about your business: your hours, your modalities, your fees, your location, your phone number.
- Be color coordinated. Keep your colors harmonious and in the background. Color should serve to highlight your information, not detract from it.
- Integrate your Web address with your other business communication pieces. Print it on your business card and your marketing brochure, and publish it in your print and online directories.
- Look at a variety of well-designed sites, to give you an idea what you want for your own. If you find that what you want is beyond the capabilities of the do-it-yourself software, you can always hire a Web designer.

Choosing Content for Your Website

Whether you produce content in-house or go to an outside provider, you will want to first take a "big picture" approach. Keep these guidelines in mind:

- Content should reflect your individual goals.
- Content should be targeted to your audience.
- Information readers want should be easily accessible on the home page.
- Background information about your business can be on the home page or clickable on an About Us tab.
- Graphics and photographs should reflect the image you want your practice to project.
- Don't bog down your page with graphics that slow your site down. Although many consumers now have computers that can handle larger amounts of data, and high-speed transmission to send and accept data, not all do.
- Don't use colored or textured backgrounds that make text difficult to read.
- Use animation and sound only to the extent that they enhance the content. Too much movement and noise can detract from your site's overall effect.

Once the basic content has been determined, it's equally important to attend to the details. Careful attention to the following will make your website user friendly:

- Check for spelling and grammatical errors, broken links, and other mistakes that can undermine your credibility.
- Always get permission for content you didn't create originally.
- Include a "last updated" message.
- If you use clickable images as navigational tools, make sure you also include text-based links on the same page.
- Don't link to unfinished pages or sections by showing an "Under Construction" sign. It's better to link to pages after you've completed them, preventing frustration when readers click for content they can't access.

"The Other Coast," artist Adrian Raeside. Permission granted for use.

- Make the "Contact Us" information easy to find, and include your location, telephone number, and e-mail address. Even if the information a client seeks is contained somewhere on your website, sometimes callers would rather ask a real person for the same information than to search for it. And if the massage profession can't offer the personal touch to clients, who can?

RESOURCES FOR INTERNET PRESENCE: CREATING A WEBSITE

PEOPLE YOU KNOW

Your Internet service provider

Local computer store

You probably know someone who has a website you like. Ask him or her who designed it.

BOOKS AND ARTICLES

Crowder, David (2007). *Building a Web Site for Dummies* (3rd ed.). Wiley.

Robbins, Jennifer Niederst (2006). *Web Design in a Nutshell*. O'Reilly.

Zohar, Amihud (2005). *Look Mom! I Built My Own Website*. Small Press Bookwatch.

ONLINE ARTICLES

Build Your Own Website: www.build-website.com

Build Web Site For You: www.buildwebsite4u.com

Small Business Bible, "Dos and Don'ts for Website Design": http://www.smallbusinessbible.org/dos_donts_websitedesign.html

Find My Host, for reviews of hosting sites: www.findmyhost.com

SOFTWARE AND DESIGN SUPPORT

Clip Art (free, public domain): www.free-clipart.net; www.clipartconnection.com; www.free-clip-art.com

Photography (stock photography that can be purchased): www.istockphoto.com; www.inmagine.com; www.corbis.com

CoffeeCup Software: www.coffeecup.com

Cool Home Pages: www.coolhomepages.com

Dreamweaver, software: www.adobe.com/products/dreamweaver

Flash software by Adobe: www.adobe.com/products/flash

GoDaddy software: www.godaddy.com

NVU software: www.nvu.com

Web Studio, software by Back To The Beach: www.webstudio.com

Who Built It is a service that lets you type in an address of a website you really like and do find out who developed it. If it's one of the more than 10,000 listed, you can contact the developer. www.whobuiltit.com

---

ABOUT ADVERTISING ON A WEBSITE

Brain, Marshall, "How Web Advertising Works," at http://www.howstuffworks.com/web-advertising.htm

Wickipedia, "Online Advertising," at http://en.wikipedia.org/wiki/Online_advertising

WebSource, "Online Advertising/Web Advertising/Business Advertising," at http://www.web-source.net/internet_advertising.htm

MASSAGE THERAPY ONLINE DIRECTORIES TO LINK TO WEBSITES

AMTA's Find a Massage Therapist®: www.findamassagetherapist.org

MassageAnywhere.com: www.massageanywhere.com

Massage Network: www.massagenetwork.com

MassageTherapy.com: http://www.massagetherapy.com/find/index.php

MassageToday: www.massagetoday.com/locator

ADVERTISING

The greatest advantages of advertising are that it allows you to control your message and your business's image and to choose when and where that message will appear. You pay for advertising, so it's important to understand how to use it in a way that pays off. If your marketing tactics include developing and running advertisements, you must decide where to place the ads and whether to use display ads or classified ads. Because most massage therapy clients will come from your local area, advertising in the business directory pages (also known as yellow pages) or in publications serving the nearby community would most benefit you. Also consider whether you can buy ad space in publications serving the particular category of clients you are targeting. For example, use sports- or fitness-related newsletters or other publications if your target group is athletes. If your target group is performing artists, consider a dance or theater newsletter.

Ultimately, the decisions about where to advertise depend on your knowledge of your clients. The better you get to know your target clients, the more information you will have for selecting where to advertise. See Figure 7.4 for a list of advertising opportunities.

FIGURE 7.4
Types of Advertising

Billboard	Links to websites
Brochure that tells about your business	Newsletters (your own, or ads in other newsletters)
Bulletin boards at local businesses	Print ads (newspaper, magazines)
Business cards	Radio
Community cable TV	Website
Direct mailers	Yellow pages
Directory listings, print and online	

Despite its cost, advertising can contribute to a successful practice. Buying an ad that will reach a large audience can be quite an expensive way of communicating. In addition, it is by definition impersonal because it is not directed to a specific individual. The impersonal nature of advertising means that some people who see or hear the ad will not be interested in what you are offering. On the other hand, advertising is a way to reach people who might not otherwise think about massage or how it can benefit them.

You might try advertising for a short period and tracking the results. The simplest way is to ask each new client where he or she learned about your practice. Keep track of how much income you earn from clients who came as a result of your advertising. If the total income from these clients equals or exceeds the cost of the ads, the advertising makes business sense.

CREATING EFFECTIVE ADVERTISEMENTS

Whether you design your own ads or pay someone else, you need to evaluate each ad idea to make sure it meets established criteria:

- What response do you want from the client after reading your ad (for example, call to schedule an appointment, attend an informational open house)?
- Does your ad contain all the information a client needs in order to respond as you intend (name of your practice, phone number, location, and type of service being offered)?
- Does the ad clearly identify your credentials and the nature of your practice?
- Does the ad appeal to the client's needs and offer a way to meet those needs? (It should tell the benefits of your work as well as features of your practice.)
- Is the ad believable and truthful?
- Is the ad pleasing to see (or hear, for a radio ad)?
- Is the ad easy to understand? Test it on friends. Ask them to read or listen to it and tell you what it is asking people to do.

PROMOTIONS

With promotions, you actively encourage making appointments. You provide an incentive that motivates people to take action. For example, by offering a discount coupon for first-time clients, you reduce the perceived risk of trying a massage, thereby increasing the number of people who will make an appointment. Or you split the financial commitment with clients and encourage them to become monthly repeaters by offering a 12-month package (one 60-minute massage each month) at 80 percent of what it would cost to buy each massage separately. Or you encourage existing clients to refer their friends by offering a bonus for each new person who books an appointment from the referral. See Figure 7.5 for an example of a coupon. Possible coupon offers include:

- First massage at 10 percent off
- Free 10-minute chair massage
- Bring a friend and split the savings: two sessions for the price of one and a half (or pay for one session and get 50 percent off a session for a second person), an idea for someone treating a friend.
- Free merchandise with massage
- Buy five massages, get one free
- Baker's dozen: buy 11 massages, get the 12th one free
- Discount of 50 percent off next visit for each new referral

CODED COUPONS

When you distribute coupons to more than one group (for example, current and former clients, or at two different health fairs), it is helpful to code the coupons in some way. For example, you could give out yellow coupons at a track meet and blue coupons at a basketball tournament. Or, you could use a letter code to identify two-for-one offers versus a percentage discount. When the coupons are redeemed, keep track of their codes. This will help you decide which kinds of offers or places of distribution give the best results. When you evaluate your plan, you will be able to tell what is working and what is not.

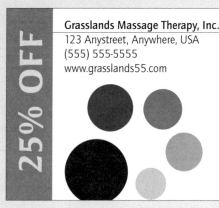

Grasslands Massage Therapy, Inc.
123 Anystreet, Anywhere, USA
(555) 555-5555
www.grasslands55.com

25% OFF

ENJOY ONE FULL HOUR OF MASSAGE
and get 25% off the regular price!

One to a customer.
Offer expires Nov. 30, 2010
Ref. 09-A

FIGURE 7.5
Sample Coupon

The places and ways you can distribute coupons are almost as unlimited as the types of promotions you can create. They include:

- health fairs
- newsletters
- newsletter for target group (such as an employer or hobby group)
- locations frequented by target groups (health clubs, hospitals)
- sports or dance events
- health-related businesses
- bulletin boards at clients' place of work
- silent auction to benefit a community organization
- flyer inserted in bulk direct-marketing mail distribution
- "trinket marketing"

Trinket marketing means you use some little trinket as a giveaway to clients and prospective clients. Choose an inexpensive giveaway that you can relate to a reason for having a massage. Have your marketing message imprinted on the item or on an attached tag. See Figure 7.6 for examples of trinket marketing. Although these ideas might seem gimmicky, many people respond well to this type of marketing because they like getting "freebies," and the trinket is something they can keep to remind them of your practice.

GIFT CERTIFICATES

When you sell a gift certificate, you win in two ways. One, you get the money as soon as you sell the certificate, and two, often the recipient of the certificate becomes a new client for you. Remember as you design or select your gift certificate format that you may be creating a first impression with its recipient. Be sure to convey the image you want for your business, and make the certificate as attractive and informative as possible.

A gift certificate should include the following information:

- The name of your business
- The address and phone number of your business
- Your business's regular working hours and "or by appointment"
- An expiration date, if one is allowed by law where you practice

Optional messages, either printed on the certificate or in a separate note, could include:

- Your business's philosophy
- The benefits of massage and bodywork
- Information about a particular modality if you specialize
- Inspirational quote
- A map with directions to your business
- Your business's marketing brochure

FIGURE 7.6
Trinket Marketing

TRINKET	MARKETING MESSAGE
Calendars	Today's a great day to have a massage. Call …
Highlighter	Seeing you is the highlight of my practice. Call …
Ruler	The value of good health is immeasurable. Call …
Flashlight	Light up your life with massage. Call …
Box of crayons	Color your world healthy. Call for a massage today.
Baby bib	Mommy, why don't you make a massage appointment today? Call …
Bag clip	Stay fresh with massage. Call …
Piggy bank	Invest in good health with massage. Call …
Rubber ducky	up for your health. (Print your number on the bottom of the ducky.)
Hot pad	Protect your health with massage. Call …
Deck of cards	Don't gamble with your health. Call …
Drawstring bag	Lighten the load with massage. Call …
Compact mirror	Massage reflects well on you. Call …
Bookmark	Mark your place on our massage schedule. Call …
Water bottle	Refresh yourself with massage. Call …

Keep a log of gift certificates that shows the purchaser's name. If possible, also record the recipient's name, address, phone number, and whether the certificate was for a special occasion such as birthday or holiday. You can use this information to send future sales promotions or to make a follow-up call if the certificate is not redeemed quickly.

Consumer Laws and Gift Certificates

Many states have consumer laws governing the sale and use of gift certificates. Some states and Canadian provinces prohibit the use of expiration dates on gift certificates. Some states say there can be no expiration dates on certificates exceeding $100 value. Some laws limit the length of time before an expiration date may be allowed. Some states do not allow service fees to be added to the cost of gift certificates. Be familiar with any laws that apply to you. To check on the laws governing gift certificates in your state, go to www.consumersunion.org and search on "gift certificates."

If you practice in a state or province that allows you to use them, be flexible. If someone wants to use a certificate after its expiration date, you will create goodwill if you accept it anyway. The potential long-term relationship with the certificate holder is almost certainly more valuable than your right to refuse the certificate. It's also up to you to let the certificate revert to the giver if it is not used by a certain date.

Be familiar with your state's consumer laws governing the sale and use of gift certificates.

CROSS-PROMOTIONS

As you develop professional relationships, you may find opportunities for cross-promotion with others. This involves you and someone else agreeing on combined promotions that benefit both of you. For example, the health club from which you get regular referrals might advertise a half-price massage from you with every new membership. Those who are attracted to the club because of the promotion might become clients for you as well.

Another example could be partnering with a diaper service to send out a mailer that

FIGURE 7.7
Partnering with Other Businesses

CROSS-PROMOTION	RELATED BUSINESSES
Seasonal promotion for aching muscles. *Offer*: One free massage for every $100 spent. *Marketing message*: "Welcome the new spring's aches with the new spring's relieving massage."	Landscape businesses Nurseries and garden centers Building contractors Club sports (soccer, baseball, etc.)
Massages for new moms and their babies. *Offer*: Two massages for the price of one, with the purchase of …. *Marketing message*: "The first year can be exhausting. Let us help with a soothing massage."	Diaper services Obstetricians/Gynecologists Photographers who take baby portraits Flower shops where the proud father will be buying a bouquet Day-care centers that welcome babies Stores that sell baby furniture, clothes, toys, baby books, strollers, etc.
Sports and fitness massage. *Offer*: Free 30-minute massage with each new membership *Marketing message*: "You do the work, we'll help you recover."	Fitness centers Sports centers Rehab clinics Golf courses Schools' athletic departments

offers "One free massage to the new mother with each new diaper subscription." You and the owner of the diaper service split the cost of the mailer and the cost of the massage (the diaper service pays you one-half of your fee). The diaper service is guaranteed a new customer, because that is the condition of the promotion, and you have an opportunity to win a new paying client after the first massage.

The key to successful cross-promotions is finding a combination of services that provides mutual benefit to both your businesses. Work with a business owner who is as enthusiastic as you are about the potential for both of you to come out winners, and you will have fun experimenting with different offers to see which one is the most effective.

The next step is negotiating the details of the cross-promotion with the other business. The transaction could be as simple as sending a promotional flier to that business's customer list, or more involved, such as offering a "package deal" to customers: a certificate for a 30-minute massage after the fourth hair styling appointment; 20 percent discount at Garden Supply Co. when you purchase a package of four massages, etc.

See Figure 7.7 for other examples of cross-promotions.

> Advertising and promotions provide the fastest results, even though they are among the more expensive strategies. Public relations activities are aimed at longer-term visibility and education.

PUBLIC RELATIONS

Public relations generates awareness of your practice. It also enhances the positive image of massage and of your practice. Public relations could include actions such as issuing a news release, giving an educational talk to a community group, and volunteering at community outreach activities. When coupled with other types of marketing communications, public relations increases the likelihood that people will try a massage at your practice. The advantage of public relations is that it only costs your time and effort. The drawback is that, in the case of a press release, you cannot control your message nor can you guarantee that your message will be publicized at all.

Send out news releases to local media about your practice's opening (include information about your credentials and on the opening's date, time, and location).

Send news releases about new services or new credentials.

Set up a booth or table at community events, health fairs, county fairs, etc.

Join local community organizations for business professionals.

Write articles for other businesses' newsletters (such as health clubs, medical practices, wellness associations, etc.).

Speak to a community group.

Distribute educational brochures about massage and/or your practice at venues where prospective clients are (health clinics, spas, health fairs, health food stores, recreation or park districts, community centers, libraries, etc.).

Volunteer for AMTA chapter activities to promote National Massage Therapy Awareness Week™.

Distribute preprinted brochures or newsletters about the benefits of massage therapy.

Write to consumer media outlets to suggest feature story ideas.

Set up a website with information about your practice and the nature and benefits of massage.

Give talks or demonstrations about the benefits of massage at health fairs, business meetings, recreation or park districts, or service and support organizations.

Give complimentary on-site chair massage at community events, in stores, at sports events.

FIGURE 7.8
Using Public Relations to Promote Massage Therapy

One of your greatest public relations assets could be membership in your professional association. When you are a member of a professional association that places high importance on educating the public and promoting the image of massage therapy, you can expect that the association will be an excellent resource for materials to help you better understand how to market and publicize your practice. Among the tools you might expect are:

- a comprehensive and credible selection of research, published articles, methods and techniques, alternative and holistic care updates, and general information related to massage therapy
- easy-to-customize news releases
- reproducible fact sheets that provide information about such topics as: the efficacy of massage; consumer demand for massage therapy; statistics and attitudes of massage practitioners toward the profession; things you should know about working with health insurance reimbursements; and information physicians should know about working with a massage therapist; and where to find research about the benefits of massage therapy
- presentation materials to simplify speaking engagements

You save time and money by becoming a member of a professional association that provides these benefits. These invaluable tools give you a solid groundwork on which to base your individualized public relations efforts to health care professionals and potential clients. 7.8 lists ideas you can use to promote your business and your profession through public relations.

EDUCATING THE PUBLIC

Although massage therapy is something most people have heard of, many are not quite sure about what it entails or how it might benefit them. Some may suffer from misconceptions about it that get in the way of their willingness to try it for the first time. Thus, a logical way to develop a client base is to educate the public.

Educating the public can involve giving talks or seminars or writing articles or news releases. If you do not like writing or public speaking, however, you still can provide information by setting up a booth at a health fair or distributing articles you have found informative. Whatever techniques you use, be sure your information explains the benefits of massage. At the same time, take care that the benefits you describe are those validated by scientific research. If you believe a certain benefit is due to massage, but that benefit has not yet been substantiated through research, say "it is generally believed" or "anecdotal evidence suggests that …".

Educational presentations can refute prospective clients' misconceptions about massage and alleviate their fears about having massage for the first time.

NEWS RELEASES

If you have information that is newsworthy, it's possible that a local newspaper, magazine, or radio or TV station would print or broadcast it. Attributes that make an item newsworthy include: it's educational, it's an –est of some sort (newest, largest, highest number), it's helpful, or it's timely. See Figure 7.9 for a sample format of a news release.

When writing a news release, always include:

- your name and phone number where you can be reached
- headline that tells what's newsworthy
- dateline (gives city, state, and date)
- a paragraph that tells who, what, when, where, and why
- boilerplate information. This is information that gives reporters background information about your practice and other general but relevant information.

Keeping Ties with Media Contacts

Maintaining contact with people who choose whether to print your news release or not can be helpful in terms of bringing your news to their attention. Knowing people doesn't guarantee that your news will be printed, but your already-established credibility with them will increase the chances that they will at least notice and consider what you've sent them.

The following ideas[2] can help you establish and maintain contacts before you need them:

1 Develop a list of health, fitness and beauty editors, and reporters, and keep it current. As you develop a relationship with them, jot down notes about their preferences and interests.
2 Get to know the types of stories they cover, their deadlines, and how they work. Don't pitch stories to them that don't fit their criteria.
3 Invest in professional photos of your business's interior. Make sure the photos reflect the image you want to convey.
4 Have a fact sheet about your business on hand at all times, as a one-page reference to answer "who, what, when, where and why." This is considered a backgrounder.
5 Regard any member of the press as your most hard-nosed critic. Pay close attention to how you package and deliver your information. You cannot control what they

FIGURE 7.9
Format for a News Release

FOR IMMEDIATE RELEASE

Contact: [massage therapist's name]
                    [name of practice]
                    [daytime/evening telephone number]
                    [Name of Business]

Announces … [Event]

CITY/STATE/DATE – [Name of business], a member of [name of professional association], [describe announcement/event].

[In next paragraph, use your own words in a quote that explains or adds color to the introductory paragraph, or use a supportive quote by a recognized expert whose permission you have to include the quote in your news release.]

[Use all or part of a standard "boilerplate" statement. For example, AMTA's boilerplate states: The American Massage Therapy Association® (AMTA®) is a professional association of more than 57,000 members. AMTA professional members have demonstrated a level of skill and knowledge through education and/or testing and must meet continuing education requirements to retain membership. AMTA provides information about massage therapy to the public and works to improve the professional climate for massage therapists. The association also helps consumers and healthcare professionals locate qualified massage therapists nationwide, through AMTA's Find a Massage Therapist® free national locator service available at www.findamassagetherapist.org or toll-free at 888-843-2682 [888-THE-AMTA].]

[Add boilerplate about your own business.]

[3 number symbols indicate the end of the release.]

write. Return their calls and attend to their queries immediately. They are on constant deadline, and your response time will influence whether or not they use you for future stories.

6   Invite members of the press to try new modalities or services you offer. However, be aware that most employers have policies that prohibit reporters from accepting free gifts or services. Your demonstration of a type of technique probably will have to be kept to a shorter session than you would normally provide.

7   Designate yourself or someone else as a spokesperson. This person must be able to expertly articulate information about modalities, trends, and techniques.

8   Develop a "nose for news." Know what is news and what's not. Ask yourself why someone would care, and whether the information is either new, unusual, timely, or helpful in some way.

9   When your press release gets coverage, display clippings in your lobby. When you send out press information, include these clippings. It shows the editor that you're media worthy.

10 Public relations is far more effective with a personal touch. Remember editors and reporters on special occasions. Little gestures can make all the difference.

GIVING SPEECHES AND PRESENTATIONS

People who are not sure they want to pay for a massage may still be open to learning about massage or related topics. You can reach people with some level of interest by holding a seminar or workshop. People who are not sure they want to pay for a massage may still be open to learning about massage or related topics. You can reach people with some level of interest by holding a seminar or workshop. Speeches help to generate awareness of your expertise and your practice. A well-delivered speech signals the personal professionalism that carries over into your practice.

When you accept a speaking engagement, choose a topic with which you are comfortable. Examples might be benefits of massage, massage of pregnant women or infants, or a particular modality. Prepare an outline and practice what you will say. Time yourself, and be sure to allow time for questions.

Know how to respond during a question-and-answer session if you do not know or are unsure of the answer to a question. Offer to take the person's name and phone number and call with the answer later. This is a great chance to follow up with someone interested in what you have to say. It also builds trust among the audience. Your audience sees that you give information only when you are sure of its accuracy.

For any type of presentation you give, take along plenty of business cards and brochures. People will pick up brochures on topics such as self-help. If your name and phone number are on the brochure, some of the audience members might call you later.

Publicizing Your Upcoming Presentation

You will want to do justice to your time in preparing your presentation by publicizing it in appropriate places, far enough in advance, to attract a suitable audience. Guidelines that can help you publicize your presentation in advance include:

1 Post information about your upcoming presentation in your treatment rooms and lobby, and at stores, community gathering areas, libraries, etc.
2 Tell all your clients.
3 Send news of your event to local papers and alternative health tabloids, and to local TV and radio stations. Send information far enough in advance to beat their deadlines for publication.
4 At the event, ask attendees to sign up on your mailing list so you can notify them of future events.

RESOURCES FOR HANDOUTS AND PRESENTATIONS

American Massage Therapy Association, 500 Davis Street, Suite 900, Evanston, IL 60201; www.amtamassage.org

Hemingway Massage Products; 815-877-5590; www.hemingwaymassageproducts.com

Information for People, P.O. Box 1038, Olympia, WA 98507-1038; 800-754-9790 or (360) 754-9799; www.info4people.com

NEWSLETTERS

Food for Thought Health News: 727-446-8405

Staying in Touch, 877-634-1010: www.stayingintouch.net

TopHealth: The Health Promotion and Wellness Letter: www.toptopics.com

---

NETWORKING AND REFERRALS

Most service businesses receive a large portion of their clients from recommendations— referrals from other professionals or word of mouth from satisfied clients. This strategy certainly applies to massage therapy. Many people are uncomfortable picking a name out of the yellow pages as a way to choose a massage therapist. The major ways of getting referrals are to use networking skills.

When you are getting started, networking requires focused, concentrated effort. Your efforts at networking should encompass relationship-building with your clients, your colleagues, other business and professional people who may be sources of referrals, and groups that represent your target clients.

Networking starts with meeting people and letting them know what you do. Be prepared to present the benefits of massage. Be ready to answer the common query, "What do you do?" by developing a response that defines your practice in one minute or less. You might even plan how to demonstrate a few techniques that establish your credibility as a skilled massage therapist. You can introduce yourself in person, with a letter (such as the one shown in Chapter 6, Figure 6.24), or by asking your clients to refer their friends and making client referral cards available. See Figure 7.10 for a sample client referral card.

Networking is the shortest distance to word-of-mouth marketing, the least expensive and most effective form of advertising.

FIGURE 7.10
Sample Client Referral Card

Massage therapists have an advantage over people in some other professions: people are generally curious about massage. When you introduce yourself as a massage therapist, many people immediately will have questions for you or be able to relate to the benefits you offer. Networking continues as people become acquainted with you and your practice and learn to appreciate your professionalism and other good qualities.

When you network successfully, people want your name and phone number so they can make an appointment or refer clients to you. Thus, it is important to have business cards and stationery that convey the desired image of your practice. Figure 7.11 shows a sample business card.

People notice and care about whether those with whom they are networking are sincerely interested in them or just trying to get ahead. When you plan your networking, keep in mind all your usual ethical and etiquette standards. Listen to others as well as promoting yourself. If you want to meet people by getting involved in a professional, charitable, or other organization, do it with sincerity and enthusiasm for the task at hand, as well as for the potential to promote yourself. When someone refers a client to you or praises your practice, be sure to thank the person, preferably in writing. For additional ideas on how to promote your business using referrals and networking, see Figure 7.12.

As you expand your practice, continue networking with clients and others. The longer you have been a massage therapist, the easier networking becomes, because your circle of acquaintances keeps expanding. Try to make a habit of meeting someone new every day.

FIGURE 7.11
Sample Business Card

FIGURE 7.12
Using Networking and Referrals

Carry business cards and informational brochures with you wherever you go.

Join professional organizations and business organizations, such as your chamber of commerce, local business association, and Better business Bureau.

Regularly attend professional and business organization meetings; become involved on a committee.

Present a talk or workshop to an organization to which you belong.

Actively participate in professional associations.

Participate in breakfast clubs or similar networking groups. If one isn't available in your community, consider starting one.

Participate in health fairs.

Tell your physician, dentist, and chiropractor about your practice and how it has helped clients; ask for referrals.

When clients express satisfaction with their progress, ask if you may write or speak with their physician about your practice and how it has helped them.

Participate in or otherwise support groups that represent your target clients (for example, sports associations or track clubs if you want to target athletes; parenting groups if you want to emphasize prenatal or postnatal care or infant massage; social organizations or support groups if you want to target people in related categories).

Send letters to health care professionals, requesting referrals.

Always send a thank you for a referral, even if the person referred to you doesn't make an appointment.

THE RIGHT ATTITUDE

Teachers of sales skills agree that selling starts with attitude. You have to believe in yourself and in what you are selling. Here are some ways to arrive at that self-confidence:

- Reflect on what you learned in your massage therapy training and continuing education. What specific things were you taught? Which of them do you believe are helpful? Which are you especially good at? Imagine yourself doing those things, and reflect on how the client feels. Are you providing the client with something valuable?

- Reflect on massages you have received. How did you feel? How did it help you? Would someone else be able to benefit in similar ways? How do your skills compare with those of the practitioner you enjoyed the most?
- Reflect on what you know about the benefits of massage. Are you familiar with the efficacy studies on massage? Have you measured results, or have clients indicated positive change due to your care? What is your rationale for believing massage is beneficial? Would another person appreciate knowing about these potential benefits?

Whenever you have an opportunity to sell someone on the benefits of what you do, start from this understanding. You will be more confident if you remember that marketing massage does not mean convincing others to buy something they do not need; rather, you are enabling them to receive something that will contribute to their health and well-being.

Although some people associate selling with talking, you will be most effective if you listen well. When others talk, listen for the needs they express. If you see how your practice can help with those needs, you can offer a solution. People appreciate being convinced when its aim is to help them.

A really effective tool every massage therapist should have at his or her disposal is the 30-second "elevator speech" that describes what you do as a massage therapist. These short verbal explanations are called elevator speeches because they're the length of a short presentation you could give to someone during an elevator trip between floors. The ability to quickly and confidently present a sales message about your business will come in handy in many opportunities. Figure 7.13 contains three examples of an elevator speech. Experiment with different speeches until one or two feel comfortable to you.

FIGURE 7.13
Sample Elevator Speeches

"You've never received a massage? May I tell you why I became a massage therapist? I learned that soft tissue kneading not only feels good but also helps reduce stress levels and aches. Clients who have been coming to me regularly for several years tell me that the good effects of massage are even better over the long-term. I'd love to show you what a massage feels like. Would you like to start with a 30-minute appointment?"

"People have mostly associated massage with rest and relaxation, but recent research has shown even more benefits. Massage has been known to help people sleep better. It's also been credited with helping reduce certain types of pain. Some people who get massages have been able to reduce their reliance on pain medication. If you'd like to book an appointment, we'll spend a few minutes at the first appointment to discuss how you'd like massage to help you, so I know what you're looking for."

"If you sit at a desk all day—particularly if you sit at a computer screen—you'll find that massage therapy can really be helpful. A chair massage, where you keep all your clothes on, and just lean forward in a chair made especially for massage, allows me to massage the areas where most office workers feel tension—your neck and shoulders, your back, your hands and wrists. Would you like to try one?"

STAGES OF BUSINESS

Every practice will have different marketing goals for different stages of business. When you first open your practice, your focus will be on gaining new clients. Once you have clients, your focus will be on keeping them and encouraging repeat business. When a client leaves, you will want to understand whether there was anything you can do to regain their business. Often you will be marketing at all three stages of business development at the same time.

BUILDING YOUR CLIENT BASE

Once you have announced your practice's opening, you will build on that communication by using all of the strategies discussed previously in this chapter: advertising, promotions, public relations, and networking. The strategies you choose will depend on the type of business you start, your target market, and your budget. General steps you will modify to suit your own practice include:

1 Become familiar with the individuals and organizations most likely to share common interests with your business goals.

2 Introduce yourself to individuals and organizations whose members or client groups might also be clients of yours.

3 Choose a mix of strategies designed to achieve short-term results as well as long-term growth. For instance, advertising and promotions provide the fastest results, even though they are among the more expensive strategies. Public relations activities are aimed at longer-term visibility and education.

4 Once you have chosen appropriate strategies, choose tactics aimed at achieving your particular goal.

If your practice is in a clinical setting, do not underestimate the strength of citing the results of scientific research. Your awareness and use of evidence-based research will help establish your credibility with health care professionals whose training and education are based on the clinical model. Being familiar with the latest studies in your area of specialty will help strengthen your ties with the clinical community and earn referrals from them. For examples specific to massage practices in different types of settings, see the two Spotlight on Business features in this section. Whatever your practice's focus, combine types of organizations, strategies, and tactics in ways that will best connect with the clients you are trying to reach.

SPOTLIGHT ON BUSINESS

How to Seek Clients in a Clinical/Rehab Setting

1 Become familiar with places of business whose clients you would like to work with.
   - Look in the yellow pages and search online for rehab clinics, sports clinics, athletic training facilities, hospitals, sports facilities, etc.
   - Make a list of organizations you would like to concentrate on, and learn more about what they do and who you might contact there.

2 Choose a mix of strategies designed to achieve short-term results as well as long-term growth.
   - Send a letter introducing yourself and stating your qualifications as well as your interest in earning client referrals from them.
   - Attend seminars, networking groups, and other meetings where you would be likely to meet others who work with the type of client you are interested in.
   - Join associations and interest groups related to your professional interest.
   - Use direct mail.
   - Partner with a clinical specialist in developing research methodology that would test the efficacy of massage in a particular area. (See Chapter 8 for more information about conducting research.)

3 Once you have chosen appropriate strategies, choose tactics aimed at achieving your particular goal.
   - Customize letters that highlight recent research that shows how massage therapy might be helpful to clients. In all cases, include at least a brief description of the research methodology used, such that the reader is assured of the research's scientific validity.

- Enclose article reprints when appropriate, but summarize the article in a cover note rather than expect that the recipient has (or will take) the time to read the entire article unless he or she first is motivated to do so.
- Develop a website on which you post current research related to your type of practice, and refer your contacts to your website for the latest information.

How to Seek Clients in a Wellness Setting

1 Get to Know Wellness Professionals/Let Them Get to Know You
   - Become active in your local chapter of Wellness Councils of America.
   - Attend national or regional conferences of the Association of Worksite Health Promotion (AWHP).
   - Join the local chamber of commerce
   - Give talks to organizations on topics such as ergonomics, relaxation, and different types of massage.
   - At a company, the person who handles wellness benefits might be a director of wellness, a director of work and family benefits, or a human resources director.
   - At a hospital, first distinguish between wellness programs for patients and wellness programs for employees or staff. There might be a wellness committee, directed by Human Resources. Many hospitals have or are developing community-based wellness centers for integrated care.
   - At a university or college, the staff/faculty wellness program might reside in a Department of Health & Psychological Services, and be headed by a wellness coordinator.
2 Introduce Yourself
   - When you have a contact person's name, send that person and letter and then follow up with a phone call and request an appointment to talk about how you could help. In the appointment, give a demonstration of your services.
   - Initial questions to ask: Do you have a wellness program? Are you thinking of implementing one? Are you familiar with seated massage?
3 Negotiate a Profitable Working Relationship
   - Employee participation is higher if the company's budget pays for them to receive on-site seated massages, vs. if the employee pays partial costs.
   - Suggest the company pay you by the hour rather than by the massage, because you will have transition times between massages that are otherwise unpaid.
4 Conduct Your On-site Business Professionally
   - Plan for three 15-minute massages per hour. You need five minutes between massages to sanitize chair after previous client, greet the new client, establish rapport, ask questions about contraindications, and adjust the chair.
   - It's important to be efficient without conveying an assembly-line approach.
   - Be a role model for self-care. If you work a seven-hour day, that's 21 clients a day – make sure to take necessary breaks, drink fluids, and use proper biomechanical posture and movements.
5 Find out if companies' health plans include flex benefits, and if employees can use their pre-tax flex benefits for massage therapy and bodywork.
   - If so, ask how you can communicate that fact to employees.
   - Find out when the flex benefit account is closed out each year, and send a notice to employees two months before to remind them how they can prevent those benefits from going to waste.

Source: "Practice-Building Tips: Working in Medical and Wellness Settings." © 2001 American Massage Therapy Association.

RETAINING CLIENTS

All massage practices are made up of clients who came for just one appointment and those who are repeat clients. Your goal is to convert as many first-time appointments to continuing clients as possible. According to a 2007 report conducted on behalf of AMTA, most practices see about one-third new clients and two-thirds repeat clients (Figure 7.14).

FIGURE 7.14
New vs. Repeat Clients

Massage therapists see an average of 41 clients per month. Of those clients:

New clients = 35% **35%**

Repeat clients **65%**

Source: 2007 *Massage Therapy Industry Evaluation Trend Report*, November 2007, conducted by North Star Research on behalf of American Massage Therapy Association.

Keeping clients is easier and less expensive than winning new ones. Clients keep coming back when they feel they have a professional, beneficial relationship with you. Therefore, efforts to encourage ongoing client relationships are often called "relationship marketing." Relationship marketing includes all the ways you strengthen your professional ties with clients, including client education and follow-up.

Relationship marketing requires the best of personal selling methods: listening to clients, taking notes, and carefully assessing clients' needs. At the end of each session, evaluate the client's situation. Encourage the use of other therapies and products if you believe they will enhance the client's well-being.

Stay in Touch with Clients

Chances are, many clients do not fully appreciate all the ways they can benefit from the services and products your practice offers. This situation offers a great opportunity for you. You can foster ongoing relationships through education of your clients. Remember that education is a long-term process, one that needs constant attention.

Many practitioners request feedback about a client's experience with the massage session, particularly after a client's first visit. Even if the client indicates satisfaction, some clients will not come back unless you follow up with them. Client follow-up is a good way to demonstrate that you care about your clients and want them to have a positive experience with your practice. It also shows that you follow through with the care plan, including return visits.

Remember, it is much easier and less expensive to keep your existing clients coming back than it is to attract new clients. (See Figure 7.15 for a list of ideas.) It is your existing clients who already know about you and about massage. Repeat clients are your practice's most valued asset. Not only do you already have their business, but they can be your best source of referrals. By providing your existing clients with a consistently high level of service and care, you allow them to trust that anyone they refer also will be pleased.

Through your marketing communications, your clients will form an impression about you and your practice. But no matter what marketing communications techniques you use, remember that the most important element of marketing your practice is you. People will respond to your skill, your professionalism, your enthusiasm, and your concern for their well-being. Do what it takes to project a positive, caring attitude, and clients will keep coming back for more.

Grow Your Practice

What makes a massage therapy practice grow? It is a dynamic combination of you, your practice, and your clients. When you want your practice to grow, take some time to review how far you have come and decide how to build on what you have learned. You may decide to move from part-time to full-time, add services and products, specialize, hire employees, or pursue related opportunities such as teaching or research.

In developing a growth strategy, it is important to define what "part-time" and "full-time" mean for a massage therapist. Massage is physically hard work. No one can be expected to spend 40 hours a week providing massages. Rather, a full-time massage therapist is closer to a volume of about 17 paid massage hours per week, with the rest of the 40-hour week spent doing such things as paying bills, doing paperwork, and following up with clients.

If you are expanding from part-time to full-time practice, some of the steps you might consider include:

- Rent an office if you now work out of your home.
- Increase your number of massage hours (setting up office hours and planning to be there to accept walk-ins).
- Hire massage staff—employees or independent contractors—to expand the massage hours you offer or locations at which you work. For more detail on hiring and managing, see Chapters 5 and 6.
- Hire support staff to help with phone calls and paperwork.
- Set up a business relationship with another massage therapist who has an established client base.
- Buy an existing massage therapy practice, or buy the physical assets of a practice.
- Expand by accepting insurance clients. For more detail, see Chapter 6.

Moving to full-time status requires that you serve more clients, and might also include increasing the frequency of appointments with your existing clients.

> If you decide to expand from part-time to full-time, remember that 17 hour-long massages a week means full-time by the time you add in your non-massage activities like paperwork and client follow-up.

THE STRATEGIES AND TACTICS SHOWN HERE CAN BE TAILORED TO A MASSAGE PRACTICE AT ANY STAGE OF GROWTH.

Before the appointment, call the client or send a reminder postcard or e-mail with a reminder of the appointment day and time.

Spend extra time in intake to find out what could make the client a repeat customer.*

Increase the likelihood that clients will evaluate their experience in a positive way by discussing their expectations before the session begins.

Vary your techniques and style. If you give the same massage, in the same sequence, every time, it will become repetitive and possibly boring for both you and the client.

Take courses in new modalities and techniques from time to time, to keep your work and style fresh to clients.

Learn about the client's life habits before the session begins. This will help you tailor your service to each client's needs.

Offer 10 percent discount to clients if they rebook the same day as they are in for a massage.*

Keep a "public calendar" openly visible that clients can see that shows the times (not names) booked, as a reminder to schedule themselves. It reminds them, it reminds you.*

Provide a level of service that makes clients feel nurtured—promptness at appointments, clear explanations, a glass of water, a warm washcloth at the end.

FIGURE 7.15
Practices That Keep Them Coming Back

FIGURE 7.15
(continued)

Focus completely on the client when in session. At the end of the session, request feedback to gather impressions about the client's satisfaction. (This can help the client notice such benefits as relaxed muscles or reduced pain.)

If you work at a salon, in slow moments, offer free mini (sample) chair massages to nail and hair clients, explaining the benefits of massage.*

Formulate a care plan utilizing formal records such as SOAP notes to help you and the client keep track of progress.

Tell clients about the benefits they can derive if they receive massages more frequently.

After the session, ask when, not if, the client wants to come back.*

Teach self-care measures for clients to use at home between visits.

Before clients leave, encourage them to book their next appointment. For example, say "You are in great shape. Once a month would really make a difference for you," or, "Until you are no longer in acute pain, let's do twice a week for several weeks. Then we can reevaluate and maybe move to once a week." Some clients with busy schedules like the idea that, routinely, a certain day and time are committed for massage.

Provide literature about massage and any other services offered by your practice for client to take home or read while they're waiting for their appointment.

Ask if there is anything they would like more or less of (like a scalp massage) at their next appointment so you can note it and make sure to address it next time.*

Give a small gift, like a square of dark chocolate, a candle; send a thank you.*

No gimmick—just go above and beyond. Inform them at the beginning of the session that this time and space is theirs.*

Offer special packages for clients, such as discounts for a series of massages, a tenth massage at half price, a free session after a client has brought in five referrals, etc.

Consider collaborating with other alternative health professionals to offer a lecture series.

Give all first-time clients a $10 discount as a thank you and as an incentive to refer.*

Have a program allowing incremental discounts to each client who sends you business.*

Stay on top of continuing education so therapy is highly effective; show people there's more to massage than relaxation.*

In a prominent place, display a card saying "Our business continues to grow through your referrals. Thank you for recommending us."

Always send an individual thank-you card for referrals.

* *mtj* readers' response to how they encourage repeat business (*mtj,* fall 2007, v46, no.3).

Diversify Your Practice

A massage practice can grow by selling more to its existing clients. You can do this by diversifying into new services and/or products. Clients who no longer have as much need for or interest in one service might make an appointment for something new. Likewise, the wider variety of services may attract new clients who are interested in one or more of the added offerings.

If you diversify your services with new massage modalities, be sure to share your new knowledge with your clients. Communicate this even if it is just a single thought or technique to add to what you already do. Clients may hear something they like and then be willing to try it. Use a variety of ways to let them know about your new diversified services:

- Provide marketing literature that details your background in massage, including the schools you have attended and for how many hours.
- Update your marketing literature as you continue your education. Hang new certificates on your wall.
- Send direct mail to clients.

Similarly, some massage therapists offer adjunct therapies such as aromatherapy or facials. They may offer other services as well, such as yoga classes or reflexology. To add adjunct therapies, you should obtain additional training to provide them yourself, or you may engage other qualified individuals to provide them. Be sure these adjunct therapies are consistent with the professional image of your practice.

Many massage therapists sell health-related products, from books and music to aromatherapy supplies, nutritional supplements, and essential oils. Be sure that the products you sell support the overall image you desire for your practice. Display the products attractively and be prepared to answer questions about them.

When you sell products, you may want to use some form of cross-selling. Cross-selling involves treating a mix of products and services as a package. For example, if your practice offers neuromuscular massage for $90 per session and paraffin for the hands at $20, you could offer the two for a price of $100. Similarly, you might sell a facial with a massage. As your practice increases, you may find that some percentage of your clients like these packages. Experiment with different combinations to see what appeals most to clients.

WINNING BACK CLIENTS

Not every client you see for the first time will become a repeat client. You will always do your best to create an environment that will encourage repeat business, but it is not realistic to expect that result in every case. Some clients decide massage is not for them, others can't afford a massage except infrequently, and still others find another massage therapist whose location is more convenient or whose practice suits them better for one reason or another.

The clients you are most likely to "win back" are those who have been repeat clients in the past and who, for unknown reasons, have drifted away. If you have seen a client three or more times—the client was evidently pleased enough with your massages to book several appointments—it is important to the health of your business to find out why he or she quit making appointments. Several approaches are available to you. You may:

- Call the client: "I've missed seeing you for massage, and the reason you haven't made an appointment lately matters to me. I there anything I can do to help you to make an appointment?"
- Send the client a personalized note via mail or e-mail: "Dear ____ : I have always appreciated your business, and I've noticed that you haven't been here in several months. This is just a friendly reminder that I would love to see you again. If there is anything I can do to improve your satisfaction with my practice, I would really welcome your comments. Sincerely, _____ . P.S. I am willing to book appointments on Saturdays and week nights."

- Send a coupon to encourage rebooking. The coupon include a note that says something like: "Don't be a stranger. Please use this 15% discount coupon to book your next appointment."
- Send a postcard survey via mail or e-mail to all former clients. The survey would be designed to anonymously elicit feedback regarding why the client has quit making appointments. Choices might include:
  · Moved away
  · Found a massage therapist closer to home or business
  · Changed to a different massage therapy practice due to (check one)
    ☐ modality offered
    ☐ price
    ☐ customer service
  · Doesn't fit in current budget
- Allow former clients the option whether to reply to survey anonymously or to give their name.
- All surveys should include the question "What can I do to earn your business again?"

Some former customers just need a reminder and an encouraging nudge to start booking appointments again. Others may have left for reasons you will never learn. The best you can do is to show sincere interest in their well-being, acknowledge to them that you have missed their business, and hope they accept your invitation to rebook.

The best win-back technique is to show a sincere interest in clients' well-being, let them know you miss their business, and invite them to come back.

RECOVERY STRATEGIES

It's the rare practice that starts out strong and continues to improve without encountering a major or minor downturn at some point. When it happens to you, it's important that you recognize the danger signs in time that you can do something about remedying the problems.

Red flags can be obvious or subtle. Subtle indicators of trouble could be the fact that the phone doesn't ring as often as it used to, or your general sense that clients aren't entirely satisfied after their sessions, even if they don't voice a complaint.

The most obvious red flags are the number of clients you have booked each month, the amount of money you take in, and the level of expenses you pay out each month. Those three measurements are easy to keep track of, so you never have to be caught off-guard when your business encounters a decline. In setting up your business, you determined how many clients you will need per month in order to bring in the minimum level of income you will need, and the maximum level of expenses you can afford.

If you know how many clients you need per month and what your maximum expenses should be, you will be able to spot a business downturn before it does serious damage to your practice.

Make it easy to see trends that could spell trouble for the future health of your business by using a consistent tracking document. Highlight in one color any indicators that fall outside the parameters of where they should be, and highlight in another color the indicators that fall within your parameters. This gives you an easy visual indicator of the health of your business on a monthly basis, or make up a weekly tracking chart if you want to exert tighter control. See Figure 7.16 for a sample of what such a tracking document might look like.

When you see a trend that alerts you to trouble, you will want to analyze the factors that are causing that trend to occur. It's important to be realistic and accurate in identifying the underlying factors because clear identification will help you develop effective strategies for restoring your business to health.

It can be helpful to categorize factors according to those you can affect directly versus those that you can affect only indirectly. See Figure 7.17 for a summary of factors that could affect your business and related strategies that could help recover from business downturns.

MAINTAIN YOUR ENTHUSIASM

Recognize when your business slumps that this is a normal cycle for almost every practice.

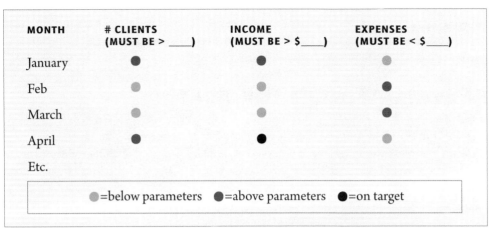

FIGURE 7.16
At-a-Glance Health of Your Business

MONTH	# CLIENTS (MUST BE > ____)	INCOME (MUST BE > $____)	EXPENSES (MUST BE < $____)
January	●	●	●
Feb	●	●	●
March	●	●	●
April	●	●	●
Etc.			

●=below parameters ●=above parameters ●=on target

FIGURE 7.17
Recovery Strategies

FACTORS AND RECOVERY ACTIONS

FACTOR	YOUR ACTIONS AFFECT DIRECTLY/INDIRECTLY	POSSIBLE STRATEGIES
Local economy	Indirectly	Become involved with economic development in your community and propose ways to help stimulate the local economy.
Services/Modalities	Directly	Take training that will enable you to provide additional modalities, which will appeal to a broader target client audience. Announce through public relations or advertising channels that your practice now offers this new service and its associated benefits.
Marketing	Directly	Assess the effectiveness of your marketing plan. Are there cost-effective ways you can reach more prospective clients? Is your client retention plan effective? Can you educate a wider audience through public relations efforts?
Customer Service	Directly	Listen closely to your customer satisfaction feedback. Examine your incidence of repeat customers. Meet with your mentor or seek supervision to help identify how you can improve your service to and relationship with clients. See Chapter 6, Creating a Therapeutic Relationship, for more information.
Financial Management	Directly	Is your budget realistic? Are you exceeding your expenses and/or under-running your income? Your marketing plan will address how to attract more clients. Your examination of expenses will identify whether there are areas where you can reduce your expenses.

When it happens to you, it's important to analyze the factors that could be causing it so that you can take steps to bring it back to its former vitality. Don't be afraid to invest the time, energy, and creativity required to keep your career healthy.

REEVALUATING YOUR PLAN

If you followed all the steps in your Career and Practice Plan, you will be prepared to evaluate your plan and your practice. Revisit that plan, and your initial hard work will help you with your next steps. Read each section of your plan, and ask questions about it. The questions shown in Figure 7.18 will help with that process. They will also help you plan how to keep your skills up to date.

FIGURE 7.18
Plan Evaluation Worksheet

Reevaluating your business and marketing plans periodically is an important step that will help keep your practice healthy. Answer the following questions about your present business situation. If you decide to change any of your business objectives or activities, revise your Career and Practice Planning Worksheet (Fig. 5.9) to reflect your new plan.

1 Do your overall goals, as stated in the plan, still describe what you want to do? If not, what do you want to change? _____

2 Do you want to continue serving the same group of clients? If not, what client group do you want to target now? _____

3 Are you interested in providing the same kinds of services? If not, what do you want to change? _____

4 Are you interested in selling the same products (if any)? If not, what do you want to change? _____

5 Are your practice location and equipment appropriate and sufficient for your activities? If not, what do you want to change? _____

6 Is your staffing adequate and appropriate for meeting your objectives? If not, what do you want to change? _____

7 Are your financial objectives the same? If not, what are your new objectives? ___

8 Do your plans still seem attainable? If not, what changes are necessary? _____

9 Overall, based on your previous answers, are you on track to achieving your objectives? _____

· If yes, what is working well for you? _____
· If not, what needs to change? _____

If your plan differs from your actual career, you need to make changes to bring the two into alignment. Perhaps you really like the way your practice has grown, even though it has not been according to plan. For example, maybe you were intimidated by the prospect of dealing with clinical establishments and thought you would avoid working closely with clinical professionals. Now, however, you find yourself working closely with several MDs and DCs and enjoying it. In this case, you can change your plan or rewrite it entirely. This will help you articulate what you want to do and will keep your activities in line with your (new) goals.

In another situation, change might be necessary for you to make progress in carrying out your original plan. For example, if you do not have enough clients to meet expenses, you will need to change your marketing strategies and tactics to generate more clients. If you are not working in the modality that most interests you, you will have to develop a base of clients who want that modality. If you have too many clients, you will have to decide whether to cut back the number of clients you serve or bring in someone who can help you with those you have. Keep in mind that clients are seeing you because of your skills and your therapeutic relationship with them. If your client base is growing, it will probably be best to refer new clients to new practitioners who join you.

Or, you might find that you made changes to your plan but did not follow through on them. As a result of your review, you may discover a need to develop new strategies and tactics.

Of course, you may also see some areas in which you are right on target. If so, congratulate yourself. Take time to be grateful for each small accomplishment on the path toward fulfilling your plans. Remember that your plan is a map of the territory, and a map is only one part of the whole. Taking a step back and getting a vision of the larger picture can help you refine your plans.

Learn from your own experience and that of others you respect. If you have been keeping careful client records, you will have good information to help you decide what is working for you. Identify the different client types and/or modalities used in your practice. Then analyze them by answering the following questions:

- Which type of client gives you the best earnings per hour?
- Which provides the most repeat business?
- Which gives you the most satisfaction?
- Which do you want to focus on?
- Where did these clients come from? (For example, if they were referrals, who were they from? If they were responses to advertising, where did they see the ads?)

You can learn from other people's experience as well. Talk to other massage therapists about what they do to build their practices. Consider whether their ideas might apply to your practice. Seek advice from others who have successfully built a practice or business. Think creatively, and look for ways to apply lessons learned by business or practice owners in other fields, as well as your own.

SUMMARY

The purpose of a good marketing plan is to make your practice visible and attract clients to it. In developing your plan, you weigh the pros and cons of how to attract clients to your business, and you choose the ways that fit your goals and your budget. Your marketing plan consists of four parts: 1) your goals, 2) your objectives that support those goals, 3) strategies for meeting those objectives, and 4) tactics for how you'll carry out those strategies.

Your target market, your budget, and where you are in your business cycle of growth influence the strategies you will choose. For instance, are you starting a new business and needing to attract all new clients, or do you want to expand an already existing practice?

Strategies you might choose from include: advertising, promotions, public relations, and networking.

Once you have selected appropriate strategies for your business, you will decide which tactics, or marketing practices, will be effective for you. These marketing practices could be carried out in one or several methods: print communications, electronic, or in person. Examples of print include brochures, business cards, gift certificates or coupons, and newsletters. Examples of electronic include websites and participation in online directories that let potential clients search for massage therapists by location or specialty. Personal selling tactics could include participation in networking and referrals to and from other health care professionals.

To determine whether your strategies and tactics continue to be appropriate for your business, you will need to reevaluate your plan on a regular basis. You might decide that you want to diversify your services or products, that you want to change your target market, or that you want to add insurance reimbursement clients. Depending on your desired changes, you would develop a current marketing plan that best supports your new goals.

Part of the need for continual reevaluation of your business is to recognize danger signs that indicate a downturn. Danger signs could include fewer clients, client complaints, or rising expenses. The key to implementing a recovery strategy is identifying the problems early enough to fix them. When you look at the causes of the problems, you will find that some of the fixes are within your control and others aren't. By understanding which problems are within your control, you will be able to develop a revitalized marketing plan and recovery strategy that puts your business back on the road to good health.

REVIEW QUESTIONS

1 What are the four primary parts of a marketing plan, and what is the purpose of each part?
2 Name at least three marketing strategies you can use to develop and maintain a client base.
3 Give at least one example of a tactic that would be appropriate for each type of marketing strategy.
4 What are the pros and cons of different marketing strategies?
5 What is the difference between a feature and a benefit? Give an example of each.
6 What are two warning signals that your practice is experiencing a downturn?
7 What are examples of recovery strategies that could help your business if you experience a downturn?

ENDNOTES

1 Adapted from "Do It Yourself: How to Create Your Own Web Site," mtj, Fall 2004, 114.
2 Adapted from Deleage, Freqerique, "Are You Making the Most of Your Spa's Media Potential," Pulse, May-June 2001.

Chapter 8

Connecting with the Professional Community

When you graduate from massage training, your certificate should say, "Congratulations—your training has just begun." You're now a part of a wider community of professionals who care just as much about massage therapy as you do.

CHAPTER OVERVIEW

- Qualities of a Professional
- Perspectives on Allied Professions
- Continuing Education
- Research
- Professional Supervision
- Professional Development Business Plan
- Summary

CHAPTER OBJECTIVES

1 Identify agencies, professional associations, and other allied professions that massage practitioners commonly do business with.
2 Identify the role of professional associations for massage practitioners.
3 Identify strategies for effective communication with other professionals regarding client care and networking.
4 Identify strategies for conflict resolution in relationships with other professionals.
5 Identify characteristics of effective interaction in groups and organizations.
6 Identify strategies to attain new knowledge.
7 Demonstrate the ability to read and critically evaluate technical information found in health-related journals.
8 Describe the importance of evidence-based research to the massage profession.
9 Explain the need for using professional supervision when appropriate.
10 Incorporate professional development goals into your business plan.

BEING A PROFESSIONAL

You are, or soon will be, a member of the profession of massage therapy. It's a weightier statement than it might at first appear. Being a professional is both a privilege and a responsibility. This section explores the breadth of opportunities open to you. It will help you expand your presence within the profession and your value to it. Gaining your certificate or diploma from a well-respected program is, as you might suspect, the tip of the iceberg.

Being a professional opens the door to personal and career growth in many ways, and expands your opportunities to extend your skills and gifts to benefit of the greatest number of people. Your decision to be a massage therapist should not be based solely upon your individual personal values and preferences but on those values, judgments, and ethical commitments shared by the profession of which you are a member. This provides the collective wisdom and advice from a broad base of professionals and can be a measure to govern professional behavior.

Three primary components of professionalism are:

1 Your professional association
2 Continuing education
3 Research and advocacy

ELEMENTS OF PROFESSIONALISM

Regardless of the profession, professionals share a set of common values and beliefs (Figure 8.1). It's easy to observe, through someone's actions and words, those who have chosen to become professionals.

One decision many professionals make is to join a professional association, for the sake of their personal development as well as the growth of the profession.

> Massage therapists differ widely in their goals, aspirations, and business philosophies but are united by a shared set of professional values and beliefs.

FIGURE 8.1
Professionals vs. Nonprofessionals

PROFESSIONALS	NONPROFESSIONALS
Share a commitment to excellence.	Become complacent.
Place their clients first.	Places their egos first.
Practice their skills to the point of mastery, then keep practicing them to improve.	Believe that what they already know how to do is enough.
Take refresher courses seriously because they are eager to learn new information.	Believe their skills will never fade.
Set high standards for themselves, their colleagues, their association, and their profession.	Aim for the minimum standard, and take the path of least resistance.
Critically review their performance, always seeking ways to improve.	Look for ways to protect themselves, to hide their inadequacies and place blame on others.

YOUR PROFESSIONAL ASSOCIATION

The role of a professional association in your personal and career development can be as limited or as encompassing as you choose to make it. A professional association supports massage therapists in the decisions they make through a recognized and articulated set of professional values that all members of the field consider of utmost importance.

At its most pragmatic, professional associations offer liability insurance for their members' and clients' protection. A professional association not only supports your practice through member benefits but also helps advance the profession as a whole, with media, health care, and insurance professionals, legislative bodies, and the general public. Two of its most important benefits are the business development and support for your practice a professional association provides. When fulfilling its greatest potential, a professional association offers the environment within which you join with other professionals to further the profession through advocacy, education, and research.

One of the foremost advantages of becoming actively involved in your professional association is that you have the opportunity to collaborate with your peers in the field of massage therapy. No one else understands the challenges, the frustrations, the deep satisfaction, and the inspirational visions for the profession as keenly as you and a peer. With your peers you can fashion strategies that keep the face of your profession turned toward the future in such a way that benefits you, other massage therapists, your clients, and the public.

When choosing which professional association to join, ask the following questions about what each association offers:

1 *To what extent does it increase public awareness of the profession?*
   Does it conduct national public relations and marketing campaigns? Does it promote the profession through high visibility efforts such as AMTA's National Massage Therapy Awareness Week?

2 *Does it support massage research through the investment of time and money?*
   Does it provide leadership in establishing an agenda for massage research that will educate health care professionals on the benefits of massage and result in encouraging referral business from the medical community?

3 *Does it define and uphold ethics and standards for members?*
   Look at associations' history of development of ethics and standards for practitioners and schools in the area of certification and accreditation. Consider the rigor and peer review process required in the development and continued application of these standards.

4 *Does it foster legislative advocacy?*
   Consider to what extent it fosters a positive environment in which massage therapists can practice. Does it conduct ongoing contact with legislators and track legislation related to healing arts and complementary and alternative medicine so it can support its members' best interests?

5 *Is it member driven?*
   As a member, do you have a vote in what your association does to support the profession? Do you have the opportunity to influence change in the profession, in legislation, in the insurance industry, and in your professional association?

6 *What are its member benefits and the cost of membership?*
   In addition to its liability insurance coverage, what other benefits does the association offer? Many provide discounts on legal services, professional training, continuing education, conferences, massage therapy products and services, credit cards and other personal services. What does it offer in the way of business resources for your private practice? Does it publish a professional journal, and of what quality? Does it offer extensive opportunities for your personal involvement on a local, regional, and national level? Does it make it easy for you to participate with professional peers?

Many massage therapists maintain memberships in a national organization or association, such as American Massage Therapy Association, Associated Bodywork and Massage Professionals, or International Massage Association, and/or in an organization that serves a particular region or specialized modality or market. An example would be someone who is a member of AMTA and also a member of American Organization for Bodywork Therapies of Asia (AOBTA).

PROMOTING THE PROFESSION OF MASSAGE

Massage practitioners, as other professionals, are expected to establish and uphold standards for their profession, and to communicate those standards to others outside the profession. This increases clients' assurance that they will receive a high standard of care, which in turn benefits both you and your clients. The primary ways in which you promote your profession are through your individual behavior and through your involvement in organizations that extend the visibility of massage therapy in a positive light. Your behavior in all areas of life signal a message to all who observe you that "this is what a massage therapist is and does," even when you are not acting in the role of massage therapist.

At a minimum, you are professionally responsible to uphold your association's code of ethics and standards of practice. In addition, you promote the profession when you are enthusiastic and informative about your work. Massage practitioners can go even further in promoting the profession through such actions as:

- They can actively participate in professional associations such as AMTA and events such as AMTA's National Massage Therapy Awareness Week (the last full week in October).
- They can write letters to government officials and support the development of massage therapy directed regulation that is fair for the profession.

Your efforts make a difference in helping influence the perceptions of massage held by legislators, health care specialists in other professions, and the public. In doing so, the profession of massage grows by attracting more clients and by enabling practitioners to be successful financially as well as in body, mind, and spirit. By investing a portion of your time and skills in supporting the profession that supports you, you are improving your work environment not only for yourself, but also for your peers and for those who follow in massage training.

PERSPECTIVES ON ALLIED PROFESSIONS

One aspect of being a professional is the interaction between and among members of your own profession, as discussed earlier. Another important aspect is the interaction with members of allied or related professions in a way that promotes cooperation and collaboration among members of the medical and complementary/alternative medicine professions.

One reason it's important to relate to members of allied professions, as well as within your own, is that you can be a spokesperson who builds bridges when differing perspectives arise. When Ruth L. Kirschstein, M.D., Acting Director of the National Center for Complementary and Alternative Medicine, appeared before the Senate Subcommittee on Labor-HHS-Education Appropriations, to request NCCAM's 2008 budget,[1] she had these words to say about the importance of allied professionals learning about each other:

> Driven largely by consumer demand for CAM, integrative medicine—which can be defined as a health care approach that makes use of all appropriate evidence-based disciplines, therapies, and health care professionals to achieve optimal health and healing—is rapidly becoming a major force shaping health care systems in the United States and around the world. At the same time, studies continue to show that open communication between conventional medical practitioners and their patients about

CAM use is uncommon. Such communication is vital to ensure well-coordinated, comprehensive, and safe care.

Many in the general public do not have a clear understanding of the relative merits of massage therapy (let alone the different modalities within this profession), physical therapy, chiropractic, osteopathy, naprapathy, naturopathy, homeopathy, acupuncture, and other professions. The same is true of professionals within each of those fields, and it's possible that you don't have any greater understanding of their profession than they do of yours. The more you interact with members of allied professions, the more opportunities you have to educate them and to learn about their professions from their perspectives.

> It's likely that members of other professions also dedicated to health and well-being know as little about massage therapy as you know about their profession. Getting to know them gives you an opportunity to educate them, as well as learn about them.

RESOURCES FOR ALLIED PROFESSIONS

Note: This list is not intended to be exhaustive, but it contains contact information for some of the professions with which you might come into contact.

UNITED STATES

American Chiropractic Association (ACA), 1701 Clarendon Blvd., Arlington, VA 22209; (703) 276-8800; www.amerchiro.org

American Occupational Therapy Association (AOTA), 4720 Montgomery Lane, Bethesda, MD 20824-1220; (301) 652-2682; www.aota.org

American Osteopathic Association, 142 East Ontario Street, Chicago, IL 60611; (800) 621-1773 or (312) 202-8000; www.osteopathic.org

American Fitness Professionals & Associates (AFPA), P.O. Box 214, Ship Bottom, NJ 08008; (609) 978-7583; www.afpafitness.com

American Physical Therapy Association, 1111 N. Fairfax Street, Alexandria, VA 22314-1488; (800) 999-APTA; www.apta.org

International SPA Association (ISPA), 2365 Harrodsburg Rd., Suite A325, Lexington, KY 40504; (859) 226-4372; www.experienceispa.com

National Athletic Trainers' Association (NATA), 2952 Stemmons Freeway, Dallas, Texas 75247-6916; (800).TRY.NATA (800-879-6282); www.nata.org

National Strength and Conditioning Association (NSCA), 1955 N. Union Blvd., Colorado Springs, CO 80909; (719) 632-6722 or (800) 815-6826; www.nsca-lift.org

CANADA

Canadian Chiropractic Association, 1396 Eglinton Ave. West Toronto ON M6C 2E4; www.ccachiro.org

Canadian College of Osteopathy, 39 Alvin Avenue, Toronto, Ontario, Canada M4T 2A7; (416) 323-1465; www.osteopathy-canada.com

Canadian Massage Therapist Alliance, 365 Bloor Street East, Suite 1807, Toronto, Ontario, Canada M4W 3L4; (416) 968-2149; www.cmta.ca/

Canadian Medical Association, 1867 Alta Vista Drive, Ottawa, ON, Canada K1G 3Y6, 613-731-9331; www.cma.ca

Canadian Naturopathic Association (CNA), 1255 Sheppard Avenue East, North York, Ontario, Canada M2K 1E2; (416) 496-8633; www.naturopathicassoc.ca

Canadian Touch Research Center, 760, Saint-Zotique Street East, Montreal, Quebec, Canada H2S 1M5; (514) 272-2254; http://www.ccrt-ctrc.ca/

SCOPE OF PRACTICE

Understanding your own scope of practice is fundamental to massage therapists' careers, and it is especially important when communicating with members of allied professions. Scope of practice is defined by whatever legal body has authority to specify the services a member of the profession may or may not perform. The legal authority will vary from jurisdiction to jurisdiction—it may be a state, a province, or a national government. States might impose more stringent rules than a national regulatory body, and municipalities more stringent than states, all levels of which practitioners are required to follow. To operate outside this scope would constitute a violation of law. (See Chapter 1 for more detail.)

In addition to the legal scope of practice every practitioner must adhere to, every profession defines its own scope of practice. This is for the purpose of sharing a common language and understanding among peer professionals, but it does not take the place of the officially defined scope of practice that regulates practice in specific states, provinces or municipalities.

In most jurisdictions, a massage practitioner is not allowed to "treat," "diagnose," or "prescribe." However, massage therapists are allowed to practice certain services in some states that other states prohibit. Being knowledgeable about the scope of practice of other allied professions in your state would contribute to your professional breadth of understanding.

Regardless of scope of practice, every massage therapist and has a personal responsibility to practice only to the extent of his or her education, training, and qualifications. An experienced massage therapist will undoubtedly practice a wider range of services, still within the given scope, than will an entry level practitioner.

BUILDING BRIDGES BETWEEN PROFESSIONS

You will want to communicate professionally and to establish networking relationships that mutually benefit you and your allied peers. Therefore, you will want to have a basic understanding of each profession's scope of practice (which may vary from state to state), the profession's basic concepts of practice, and its members' level of professional training. Just as it is important for you to know how many hours of training a particular specialist is required to have, it is important that you educate your professional counterparts about how many hours of massages you have provided, in addition to your core training.

A key to communicating effectively with members of allied professions is in understanding the other specialist's terminology and depth of training. For example, the term "range of motion" can be the basis for honest miscommunication between a massage practitioner and a physical therapist (PT). As a massage practitioner, you might tell a physical therapist that you can be helpful to a client in increasing his or her range of motion. To you, this means you can increase the mobility of a client's limb to a greater range than the client could move it before having a session with you. To a PT, however, range of motion refers to an entire area of study in which the PT has a very extensive level of knowledge and training.

Another example is comparing how a massage practitioner, a physical therapist, and a chiropractor use the term "PNF" (proprioceptive neuromuscular facilitation). The massage practitioner has a basic understanding of PNF, and is probably trained in one or several contract-and-relax techniques that would be acceptably classified as PNF techniques. The PT and chiropractor, however, have undergone training in which PNF is studied as an entire complex system and in which they are trained to apply specific and sometimes sophisticated treatments to aid the client. For a massage practitioner to assume that PNF means the same thing to all specialists would lead the PT to believe that the massage practitioner is not knowledgeable about the level of training required by a PT.

CONFLICT RESOLUTION

A misunderstanding between professionals can be remedied if both parties focus on the similarities rather than on the differences between them, and recognize that they both want to achieve the same thing: a more healthful outcome for the client.

Approach a dialogue with a peer professional from the point of view of wanting to clarify what he or she is communicating to you. As in the examples of "range of motion" and "PNF" above, sincere dialogue about what each person means by this terminology will go a long way toward fostering appreciation of the other specialist's intent.

The basic goal in establishing productive working relationships that enhance the perception and quality of each other's work is to develop a genuine appreciation for what another specialist's strengths are. You can enhance each other's professional image by understanding how your two professions complement each other. For instance, many chiropractors appreciate the increased mobility a massage can give a client, which can allow the client's chiropractic session to be more effective than it might have been without a prior massage.

Be aware that you might encounter overlapping areas of work between your scopes of practice. When this is the case, simply acknowledge that although some services or techniques might be common to both professions, a practitioner of one or the other profession is probably specifically qualified to a greater degree than the other to help a client in a particular way.

When you know you will be talking with a member of an allied profession, it would be helpful if you had with you written educational materials about the efficacy of massage that you could share. Another way you can educate members of allied professions is to offer to present educational sessions to their colleagues and staff. This could either be in the format of a prepared speech (see Chapter 7) or in an informal discussion in the office break room. Your willingness to share information that could be of benefit to their clients and to members of allied professions, and your knowledge of the benefits of massage, will aid you as well as the entire profession of massage therapy.

CONTINUING EDUCATION

Ongoing education is essential to professional growth. The organizations through which you are licensed and nationally certified, and of which you are a member, have continuing education requirements for maintaining your credentials or membership status.

In answer to the question, "In the next 12 months, what continuing education classes do you plan to take for massage therapy?"

Advanced training specific modalities	50%
Training for new modalities	67%
Massage for specific populations	39%
Ethics	25%
Business skills	17%
Massage research	7%

Source: 2007 Massage Therapy Industry Evaluation Trend Report, conducted by North Star Research on behalf of AMTA.

FIGURE 8.2
Continuing Education Massage Therapists Plan to Take

Education can be for the purpose of refreshing skills you know already or learning new ones. See Figure 8.2 for a list of the types of continuing education massage therapists said they plan to take. You might decide to expand your knowledge in depth by taking as much additional training as you can in a given specialty area. Or you might find that expanding your breadth of training—taking continuing education sessions in a variety of topics—is more suitable for you.

STRATEGIES FOR ATTAINING NEW KNOWLEDGE

Your strategy for attaining new knowledge will differ depending on whether you are pursuing formal training or informal training. Formal training is what you need to earn the continuing education credits required for you to maintain your professional credentials or membership status. Informal is the method through which you greet every experience as an opportunity to attain new knowledge. See Figure 8.3 for examples of both types of training.

Formal Training

A good time to devise a game plan for taking continuing education is when you reevaluate your business plan and when you prepare your annual expense budget. Evaluating your business plan prompts you to review your long-term goals and to set new directions for your career or business. If you have employees, you should include continuing education objectives as part of your expectations as an employer. Remember, your objectives for upgrading your skills—and the services you offer—should support your overall business goals.

Depending on your goals, you may decide to take training in a new modality, to change your career direction, or to acquire more in-depth knowledge in a specialty area you already practice. By looking at least a year in advance, you can plan ahead for the expense involved and include it in your budget. The expense of continuing education can generally be claimed as a tax deduction.

Planning ahead enables you to make the most of your upcoming training by reading related materials prior to attending the class or workshop. Then, when you are in the presence of an instructor/specialist, you will have the opportunity to ask questions about areas of the topic that might go into more depth than what is presented during class.

Also, by planning ahead you have the chance to combine your continuing education goals with your personal goals. If you want to take a spring vacation to a certain area of the country, you might research which schools of massage or chapters of professional associations are in that part of the country, and time your vacation with continuing education opportunities. Combining your education and vacation plans also helps you stretch your budget dollars further. Certain restrictions exist taxwise in combining personal and business expenses, so consult a tax accountant or go to www.irs.gov to learn the specifics that will result in the greatest advantage to you.

> The difference between formal and informal training might be compared to earning a college degree versus going to the school of hard knocks. Both are of great value.

Informal Training

Informal training is one of the self-care benefits you can build into your routine every day. Opportunities for continual knowledge attainment abound when you approach the world with an inquiring mind. Every massage session, if you focus your observation skills, gives you information about the effectiveness of your touch techniques on the client. Every conversation with a client offers new opportunities for you to refine your communications and customer service skills. Conversations with peers or other professionals introduce topics that you might want to research further.

You might want to "formalize" informal training by scheduling 30 minutes a day specifically for knowledge attainment. This could consist of reading a journal, listening to a tape, watching a video, and reading information online. You might want to assign yourself a "topic of the month" and learn as much as you can about a particular topic.

At the end of every day, get in the habit of asking yourself, "What new thing did I learn today?" and "What do I want to learn tomorrow?"

FIGURE 8.3
Strategies for Attaining
New Knowledge

TIPS FOR ACQUIRING FORMAL TRAINING

When you prepare your annual budget is a good time to think about your formal training strategy. What are your long-term goals, and what type of training do you need to achieve them?

Balance your technical training (new modalities and skills) with business and marketing training.

When you are selecting a class, consider how it qualifies for your needs:

1 Look at the instructor's qualifications. It is acceptable to contact an instructor ahead of time and ask about learning objectives or to get a feel for the instructor. You will spend a lot of money and time on education, so make sure you do your homework and find out if the class and instructor are the right fit for you.
2 Make sure the course is accepted by your state if your state requires continuing education.
3 Make sure it is offered by an NCB provider if you are obtaining continuing education for your national certification.

Combine the training you need (for maintaining your credentials) with the training you want. If you feel you need a basic accounting course for the good of your business, see if you can also take a course that stimulates your creativity or your physical movement needs.

Explore the opportunities for taking online training. Ask colleagues for their recommendations. By taking an online course, you're a click away from earning continuing education certificates whenever you have a few hours at home or between clients.

If you work with employees, include continuing education as one of their performance objectives. Highlighting the importance of education and training sets a professional tone for your business. Allowing flexible work practices that encourage time off for training even further emphasizes the importance of growing in skills and knowledge. Or considering bringing the training "in house" for the staff. It not only enhances knowledge but builds community within your practice.

TIPS FOR ACQUIRING INFORMAL TRAINING

All you need is an inquiring and creative mind.

Every conversation with a client is an opportunity to hone your customer service skills or practice an elevator speech to promote a new aspect of your business.

Set aside a certain amount of time—say an hour a week—to read journals or massage research studies. Make a point of telling at least one person about something new you learned.

Choose a "theme of the month" – maybe massage research, nutrition, or third-party billing – and learn all you can in a 30-day period about that particular topic.

Buy, rent, or borrow training DVD/videotapes and set aside regularly-scheduled time to watch them.

RESOURCES FOR CONTINUING EDUCATION

Massage schools

Community colleges

AMTA's continuing education calendar: www.amtamassage.org

Massage Therapy Journal advertising

Massage Magazine advertising

Massage Today at www.massagetoday.com

NCBTMB's continuing education provider listings: www.ncbtmb.com

Research institutes

RESEARCH

The volume and importance of research in the field of massage therapy has grown in recent years. It is only recently, when the public has turned to more nontraditional forms of health care and wellness, that massage has become more popular. This has led to questions about the use, safety, and efficacy of massage by health care professionals in the allopathic, or medical, community, which in turn has contributed to the increase in research on massage.

Do not put off by the term *research*. Do not assume that the realm of research is the exclusive domain of scientists and people who already known how to conduct research. There is no ivory tower in which a few very serious and intelligent people carry out the important studies that identify the measurable and observable effects of massage. You, too, are invited—even encouraged—to join the research process. Even if you are not trained as a researcher or scientist by education, your entry into the field of research is warmly welcomed by the research community—the prerequisite is just your level of interest. Not only have research opportunities and funding increased in recent years, but so have the support materials and supportive climate to help massage therapists become players in this important and growing field.

The climate of massage therapy research is one of careful balance between choosing areas of study that hold the greatest promise of improved lives, and restraint from attributing more benefits to massage than have been proven by scientific studies. This caution was articulated by Margaret Chesney, Ph.D., in her keynote speech at the North American Research Conference on Complementary and Integrative Medicine:[2]

> Be bold in what you try, cautious in what you claim, and thoughtful about what you do. Express your purpose in a way that inspires commitment, innovation, and courage. We need you to contribute your part to the whole, as we work together to add to the fabric of knowledge about CAM and create a new, comprehensive health care.

Recent developments within the scientific health care community have made such participation opportunities possible.

INCREASED OPPORTUNITIES FOR RESEARCH

Momentum has built in recent years that bodes well for the availability of increased research in massage therapy. One example is that the National Center for Complementary and Alternative Medicine (NCCAM) of the National Institutes of Health (NIH) committed $121.6 million to CAM research in 2008, more than six times its funding in 1998. Another is the formation of groups and the convening of conferences whose exclusive focus is massage therapy research. An early leader in the commitment to devote resources to

All is takes to support the profession's need for massage therapy research is a sincere interest in learning more. Learning aids and training workshops are tailored to massage therapists who have no prior research background.

Researchers should be "bold in what you try and cautious in what you claim." -Margaret Chesney, Ph.D.

massage therapy research was the Massage Research Agenda Workgroup (MRAW), convened by the Massage Therapy Foundation in 1999, which identified specific areas of study and goals for massage therapy research. The 2005 "Highlighting CAM in Massage Therapy Research" conference, became the first massage research–related conference to be supported by an NCCAM grant to the Massage Therapy Foundation, for the purpose of convening renowned researchers and lecturers to focus on the topic of massage therapy research. Another landmark development occurred in 2005 with the creation of the Massage Therapy Research Consortium (www.massagetherapyresearchconsortium.com), a network of participating schools that support each other in developing resources to enhance the schools' capacity to conduct research and partner with outside researchers.

The need for research becomes particularly apparent in light of the fact that the Agency for Health Care Quality and Research (AHCQR), a part of the U.S. Department of Health and Human Services, decides which services and treatments will be reimbursed for people whose health care is paid by Medicaid and Medicare. Agencies such as AHCQR require credible scientific research in order to justify approving certain services for coverage. They make their decisions on the basis of published large, randomized control, double-blind and placebo-based studies that clearly show efficacy, safety, and cost-effectiveness of treatment modalities.

RESOURCES FOR ORGANIZATIONS THAT FUND MASSAGE RESEARCH

Canadian Touch Research Institute (CTRC), 760 St-Zotique Street East, Montreal, Canada H2S 1M5; 1-800-619-5463; real.gaboriault@ccrt-ctrc.org; www.ccrt-ctrc.org

Massage Therapy Foundation, 500 Davis Street, Suite 900, Evanston, IL 60201; (847) 869-5019; www.massagetherapyfoundation.org

National Center for Complementary and Alternative Medicine, P.O. Box 8218, Silver Spring, MD 20907-8218; (888) 644-6226; www.altmed.od.nih.gov/nccam/

Touch Research Institute, University of Miami, School of Medicine, Dept. of Pediatrics, P.O. Box 016820, Miami, FL 33101; (305) 243-6781; www.miami.edu/touch-research

---

WHAT TOPICS ARE RESEARCHED?

Research can help answer questions that lead to better understanding of how massage can improve people's lives. For example: Why or how does massage help premature infants gain more weight when they are massaged versus when they are not? Can massage help a person with insomnia sleep better? What effect does massage have on scar tissue? How does self-healing occur? What is the role of massage in helping a client achieve peak performance?

These are just a few of the unanswered questions that point to the need for research in the field of massage therapy. Massage practitioners want to see research in topics that will help them communicate more information to clients and that will help them expand their practices. Many massage therapists use research results in the following ways:

- To improve their skills as therapists
- To help start or grow their practice
- To learn how to better serve their clients with safe and efficacious massage.
- To validate the medical benefits of massage
- To validate the mind/body benefits of massage
- To validate acceptance of the massage therapist as a professional

IDENTIFYING BIASES IN RESEARCH

It is very difficult to conduct a study that is totally objective, devoid of all tendencies to produce a result that proves what the researcher already suspects. That is why adherence to accepted research methods is so important. If you take a course in research methods and you become conversant with the factors that affect a study's validity, you will start to read the results critically. It is possible, in a study that is not conducted according to accepted research methods, for biases to be introduced. The ethical intent of a researcher is to remove all bias in a study. Questions to determine the validity of research results, and possible sources of bias, include:

- How were the sample participants chosen?
- Was the sample size large enough from which to draw statistically valid conclusions?
- Was there a control group?
- What level and quality of statistical analysis was performed?
- Did the study participants know the source of the study's funding?
- Did the funding for the study come from a commercial source that might have unintentionally introduced a bias in the study's construction?
- Have the results been replicated by other scientists? (Also, can the results be replicated by other scientists? Some studies cannot be replicated because the problems researched in the original study were not well defined.)
- Would it be possible for another scientist to replicate the results?

Suggesting that you be alert to biases does not mean you should view research with a jaundiced eye—but with a critical eye that focuses on accurately understanding how the results were achieved.

> Understanding how to identify bias in research allows you to temper your understanding of a study's results according to how the study was constructed and carried out.

HOW TO FIND AND READ RESEARCH ARTICLES

The fact that the effects of massage therapy are becoming a more frequent topic of research studies is partly due to more massage therapists learning how to conduct research studies. Whether you become interested in conducting or participating in massage research, you should at least recognize the importance of reading research articles so you can extend your new knowledge to the benefit of your clients.

There are many places to find massage therapy research articles. Among them are:

- Massage Therapy Foundation posts articles that describe the importance of research, how massage therapists can become involved, and other research-related topics, as well as provides links to massage research studies: www.massagetherapyfoundation.org
- American Massage Therapy Association includes research citations in its Massage Information Center: www.amtamassage.org/infocenter/home.html
- Massage Magazine posts research summaries: www.massagemag.com/Magazine/research.php
- CAM on PubMed is a partnership of NCCAM and the National Library of Medicine (NLM) that has a search feature for complementary and alternative medicine: www.nlm.nih.gov/nccam/camonpubmed.html
- Type "massage therapy research" or "touch research" into your computer's search engine.

Unless you are already familiar with research formats and terminology (Figure 8.4), you will have to concentrate carefully on the research content rather than skim it. It helps if you are enthusiastic about the opportunity to expand your knowledge. Sit quietly for a few minutes before starting to read. Think how much more helpful you can be to your clients when you understand the most recent research results. Think of the benefits to your professional growth.

First, read the abstract, which is a summary of the study and results. Some research studies call this section the Summary or the Plain Language Summary. It gives a brief overview of the study's background, its methodology, and its main results and conclusions. It often specifies where more information is needed in order to draw more substantive conclusions.

Next, read or skim the section that describes the methods the researcher used to conduct the study. This gives you a more complete picture of what the researchers did and how they did it.

Last, look over the results section. This usually tells how the data were analyzed, provides more detail about the areas that require further study, and describes the implications of the data. Because this section is likely to contain extensive data, it might seem overwhelming at first. Read it so you can gradually become accustomed to this type of information, whether you understand the details or not. If nothing else, you will gain an appreciation for the steps the author of the research went through to collect and analyze the data in order to present it accurately for the benefit of others who are reading the results – just as you are.

When you are finished reading a study, the most important thing you can do with what you've learned is to translate its findings to your practice in a way that makes a difference to your clients, a concept known as translational research.

TRANSLATIONAL RESEARCH: BENCH AND BEDSIDE

What good is research if its results are never applied to actual practice? Acknowledging this basic tenet, the National Institutes of Health (NIH) named translational research one of their priorities. The NIH Roadmap for Medical Research[3] states:

> To improve human health, scientific discoveries must be translated into practical applications. Such discoveries typically begin at "the bench" with basic research—in which scientists study disease at a molecular or cellular level—then progress to the clinical level, or the patient's "bedside."

Scientists are increasingly aware that this bench-to-bedside approach to translational research is really a two-way street. Basic scientists provide clinicians with new tools for use in patients and for assessment of their impact, and clinical researchers make novel observations about the nature and progression of disease that often stimulate basic investigations.

What translational research means to massage therapists is that awareness must be built and processes established that facilitate bringing the benefits of newly learned knowledge to the bedside, or massage table.

Translational research describes the concept of a study starting at the bench—the research setting—and ending up helping the client—the bedside setting.

ETHICAL CONSIDERATIONS IN CLINICAL RESEARCH

Understanding how the practice of ethics applies specifically to massage therapy research is critical to becoming a trusted researcher. In short, researchers are expected to protect the rights and well-being of the study's subjects. Following World War II, standards for research ethics were developed and made official through the Nuremberg Code in 1947 and the Declaration of Helsinki in 1964 (revised in 1975). These two documents became the foundation of what is now, under the direction of the U.S. Department of Health and Human Services, the Belmont Report.

The Belmont Report proposes that the following three elements should underlie all research endeavors:[4]

Respect for persons. Respect for persons requires that people participate in research voluntarily and that they have a thorough understanding of what the study entails and their role in it. Therefore, the rules regarding informed consent for research participants are well-defined (Figure 8.5).
Beneficence. Beneficence is the concept of doing no harm. Researchers are obligated to weigh the benefits against the risks of the research and to accurately articulate those to the participants. Participants apply their own values in deciding whether to participate in the study or not.

FIGURE 8.4 Research Terminology

When reading the results of research studies, it is helpful to understand the meanings of the following terms:

ANOVA – analysis of variance. This is a statistical method that determines the effect of a test factor (such as "a 15-minute massage") on a response variable (such as "systolic blood pressure"). ANOVA analyzes variability between groups, relative to the effects, and determines whether groups of data are similar or different. This tool helps weed out differences due to normal variation from those actually produced by independent variables.

BLINDING – Performed or made without the benefit of background information that might prejudice the outcome or results. One common example is blind taste tests used in marketing studies.

EMPIRICAL – A method of inquiry that relies on subjects' experience or observation.

EXPERIMENTAL GROUP – Subjects who are receiving trial intervention.

MEAN (M OR X) – The average. The mean is calculated by adding all of the values and dividing by n, the sample size.

MEDIAN – An indicator of the middle. Half of all observed values are above the median and half are below.

N – The sample size. If, for example, 20 individuals were evaluated, then n = 20.

OBJECTIVE (WHEN USED AS AN ADJECTIVE) – Information gathered by the use of measurement tools, as in: "The summary provided objective information regarding the topic studied."

P-VALUE – When performing a T-test, a resultant p-value tells us how confident we can be in the result. For instance, "p<0.05" means there's a 5 percent chance that the means are the same and a 95 percent chance that the means are truly different. See the definition of T-test for a further explanation and example of how p-values are used.

PLACEBO – A substance, technique or protocol having no pharmacological effect but given to a subject of an experiment who supposes it to be a medicine.

RANDOMIZED – A research design in which subjects are arbitrarily placed in either the control group or experimental group.

STANDARD DEVIATION, SD OR ± – How variable the data are about the mean. The symbol ± means plus or minus.

STATISTICAL SIGNIFICANCE – A method of analyzing data that demonstrates that there is a less than 5 percent chance that the finding occurred by chance. In other words, if something is statistically significant, there are five chances in 100 that the outcome was a fluke, and therefore a 95 percent chance that the finding was not an accident.

SUBJECTIVE – Information reported by the subject or a practitioner. Generally, subjective information is less quantifiable than objective information.

TREND – Data that lean toward a certain outcome, but are not statistically significant.

T-TEST – Compares two means to determine whether they are statistically different from one another. The T-test will produce a p-value that will tell you how confident you can be in a result.

For example, when p<0.05, and the T-test indicates that the means are different, you can be 95 percent confident that the means truly are different, as opposed to merely appearing different. Researchers know that sometimes things that look different may actually be the same—or, more accurately, may have been sampled from the same pool— and appear different only to the naked eye. A good example is body temperature and blood pressure. These vital signs vary within an individual as well as between individuals. Good use of ANOVA and a T-test will indicate whether apparent differences are real or simply due to natural variation.

Justice. The concept of justice refers to fairness in the distribution of benefits and burdens. Research participants should be selected for study based on the requirements of the research question being asked and not only on their availability to participate in the study. The goal of justice is to not exploit a particular group of participants but to choose a proportionate distribution from a wide range of qualified participants.

The creation of institutional review boards (IRBS) is due in large part to the need for scrutinizing each proposed research study to assure that it meets academic, scientific, and ethical standards. An IRB is comprised of at least five representatives, one of whom may not be from the institution sponsoring the IRB, and another who focuses on nonscientific issues. The IRB can decide to approve, require modification, or disapprove a study.

FIGURE 8.5
Elements of Informed Consent for
Research Studies

PURPOSE OF RESEARCH PROJECT: the reason for doing study & for selecting subject.

PROCEDURES: exactly what participation involves.

POTENTIAL RISKS: an accurate description of any potential negative consequences of participation in the study.

POTENTIAL BENEFITS: an accurate description of the potential benefits of participation to the individual and/or society.

ALTERNATIVES TO PARTICIPATION: any alternative procedure that could be used instead of participating in the study.

CONFIDENTIALITY: how the subject's identity will be protected in collection, storing, and reporting research information.

REQUEST FOR MORE INFORMATION: participants are provided contact information so they may ask questions at any time during the research process.

REFUSAL OR WITHDRAWAL: assurance that participants can refuse to participate or withdraw from the study at any time.

INJURY STATEMENT: measures that will be taken is participant is injured at any point during the study.

CONSENT STATEMENT: verification that the individual consents to participate in the study.

SIGNATURES: signature is required of the participant or a legal guardian, and a witness. Informed consent forms are considered legal documents.

Source: Adapted from Cynthia Piltch and Martha Brown Menard, "Research and Practice Ethics," *mtj,* spring 2007, 164. Used with permission.

HOW TO PARTICIPATE IN RESEARCH

Opportunities to participate in research are available through many avenues. It is not imperative that you be good at all areas of research. Knowing your abilities and strong suits, and working cooperatively in your collaboration with others, are tremendous assets.

The first step in participating in research is to become research savvy through education and study of the current state of massage therapy research. Some of the ways in which you might do that include:

1 *Take a course on research methods.* Many colleges and universities offer courses on research methodology and statistics. Workshops are held at national conventions and state chapters of professional associations.

2   *Submit a Case Report.* Students and practitioners are encouraged to submit case reports in which they focus on one small area of study. In student case report contests, the Massage Therapy Foundation asks students to: review the literature about a particular condition, create and implement a treatment plan for one client, write up the results in which the student discusses implications of the outcome, and offer suggestions for future study.

3   *Review research that has been done.* Look at the sources listed in Resources to access the latest information. Reviewing what research has been done may lead to new research questions. This may also lead to questions about the mechanisms of how massage works; new potential uses or interventions for massage; how massage may interface with other allied health care modalities; etc.

4   *Learn how to put together a good research proposal.* Use the organizations and sources listed in Resources to gain the information you need about how to write a research proposal.

5   *Find out deadlines for research application proposals and submit your proposal.*

RESOURCES FOR RESEARCH

BOOKS AND TOOLS

Dryden, T., & Achilles, R. (2003). *Massage Therapy Research Curriculum Kit.* Evanston, IL: Massage Therapy Foundation.

Field, Tiffany (2006). *Massage Therapy Research.* Elsevier.

Hymel, Glenn (2006). *Research Methods for Massage and Holistic Therapies.* Mosby.

Menard, Martha Brown (2004). *Making Sense of Research: A Guide to Research Literacy for Complementary Practitioners.* Toronto: Curties-Overzet.

Rich, Grant Jewell (2002). *Massage Therapy: The Evidence for Practice.* Elsevier Health Sciences.

ARTICLES, COLUMNS, DATABASES

Harvey, Michael (2001). "5 Steps to Getting the Most from Research Articles." *Massage Magazine*, March/April 2001, 165–166, 168–172.

Hymel, Glenn (2003). "Advancing Massage Therapy Research Competencies: Dimensions for Thought and Action." *Journal of Bodywork and Movement Therapies* (7)3, 194 – 199. Revised paper originally presented as poster at Annual Meeting of American Massage Therapy Association in Quebec, Canada.

IN-CAM Outcomes Research Database: http://www.incamresearch.ca/index. php?id=52,0,0,1,0,0&lng= (search on "IN-CAM outcomes research" if this URL does not work). Hosts outcome measures of particular importance to CAM research.

Jonas, Wayne B. (2001). "The Evidence House: How to Build an Inclusive Base for Complementary Medicine." *Western Journal of Medicine, 175*, 79–80.

Massage Magazine: www.massagemag.com (search on research)

Massage Therapy Foundation: www.massagetherapyfoundation.org (go to Library, then Articles of Interest)

mtj column *Research Literacy,* by Martha Brown Menard and Cynthia Piltch: www. amtamassage.org (search on research literacy)

National Center for Complementary and Alternative Medicine: http://nccam.nih. gov/research/

Thompson, Diana, & Ravensara Travillian (2006). "Can Research Make Us Better Massage Therapists?" *Washington Massage Journal:* www.amta-wa.org

Woolf, S. H. (2008) "The Meaning of Translational Research and Why It Matters." *JAMA*, 299: 211–213.

ORGANIZATIONS

Canadian Massage Therapy Research Network (CMTRN): www.cmtrn.ca/

IN-CAM: Canadian Interdisciplinary Network for Complementary and Alternative Medicine Research (IN-CAM): http://www.ucalgary.ca/news/march2008/IN-CAM

Massage Therapy Foundation: www.massagetherapyfoundation.org

Massage Therapy Research Consortium: www.massagetherapyresearchconsortium.com

National Center for Complementary and Alternative Medicine (NCCAM): www.nccam.nih.gov

National Institutes of Health (NIH): www.nih.gov

Osher Research Center, Harvard Medical School, Division for Research and Education in Complementary and Integrative Medicine: www.osher.hms.harvard.edu

Touch Research Institute: www.miami.edu/touch-research/

PROFESSIONAL GROWTH THROUGH SUPERVISION

In Greek mythology, Mentor was the teacher and guide of Telemachus, the son of Odysseus. "Mentor" actually was Athena, the goddess of wisdom, in disguise. The symbolism implied is that a mentor role is one of benevolent, guiding wisdom. A mentor/mentee relationship is often used in the massage therapy profession. Many massage therapists find they need someone to help them sort out the behaviors and feelings they experience while interacting with clients. They get this help from supervision—that is, a process of learning by discussing work experiences with peers or a more experienced therapist.

A mentor, in relation to a mentee, is a person of higher ranking within an organization or profession, with greater experience or knowledge and a commitment to supporting the development of a mentee's career. A mentor serves as a role model who offers acceptance, confirmation, protection, and even friendship to the mentee. A mentor listens, observes, asks, counsels, coaches, and challenges the mentee.

Massage therapists can use any of three kinds of supervision:

1 *School clinic supervisor.* This type of supervision usually focuses on the notes written after the student/client session. It may or may not be technique related. These supervisors help students understand where the students need to develop, or grow.
2 *Group supervision.* This is also called peer supervision. It could involve one-on-one supervision with a colleague or could consist of a group of massage therapists coming together to talk through client issues they are experiencing. The therapists offer advice to each other based on their own experiences.

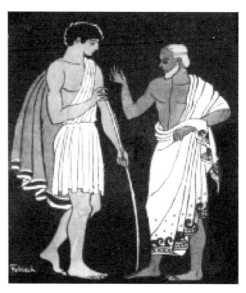

The word mentor comes from Greek mythology, in which Athena, goddess of wisdom, disguised herself as a man named Mentor and served as instructor and guide to Telemachus. This image is of *Telemachus and Mentor* by Pablo E. Fabisch, from *Les Adventures de Telemaque* (1699).

3 *Professional supervision.* A trained mental health professional who knows the theory of client-therapist relationships acts as a guide through a massage therapist's self-examination of professional issues. Ideally, a professional supervisor is trained in massage and the relationship issues it can bring out.

Because of the confidential nature of massage, the actual supervision is done outside the session. Supervision can help with many of the client issues that massage therapists encounter, from client hygiene or lack of cooperation, to a therapist's anger or other feelings aroused by a client's behavior. The supervisor also can help the massage therapist address particular issues related to specific client types. Supervision issues may fall into three categories:

1 Client-therapist relationship
2 Client's psychological and physical well-being
3 Massage therapist's psychological and physical well-being

Supervisors who have more experience than the massage therapists they supervise can provide options for how a massage therapist can handle a situation the next time it arises.

When you are looking for a supervisor, keep in mind that some states have qualifications for supervision. For example, Oregon's mental health board keeps a list of professional supervisors who are certified by the state in the mental health field. Check with your state board for such a list, ask your school for advice and recommendations, or look for a counselor who is trained in massage. Also, note that the expense of paying for a supervisor generally is tax deductible.

PROFESSIONAL DEVELOPMENT IN YOUR BUSINESS PLAN

FIGURE 8.6
Professional Development
Business Plan

As discussed in Chapter 5, creation of a business plan helps you define your goals and create plans for how those goals can be achieved. Professional development is appropriately included in a business plan because achievement of goals in this area is critical to the success of your practice. Figure 8.6 shows the section of the Career and Practice Planning Worksheet that pertains to professional development.

PROFESSIONAL DEVELOPMENT (EXCERPT FROM FIGURE 5.9, CAREER AND PRACTICE PLANNING WORKSHEET)

Professional Advocacy

Issue of importance to the profession   *How you plan to become involved with this issue.*

_____   _____

_____   _____

What is your plan for educating consumers about the profession of massage? _____

_____

_____

Allied Professions

List the allied professions with whom you plan to develop professional relationships. _____

_____

_____

_____

FIGURE 8.6 (continued)

What is your plan for developing professional relationships with allied professions? _____
_____
_____
_____

What is your plan for maintaining these relationships? _____
_____
_____
_____

Continuing Education

Formal Training

1 List the continuing education requirements for renewal of your credentials. _____
   _____

2 What courses or training classes do you plan to take over the next three years?

	Name of course	Cost	Location
Year one	_____	_____	_____
Year two	_____	_____	_____
Year three	_____	_____	_____

Informal Training

How do you plan to continue your education through informal methods? _____
_____
_____

Research

1 What is your plan for becoming research literate? _____
   _____
   _____
   _____

2 What is your plan for becoming involved in massage therapy research? _____
   _____
   _____
   _____

3 What is your plan for incorporating massage therapy research into your practice for client education? _____
   _____
   _____
   _____

Supervision

1 What is your plan for incorporating professional supervision into your practice development? _____
   _____
   _____
   _____

2 What is your plan for providing supervision to a colleague for his or her practice development? _____
   _____
   _____
   _____

SUMMARY

Many massage therapists consider professional development to be among their highest priorities. To extend your time and energy to professional growth beyond your skills as an employee or business owner, you enhance your individual experience as well as contribute to the entire profession. Three areas that offer rich and satisfying opportunities for professional growth include joining a professional association, taking continuing education, and supporting research.

Your professional association offers many opportunities and benefits. When selecting which professional association you will join, consider its business development and practice support, and its contribution to the profession in terms of media exposure, legislative advocacy, quality of continuing education, opportunities to collaborate with your peers, and promoting massage to the general public and to allied professions.

You can build bridges with massage therapy's allied professions, such as chiropractic and physical therapy, as an individual as well. Relating positively to other professionals allows you to expand your business, as well as build productive alliances and extend your knowledge. By learning about the scope of your allied professionals' training and understanding the basics of their terminology, you will be able to educate them effectively about how massage therapy complements their clients' wellness or rehabilitation needs.

Another way in which to enhance your profession is to take advantage of continuing education opportunities. A specified number of continuing education credits over a given period of time are mandated by many professional organizations in the United States and Canada as a requirement of maintaining professional status as a member. Learning takes place in formal settings, such as classes and workshops, as well as informally. Adopting an attitude that views everyday experiences as learning opportunities allows you to expand your knowledge and your perceptions far beyond the classroom experience.

One area of continuing education that has become more important in recent years is massage therapy research. Many massage therapists believe additional research about the efficacy of massage will help them improve their skills, validate the medical and body/mind benefits of massage, and help expand the acceptance of massage therapists as professionals. As a massage therapist, you may want to become involved in conducting or participating in research, or as a reader of massage therapy research that you can apply to the benefit of your business. Opportunities for both are growing rapidly, and many support tools are available to the massage therapist who has never participated in research before.

Another area of professional development that many massage therapists find valuable is using a practice called supervision. Engaging the assistance of a professional supervisor allows you to sort out the behaviors and feelings you experience while interacting with clients. You would work with individual or group support, with experienced supervisors who can help you reflect on your experiences with clients. Feedback from a supervisor can help you enhance your therapeutic relationship with clients, improve your self-care, and improve the health of your business.

Growing as a professional within your own community of peers, community-wide, association chapter-wide, nationwide and worldwide, allows you to communicate how much you care about the massage therapy profession. An immense potential exists for extending the benefits of massage by focusing on the good of all, which includes the public, health care professionals, and your peers. Professional growth will make your career that much more rewarding.

REVIEW QUESTIONS

1 Identify agencies, professional associations, and other allied professions that massage practitioners commonly do business with.
2 Identify the role of professional associations for massage practitioners.

3 Identify strategies for effective communication with other professionals regarding client care and networking.

4 Identify strategies for conflict resolution in relationships with other professionals.

5 Identify characteristics of effective interaction in groups and organizations.

6 Identify strategies to attain new knowledge.

7 Demonstrate the ability to read and critically evaluate technical information found in health-related journals.

8 Describe the importance of evidence-based research to the massage profession.

9 Explain the need for utilizing professional supervision when appropriate.

10 How would a massage therapist benefit from using professional supervision?

11 What professional development goals will you include in your business plan?

ENDNOTES

1 Ruth L. Kirschstein, M.D., Acting Director, National Center for Complementary and Alternative Medicine, appeared as a witness before the Senate Subcommittee on Labor-HHS-Education Appropriations (June 22, 2007) to request 2008 budget. Retrieved from http://nccam.nih.gov/about/offices/od/directortestimony/0607.htm

2 Margaret Chesney, Ph.D., deputy director of NCCAM, keynote speaker at North American Research Conference on Complementary and Integrative Medicine (May 2006, Edmonton, Alberta, Canada). Retrieved from http://nccam.nih.gov/news/newsletter/2006_summer/conference.htm

3 NIH Roadmap for Medical Research, Translational Research, available at http://nihroadmap.nih.gov/clinicalresearch/overview-translational.asp

4 Piltch, C., and Brown Menard, M. (2007). Research and practice ethics. mtj, 46(1), 161–165.

Appendix A

Shared Wisdom quotes from
The Business of Massage,
First Edition, 2002

The margin notes of advice from massage therapists throughout the United States and Canada that were printed in the first edition of The Business of Massage *communicated not only a wealth of knowledge but a wish that all new massage therapists would also become successful. Their good words are reprinted here in the same spirit.*

CHAPTER 1: TAKING STOCK OF YOUR CAREER OPTIONS

"Attitude and determination are so important. Study to gather all the knowledge you can from what is presented to you. Don't just study enough to pass tests. The real test is when you apply service to the clients, so store all the information you can to ensure safe, therapeutic, and professional services." – CARRIE BADKER, *"Carrie's Kadesh" School of Massage, Mitchell, South Dakota*

"To succeed in business you must first succeed in your own life. The successful massage business owners I know present a cheerful countenance and infectious enthusiasm, and are grounded in the belief in the value of what they are doing. They have resolved their personal issues to the point that their daily presentation lacks signs of anger and hostility. Their personal lives are stable. They are wholesome, outgoing people lovers. Doing the personal work early creates the situations that lead to a successful business." – ED DENNING, *Stark State College of Technology, Canton, Ohio*

"Be patient during the first year in practice. The first year is a good time to focus on technique and skill proficiency, as well as to develop a personal niche. Time spent in a supported environment, such as a chiropractic or multi-professional office, allows for development in these areas without the additional pressure of business development, marketing and advertising. It also allows time to build a client base and the funding necessary for private practice and increased business expenses." – ANN MARIE ENGSTROM, *Rising Spirit Institute of Natural Health, Atlanta, Georgia*

"Anyone who has been in the field of massage therapy and bodywork for more than five years has done a lot of personal growth work. Some types of practices place greater emphasis on the mind/spirit aspects of massage, and some on the physical aspects. When a person has a foot in both camps – when the session is nurturing, kind, and healing, as well as physically excellent – the more value it imparts to the client and to the world at large." – JUDY DEAN, *Agua Dulce Center and Spa, Prescott, Arizona*

"I have found that the fastest way to establish credibility with the medical community is to have them see that you are not just someone seeking referrals, but a fellow healthcare practitioner who can make a difference to his or her patients. They are used to empirical evidence and double-blind studies that prove efficaciousness." – BOB HAASE, *School Director, Bodymechanics School of Myotherapy & Massage, Olympia, Washington*

"If you worked in a spa for even one year, you would triple your experience in hands-on/technical skills and strengthen your ability to relate to new clients, relative to any other work experience. Spas offer very eclectic experiences which relate to health and wellness." – DI TRIESTE, *Corporate Spa Treatment Director, Canyon Ranch Health Resorts, Tucson, Arizona*

"If you want to develop a specialty in canine massage, spend as much time as you can learning dog behavior, visit with veterinarians, go to dog shows and doggie day care, and take a certification program whose teachings include anatomy, pathology, and lots of hands-on massage." – RHONDA REICH, *Boulder College of Massage*

CHAPTER 2: LAUNCHING A SUCCESSFUL PRACTICE

"Do the math: After adding up the amount per month you would be paying as percentage to a clinic, you will see that it is possible to pay rent on your own office space. (For example, in a 60/40% split that is usual in a clinic type establishment, 40% on a $45 massage = $18 × 20 massages per week – considered full-time = $360 per week × 4 weeks in a month = $1,440 paid per month to the establishment out of *your* income.) In your own practice, you receive the entire $45, and the rent you would pay on office space would usually be much less than $1,440." – LAURIE MCCUISTION, *Licensed Massage Therapist, Magna, Utah*

"If you want to buy an existing practice, consider the option of renting to own. You might agree with the owner that you will run the practice for one year and give the owner 80% of your fees, which accrue to the purchase. At the end of the year, you own the business. Or, if you have decided at the end of the year that you don't want the business, the owner keeps what you have already paid in. The agreement should be in writing. This provides subsistence living for you (the buyer) the first year, but it allows for gradual payment and the smooth and gradual transition from the first owner." – BARRY ANTONIOW, *Kiné-Concept Institute – Maritimes, Fredericton, New Brunswick, Canada*

"Number One Rule: Don't quit your day job too soon! Once you have met your break-even point three months in a row, it is fairly safe to quit the day job and put all your energy into growing your business to full-time. Building a solid clientele requires time, because word-of-mouth is still the best marketing. Don't put yourself in the position of not being able to pay rent or buy groceries because you quit your day job before you had enough clients to support you." – PEGGY SMITH, *BMSI Institute, Overland Park, Kansas*

"When setting up a business, don't be shy, *be visible*. Choose, for example, storefront office space; advertise in the yellow pages, in the newspaper, in alternative newspapers. Participate in health fairs and give demonstrations at your local health food store. Visibility is a great strategy." – CHRIS HOFFMAN, *Finger Lakes Community College, Canandaigua, New York*

"Don't wait until after graduation to begin looking at the reality of finding work as a professional. Find out the costs of oil and business cards, call three publications and obtain the costs of advertising, provide the name, address, and contact person of three establishments where you might get a job as a massage therapist." – SUE BROWN, *Illinois School of Health Careers, Chicago, Illinois*

CHAPTER 3: MANAGING YOUR PRACTICE

"Don't assume you do not have to pay quarterly taxes your first year of self-employment. If you wait until the end of the tax year you may find that if you owe taxes for your self-employment earnings, you will also owe penalties. If you owed $1,000 for example, IRS would expect you to pay $250 to them each quarter. If you wait and pay it all at the end of the year, you will owe penalties for paying the first quarter 10 months late and the second quarter 7 months late and the third quarter 4 months late! It is worth the money and time to talk to an accountant as you set up your business to avoid these mistakes." – PEGGY SMITH, *Licensed Massage Therapist, and director of BMSI Institute, Overland Park, Kansas*

"Chart every single session, regardless of the intent of the session (relaxation or rehabilitation), regardless of the payor (cash or insurance), and regardless of the health of the client. The chart entry can be as simple as: '2–2–03, full body Swedish massage, client prefers pillow under hips when prone,' or as complex as a SOAP chart. If we are to be treated as healthcare providers, we are to behave as such. Think of it this way – a doctor would never consider skipping out on charting an annual physical just because the patient was in good health." – DIANA THOMPSON, *author of Hands Heal: Communication, Documentation, and Insurance Billing for Manual Therapists, Seattle, Washington*

"A massage therapist must find common ground with the medical community in their communication of what it is they do and how long it will take. When a massage therapist starts talking energy and meridians, the doctor's eyes will glaze over. Tell them what you can do for their patient in anatomical and physiological terms and your specific care plan for a given medical condition. Help them feel comfortable that referring a patient to you was the right things to do." – BOB HAASE, *School Director, Bodymechanics School of Myotherapy & Massage, Olympia, Washington*

"It's been my experience that, even when someone else is available to answer the phone at my practice, clients prefer to talk with me personally when they call to book an appointment. It might not be the most efficient way to schedule appointments, but I think my willingness to honor the client's preference to book with me personally helps strengthen our therapeutic relationship and promote ongoing business with those clients." – IAN KAMM, *Sutherland-Chan School and Teaching Clinic, Toronto, Canada*

CHAPTER 4: CREATING A SENSE OF PLACE

"Keep your targeted client type in mind as you make decisions about your office design and image. A medical doctor once told me, 'I'm afraid that when I send a patient to an unknown massage therapist for a shoulder injury, they will have incense burning, music of whale sounds playing, and then stick a candle in the patient's ear and light it. I want to know that the therapist's office looks professional." – BOB HAASE, *School Director, Bodymechanics School of Myotherapy & Massage, Olympia, Washington*

CHAPTER 5: CREATING A THERAPEUTIC RELATIONSHIP

"By far the most useful business tool is understanding who your clients are – what is their model of the world, what do they believe in, how do they think, and what are their priorities in life? Point out to them – through your advertising, by how you dress, how you decorate your office – that you understand and respect them for who they are. In effect, meet them at their model of the world instead of expecting them to meet you at yours." – CRAIG MCLAUGHLIN, *Mountain Heart School of Bodywork, Crested Butte, Colorado*

"Teach students that this is a people business and the client comes first. Don't worry about how large a tip is – do your best, love what you do, and the rest will follow." – SISTER M. JANINE RAPHOWSKI, *Center for a Balanced Life Inc., West St. Paul, Minnesota*

"Be in touch with how you feel about people. People who have been bartenders and cocktail waitresses before becoming massage therapists do not have to go through the angst that others do – they've interacted with the public; they have learned tolerance for human frailty. Know your boundaries – what you can and cannot do and what you will and will not do." – JUDY DEAN, *Agua Dulce Center and Spa, Prescott, Arizona*

"1) Give your client your total attention for the time they are with you. Keep your boundaries clear and clean; 2) Don't use the little flower-shaped soaps in the bathroom when you make a home visit. They are only for show. ☺" – JANIS LEGENDRE, IUPUI – *Indiana University, Purdue University, Continuing Studies, Indianapolis, Indiana*

"Be sure to give each new client a check-up call one or two days after their first visit. This way you can answer any questions that have come up for them since their first massage with you. This is a courtesy call – you are not asking them to rebook an appointment with you. It shows you care." – JOCELYN GRANGER, *Ann Arbor Institute of Massage Therapy, Ann Arbor, Michigan*

"Be on time! Making clients wait gives them a bad impression before they even make it to the table!" – LAURA ALLEN, *The Whole You School of Massage & Bodywork, Rutherfordton, North Carolina*

"Always be on time and prepared." – PAULA CURTISS, *Healing Hands School, Pala Loma, Valley Center, California*

"I find that substantiated, rehearsed responses to commonly asked questions not only promote one's professionalism but also promote the integrity of the entire massage therapy profession." – GREG ST. JACQUES, *Director, Central Mass School of Massage and Therapy, Spencer, Massachusetts*

CHAPTER 6: PRACTICING SELF-CARE

Continued education regarding body mechanics should be stressed to all students who are studying massage therapy. The correct use of body mechanics can help the longevity and successfulness of their business or career. It can make or break them. I've been practicing massage for over 25 years, and with the correct use of body mechanics, I am still going strong. Have a fellow massage therapist watch you as you give a massage." – SANDY FRITZ, *Health Enrichment Center Inc., Lapeer, Michigan*

CHAPTER 7: SPREADING THE WORD

"Have a professional attitude at all times. When in public project an image that is positive. You never know when you will run into a present client, and everyone is a potential client, so be prepared with a positive, professional attitude – a smile and business cards." – JEANNE TRONIAO, *Massage Training Institute of Bakersfield, Bakersfield, California*

"Give incentives: Offer discounts like $10 off first session and give a 'punch card' where every sixth session is free. This gets the client in the door and keeps them coming. Sure, you will be doing a lot of free massages at times, but isn't that better than doing no massages!" – LAURIE MCCUISTION, *Licensed Massage Therapist, NCTMB, Magna, Utah*

"The single most important concept about advertising is that it should be cheap enough to be able to continue for a long time. Clients may see your ad running for months before responding to it. If the ad disappears quickly, they might think your business has failed." – IAN KAMM, *Sutherland-Chan School and Teaching Clinic, Toronto, Ontario, Canada*

"Reward your clients for doing your advertising. Offer them incentives for referring new clients to you. I give my clients a $5 gift certificate for each person they refer." – DORI L. FACEMYER, *Oakes Massage Therapy College/Stark State College, Malvern, Ohio*

"Do seated massage on TV talk shows and public access channels. It costs nothing, educates the public about massage and your business (people see who you are and what you do) and catches people's attention when they are channel surfing since most people have never seen a massage chair." – KAREN CRAIG, *The Massage Institute of Memphis, Memphis, Tennessee*

"To build a good referral base, start while you're a student. Your scope of practice is small and you will come across clients in need of psychotherapy, chiropractic, counseling, podiatry, dentistry, OB/Gyn, etc. Meet these professionals face to face and you will be able to build a referral base that will refer back to you." – KIMBERLY WILLIAMS, *Southeastern School of Neuromuscular & Massage Therapy, Inc, Charlotte, North Carolina*

"Evaluate your return client percentage. If 50 percent or less of your clients do not schedule an appointment within three months it is time to consider taking a business strategies course." – VAN DELIA, *Onandaga School of Therapeutic Massage, Syracuse, New York*

CHAPTER 8: CONNECTING WITH THE PROFESSIONAL COMMUNITY

"If you wish to get involved in research, you should contact your local hospitals, local research centers, colleges and universities, and/or key practitioners in your geographic area. Read the newest studies and see if any are being done in your area. You could perhaps do a small study within your practice – be in touch with the AMTA Foundation about how to do this." – JOHN BALLETTO, NCTMB, *President, AMTA Foundation*

INDEX

A

Accountants, 111, 131, 144, 145, 166, 168, 184, 186, 221
Accreditation *See* Massage schools and training programs
ADA *See* Americans with Disabilities Act (ADA)
Advertising, 226, 234–235
Agency for Health Care Quality and Research (AHCQR), 267
Allied professions, 260–263, 276
    improving communication among, 263, 276
    list of allied professions, 261
    resources for allied professions, 261
Allopathic (medical) model of health, 40
Alternative therapies *See* Complementary and alternative medicine (CAM)
American Journal of Health Promotion, 11
American Massage Therapy Association (AMTA)
    code of ethics for the profession, 41
    compound interest rate schedule on website, 157
    contact information, 32
    Find a Therapist Directory, 55
    for latest statistics on demand for massage, 135
    membership as professional credential, 30
    performance standards guidelines, 42–43
    research citations in Massage Information Center, 268
    role and importance as a professional association, 259–260
    source for information on how to start a workplace massage program, 14–15
    source of information about regulations on credentials in U.S., 28
    survey 2006 provides information on doctor referrals, 16
American Organization for Bodywork Therapies of Asia (AOBTA), 260
Americans with Disabilities Act (ADA), 73, 76, 147, 152
AMTA Massage Therapy Industry Fact Sheet (2005), 7
Antoniow, Barry. "Insurance" in *Kiné-Concept Institute Business Success Workbook*. New Brunswick, Canada: Kiné Concept Institute Maritimes. n.d. , 134
Apprenticeships *See also* Employee, Working as
Associated Bodywork and Massage Professionals (ABMP), 30, 32, 41, 259–260
Associations, Professional *See* Professional associations
Attorneys, 72, 79, 111, 145

B

Balance sheets, 174–175
Bookkeeping *See* Business recordkeeping
Boundaries *See also* Clients; Confidentiality; Ethics; Therapeutic relationships
    as behavioral guidelines with clients, 43
    boundary violations, 47–48
    business policies help set boundaries, 141
    confidentiality, 43–44
    counseling and advising clients, 46–47
    draping, 44–45, 142
    dual relationships, 46–47
    ethics and, 40, 43–48
    personal safety and security, 45
    resources for ethics and boundaries, 47
    working in clients' homes, 45–46
Business Insurance for Better or Worse (Insurance Information Institute), *Massage Therapy Journal*, Spring 2004.
Business licenses, permits, fees, taxes
    business licenses and professional licenses are different, 130
    business licenses may have special requirements for massage therapists, 130, Spotlight on Business: Selected business license/permit fees, 131
Business of Massage (The): The Complete Guide to Establishing Your Massage Career.1st ed. AMTA, 2002, 289–294

Business ownership structures
    business structures pros and cons, 107
    cooperatives, 106, 107
    corporations, 106, 107, 109, 111, 160
    limited liability companies (LLC), 106, 107, 109
    partnerships, 106, 107, 109, 111, 160
    resources for forming a corporation or partnership, 111
    sole proprietorships, 106, 107–108, 109, 160
    Spotlight on Business: Get to know your SBA Business Development Center, 111–112
Business plans *See also* Financial planning
    completing a business plan: Career Planning & Practice Planning Worksheet, 114–125
    evaluating the business plan: Career Planning and Practice Planning Worksheet, 160
    financial planning, 155–159
    formulating goals and objectives, 113, 126
    importance of business planning, 112–113, 160
    major sections of a business plan, 160
    reevaluating your business plan, 254
Business policies and procedures, 141–143
    employee policies, 217–219
    typical categories of business policies, 142
Business recordkeeping *See also* Financial management, Taxes; Client records management
    bill collecting, 180–181
    business tax deductions (write-offs), 182–186
    financial records, 166–168
    importance of good recordkeeping, 166, 222
    income reporting, 182
    invoicing, 179–181
    mileage log for business tax deduction, 184
    resources for filing tax returns, 186
    tax forms (Federal), 186
    tax withholding guidelines, 181
    types of financial reports, 173–178
    using professional bookkeeping services, 168

C

CAM *See* Complementary and alternative medicine
Canadian Massage Therapist Alliance, 28
Career options *See also* Career settings; Employee, Working as; Self-employment
    career trends, 5, 37
    lists of career options and settings, 5, 7, 10–11, 37
    questions to ask when considering options, 10–11
    self-evaluation to help in making choices, 32–37
Career Planning and Practice Planning Worksheet (business plan), 114–125, 254–255
Career settings *See also* Career options
    clinical/rehab settings, 246–247
    corporate/franchise settings, 10, 22–24, 37
    integrative health care settings, 5, 16–18
    spa settings, 5, 20, 21
    specialty settings, 26–28
    sports/fitness settings, 5, 10, 18–20
    wellness programs and settings, 5, 10, 11–15, 247
Carpal tunnel syndrome, 89–90, 216
Cash flow statements, 176–178
Certification
    International Association of Equine Sports Massage Therapists certification, 25
    National Certification Board for Therapeutic Massage & Bodywork (NCBTMB), 29, 31
    Nationally Certified in Therapeutic Massage & Bodywork (NCTMB) credential, 29
    Nationally Certified in Therapeutic Massage (NCTM) credential, 29
Chair massage, 14, 15
    resources for chair massage, 15

THE OASIS WITHIN